D1266692

WHICH PEOPLE'S WAR?

WHICH PEOPLE'S WAR?

NATIONAL IDENTITY AND CITIZENSHIP
IN BRITAIN 1939–1945

SONYA O. ROSE

OXFORD
UNIVERSITY PRESS

OXFORD
UNIVERSITY PRESS

Great Clarendon Street, Oxford OX2 6DP

Oxford University Press is a department of the University of Oxford.
It furthers the University's objective of excellence in research, scholarship,
and education by publishing worldwide in

Oxford New York

Auckland Bangkok Buenos Aires Cape Town Chennai
Dar es Salaam Delhi Hong Kong Istanbul Karachi Kolkata
Kuala Lumpur Madrid Melbourne Mexico City Mumbai Nairobi
São Paulo Shanghai Taipei Tokyo Toronto

Oxford is a registered trade mark of Oxford University Press
in the UK and in certain other countries

Published in the United States
by Oxford University Press Inc., New York

© Sonya O. Rose 2003

The moral rights of the author have been asserted
Database right Oxford University Press (maker)

First published 2003

All rights reserved. No part of this publication may be reproduced,
stored in a retrieval system, or transmitted, in any form or by any means,
without the prior permission in writing of Oxford University Press,
or as expressly permitted by law, or under terms agreed with the appropriate
reprographics rights organization. Enquiries concerning reproduction
outside the scope of the above should be sent to the Rights Department,
Oxford University Press, at the address above

You must not circulate this book in any other binding or cover
and you must impose this same condition on any acquirer

British Library Cataloguing in Publication Data

Data available

Library of Congress Cataloging in Publication Data

Data available

ISBN 0-19-925572-5

1 3 5 7 9 10 8 6 4 2

Typeset by SNP Best-set Typesetter Ltd., Hong Kong
Printed in Great Britain
on acid-free paper by
Biddles Ltd.
Guildford and King's Lynn

Acknowledgements

I have been working on this book for a number of years. As do many historical studies, this one changed over time. It began as a kind of interlude right after I finished a book on gender and labour in the nineteenth century. I meant for it then to be a quite limited study of the impact on British women of the American presence in World War II. I became interested in the topic when I discovered a letter in my long deceased father's diary. But as I delved into the relevant archives, I found myself unable to ignore the material that kept cropping up concerning citizenship and national identity. Eventually, those issues became central to me, and this book is the result.

My father, Louis Razinsky, died when he was 42 and I was 15 years old. He had served as an enlisted flight surgeon in the US Air Force during World War II. Sometime in 1991 I was cleaning my study and came across his diaries, buried in a box of memorabilia written during the time he was stationed in England at Bovingdon Air Base just north of London. He went to England in the spring of 1942 and his daily journal recounted what was going on at the base, how he dealt with the wounded men returning from missions and grieved for those who failed to return. It also was a travel diary that recorded the English villages he had visited when on leave. There are two such journals. I was putting them away after I had read them when from the back of one dropped a carbon copy of a letter purportedly written by a prostitute to the medical personnel at the base. She cautioned the staff to encourage the men to use condoms when they had sexual relations, and to choose for partners only professionals who not only knew their trade, but also kept themselves disease free. And she warned against the habit of men going with the 'amateurs', the 'good-time girls', who frequented the areas around the base and congregated on the streets of towns in many areas of the country. The letter closed with the author's statement that she had not always been a prostitute, but was a woman who had fallen on hard times. She had been married to a physician who had died, leaving her penniless.

I put the letter down and picked up the phone to call a colleague in England. Who, I asked, is working on prostitution in World War II? My thought was to send the letter to such a scholar. My friend, Leonore Davidoff, said that she really didn't know anyone, and suggested, 'You do it'. And that started this journey onto the World War II home front. As I researched the topic of women's sexual engagements and the public commentary about such women, I kept coming across references to 'good citizenship', and became increasingly intrigued with the hopes and fears that were expressed about Reconstruction. Reading this material also rekindled a somewhat longer-term interest of mine in patriotism and national identity. These issues moved the project onto ground that was new for me, extending the scope of a project that took much longer to complete than I ever would have imagined.

Because I have been working on this study for about ten years, I have incurred many debts. Conversations with friends and colleagues, students who have worked with me, institutional support, and the assistance of a number of archivists and staff members all have contributed to this project, although of course, I alone am responsible for its outcome. I worry that inadvertently, I will neglect to mention my debt to someone.

I want to acknowledge the significant social, emotional, and intellectual support of many of my colleagues at Michigan and friends in Ann Arbor. Some of them read and commented on various drafts; others listened to my ideas and shared theirs— sometimes challenging my approach. Some who read, listened, and challenged were joined by others to offer their friendship through the ups and downs that inevitably accompany the processes of research, writing, and publishing that are involved in producing a book such this. I especially want to thank Susan Douglas, Carroll Smith-Rosenberg, Geoff Eley, Kathleen Canning, Julia Adams, Todd Endelman, David Scobey, Bill Rosenberg, Ron Suny, Maris Vinovskis, Ernie Young, Vic Lieberman, Peggy Somers, Fred Cooper, Kali Israel, T. R. Durham, Alvia Golden, Elie Rosenberg, and Val Kivelson. Colleagues from afar also read, commented, sympathized, criticized, and/or just listened. I cannot imagine what the last several years would have been like without the presence in my life of Bill Schwarz, Catherine Hall, Penny Summerfield, Keith McClelland, Angela Woollacott, Philippa Levine, Susan Kent, Jim Epstein, and Leonore Davidoff. Martin Francis, James Vernon, Hal Smith, Laura Tabili, Laura Fradet, and Eileen Boris provided crucial suggestions and friendship at various points as this work evolved. My new friends and colleagues Stefan Dudink and Karen Hagemann were central to the creation and refinement of one of the chapters of this book and to what I plan to do next. In different ways each of you is present in the pages of this book. And then there are the graduate students who assisted me at various points during this project's long incubation, and who, more than they can imagine, have enormously enriched my life at Michigan. They include Alice Ritscherle, Joel Purkiss, Genie Deerman, Chandra Bhimull, Andy Donson, Caitlin Adams, Liz Buettner, Becky Conekin, and Michelle Harper. Thanks go as well to Pax Bobrow, Sarah Womack, and Jennifer Badner for their help.

I am deeply grateful to the staff members of the various libraries and archives that provided the sources undergirding the book's arguments. I cannot thank enough the staff at the Public Records Office at Kew. It is extraordinary given the demands of the variety of researchers from across the globe who descend on them every day that they can remain as helpful and personable as they have seemed to me. I also want to acknowledge the help of archivists and staff members at the Modern Records Centre at the University of Warwick and at the BBC Written Archives Centre in Reading who were helpful throughout the life of the project even to the point of helping me to check references at the end; the Religious Society of Friends Library, the British Library (especially its Colindale branch and the India Office), the Imperial War Museum, Mass Observation Archive at the University of Sussex, and various county and city records offices.

This book would not have been possible without research funds provided by the College of Literature, Science, and the Arts, the Horace H. Rackham School of Graduate Studies, the Institute for Research on Women and Gender, and the office of the Vice Provost for Research, all at the University of Michigan. I also want to thank Pat Preston in the Department of Sociology who has helped me and the students who have worked with me in many ways. I began this research when I was still a faculty member at Colby College. The college provided research funds and a supportive environment. It is especially the latter that I have never forgotten.

Earlier versions of parts of this book have already appeared. I thank the American Historical Association for permission to reproduce in revised form sections of my article, 'Sex, Citizenship, and the Nation in World War II Britain', appearing in the *American Historical Review*, 103 (October 1998), 1147–76; Blackwell Publishers Ltd., for permission to include some of the material in revised form in my essay, 'Race, Empire, and British Wartime National Identity, 1939–45', in *Historical Research*, 74 (May 2001), 220–37; Taylor & Francis Limited (http://www.tandf.co.uk) for permission to include in revised form sections of my article, 'Women's Rights, Women's Obligations: Contradictions of Citizenship in World War II Britain', that appeared in *European Review of History*, 7 (Autumn 2000), 277–90.

I want to acknowledge the following for giving permission to quote from their work or reproduce images for which they hold the copyright: Maggie Noach Literary Agency and the Estate of Emlyn Williams, Mrs Louie Williams (née White), Hulton Getty Photo Archives, The Copyright Unit, Her Majesty's Stationery Office, Atlantic Syndication, ISTC, and the Centre for the Study of Cartoons and Caricature at the University of Kent.

Ruth Parr and Anne Gelling of Oxford University Press have been wonderfully supportive, encouraging, and incredibly efficient.

Finally, I owe an enormous debt of gratitude along with boundless love to my family. My adult children on the East Coast and my husband's on the West Coast have been amazingly tolerant of my obsession with this work. Marc Orleans's creativity and diverse musical talent have inspired me. Laura Orleans's humanity and her proficiency and dedication to her work have made me very proud. Emma

ACKNOWLEDGEMENTS

Orleans York and Isaac Orleans York have blessed my life. And then there is Guenter. His love, understanding, strength, and humour have sustained me. That we have grown closer over the last few years means everything, and I dedicate this book to him, as well as to the memory of my father.

S.O.R.

Ann Arbor, Michigan
July 2002

Table of Contents

List of Illustrations

Abbreviations

ABCA	Army Bureau of Current Affairs
AEU	Amalgamated Engineering Union
ARP	Air Raid Patrol
ATS	Auxiliary Territorial Service
BFBPW	British Federation of Business and Professional Women
BUF	British Union of Fascists
ILP	Independent Labour Party
JPCs	Joint Production Committees
MOI	Ministry of Information
NUWM	National Unemployed Workers' Movement
PEP	Political and Economic Planning
RIOs	Regional Intelligence Officers
SNP	Scottish National Party
UGCC	United Gold Coast Convention
WAAFS	Women's Auxiliary Air Force Service
WEA	Workers' Education Association
WGPW	Women's Group on Public Welfare
WLA	Women's Land Army
WPPA	Women's Publicity Planning Association
WRNS	Women's Royal Navy Service
WVS	Women's Voluntary Services

1

Introduction

NATIONAL IDENTITY AND CITIZENSHIP

The British home front in World War II continues to be a source of both fascination and nostalgia even for those who were born long after the war had ended. It was a time when the British pulled together to defeat the Nazi enemy in a war that until the middle of 1944 had produced more deaths among civilians in Britain than among those who were in the fighting services. After the fall of the European allies in the spring of 1940, when Great Britain was militarily isolated in Western Europe, the country feared Nazi invasion for more than a year. But these facts and dates do not capture what it was about the war on the home front that has been such a compelling source of interest for historians, ageing survivors and their families, and others who had little or no direct association with the people who participated in it.

World War II is remembered through film, posters, songs, and fiction as a time when civilians mustered their energies to 'do their bit', and to 'keep smiling through'; and for many, or so one might imagine, it was when young people had 'the time of their lives', learning the jitterbug and American slang, or, if they were school-children, and if they had not been evacuated to the countryside, they were given a few days off because their school had been damaged in a raid.[1] And some remember stories about the rationing and the shortages of beer and of just about everything else needed for a bit of relaxation at the end of an exhausting day.

Recalled are often signal events like Dunkirk, the Battle of Britain and the Blitz, D-Day, and the VE Day celebrations; or a complex potpourri of sounds, especially the loud and deep wail of air raid sirens, the droning planes overhead, and the frightening whistle of a bomb as it plummeted through the air. They see blurred images of people watching the night sky, or picking through the rubble in the early light of morning. World War II is remembered as Britain's 'Finest Hour'—when people, both the 'ordinary people' and the privileged put aside their everyday

---

[1] For an excellent analysis of film and collective memory, see Geoff Eley, 'Finding the People's War: Film, British Collective Memory, and World War II', *American Historical Review*, 106 (June 2001), 818–38.

involvements and individual concerns, joined hands, and came to the nation's defence. Public memories of the war continue to recall this as a historical moment when the nation was truly united.

As historian Lucy Noakes has put it, it was a time when people's 'lives seemed to be "a part of history", a time when they were living through momentous events'.[2] Contributing to this sense of being witness to momentous times, the most powerfully compelling historical memory of wartime Britain was that Britons felt that they were an integral part of a community—a national community. But how was this wartime national community understood then? What did it mean to be British in the People's War? How was a unitary British national identity articulated and with what consequences?

Which People's War? examines how national belonging was envisaged in the public culture *at the time*. It probes the dimensions and contours of that wartime cultural configuration and its significance. It asks who was included and who was excluded and how and with what consequences those inclusions and exclusions were articulated. It questions how the British understood their nation as a people— a singular people—the people fighting 'the People's War', as World War II was and still is popularly named. And it examines the several meanings of citizenship elaborated in various discussions concerning the British nation at war. The chapters that follow investigate the powerful constructions of national identity and understandings of citizenship circulating in Britain and reveal their multiple and contradictory consequences within the wartime conjuncture itself. *Which People's War?* exposes the fragility of a unitary national identity, even during a war that involved total mobilization of the country's citizenry and that cost 400,000 British civilian lives.

Wartime Depictions of Nationhood and Britishness

Public officials responsible for civilian morale and participants in discussions about Britain's post-war future, as well as artists and writers (especially those under the tutelage of the Ministry of Information), portrayed the nation as composed of self-sacrificing, relentlessly cheerful, and inherently tolerant people who had heroically withstood the Blitz and were stalwart as they coped with the material deprivations of a war economy.[3] Britain was depicted by numerous social commentators as

[2] Lucy Noakes, *War and the British: Gender, Memory and National Identity* (London: I. B. Tauris, 1998), 3.

[3] For a discussion of the significance and centrality of these depictions of British national character and behaviour both during the war and afterward, see Angus Calder's insightful study, *The Myth of the Blitz* (London: Jonathan Cape, 1991). Echoing the characteristics of Britishness/Englishness referred to here, Jeffrey Richards has maintained that in almost every wartime film there were three qualities that were depicted as central strands of national character: sense of humour, tolerance, and stoicism or emotional restraint. See Jeffrey Richards, 'National Identity in British Wartime Films', in Philip M. Taylor (ed.), *Britain and the Cinema in the Second World War* (London: Macmillan, 1988), 58.

engaging in a war being fought by and for a country imagined as a unified land of 'ordinary people'. It was a nation whose historically characteristic, identifying virtues emerged along with what Angus Calder called 'the myth of the Blitz'—one in which the ' "people", improvising bravely and brilliantly', had fought off the German Luftwaffe and had withstood its fire.[4] A *Picture Post* photograph of May 1941, for example, portrayed 'The Man the Nazis are Trying to Rattle: A British Citizen of 1941'. It shows a working-class man wearing a cap and overcoat sifting through rubble. The caption declares, 'He is the English city dweller. His home is the Nazi bombers' target. His few poor possessions, bought with the savings of years, are their military objective. And when a bomb falls, and makes of his home a shapeless heap of bricks, he calmly salvages what he can and starts afresh.'[5] The mythical notion that the British of all classes remained stalwart in the face of nightly bombings was actively being created as it contributed to the redefinition of the nation.

J. B. Priestley's radio broadcast following the evacuation of British troops from Dunkirk months prior to the Blitz and George Orwell's famous essay on patriotism both captured and helped to articulate the meanings of the nation being elaborated during the war. Priestley suggested that Dunkirk was 'very English . . . in the way in which, when apparently all was lost, so much was gloriously retrieved'.[6] Unlike the Germans, he proudly declared, 'the English' (Priestley said he really meant 'British') are able to create an 'epic of gallantry' from what starts as a 'miserable blunder'. As Calder has argued persuasively, the idea that the British traditionally have rescued victory from the jaws of defeat is clearly mythological.[7] Priestley proposed that what was so 'characteristically English' about this particular epic

was the part played in the difficult and dangerous embarkation—not by the warships, magnificent though they were—but by the little pleasure-steamers. We've known them and laughed at them, these fussy little steamers, all our lives. We have watched them load and unload their crowds of holiday passengers—the gents full of high spirits and bottled beer, the ladies eating pork pies, the children sticky with peppermint rock. Sometimes they only went as far as the next seaside resort. But the boldest of them might manage a Channel crossing, to let everybody have a glimpse of Bologne.[8]

Priestley used populist language to depict the little 'boats' who went to rescue the soldiers fleeing Dunkirk, as 'ordinary people'.[9] By focusing on the 'little pleasure-steamers' and depicting them through working-class and lower middle-class

---

[4] Calder, *Myth of the Blitz*, 125.

[5] 3 May 1941, in Tom Hopkinson (ed.), *Picture Post 1938–1950* (London: Chatto and Windus, 1984), 89.

[6] J. B. Priestley, 'Broadcast from June 5, 1940', in Priestley, *Postscripts* (London, 1940), 2.

[7] Calder, *Myth of the Blitz*, chap. 1.   [8] Priestley, *Postscripts*, 2.

[9] Thanks to Geoff Eley for pointing out Priestley's use of populist rather than socialist class imagery in this passage. For an insightful study of J. B. Priestley's conceptions of Englishness, see Chris Waters, 'J. B. Priestley 1894–1984, Englishness and the Politics of Nostalgia', in Susan Pedersen and Peter Mandler (eds.), *After the Victorians: Private Conscience and Public Duty in Modern Britain, Essays in Memory of John Clive* (London and New York: Routledge, 1994), 209–26.

cultural imagery, Priestley conjured up the heroism of the ordinary people of Britain in a narrative not unlike the children's story 'The Little Engine that Could'.

George Orwell also depicted the nation as comprised of ordinary people when he wrote,

We are a nation of flower-lovers, but also a nation of stamp-collectors, pigeon-fanciers, amateur carpenters, coupon-snippers, darts-players, crossword-puzzle fans. All the culture that is most truly native centres round things which even when they are communal are not official—the pub, the football match, the back garden, the fireside and the 'nice cup of tea'.[10]

Implicitly contrasting the British with the Germans, Orwell used this characterization of Britons in their private lives to make the point that these ordinary, pub-going, and flower-loving people were not innately drawn to nationalism or to participating in affairs of state.[11]

Portraying the British people as characterized by diversity rather than a 'mass mentality', he also remarked on the deep class divisions in this 'land of snobbery and privilege, ruled largely by the old and silly. But in any calculation about it one has got to take into account its emotional unity, the tendency of nearly all its inhabitants to feel alike and act together in moments of supreme crisis'.[12] In spite of its diversity and its abrasive class hierarchy, Britain, he maintained, is like a family that 'closes ranks' upon the approach of an enemy.[13] Thus, Orwell depicted Britain as composed of people not innately given to heroic public deeds but who, despite deep class divisions and their heterogeneous pastimes, were able to put aside their differences and their individual interests to defend the nation.[14]

There were numerous 'odes' to Britain written during the period that celebrated the 'natural' bonds that joined Britons into one people in spite of the British class system. Journalist Thomas Burke, in an essay published in the *Preston Herald*, for example, singled out the pub tradition as both representing and fostering 'true democracy'.

When you enter the pub, whatever you may be in the outside world, you are, for the time being, a common member of a classless pub . . . The pub is the place where all are equal; where the member of a Pall Mall Club and the Working Men's Club are just customers, neither receiving more attention than the other . . . In that centre of mutual tolerance and

---

[10] George Orwell, *The Lion and the Unicorn: Socialism and the English Genius* (London: Secker and Warburg, 1941), 15.

[11] For a discussion of Orwell, and other left-leaning commentators who idealize the heterogeneity of the 'English', see Miles Taylor, 'Patriotism, History and the Left in Twentieth-Century Britain', *Historical Journal*, 33 (Sept. 1990), 971–87.

[12] Orwell, *Lion and the Unicorn*, 33.

[13] I will explore further the familial metaphor in Chapter 4.

[14] Simon Featherstone argues provocatively that the myth of unity despite diversity articulated in World War II literature is a central component of the literary construction of 'nation as pastoral' that exposes division as it seeks to deny it. Featherstone, 'The Nation as Pastoral in British Literature of the Second World War', *Journal of European Studies*, 16 (Summer 1986), 155–68.

the operation of our easy English good humour, men recognise not their difference, but their common nature . . . The bar . . . is almost the only place where you find not only demo-cracy in being but true Socialism in practice. The bar makes people what they should be—kind, impulsive, and generous without calculation.[15]

Significantly, this is a masculine representation of the English tradition of community life—surely in 1940s Britain whether or not one was male or female mattered when entering a pub. But this masculine representation conveyed the sense that the pub was at the heart of English life, and, therefore, so too was the 'democratic spirit' that obliterated class feeling from the essence of the nation. Burke's disquisition on the pub and Orwell's statements about patriotism portrayed the nation as a unified if not homogeneous community. Such portraits of national unity suggested also that those who best represented Britain at war were not exceptional individuals but rather were everyday, ordinary people; those who were 'doing their bit'. Even the Queen's daily routine was described as having been radically reorganized, affected by rationing and wartime economizing, with 'the victory of the Allies as its foremost aim'.[16]

The spirit of everyday sacrifice by ordinary people was portrayed in *Diary for Timothy*, the Humphrey Jennings documentary made in the closing months of the war, which focused on baby Timothy, born on the war's fifth anniversary, 3 September 1944. Timothy signified the future, and the script signalled to the film's audience that the sacrifices were being made for them and for their children's future. Suggesting that Britain was on the threshold of the war's end, the film portrayed the nation as being represented by particular key figures. There was Peter, a pilot, convalescing in hospital after having been wounded during D-Day; Geronwy, a coal miner who had been injured in a mining accident; a gentleman farmer, Alan, who had sacrificed significant portions of his grazing land in order to grow food for the war effort; and Bill, an engine driver who carried the crucial supplies of ammunition, fuel, and food. Together they represented the unified war effort. Michael Redgrave, narrating the film, informs the baby and the film's audience that 'these people are fighting for you'.[17] Like the depiction of the pub as the heart of the nation, Jennings's film also portrayed the nation with gendered imagery. It celebrated masculine sacrifice with its focus on the four male characters, while Timothy's mother, the only female figure of note in the film, exemplified the maternal.

Feminist scholarship has suggested the centrality of gender distinctions to nationhood. Literary theorist Anne McClintock has proposed, for example, that 'all nations depend on powerful constructions of gender. Despite many nationalists' ideological investment in the idea of popular *unity*, nations have historically

[15] Thomas Burke, 'Democracy in Being; In the Bar All are Equal', *Preston Herald*, 19 Mar. 1943, 7.
[16] Arthur Nettleton, 'The Queen's Household in Wartime', *Woman's Own*, 9 Mar. 1940, 11.
[17] Humphrey Jennings, *Diary for Timothy*, Crown Film Unit, 1945.

amounted to the sanctioned institutionalization of gender *difference*.[18] While women have been excluded from being full citizens of the nation-state and have been depicted in political theory from the ancient world through the Enlightenment as unworthy or inappropriate to assume the rights and obligations of citizenship, images of women have often symbolized the nation.[19] Furthermore the status of women has been a central theme in nationalist discourses.[20] Yet most scholars have argued that nations are constructed as fraternities; as being characterized by male bonds, largely because of the significance of war (that most gendered of activities in which states engage) to their development.[21] Women have generally been included within the nation in their status as mothers—as reproducers of the race, rather than as political participants in civil society.[22] As I will discuss further in Chapters 3 and 4, complex issues of gender crucially framed discourses of nationhood and citizenship in World War II Britain and were central to the portrayal of the 'home front' and the heroism of its ordinary people.

There were numerous portraits depicting the nation as a unified community of ordinary people contributing to the war effort. These characterizations made 'the common man' central to the nation at war, celebrated diversity, implicitly advocated tolerance, and recognized Britain as a class- and gender-divided society but denied that it mattered to national unity—to the image of the British as essentially one people. This vision of World War II British patriotism provided the parameters

---

[18] Anne McClintock, *Imperial Leather: Race, Gender and Sexuality in the Colonial Context* (London and New York: Routledge, 1995), 353.

[19] For the contested use of feminine allegorical symbols during the French Revolution, see Lynn Hunt, *Politics, Culture, and Class in the French Revolution* (Berkeley and Los Angeles: University of California Press, 1984), esp. 60–2, 90–4; Joan Landes, 'Representing the Body Politic: The Paradox of Gender and the Graphic Politics of the French Revolution', in Sara E. Melzer and Leslie W. Rabine (eds.), *Rebel Daughters: Women and the French Revolution* (New York and Oxford: Oxford University Press, 1992), 15–37. On the transformation of female symbols of the nation to suit nationalist purposes, see George L. Mosse, *Nationalism and Sexuality: Middle-Class Morality and Sexual Norms in Modern Europe* (Madison: University of Wisconsin Press, 1985), chap. 5, and McClintock, *Imperial Leather*, 352.

[20] See e.g. Deniz Kandiyoti, 'Women and the Turkish State: Political Actors or Symbolic Pawns?', in Nira Yuval-Davis and Floya Anthias (eds.), *Woman—Nation—State* (Basingstoke: Macmillan, 1989), 126–49; Deniz Kandiyoti, 'From Empire to Nation State: Transformations of the Woman Question in Turkey', in Susan Jay Kleinberg (ed.), *Retrieving Women's History: Changing Perceptions of the Role of Women in Politics and Society* (Oxford and New York: Berg, 1988).

[21] Mosse, *Nationalism and Sexuality*, 91; Andrew Parker, 'Introduction', in Andrew Parker *et al.* (eds.), *Nationalisms & Sexualities* (London: Routledge, 1992), 6–7; McClintock, *Imperial Leather*, 352–3.

[22] For a path-breaking work on this issue for England, see Anna Davin, 'Imperialism and Motherhood', *History Workshop Journal*, 5 (Spring 1978), 9–65. For Russia, see Elizabeth Waters, 'The Modernisation of Russian Motherhood, 1917–1937', *Feminist Review*, 33 (Autumn 1989), 3–18. On republican motherhood and the French Revolution, see Joan Landes, *Women and the Public Sphere in the Age of the French Revolution* (Ithaca, NY and London: Cornell University Press, 1988). On republican motherhood in the USA, see Linda Kerber, 'The Republican Mother: Women and the Enlightenment', *American Quarterly*, 27 (1976), 187–205. On the centrality of women as mothers, but not as wives or citizens, to the making of the Irish republic, see Sarah Benton, 'Women Disarmed: The Militarization of Politics in Ireland 1913–23', *Feminist Review*, 50 (Summer 1995), 148–72.

for defining the nation as a *community* 'imagined as a deep, horizontal comrade-ship', to use Benedict Anderson's words.[23]

Such representations of nationhood were understood by the Government, the press, as well as many members of the public at large to be crucial to morale and to generating the massive public support that was needed for the war effort. But what is it about war that makes 'the nation' capable of inspiring passionate loyalty? To answer this question, we need to understand conceptually what nations are and how they become sources of personal identification capable of generating passionate loyalty.

Nationhood, National Identity, and War

As a number of scholars have argued, war between and among states has been crucial to generating the conception of nationhood as a political collectivity that is 'one and indivisible'.[24] I use the word 'nationhood' here, following sociologist Rogers Brubaker, to indicate that I am not adopting a view of 'the nation' that conceives of it as a concrete entity. Rather 'the nation' is a 'central and protean . . . category of modern political and cultural thought, discourse, and practice'.[25] It is a mode of practice that constructs a people as an actually existing unitary entity.[26] The nation is a reification, a conceptual abstraction, but through representations and rhetoric it appears to exist in a concrete form.

These representations and rhetorics work to generate what we might term the pull of unity—of absolute belonging—the desire to be part of a grand, unified collective. This study will show, ironically however, that as the cultural images portraying nationhood as a unitary collective identity dominate civic culture, their centrality in the public imagination produces the possibility for the kinds of

---

[23] Benedict Anderson, *Imagined Communities: Reflections on the Origin and Spread of Nationalism*, rev. edn. (London: Verso, 1991), 7.

[24] Jean Bethke Elshtain, *Women and War* (Chicago and London: University of Chicago Press, 1995), 256. From a different perspective, see Charles Tilly, who argues the centrality of war to national state-making in *Coercion, Capital, and European States, AD 990–1992*, rev. edn. (Cambridge, Mass. and Oxford: Basil Blackwell, 1992).

[25] Rogers Brubaker, *Nationalism Reframed: Nationhood and the National Question in the New Europe* (Cambridge: Cambridge University Press, 1996), 10.

[26] See Brubaker, *Nationalism Reframed*, 15. The study of nationalism(s) has produced an extensive literature. The approach that I use in this study draws heavily on Benedict Anderson, *Imagined Communities*. Other helpful discussions include: Partha Chatterjee, 'Whose Imagined Community?', in Partha Chatterjee, *The Nation and Its Fragments: Colonial and Postcolonial Histories* (Princeton: Princeton University Press, 1993), chap. 1; Ronald Grigor Suny, *The Revenge of the Past: Nationalism, Revolution and the Collapse of the Soviet Union* (Stanford, Calif.: Stanford University Press, 1993), chap. 1; Katherine Verdery, 'Whither "Nation" and "Nationalism"?', *Daedalus*, 122 (Summer 1993), 37–46. See also: Craig Calhoun, *Nationalism* (Minneapolis: University of Minnesota Press, 1997); Geoff Eley and Ronald Grigor Suny (eds.), *Becoming National: A Reader* (New York and Oxford: Oxford University Press, 1996), Introduction, 3–37.

conflicts that in the last third of the twentieth century came to be known as 'identity politics'—a politics of making claims to respect, recognition, rights, and inclusion based on group membership.[27] For example, as Chapter 6 will show, members of the armed forces from Scotland insisted on wearing the kilt as formal military dress rather than the uniforms of the British army, and the Welsh (in addition to the Scottish) protested when the BBC referred to the country as England. The pull to unity, then, was accompanied by the pull to resist that incorporation in the name of particularity, difference, or group distinctiveness.

Defying a unitary sense of 'we-ness', definitions of nationhood and representations of national identity produce an array of multiple, unintended meanings for and interpretations by people in differing circumstances and social locations. As Chapter 2 will suggest, for example, the slogan 'equality of sacrifice' inspired protests by people in the working classes about upper-class privilege. Such meanings and interpretations are made possible and are shaped by the historically particular constraints and opportunities structuring peoples' lives. Thus, even in Britain, even during the war, in a time now remembered in popular memory as one in which the people of the country were of one mind and were fully unified around the war effort, there was defiance, resistance, and indifference. Representations of the nation, then, are not always successful in creating a single frame through which people see themselves as national beings, even in the face of total war. Why might this be so? To answer this question, I turn to some helpful theoretical discussions of national identity and nationhood.

Any particular specification of nationhood never exhausts what its language is intended to signify—there is always an excess available to be given meaning by other languages of group identification or 'we-ness'. Cultural theorist Stuart Hall explains that such constructions of nationhood and national belonging 'emerge within the play of specific modalities of power, and thus are more the product of the marking of difference and exclusion, than they are the sign of an identical naturally-constituted unity—an "identity" in its traditional meaning (that is, an all-inclusive sameness, seamless, without internal differentiation)'.[28] For example, British masculinity was constructed against the hyper-masculine Nazi 'other' as

[27] For a discussion of the discourse of 'identity' and 'identity politics', see Craig Calhoun, 'Social Theory and the Politics of Identity', in Craig Calhoun (ed.), *Social Theory and the Politics of Identity* (Cambridge, Mass. and Oxford: Basil Blackwell, 1994), esp. 20–6. For a provocative critique of the concept of 'identity' as it is used currently in social theory, see Rogers Brubaker and Frederick Cooper, 'Beyond "Identity"', *Theory and Society*, 29 (Spring 2000), 1–47. For some of the recent debates concerning what Charles Taylor has called 'the politics of recognition' and multiculturalism, see the essay by Taylor, 'The Politics of Recognition', and responses to it in Amy Gutmann (ed.), *Multiculturalism: Examining the Politics of Recognition* (Princeton: Princeton University Press, 1994); Susan Miller Okin, *Is Multiculturalism Bad for Women?* and the essays responding to Okin's essay (Princeton: Princeton University Press, 1999).

[28] Stuart Hall, 'Introduction: Who Needs Identity?' in Stuart Hall and Paul du Gay (eds.), *Questions of Cultural Identity* (London: Sage Publications, 1996), 4.

Chapter 5 will suggest, and as Chapter 3 will show, the 'good citizen' and true Briton were conceived in opposition to those within the country who were described as selfish and self-serving. This complexity and the diversity of possible meanings inherent in the discourse of nationhood means that it is always a possible site of contestation.

While rhetorical constructions of the nation can and do produce alternative meanings, these alternatives are not, however, limitless. They are constrained by the events, structures, and relations in and through which they are articulated. The chapters of this book provide ample evidence that there were a variety of unantici-pated and deeply ironic repercussions of the articulation of a unitary collective national identity in the years of World War II.

Although this study suggests the impossibility, even in a period of total war, of fully and fixedly representing the nation as a unitary 'we', I will argue that even the necessarily failed or inadequate depictions and attempts to fashion a singular iden-tity—a one-size-fits-all image of Britishness or Englishness—reinforced the signi-ficance of the nation as an object of personal identification. As people contested the images of Britain on offer, or used them to serve sectional interests, they deployed languages inflected by the wartime discourses about nationhood and citizenship that contributed to a reconfigured, emotionally charged political culture.

Linda Colley has suggested that identities are not like hats—one can wear more than one at a time.[29] While that is a helpful image, or counter-image, it does not go far enough to fully capture the complex ways that national identity meshes with other identities, especially during a war. Representations of national identity in wartime either subsume or deny the significance of other identities.

Rhetorics of nationhood are strategies deployed to manage or organize the dif-ferences among people that have come to be sites of collective identity formation so that individuals see themselves as national beings regardless of their other loyalties and preoccupations. As sociologist Craig Calhoun has written, 'nationality . . . becomes one large categorical identity that encompasses many smaller categories ("tribes", ethnic groups) each of which may be organized internally on the basis of further categories and complex networks of interpersonal relationships'.[30] In other words, nationality is a master social category. In certain historical circumstances, this master category, the national 'we', becomes a politically and emotionally pow-erful vision. War has been just such a time.

In World War II the potency of the national 'we' was stimulated by particular images of the nation as a community. Benedict Anderson's path-breaking idea that the nation is an imagined community remains, in spite of critiques of aspects of his analysis, an exceptionally helpful analytical tool for understanding

---

[29] Linda Colley, *Britons: Forging the Nation 1707–1837* (New Haven and London: Yale University Press, 1992), 6.

[30] Calhoun, *Nationalism*, 39.

nationhood.[31] Most scholars have come to agree that nations, indeed all communities, are imagined. As Etienne Balibar, in a theoretically astute discussion suggests, *'Every social community reproduced by the functioning of institutions is imaginary,* that is to say, it is based on the projection of individual existence into the weft of a collective narrative'.[32]

Community may be understood to be the outcome of the process of collective identification; it is made through practices that establish who 'we' are as a collective body.[33] As is the case with group identities generally, communal identities are forged as people take action together and as they deploy cultural tools to manufacture a sense of 'we-ness'.[34]

Historically when, why, and how the 'nation' became the object of joint identification has been a long-standing source of scholarly debate, a debate that I will not reproduce here.[35] Rather, it is important to consider what kind of 'imagined community' is the nation, and how war might activate its salience for the citizens of a nation-state.

In words that are especially applicable to how the World War II British nation was culturally constructed, social theorist Etienne Balibar suggests that in being constituted as a community, the nation is defined as 'the people'.[36] And as he insists, 'such a people does not exist naturally'.[37] No nation is 'ethnically pure' and no nation is free of class and other forms of inequality. The nation, then, may be understood as an ideological discourse that produces 'the effect of unity by virtue of which the people will appear, in everyone's eyes, "as a people", that is, as the basis and origin of political power'.[38] At its heart, and nowhere was this more particularly the case than Britain in World War II, 'the nation' is often a populist and always a utopian fantasy.[39] Like all ideologies, it is at once a historically shaped cultural construction

---

[31] See e.g. Chatterjee, *The Nation and Its Fragments*, 4–6.

[32] Etienne Balibar, 'The Nation Form: History and Ideology', in Etienne Balibar and Immanuel Wallerstein (eds.), *Race, Nation, Class, Ambiguous Identities* (London and New York: Verso, 1991), 86–106 (emphasis in the original).

[33] Richard Sennett, *The Fall of Public Man* (New York: Vintage Books, 1974), 222.

[34] See ibid. and also see Rick Fantasia, *Cultures of Solidarity: Consciousness, Action, and Contemporary American Workers* (Los Angeles and Berkeley: University of California Press, 1988), 17. At the most elementary level, national consciousness or national identity is similar to other kinds of identities, and Rick Fantasia's discussion of class consciousness, what he terms 'cultures of solidarity' is helpful in thinking about the similarities and differences of national and more local communal identities.

[35] For good overviews of this literature, see Geoff Eley and Ron Suny, 'Introduction: From the Moment of Social History to the Work of Cultural Representation', in Eley and Suny (eds.), *Becoming National*, 3–38; Calhoun, *Nationalism*, esp. chap. 1.

[36] Balibar, 'The Nation Form', 93.   [37] Ibid.   [38] Ibid. 93–4.

[39] For a discussion of populism and the relationship of individuals to political community and 'the common good' in the United States, see Robert N. Bellah et al., *Habits of the Heart: Individualism and Commitment in American Life* (New York: Harper & Row, 1986), chap. 10; for a discussion of populism in British political discourse in the 19th century, see Patrick Joyce, *Visions of the People: Industrial England and the Question of Class, 1848–1914* (Cambridge: Cambridge University Press, 1991).

meant to apply broadly and a cultural concept that answers the question for individuals, 'who am I'? Thus, it produces both an individual and a collective identity.

The term 'identity' suggests the powerful emotional attachment that the ideology of nationhood can forge. As Balibar, borrowing from the philosopher Fichte, has put it, 'the "external frontiers" of the state have to become "internal frontiers" or—which amounts to the same thing—external frontiers have to be imagined constantly as a projection and protection of an internal collective personality, which each of us carries within ourselves and enables us to inhabit the space of the state as a place where we have always been—and always will be—"at home".'[40] In other words, the nation is imagined as an essentially unchanging place of like-minded people where we experience the emotional security of being perpetually at home.

Understanding nationhood as an ideological discourse that produces a common belief that the national community is *one* people and creates subjects who understand or experience themselves as national beings suggests why it is that war can so powerfully activate and make central national identity. As the 'external frontiers' of the nation are threatened, so too, are the 'internal frontiers' of individuals. When in World War II mothers sent their sons off to war, they were doing so not because they were mothers but because they were British mothers. As the bombs rained down on British soil, destroying British houses, British monuments, factories and ports, citizens of Britain understood at some very deep level that their personal lives and well-being were at risk only because of their national belonging. They shared at least that much in common with everyone, and this recognition of common jeopardy contributed mightily to making national identity particularly meaningful for individuals.[41] And when there exists no shared sense of individual jeopardy because the war is being fought elsewhere, the Government attempts to persuade its people that their fathers, sons, and brothers are fighting for their personal safety as well as for the long-term security of the nation.

National communal identification in wartime is enhanced by the fact that, as the scholar Elaine Scarry has argued, war is a contest involving two and only two contestants whose outcome will result in one contestant remaining. In war, she has suggested, 'each side works to bring the other side to the latter's perceived level of intolerable injury faster than it is itself brought to its own level of intolerable injury'.[42] Or, as historian Michael Geyer in his mediation on military history

---

[40] Balibar, 'The Nation Form', 95.

[41] A similar argument is implicit in Paul Gilroy's discussion of the role of the memory of terror and bondage 'in securing the unity of the communities of sentiment and interpretation which black culture helps to reproduce'. See *The Black Atlantic: Modernity and Double Consciousness* (Cambridge, Mass.: Harvard University Press, 1993), chap. 6.

[42] Elaine Scarry, *The Body in Pain: The Making and Unmaking of the World* (New York and Oxford: Oxford University Press, 1985), 89.

maintains, war is about 'death—man-made mass death, neither natural nor individual death'.[43]

The heightened significance of national identity in people's everyday lives in wartime provides the possibility that they will experience either of two opposite emotionally charged responses. On the one hand, civilians may oppose the war and refuse to support their Government. Or, on the other hand, as was the case in World War II Britain, they may unite in solidarity with their Government. But in either case, they do so in defence of 'the nation'.

As numerous scholars have pointed out, there is an important distinction between states and nations. Hugh Seton-Watson, for example, has argued that 'states can exist without a nation, or with several nations, among their subjects; and a nation can be coterminous with the population of one state, or be included together with other nations within one state, or be divided between states'.[44] States are institutions and institutionalized practices, while as I have suggested earlier, 'nations' are the effect of discourses of nationhood, discourses with tremendous emotional power. Thus, it is the vision of the nation that generates strong emotional responses and loyalties, not necessarily the state or the government. Citizens may fervently protest or avidly participate in war in the name of 'the nation'.

This is not meant to imply that *all* citizens become passionately involved—certainly some may be relatively unconcerned with the course of events; and as happened in Britain during the Blitz, some took advantage of other people's tragedies for their own gain, while others declared a conscientious objection to participating in the war. And as I will have occasion to show throughout this book, national symbols can be deployed for fundamentally sectional aims. But unlike 'ordinary times', wartime creates conditions likely to stimulate passionate identification with the nation on the part of relatively large numbers of people.

Numerous scholars have attempted to reckon with the emotional power of 'the nation'—of imagery that produces in individuals a passionate identification with and an immediate sense of belonging to a national community. The issue of emotional attachment to an imagined national community was a central question that Benedict Anderson raised, but did not successfully answer.[45] To do so requires a psychological theory of emotion and identification, or to use Stuart Hall's words, a theory of 'the practices of subjective self-constitution'.[46] I will not pretend to advance such a theory here. In fact, I am not necessarily convinced by the specifics of the

[43] Michael Geyer, 'War and the Context of General History in an Age of Total War: Comment on Peter Paret, "Justifying the Obligation of Military Service", and Michael Howard, "World War One: The Crisis in European History"', *Journal of Military History*, Special Issue 57 (Oct. 1993), 161.

[44] Hugh Seton-Watson, *Nations and States* (London: Methuen, 1977), 1.

[45] Essentially Anderson wonders what makes it possible 'for so many millions of people, not so much to kill, as willingly to die for such limited imaginings', as the nation. Anderson, *Imagined Communities*, 7.

[46] Hall, 'Introduction: Who Needs Identity?', 13. See Hall's discussion of this issue, 13–17.

various psychoanalytic theoretical explanations for the origins of the emotional power of national identity on offer. But scholars whose work has been informed by psychoanalytic theories seem to have an important purchase on at least describing the phenomenon.[47]

Literary critic Lauren Berlant has suggested, for example, that the discursive practices creating collective consciousness, what she terms the 'National Symbolic', bind 'regulation to desire, harnessing affect to political life through the production of national fantasy'.[48] The ideological work of nationhood does more than inculcate certain beliefs or political values. It integrates these beliefs and values into an emotional process involving 'the affects of love and hate and representation of the "self".'[49] And it is in wartime, I am arguing, that this ideological work is especially trenchant in generating emotional attachment to the nation.

The strength of these attachments, however, does not mean that representations of the nation are actually successful in making individuals see themselves as fully national beings. The seeming oneness of national identity itself produces desire, because it is 'always incomplete'.[50] As I suggested earlier 'the nation' is an abstraction that produces the pull of unity. But those others in one's 'homeland' are in actuality a diverse lot; uniformity is an impossibility and unity is never total. Political theorist Renata Salecl, using Lacanian psychoanalytic language, explains that it is through fantasy that the psyche attempts to symbolize or complete what cannot be symbolized or made whole.

In the fantasy structure of the homeland, the nation (in the sense of national identification) is the element that cannot be symbolized. The nation is an element in us that is 'more than ourselves,' something that defines us but is at the same time undefinable: we cannot specify what it means, nor can we erase it . . . The homeland is the fantasy structure, the scenario, through which society perceives itself as a homogeneous entity.[51]

And in war, in a contest to 'out-injure' the other, the national body as a national fantasy is both literally and figuratively in danger of destruction.

Even though it may seem self-evident that war heightens the significance of the nation as an object of identification making national subjects passionate about their embattled country, the process of national identity formation is not automatic. It is, as I suggested before, produced by ideological work. And the particular

[47] For a provocative recent attempt to use Freudian and Lacanian analysis to inform an understanding of national identity, see Antony Easthope, *Englishness and National Culture* (London and New York: Routledge, 1999).

[48] Lauren Berlant, *The Anatomy of National Fantasy: Hawthorne, Utopia, and Everyday Life* (Chicago: University of Chicago Press, 1991), 5.

[49] Balibar, 'The Nation Form', 94.

[50] See Easthope, *Englishness and National Culture*, 47.

[51] Renata Salecl, 'The Fantasy Structure of Nationalist Discourse', *Praxis International*, 13 (Oct. 1993), 216–17. For a similar, Lacanian-based discussion that is focused on Englishness, see Easthope, *Englishness and National Culture*.

symbols, themes, and rhetorical strategies—the ideological discourses current in a particular war—are shaped by the specific cultural and social contexts in which they are generated.

While certainly the propaganda arms of the Government are significant in generating the national meanings that circulate, they do not operate in a cultural vacuum, nor is the process of national identity formation simply dictated by those with formal political power. Rather, ideas about the nation and the symbols by which it is represented are in dialogue with a range of cultural meanings. And these symbols and meanings are reworked in various ways by people differently located in society who join in the national conversation.

The fact that World War II followed a depression in which there was massive though uneven unemployment and poverty—there were still a million unemployed at the beginning of the war—was highly significant in shaping the terms of the discussion about the nation and its future. That the enemy was Nazi Germany, and that much of the rhetoric about Great Britain and its empire was shaped in opposition to images of Nazi Germany clearly had a role in fashioning national imagery, as did historically long-lived understandings about Great Britain as both a white nation and an imperial power, subjects that are taken up in Chapter 7. That labour to produce the tools of war was in such great demand that women were conscripted into industry and some men were excused from military service to remain on their jobs at home also affected how gender and nation were linked in various representations and debates as I discuss in Chapters 4 and 5.

The Meanings of Citizenship

During the war the term 'citizenship' appeared in a variety of disparate discussions. These discussions ranged from, for example, the nature of wartime service and issues of equity, to arguments about the need for youth groups, debates about reconstruction, and even to admonitions about sexual propriety.[52]

Patriotic discourse in World War II centrally featured the idea that the members of the national community were self-sacrificing citizens, the focus of Chapter 3. Entreaties that individuals should be self-sacrificing, placing the community's interests and needs above their own were omnipresent in the media. Daphne du Maurier, the popular fiction writer, wrote in the *Sunday Chronicle* in early August 1940, during what was to become known as 'the Battle of Britain', 'We Can Face this Challenge!'

---

[52] I will discuss this more fully later in Chapter 2. Also see my essay, 'Sex, Citizenship and the Nation in World War II Britain', *American Historical Review*, 103 (Oct. 1998), 1147–76. For a study that addresses the issue of citizenship in World War II Britain, see David Morgan and Mary Evans, *The Battle for Britain: Citizenship and Ideology in the Second World War* (London and New York: Routledge, 1993).

Is it too late to root out the germ of selfishness from human nature and to cultivate the seed of generosity instead? . . . The ordinary man, woman and child can face up to this challenge and be victorious. The fight is not spectacular. It is a silent struggle between self and Spirit, and the voice of the Spirit is the voice of God. We can listen to either . . . The secret of high morale lies in personal victory over every selfish thought, every narrow prejudice that creeps stealthily into our hearts and minds in time of trouble.[53]

In the following months, the people of Britain proved that they could face that challenge, or at least that was the image that developed in the self-representations produced during and after the Blitz. A Ministry of Information (MOI) pamphlet published in 1941 proclaimed that when 'the mighty hordes of Hitler lined the French Channel coast, facing the white cliffs of England . . .'

What happened? The defences were manned in time. The attack by air was smashed . . . the greatness of a free people proved itself. The strength of character that Churchill trusted—that character that enabled him to rally his people—came out, in every street, in every home . . . the entire industrial population of the British Isles and of the British Commonwealth rose as one man and hurled itself . . . into the fight against the Nazis. Workers, foremen, managers—men and women—all 'went at it' flat out, hour upon hour, by day and by night.[54]

The MOI pamphlet proclaimed that there 'was hardly a class in the community but had thrown aside its privileges', and that the 'British working men and women have willingly surrendered cherished rights'.[55] The victorious fight was made possible because the people put aside their 'privileges' and 'their cherished rights' to defeat the enemy. Such references to the crucial importance of self-sacrifice (and the suspension of group perquisites) were often linked to the idea of citizenship in wartime debates and pronouncements.

Citizenship is one of the most ambiguous concepts in contemporary academic parlance.[56] It is a term generally denoting the relationship between individuals and the nation as well as between individuals and the state—a term that has broadly symbolic as well as more narrowly juridical meanings. In addition to describing the formal rights and duties of membership, it can have multiple and contested meanings.

Crucially citizenship is a membership category, defining who does and does not belong to a particular (national) community. In this sense, citizenship is a synonym for nationality, but it is one that is formally linked to the notion of rights that accrue

---

[53] Daphne du Maurier, 'We Can Face This Challenge!', *Sunday Chronicle*, 11 Aug. 1940, 4.

[54] Factories of Freedom', Ministry of Information, 1941. At the Imperial War Museum, London, 3–4.

[55] Ibid. 7, 11.

[56] For a provocative theoretical discussion of citizenship, see Margaret Somers, 'Citizenship and the Place of the Public Sphere', *American Sociological Review*, 58 (1993), 587–620. For a series of useful essays, see Bryan Turner, *Citizenship and Social Theory* (Newbury Park, Calif.: Sage Publications, 1993). On feminist debates on citizenship, see Ruth Lister, *Citizenship: Feminist Perspectives* (New York: New York University Press, 1997), 7.

to members, and to the obligations they owe to the state in return. Rules of membership and the specification of rights and duties constitute the juridical aspects of citizenship.[57]

In the universalizing tradition of liberalism, citizenship is often taken to mean a 'status' attached to which are particular rights and obligations. Until recently the obligations of citizenship have received less attention than have rights by political commentators and scholars working within the framework of liberal political theory.[58]

The concept of civic obligations, important to discussions about British citizenship in World War II, is more central to scholars and others who criticize liberalism, many of whom rearticulate ideas from classical republicanism. In the tradition of republicanism, civic humanism, and in more recent communitarian derivations, citizenship is a practice—a practice in which the citizen acts in the interest of the common good, putting aside his (in the classical and civic humanist tradition, only males were citizens) individual interests.

These different theoretical traditions defining citizenship have been crucially important in political practice at various points in the history of modern Europe since the seventeenth and eighteenth centuries. It is also the case that the language of citizenship has varied historically, and similar languages can and have taken on radically different meanings with substantially important consequences for people's lives. The questions that a historian might ask about these traditions and languages concern how and why particular dimensions of citizenship came to be significant at different historical points; what meanings of citizenship inform those dimensions at particular moments and to whom do they apply, and what uses are made of them and with what consequences? These questions are central to this book.

Citizenship, I would suggest, may usefully be defined as a *discursive framework* explicating the juridical relationship between people and the political community. It is a multidimensional framework that provides the basis upon which people can make claims on the political community concerning juridical rights and duties, political and ethical practices, and criteria of membership. By suggesting it is a

[57] For an important analysis of how nationhood influenced citizenship as a formal institution or juridical relationship securing membership in France and Germany, see Rogers Brubaker, *Citizenship and Nationhood in France and Germany* (Cambridge, Mass.: Harvard University Press, 1992), esp. chap. 1 and his discussion of citizenship as an instrument and an object of social closure—defining the rules of inclusion and exclusion of membership in the nation.

[58] A notable exception is the scholarship of American historian Linda Kerber who investigates the gendering of civic obligations in US history. See *No Constitutional Right to be Ladies: Women and the Obligations of Citizenship* (New York: Hill and Wang, 1998). Also see 'The Meanings of Citizenship', *Journal of American History*, 84 (Dec. 1997), 833–52. Kerber, however, focuses on those obligations that are state-enforced. As we shall see, in World War II Britain, the 'obligations of citizenship' that occupied so much space in public discussion were not necessarily statutory, but were moral 'oughts' rather than legal 'musts'.

framework that serves as a basis for claims-making, I mean to suggest that citizenship as an idea has been taken up and modified in different historical situations so that even those who traditionally were not imagined as citizens could use the framework of citizenship to demand certain protections or to secure certain benefits or to be guaranteed particular capacities.[59] It is on the basis of the discursive framework of citizenship that the state or community can expect or demand reciprocity from its members.

Significantly, the discursive framework of citizenship creates both legal and political subjects. The laws pertaining to citizenship that specify who can and who cannot belong to the nation-state and the formal rights and obligations of citizen/members create legal subjects. They stipulate who is subject to certain rights and duties. Crucially important, the discursive framework of citizenship also produces political subjectivities. People enact these subjectivities as they contest meanings and make claims on the political community, drawing upon the meanings made possible by the discursive framework.[60]

One of the fundamental characteristics of modern (liberal) citizenship is that it stipulates, in theory a universal subject. A citizen is a citizen—the same as any other citizen—regardless of whatever else he or she might be. Therefore all citizens, in theory, have the same entitlements and obligations. Liberalism (and the form of citizenship associated with it) promises to apply universally to all and offers a vision of inclusion. But, of course, its history has been marked by exclusions based on gender and race that stem from the capacities imagined in liberal theory that characterize the universal political subject, as political theorists Uday Mehta and Carole Pateman in different ways have suggested.[61] The strategies of liberal exclusion, as Mehta calls them, quite possibly derive in some way from ideas about 'civic virtue' in the tradition of civic humanism or classical republicanism, thus joining liberal citizenship to an aspect of republican citizenship. These strategies select out for inclusion

[59] Frederick Cooper, Thomas C. Holt, and Rebecca J. Scott, *Beyond Slavery: Explorations of Race, Labor, and Citizenship in Post-Emancipation Societies* (Chapel Hill and London: University of North Carolina Press, 2000), Introduction. My definition of citizenship is similar although not identical to one offered by Lauren Berlant, who suggests that 'citizenship is a status whose definitions are always in process. It is continually being produced out of a political, rhetorical, and economic struggle over who will count as "the people" and how social membership will be measured and valued.' See *The Queen of America Goes to Washington City* (Durham, NC and London: Duke University Press, 1997), 20.

[60] These ideas are indebted, in part, to theorizing in the Foucauldian tradition. See esp. essays in Graham Burchell, Colin Gordon and Peter Miller (eds.), *The Foucault Effect: Studies in Governmentality* (Chicago: University of Chicago Press, 1991). See esp. Graham Burchell, 'Peculiar Interests: Civil Society and Governing "The System of Natural Liberty"', 119–50. Also see Giovanna Procacci, 'Omnes or Singulatum? Citizenship as Government Strategies', paper presented at the CSST Faculty Seminar, University of Michigan, 28 Jan. 1999.

[61] Uday Singh Mehta, *Liberalism and Empire: A Study in Nineteenth-Century British Liberal Thought* (Chicago: University of Chicago Press, 1999), esp. chap. 2; Carole Pateman, 'The Fraternal Social Contract', in Carole Pateman, *The Disorder of Women: Democracy, Feminism, and Political Theory* (Stanford, Calif.: Stanford University Press, 1989), 33–57.

persons who are believed to possess the qualities to be 'good citizens', that is, those who, on the basis of personal characteristics (or what Mehta calls an 'anthropological minimum') can be trusted to fulfil the formal and informal obligations of community members. Independence and rationality are two such characteristics that have been the basis for the exclusion of non-whites, the economically indigent, and women. The ambiguity in the discursive framework of liberal citizenship, centred on its pretensions to universality and coupled with its strategies of inclusion and exclusion, has historically provided fertile ground on which individuals could make claims for inclusion.

In addition the components of the discursive framework of citizenship permit many possibilities for interpretation; that is there are multiple possible meanings generated by the terms citizen or citizenship, the language of rights, the rhetorics of obligation. Particular inflections of these terms and languages may be broadly emphasized and/or hotly contested depending upon the particular historical and cultural circumstances with which they are articulated. Historically gender and race have been central to such contestations about the dimensions and meanings of citizenship; about rights, obligations, membership, and moral and political practices. Thus, in World War II a discourse of 'rights' for women was given renewed vigour, in part because in wartime Britain the Government focused so pointedly on the various obligations that women as well as men owed to the nation as I argue in Chapter 4.

Although there were discussions and debates about legal rights and obligations, significantly a feature of the World War II discursive framework of citizenship focused on issues of morality and ethical behaviour. A BBC discussion presented on the Scottish News Hour concerning training for citizenship, for example, involved the following exchange:

Joseph F. Duncan: . . . If citizenship is anything, it's a thing of the spirit. It's a part of a person's character. . .

Lord Provost Darling: You must be taught to feel . . . and feel the right way. Emotion comes into it. Conscience comes into it. A good citizen is a man with a sense of his obligations as well as his rights. That's what we've kept on forgetting. Duties as well as privileges.[62]

Being a 'good citizen' then had to do with actively expressing a commitment to the nation by voluntarily fulfilling obligations and willingly contributing to the welfare of the community.

This vision of citizenship, while it came into full flower in World War II, had its roots in a number of philosophical traditions. These included classical republicanism with its emphasis on citizenship as an activity or practice and British

---

[62] Scottish Half Hour, 'Discussion on Training for Citizenship', 15 Sept. 1942, Radio Talks Scripts Film T 157, p. 3. at the BBC Written Archives Centre, Caversham Park, Reading.

idealism which, as historian Jose Harris has suggested, stressed 'corporate identity, individual altruism, ethical imperatives and active citizen-participation'.[63] Such ideas were promulgated by intellectuals such as R. H. Tawney and Harold Laski, and in the writings of Ernest Barker, the first professor of political science at Cambridge.[64]

During the war, active citizenship was linked to 'social responsibility' and participation in civil society or in public affairs. For instance, an editorial in a Coventry newspaper in 1943 discussed a meeting held among leaders of civil defence organizations 'and other interests in city life . . . to consider how best the spirit of service so nobly typified by civil defence personnel in the stress of air raids, can be perpetuated in the days of peace and used for the good of Coventry'.[65] The editorial contrasted the apathy towards civic responsibility that characterized Coventry in the past, when 'too many people have been immersed in their own affairs, and responsibility to citizenship has too often begun and ended with the payment of rates'.[66]

In a similar vein a correspondent wrote in *The Land Worker*, the journal of the Agricultural Workers' Union, of the growing interest on the part of villagers in local affairs. He maintained:

We have . . . working together for the common good, a number of people who had, until the war threw them together, been of the kind who 'can't be bothered' with the running of their own lives.

The village is becoming conscious that it is a part of the scheme of things.

If every village in this country would do as much, what a difference it would make. How much more power the 'common people' would have. And what a difference there would be in the results of future elections![67]

And, celebrating the possibility that in Coventry an organization would be formed by community leaders to promote the perpetuation of 'the spirit of service' in the

---

[63] Jose Harris, 'Political Thought and the Welfare State, 1870–1940', *Past and Present*, 135 (1992), 137. Harris argues that idealist thought profoundly influenced British political and governmental culture from the Edwardian period into the 1940s.

[64] Richard Weight and Abigail Beach, 'Introduction', in Weight and Beach (eds.), *The Right to Belong: Citizenship and National Identity in Britain, 1930–1960* (London: I. B. Tauris, 1998), 2. See also Sandra M. den Otter's lucid discussion of Idealist thought in *British Idealism and Social Explanation: A Study in Late Victorian Thought* (Oxford: Clarendon Press, 1996).

[65] 'The Spirit of Coventry', *Coventry Evening Telegraph*, 29 May 1943, 4.

[66] Ibid. For research on post-war Coventry, see Nick Tiratsoo, *Reconstruction, Affluence and Labour Politics: Coventry 1945–60* (London: Routledge, 1990). For a discussion of the eventual setting up of the Coventry Guild of Citizens towards the end of 1943 and the variations among Coventry's population in its concerns as the war drew to a close, see Tony Mason and Peter Thompson, ' "Reflections on a Revolution"? The Political Mood in Wartime Britain', in Nick Tiratsoo (ed.), *The Atlee Years* (London and New York: Pinter, 1991), 54–70, esp. 60–5.

[67] Wallace Arter, 'War—and the Village', *The Land Worker*, Mar. 1940, 6.

days of peace, the previously quoted editorial in the *Coventry Evening Telegraph* proclaimed: 'Few people would deny that there has been lacking in Coventry in the past the sense of civic responsibility and the desire to serve. . . it has taken great misfortune to show us that a new age will require a new spirit, and that bricks and mortar alone will not make a new city.'[68] Indeed, a Guild of Citizens claiming over 600 members in numerous local branches was formed.[69] Thus, the war years reactivated and gave renewed emphasis to the idea of good citizenship as involving voluntary fulfillment of obligations and willingness to contribute to the welfare of the community.

Citizenship during this period, then, was predominantly understood to be a moral or ethical practice that was deemed crucial for national survival. Membership in the British nation during wartime, in theory, meant the transformation of private individuals into public, civic participants.[70] As is suggested by the emphasis on self-sacrifice in depictions of the nation as well as in prescriptions for citizenship, and as historians Richard Weight and Abigail Beach have so cogently argued, ideas of citizenship and those of national identity became closely intertwined during the war. Furthermore Weight and Beach propose that during the period national identity and citizenship were regarded in Britain as 'complementary, if not virtually indivisible, by many different groups'. Because the nation was believed to be a moral community of good citizens, it would emerge victoriously from the war and a new Britain would follow in its wake. The link between moral or ethical notions of citizenship and national identity is explored further in Chapter 3.

Purpose and Place of this Book

There have been a number of important studies of Britain in World War II that I have drawn upon in writing this book. Angus Calder's monumental survey of life in Britain during the war years, published in 1969, is an unparalleled resource that investigates in great detail the social history of the home front in its political and military context, revealing the political and social tensions that persisted throughout the period.[71]

More specialized works have importantly informed this project, as well. Penny Summerfield's landmark social history of women workers, Lucy Noakes's analysis of gender and national identity, Sian Nicholas's study of the BBC, and Ian

---

[68] *Coventry Evening Telegraph*, 29 May 1943, 4.

[69] Mason and Thompson, 'The Political Mood', 62–3.

[70] Mabel Berezin suggests that the fusion of public and private selves was a crucial component of Mussolini's Fascist Italy. See *Making the Fascist Self: The Political Culture of Interwar Italy* (Princeton: Princeton University Press, 1997). The difference lies, however, in the British stress on the active political participation of citizens in the national community.

[71] Angus Calder, *The People's War: Britain 1939–1945* (London: Pimlico, 1992).

MacLaine's work on the Ministry of Information all have provided crucial background and insights within which this study is situated.[72]

But the purpose of this study differs from works such as these in that it is meant to be neither a general social or cultural history of wartime Britain nor a close analysis of a particular institution or arm of government, nor is it specifically focused on gender, although issues of gender are central to several of its chapters. It differs also from Calder's *Myth of the Blitz*, that wonderfully provocative analysis of the complex reality that was 'purified' through the mythological story of the Blitz, although the book is centrally concerned with a crucial aspect of that myth. The book's place in the extensive historiography of World War II Britain and its aim as historical analysis is to foreground the numerous possibilities for social transformation unleashed by and through the processes of national identity formation and the construction of the meanings of wartime citizenship. The idea that the British were one people fighting a people's war dominated popular culture, and it is this vision that continues to inform post-war nostalgia. It is helpful to think about the dominance of such perspectives in the cultural productions of the time using the concept of 'hegemony'. Understanding the domination of the idea that the British were a singular people fighting a people's war as a hegemonic cultural formation conveys the sense that the dominance of these ideas was not total; the ideas did not form an unvarying, uniform orthodoxy. Hegemonic power both produces and contains possibilities that make it always unstable and capable of metamorphosis, reinforcing or unleashing political and institutional currents that run counter to it. This book analyses the meanings of nationhood and citizenship within this theoretical understanding of hegemonic cultural constructions.[73]

The main debates about the period of World War II that have dominated a great deal of historical argumentation primarily concern the question of whether or not a new political consensus emerged during the war that was the basis for post-war social and economic reform; consideration of the extent of popular engagement in the dominant wartime national spirit and whether the nation became more unified across class and other social divisions; and controversy over whether or not the war constituted a turning point in various particular arenas of British life. Although there are different specific facets of each of these debates, they raise the more general question, what difference did the war make?[74] While my aim in writing this book

[72] Penny Summerfield, *Women Workers in the Second World War: Production and Patriarchy in Conflict* (London and Dover, NH: Croom Helm, 1984); Noakes, *War and the British*; Sian Nicholas, *The Echo of War: Home Front Propaganda and the Wartime BBC, 1939–45* (Manchester: Manchester University Press, 1996); Ian McLaine, *Ministry of Morale: Home Front Morale and the Ministry of Information in World War II* (London: George Allen & Unwin, 1979).

[73] Stuart Hall, 'Gramsci's Relevance to the Analysis of Racism and Ethnicity', *Journal of Communication Inquiry*, 10 (1986), 5–27.

[74] See the book of essays by that title edited by Brian Brivati and Harriet Jones (eds.), *What Difference Did the War Make?* (London and New York: Leicester University Press, 1993).

has not been to address the specifics of these debates directly, the analysis offered here will give a new vantage point for assessing them.

The argument that there was a new political consensus brought about during the war was articulated most forcefully by Paul Addison in *The Road to 1945*.[75] It was Addison's view that the political consensus that emerged in the 1940s moved the political parties into greater agreement about the necessity for social reform and was backed to a significant extent by public opinion.[76] The country, he suggests, was more politically polarized in the years prior to the war than it was to become in the 1940s. A new middle ground, resulting in the formation of a moderate welfare state was the product. Addison's thesis has been subject to considerable criticism and substantial new historical work showing that there was significant political controversy during the war years. Stephen Brooke has documented that it was Labour members of the wartime Coalition, insisting on the necessity for reforms they had been backing before the war, that contributed to the wartime political shift.[77] Kevin Jefferys has argued that there was considerable disagreement between the political parties over welfare reform, and that the Conservative Party only began to modify its position in response to its defeat in the June 1945 election, not as a consequence of the experience of war.[78] Jose Harris provided evidence that consensus was actually a contrived myth.[79] Rodney Lowe has convincingly argued that in general there was consensus on broad and sometimes vague principles, but not on implementation.[80]

While this book does not deal with party politics and thus does not bear on the political consensus debate, it is relevant to the continuing arguments about a related point—the extent to which the British people participated in and experienced a new social solidarity, on the one hand, and supported social reform and visions of a 'new Britain' as a result of their wartime experiences, on the other. Numerous

---

[75] Paul Addison, *The Road to 1945: British Politics and the Second World War*, rev. edn. (London: Pimlico, 1994). Addison's 'Epilogue: The Road to 1945 Revisited', in the revised edition of the book, originally published in 1975, written in response to his critic clarifies that what he meant by consensus was a 'Whitehall consensus', not a social consensus or a political party consensus.

[76] Others who have made the claim that there was a dramatic shift during the war in popular political attitudes or a new political mood include: Kenneth O. Morgan, *Labour in Power 1945–1951* (Oxford: Clarendon Press, 1984); Arthur Marwick, *Britain in the Century of Total War: War, Peace and Social Change, 1900–1967* (Boston: Little and Brown, 1968). For an intelligent and provocative restatement of the idea of a shift of 'mood', see James Hinton, '1945 and the Apathy School', *History Workshop Journal*, 43 (Spring 1997), 266–72.

[77] Stephen Brooke, *Labour's War: The Labour Party during the Second World War* (Oxford: Clarendon Press, 1992).

[78] Kevin Jeffries, 'British Politics and Social Policy during the Second World War', *Historical Journal*, 30 (Mar. 1987), 123–44.

[79] Jose Harris, 'Political Values and the Debate on State Welfare', in Harold L. Smith (ed.), *War and Social Change* (Manchester: Manchester University Press, 1986), 239.

[80] Rodney Lowe, 'The Second World War, Consensus, and the Foundation of the Welfare State', *Twentieth Century British History*, 1 (1990), esp. 161–9.

scholars have provided evidence and argument countering the image that class and other social differences were blurred during the war and that the British actually experienced themselves as a community. Others suggest that there was much less engagement in and enthusiasm for post-war reconstruction planning on the part of 'the ordinary people' than had been thought.

Henry Pelling, for example, maintained that apathy returned after the Blitz and workers' engagement in the war effort dampened as victory became more likely.[81] Angus Calder argued that the 'myth of the Blitz' omitted any references to the black market, widespread looting after bombings, the labour unrest and absenteeism, and periods of low morale documented in Home Security reports.[82] Kenneth O. Morgan suggested that there was much less wartime unity than the images imply, and that the war hardened rather than dissolved social distinctions. Rodney Lowe argued, in a balanced appraisal, that the majority of the British public were 'ill-informed, lacked "social solidarity", and supported neither state intervention nor altruistic welfare policies', although there was a 'thinking minority' who supported such politics and policies.[83] In these accounts, the images of solidarity and broad participation in and engagement with civil society are countered by a different reality. What people were actually doing, saying, or feeling was not consonant with the picture of public opinion prevalent in popular culture at the time and implicit in the 'consensus' analysis. While, according to Rodney Lowe, 'consensus—defined as an historically unusual degree of agreement—was not a mirage . . . its nature was constantly evolving and it had distinct limitations.'[84]

Several historical works, especially by historians Steven Fielding, Peter Thompson, and Nick Tiratsoo forcefully challenge the belief that 'ordinary people' actively yearned for and were engrossed in visions of a 'new Britain' that could become reality after the war was over.[85] Basically, they argue that rather than the war transforming people 'from private individuals uninterested in wider events into active citizens seeking to influence public affairs', the evidence based on public opinion assessments done during the war show that 'most people remained preoc-

[81] Henry Pelling, *Britain and the Second World War* (London: Penguin, 1970).

[82] Calder, *The Myth of the Blitz*.

[83] Kenneth O. Morgan, *The People's Peace* (Oxford: Oxford University Press, 1990), 18; Lowe, 'The Second World War', 175, 177. For an excellent critique of such arguments, see Geoffrey Field, 'Social Patriotism and the British Working Class: Appearance and Disappearance of a Tradition', *International Labor and Working-Class History*, 42 (Fall 1992), 20–39.

[84] Lowe, 'The Second World War', 180.

[85] Steven Fielding, Peter Thompson, and Nick Tiratsoo, *'England Arise!': The Labour Party and Popular Politics in 1940s Britain* (Manchester: Manchester University Press, 1995). Also see: Steven Fielding, 'What Did "The People" Want?: The Meaning of the 1945 General Election', *Historical Journal*, 35 (1992), 623–39; Steven Fielding, 'The Second World War and Popular Radicalism: The Significance of the "Movement Away from Party"', *History*, 80 (1995), 38–58. For thoughtful assessments of this approach, see reviews by Sarah Benton, John Marriott, and James Hinton in *History Workshop Journal*, 43 (Spring 1997), 249–72.

cupied with their private spheres and rejected initiatives to make them community-spirited'.[86] About the effect of the war on the majority of Britons, they conclude, 'Above all else, the war had been extremely disruptive and so there was a common desire that it should be followed by a period of normalcy. The priority was to re-establish home and work life on a civilian basis as quickly as possible. Wider questions seemed less pressing.'[87] While the authors acknowledge that no one wanted to return to the social conditions of the 1930s, they propose that political thinking during the time did not lead to a concrete politics of social transformation.

Finally, historians have debated whether or not the position of women advanced as a result of the war. As Penny Summerfield has noted, the debates have concerned the impact of social policy on women, women's roles in employment, and women's subjective responses to wartime opportunities. From Richard Titmuss in the 1950s to Arthur Marwick in the 1960s, social scientists argued that the war had improved women's status. But as Summerfield's thoughtful overview of the literature suggests, with regard to public policy, the outcomes for women were contradictory; regarding their position in the labour force, women's wages and particular job opportunities were not transformed by the war—only a small number of women worked in highly skilled, well-paid 'men's work'.[88] In the mid-1980s Harold Smith argued that women were anxious to return to a life of domesticity, and that if anything, there was a 'strengthening of traditional sex roles rather than the emergence of new roles'.[89] Penny Summerfield showed that women's responses to public opinion surveys were not at all clear-cut, and in her most recent analysis of oral histories aimed particularly at the issue of women's subjectivities, she argues that women articulated their wants and desires in light of the cultural constructions available to them at the time and their particular experiences. Since these were contradictory, different women responded to them in different ways.[90]

Which People's War? makes a particular kind of intervention in the debates over 'what difference the war made'. It argues that heroic, populist, and utopian constructions of national identity and citizenship dominated public and political culture during the war years.[91] But these articulations did not have singular meanings—they differed by gender, for example, and were inflected by issues of

---

[86] Fielding, Thompson, and Tiratsoo, *'England Arise'*, 213.   [87] Ibid. 39.

[88] P. Summerfield, 'Approaches to Women and Social Change in the Second World War', in Brian Brivati and Harriet Jones (eds.), *What Difference Did the War Make?* (London and New York: Leicester University Press, 1993), 65–70; for a full analysis, see Summerfield, *Women Workers in the Second World War*.

[89] Harold L. Smith, 'The Effect of the War on the Status of Women', in Harold L. Smith (ed.), *War and Social Change: British Society in the Second World War* (Manchester: Manchester University Press, 1986), 57.

[90] Penny Summerfield, *Reconstructing Women's Wartime Lives: Discourse and Subjectivity in Oral Histories of the Second World War* (New York and Manchester: Manchester University Press, 1998).

[91] See Geoffrey Field's intelligent discussion of what he calls 'social patriotism', in 'Social Patriotism and the British Working Class'.

class difference, the significance both of British imperialism and racial difference as well as regionalism to ideas about the nation, and so on. They were open to a number of possible interpretations and were consonant with a variety of courses of action both during the war and in the post-war period. They could and did generate conflict and contradiction as often as they induced social harmony and consensus; the hegemonic discourse about wartime nationhood and the new Britain that was to emerge after the war contained discrepant strands that could not be easily woven together.

Yet it is important to acknowledge that there was a left-leaning, populist, progressive shift in the dominant political culture that inundated the United Kingdom. To ask, as the critics of this point of view have been asking, exactly how many people espoused new views and allied themselves with the new spirit of citizenship is to miss something fundamental. It misses the inchoate hopes and desires that both produced and were aroused by this transformed political culture, and it mistakes what Raymond Williams might have called a 'structure of feeling' with a fully worked out political programme.

Which People's War? investigates this structure of feeling or hegemonic wartime mood, exploring its contradictions and instabilities. In other words, as an examination of the discourses concerning national identity and citizenship during the war years, it is intended to illuminate the variety of possibilities that were opened as a consequence of the wartime conjuncture. The idea that a new Britain would rise like a phoenix from the ashes of war was a powerful one that dominated the hopes and fears articulated in popular discourse. This admittedly utopian vision of renewal, however, did not delineate in very precise ways what this would entail and how it would be accomplished and who in particular would benefit from it. What it did do was to unleash desire.[92]

A Note about Sources

My research for the book is based on a variety of different sources including local, regional, and national newspapers, popular magazines, records of various ministries, data from Mass Observation, books and pamphlets, film, novels and stories, diaries and letters, radio scripts and published photographs. With almost no exception I relied on material produced during the war and did not consult memoirs, autobiographies, films, novels, etc., written after January 1946, nor did I make use of oral histories.[93] My aim in restricting myself to sources produced during the time period was to get as close as possible to what the people living then might have read,

[92] See also Sarah Benton's brief discussion of desire, 'The 1945 "Republic"', *History Workshop Journal*, 43 (Spring 1997), 252.

[93] The one exception I made, because I could find no other first-person sources for colonials living in Great Britain, was the memoir written by Ernest Marke, a man from Sierra Leone who lived in London. I refer to his recollections in Chapter 7.

heard, or seen. It was important to my sense of this project to understand how wartime experiences were filtered through the available public culture of the time, rather than to understand post-war reconstructions of those experiences. While my own readings of the wartime evidence obviously have been informed by a deluge of reconstructions both of the war and interpretations of the consequences of the war on post-war Britain, the wartime texts, with their own interpretive frames, were not produced with the knowledge or experience of 'the future'. That future was not known to the people who were living on the home front, but was rather a product of their imaginative desires, aspirations, and yearnings that shaped their wartime perspectives.

Yet the sources that I have used for this book are not without other problems of interpretation. No documents are free of distortion of some kind or other. Government documents that reveal discussions among ministry staff members about policies seem fairly straightforward. Yet we can never be certain that we know the 'real motives' behind these policies or how widely supported within the government they were. Clearly newspaper editorials and reports by journalists are a different kind of source. They selectively describe an event or series of events, and they present their own interpretations. Newspapers, then, are a vital source in assessing the public, political culture of the times, but they do not present a totally neutral, direct, and unmediated view of their subjects. All archival documents are structured not only by predilections of the authors, but also by their perceptions of their intended audiences. Furthermore, they unconsciously employ various narrative strategies, organizing their messages as, for example, romances or tragedies, and often frame their rhetorics with irony or sometimes with pathos.[94]

In order to get a sense of how 'ordinary' people were responding to what they were experiencing, I relied on a number of different sources including periodic reports from Regional Commissioners under the direction of the Ministry of Home Security, and reports on the public mood from officials working under the auspices of the Home Intelligence division of the Ministry of Information, diaries, the occasional memoir, private letters, and letters-to-the-editors of newspapers. One might ask how representative of 'the people' were these reports, diaries, or letters? I make no claim that these sources are representative. What they do is allow us some insight into some peoples' concerns, anxieties, and hopes. In other words, they shine some light onto wartime subjectivities. No claim of representativeness can be made about the people who kept diaries and memoirs and bequeathed them to the Imperial War Museum. People who write letters to the editors of newspapers certainly are not representative of the mass of newspaper readers. Letter writers are probably

---

[94] For discussions of narrativity in texts, see the essays in W. J. T. Mitchell, *On Narrative* (Chicago and London: University of Chicago Press, 1981); Hayden White, *The Content of the Form: Narrative, Discourse and Historical Representation* (Baltimore and London: Johns Hopkins University Press, 1987), esp. chaps. 1, 2, and 8.

more engaged than the ordinary reader, and/or they are likely to have had the time to devote to writing. Some of them wrote letters regularly. Others did so much more infrequently. Additionally, it is probable that editors are selective in the letters that they print. But letters to the editor are important sources nonetheless because they allow us to gain insight into how some people were responding to events. And significantly their letters and the debates in which they participated and contributed to became a part of the political culture of the time. Numerous letters to the editors about particular issues also suggest how important such issues were to newspaper readers. The letters columns were an important forum for public discussion, although undoubtedly editorial discretion was exercised about which letters would be printed as well as when the debate about a particular topic should end.

Novels, films, posters, and radio programmes present other issues for historical reconstruction and interpretation. I have used them in this work for what they were—contributions to the cultural representations and meanings that were available to the people on the home front. These representations were central to the political culture of wartime Britain which, in turn, framed how British citizens experienced the war and made sense of those experiences.

Organization of the Book

Class and the omnipresent slogans of 'equality of sacrifice' and a 'new Britain' that helped to construct the British nation as 'one people' despite social and economic inequality are the subjects of Chapter 2. I suggest that these rhetorics of nationhood stimulated expressions of what I will call, following its use in wartime documents, 'class feeling'.

Popular representations of what it meant to be a good British citizen during the war highlighted being self-sacrificing and putting the needs of others above self-interest. Chapter 3 argues that public identification and denigration of particular 'internal others' who were depicted as failing to be good citizens or were seen as 'unBritish' because they were selfish and self-interested underscored the significance of the ethics of self-sacrifice to good citizenship and Britishness. Young women and girls who frolicked with soldiers, especially African-American soldiers, were depicted in terms that defined them as selfish and irresponsible—as the opposite of the 'good citizen'. Anti-Semitic references to Jews on the home front reworked historically long-lived stereotypes in ways that highlighted the differences between being British and being alien. Constructions of femininity in public culture and the debates about women's citizenship that emerged during the war are the focus of Chapter 4. The chapter exposes the contradictory ways in which women were expected to remain female and yet participate in the war effort, and explores the possibilities for interpretation inherent in these contradictions.

Chapter 5 takes up the question of masculinity in wartime and concentrates, in particular, on how manhood was constructed for men on the home front during the war. I suggest that masculinity was composed of two seemingly opposite sets of characteristics and explore the instabilities in the meanings of manliness that existed as a consequence.

Chapter 6 explores the issues of regional differences and the distinctions among 'national cultures' within the British Isles. It shows that policies and wartime debates opened up space and provided languages through which rural dwellers could express grievances about the privileging of urban and industrial Britain in Government policy, and it examines the ironies in depictions of the rural in wartime discussions. It examines the emphasis on Englishness in constructions of national identity and the attempts to represent Britain as consisting of diverse national cultures and the 'identity politics' that occurred in Wales and Scotland in response.[95]

An analysis of race and empire in British national identity is at the centre of Chapter 7. In this last substantive chapter I explore how Britain popularly represented itself as an imperial nation and the ways that both racism and colonialism separately and in concert undermined that representation and continued to destabilize the long-term unity of the empire.

The final chapter assesses what I have learned about wartime national identity and citizenship through my examination of their elaboration in and through the various forms of social and political difference. In particular I examine the consequences of the instability of national identity and conceptions of nationhood for wartime Britain, and draw out what I see as the value of such an analysis for understanding historical processes in unsettled times such as war.

---

[95] I did not include a discussion of Northern Ireland because of its incredible complexity relative to Wales, Scotland, and England. The Government did not institute conscription in Northern Ireland, although there were recruits. Also the Ministries of Labour and Supply recruited workers from Eire, although Eire was neutral in the war. Complicating the picture as well was that the division of Ireland into the independent Southern Counties and the North, which remained part of Britain, was quite recent. The topic of British nationhood with respect to Ireland during the war is worthy of a book-length study on its own.

2

'With Axe Large and Gory'

THE WARTIME NATION AND CLASS

The war years were indelibly etched by the interplay of two seemingly opposite tendencies. There was, on the one hand, the dynamic unleashed by a powerful fantasy of national cross-class unity, coupled with the belief that the war was or would be a levelling influence. And, on the other hand, there were persistent expressions of class antagonism. This combination of desire for singularity and incessant conflict contributed to an unprecedented focus on the deep rents in the social fabric produced by economic inequalities. This chapter will suggest that discourses about the nation as one in which sharp class differences were vanquished through a united war effort fed heightened sensitivity on the part of the British public to issues of economic and social inequality. It explores these dynamics by examining the rhetorics of class awareness and antagonism that flourished in several sites. In particular, it examines contestation between capital and labour, expressions of admiration for the Soviet Union, the revelations about poverty and its consequences exposed by the evacuation, and debates about social welfare and post-war reconstruction.

It was in the immediate post-Dunkirk period and the beginnings of the Blitz that the depiction of the war as a 'People's War' took hold in public imagination. 'The People's War' was a construction promulgated by the press, radio, and film, one that profoundly shaped and was elaborated in both official and unofficial wartime propaganda.[1] It drew upon and reconfigured the narratives of a long British history of populism, with its late eighteenth- and nineteenth-century traditions of popular radicalism.[2] And it amplified languages of class that took root on the Left in the

[1] See Angus Calder, *The People's War* (London: Pimlico, 1992), 138.

[2] For an important overview of the period 1848 to 1914, see Patrick Joyce, *Visions of the People: Industrial England and the Question of Class, 1848–1914* (Cambridge: Cambridge University Press, 1991). Also see the essays in Eugenio F. Biagini and Alastair J. Reid, *Currents of Radicalism: Popular Radicalism, Organized Labour and Party Politics in Britain, 1850–1914* (Cambridge and New York: Cambridge University Press, 1991), and Eugenio F. Biagini, *Citizenship and Community: Liberals, Radicals and Collective*

inter-war years against the background of economic crisis at home and Fascism on the Continent.

Britain's entry into war followed a decade of devastatingly high unemployment—when at its worst in 1932, more than three million men were out of work.[3] Although the economic situation of the country had improved by the mid-1930s, and the unemployment rate fell, the general recovery did not change the plight of communities in the old industrial centres of the country. There unemployment rates continued to remain very high. In 1929, 4.6 per cent of those unemployed had been out of work for a year or more but that percentage rose to 26 per cent in 1935. Nearly half of the long-term unemployment was concentrated in coal, shipbuilding, iron and steel, and textiles.[4] In Jarrow, a shipbuilding town, nearly 80 per cent of men were unemployed in the middle of the decade.

Those working-class people with jobs were relatively well off because prices were low, but they experienced little economic security as seasonal fluctuations in employment persisted through the period.[5] Those who had exhausted what meagre unemployment benefits they had were especially devastated, and the dreaded means test brought public officials into their homes to make sure that they were not hiding unacknowledged sources of income. In particular, those on relief were not permitted to have a teenage child contributing to household expenses; they had to be completely dependent on the Government, and their teenage children were to be out on their own. As John Davis has put it, 'The means test was hated for its intrusiveness, its mistakes and its intrinsic scepticism but above all because it persecuted life's victims.'[6]

The plight of those who were out of work was made glaringly evident by organizations such as the National Unemployed Workers' Movement (NUWM), formed to agitate on their behalf. The NUWM, a communist-led organization, organized hunger marches to London in 1930, 1932, 1934, and 1936. In October 1936 Ellen Wilkinson, Labour MP for Jarrow, and the Jarrow Town Council organized the famous Jarrow Crusade in which marchers carried 80,500 signatures in two petitions to Parliament demanding that work should be provided for the unemployed.[7]

Identities in the British Isles, 1865–1931 (Cambridge and New York: Cambridge University Press, 1995). For the early 19th century, see James A. Epstein, *Radical Expression: Political Language, Ritual, and Symbol in England, 1790–1850* (Oxford and New York: Oxford University Press, 1994), esp. 3–28. Also Laura Mayhall suggests the significance of the language of popular radicalism to militant women's suffrage activists. See *Rethinking Suffrage: Citizenship and Resistance in Britain, 1860–1930* (New York and Oxford: Oxford University Press, forthcoming).

[3] John Davis, *A History of Britain, 1885–1939* (New York: St. Martin's Press, 1999), 216.

[4] Pilgrim Trust, *Men Without Work* (Cambridge: Cambridge University Press, 1938), 6, 9, 18.

[5] John Saville, 'May Day 1937', in Asa Briggs and John Saville (eds.), *Essays in Labour History, 1918–1939* (London: Croom Helm, 1977), 240.

[6] Davis, *A History of Britain*, 212.

[7] Joanna Bourke, *Working-Class Cultures in Britain, 1890–1960: Gender, Class and Ethnicity* (London and New York: Routledge, 1994), 20.

The publicity that the Jarrow March achieved was enormous, according to historian John Saville.[8] In 1938 the NUWM waged a series of non-violent actions just before Christmas, including 200 unemployed men lying across the road on Oxford Street stopping traffic, 100 unemployed entering the Grill Room at the Ritz to ask for tea, petitioning the king and picketing of the main railway stations on Christmas Eve. Christmas Day 1938 found 150 unemployed demonstrating outside the house of the Chairman of the Unemployed Assistance Board where they sang carols. On New Year's Eve as crowds gathered in Trafalgar Square, a procession of unemployed marched down the Strand bearing a black coffin. The demonstrations continued throughout the winter. According to Robert Graves and Alan Hodge, while they yielded no change in Government policy, they did attract widespread press coverage and public attention.[9] One million men were still unemployed as Britain went to war.

It is no wonder, then, that the slogan 'equality of sacrifice', coined very early in the war as a 'morale measure' by the Government, was so widely adopted in wartime debates. It was generally recognized that the war would involve civilians in unprecedented ways, and that much would be demanded of them. The notion that in wartime there should be equality of sacrifice contributed to the construction of the war as a 'People's War'. And regardless of how much or how many individuals may actually have 'shirked' their duties or taken advantage of the war for private gain, popular opinion increasingly endorsed an egalitarian morality and condemned its opposite.[10]

The message about 'equality of sacrifice' was delivered by the media in many ways. One was to portray the elite, often symbolized by royalty, as taking an active part in 'The People's War'. The *Glasgow Herald*, for example, featured a picture of the Duke of Buccleuch's son, with a caption explaining that the picture was of the Duke's heir, a student at Eton, doing factory work on the weekends.[11]

Embodying the presumption that there should be equality of sacrifice, anti-aristocratic rhetorics that in the past had denounced 'privilege' were reworked during World War II to condemn 'special interests' and to denounce those who demanded and got special consideration. In the winter of 1940, for example, *Sunday Pictorial* featured a series on the 'Other Half'—those who 'put their own interests first'.

There have always been class distinctions, Peter Wilson, the article's author, wrote 'but there's a war on now, and we have to pull together—rich or poor. That's how victory will be ours.' In the news story, Wilson focused on 'the BAD among the rich.

[8] Saville, 'May Day 1937', 240.

[9] Robert Graves and Alan Hodge, *The Long Week-End: A Social History of Great Britain, 1918–1939* (New York: W. W. Norton, reissued 1994; originally published 1940), 391–3.

[10] See Paul Addison's discussion, *The Road to 1945: British Politics and the Second World War*, rev. edn. (London: Pimlico, 1994), 131–2.

[11] *Glasgow Herald*, 16 July 1940, 2.

1. Jobless protest, 11 January 1939.
Hulton Archive

For there are those who uselessly squander their money—and their time. The gents who eat too much. Drink too much. And don't sleep enough.'[12]

In a following issue of the newspaper, he condemned 'The People Who Get the Easy Jobs', identifying them as 'that rotten section of all classes' who 'use their underhand influence'.[13] Although the writer suggested that there were 'rotten sections' in all classes, he focused his censure implicitly on those in the upper levels of society: a 'couple of elegant young men' without military qualification who after less than a week were transferred from a training unit to another regiment with commissions; those who 'wangled "cushy" staff jobs'; and a woman who lasted only ten days working for a civil defence organization because 'she "wasn't accustomed" to rough work like scrubbing floors'.[14]

Underscoring the message a week later, the paper told the story of an admirable young man who had 'turned his back on a life of comfort so that he could face starvation and learn about life'. The writer commented that 'in this new world there will be no place for the idler, relying on his father's money to evade his own responsibilities and duties in life'.[15]

The writers used such expressions of egalitarian morality to condemn immoral, self-interested behaviour on the part of elites, but not the social order that privileged them in the first place. The rhetoric of 'equality of sacrifice', while emphasizing the existence of unequal advantage, primarily implored those in positions that would enable them to demand special treatment not to abuse their privilege. As a Home Intelligence report put it, it is 'unfairness' that people resent.[16] But while the social order was not explicitly criticized, there was a hint in the last example that a 'new world' was coming in which selfish individuals would no longer fit or be welcome. The call for a 'new Britain' was a powerful trope of social transformation that figured prominently in wartime rhetoric. In this particular version, the lions would lie down with the lambs, but there would still be lions and lambs.

Condemnation of privilege in the press was persistent across the country and throughout the war. The *Western Mail & South Wales News*, for example, took aim against women who were not 'pulling their weight as they should'.[17]

Recently I went to an afternoon reception given by a young married woman who, by virtue of her unearned income, stands to win or lose everything by the issue of this war. I am afraid she is not endowed with the capabilities to earn her living should she lose her fortune. Was she aware of the seriousness of the situation? I judged she was not when I looked at the delicacies, including caviare [*sic*] (which she had sought and found with the painstaking

[12] Peter Wilson, 'The Other Half!', *Sunday Pictorial*, 28 Jan. 1940, 8.
[13] 'The People Who Get the Easy Jobs!', *Sunday Pictorial*, 4 Feb. 1940, 18.
[14] Ibid. [15] *Sunday Pictorial*, 11 Feb. 1940, 19.
[16] Home Intelligence Weekly Reports, 7–14 May 1941. PRO/INF 1/292 1A.
[17] A Working Mother, 'Are We Women Pulling Our Weight', *Western Mail & South Wales News*, 17 Feb. 1942, 3.

industry of an ant), which even in peace-time would not have disgraced the table of an epicure.[18]

Such women, the reporter argued, were not typical of British women more generally, 'but that she exists even in small number must not be allowed in total war'.[19] Like the appeals to women to answer the call of their country by moving to jobs where they were needed, joining the service, or taking on new responsibilities, these entreaties suggested that equality was expected 'for the duration only'.

Yet the discourse of equality of sacrifice gave wide scope for the expression of resentment by those who claimed to be experiencing particular hardships and were not members of the more privileged classes. *Sunday Pictorial*, for example, produced the following headline to accompany a feature story, 'Rich Hotels Turn People Away during Air Raids'. The article appeared in late September 1940, in the midst of the Blitz. The story told of a reporter and his 'girl companion' who went to Claridge's Hotel to investigate how 'ordinary working people' were received if they requested shelter at luxury hotels to 'escape the bombs'. The couple asked if they could stay in the hotel shelter and were told to go to a public shelter because the one at the hotel was for residents only. When they then asked if they might rent a room so they could use the shelter, they were told that the hotel was full. The article concluded by saying that they received the same treatment at the Berkeley Hotel.[20]

Such complaints worried the Ministry of Information, in charge of home front morale, because ministry officials understood their articulation as expressions of 'class feeling'. Home Security saw such class feeling as a threat to national unity and continued throughout the war to report its occurrence. For example, in July 1940 one Regional Commissioner wrote in his report,

The betrayal of France has sunk deep into the popular mind, and has produced some danger of class feeling. It is realised that in Norway, Holland, Belgium and France the pro-Nazi elements were always on the Right. If national unity is to be preserved, nothing is more important than that any suspicion of favouritism to the well-to-do should be sedulously avoided . . . It is important that any appeal to class feeling should be avoided by those who share the responsibilities of Government.[21]

In the autumn of 1941, two Home Intelligence Officers reported that there were expressions of growing ill-feeling caused by the sight of numbers of young officers' wives 'sitting about in the hotels of coastal and country towns, and in no way assisting the war effort'.[22] And in July 1943, Home Intelligence reported that those in need of obtaining domestic help had expressed the feeling that 'people with money and

---

[18] A Working Mother, 'Are We Women Pulling Our Weight', *Western Mail & South Wales News*, 17 Feb. 1942, 3.
[19] Ibid.   [20] *Sunday Pictorial*, 22 Sept. 1940, 4.
[21] 'Report of the Commissioner for the Two Months ended July 13, 1940', Region 6, Policy Regarding Monthly Reports. PRO/HO 199/410.
[22] INF 1/292 B, 6–13 Oct. 1941.

influence' can get as much help as they need. The report confirmed that some people were, in fact, doing quite well quoting from a letter recorded by Postal Censorship: 'We are two in the family, the Colonel and myself, and my little boy of eleven and a half in the holidays, and my older son on leave occasionally. I keep a cook (middle aged), two young girls under her and a very nice head housemaid (also middle aged) and an under, and two in the pantry.'[23]

Food rationing was a popular measure that the Chamberlain Government announced at the end of November 1939 and inaugurated in the new year. A Gallup Poll earlier in November showed that six out of ten people believed rationing to be necessary.[24] And as many scholars have pointed out, rationing was popular with the working classes, as was Lord Woolton, who served as the Minister of Food from April 1940 to November 1943. But as Angus Calder has argued, while food rationing was popular, it was hardly fair.[25] Calder focuses on the fact that the rationing system paid no attention to how much food different people needed, or to regional and occupational differences in diet. But more to the point of this chapter, food consumption was a focal point of 'class feeling'.

In January 1941, for example, *Sunday Pictorial* carried the headline 'Cheap Meal Cheats' reporting that well-to-do people were said to be 'using a feeding centre to obtain cheap meals and dodge meat rationing'.[26] There were recurrent complaints published in the newspapers about wealthy people who could spend lavishly at restaurants, and about leisured women who could command tables at lunch time forcing office workers to miss their noon meal. Class sensitivity on this point is evident in an article in *Daily Sketch*, a paper with a Conservative readership. 'To most people . . . it will come as a surprise to learn that a certain amount of "luxury feeding" is going on. It will be a surprise because few have seen it; and few have seen it because there is very little of it. High and Low, rich and poor, have faithfully honoured the principle of equality of sacrifice. The dishonourable exception are insignificant in number.'[27] The article contributed to the construction of the nation as a class-unified community, even as it smacked of what may be called politically motivated defensiveness about it.

The release of Oswald and Lady Mosley from prison in November 1943 was notable in that regard.[28] Shortly after the Mosleys' release from prison, Home Intelligence regional officers from around the country reported widespread hostility and open protest about the Home Secretary's action. The Southwest regional officer reported that workers, believing that the Mosleys' wealth secured their

---

[23] Home Intelligence Weekly Reports, 29 June to 6 July 1943. INF 1/292 Part 3C.
[24] Cited in Calder, *The People's War*, 71.   [25] Ibid. 405.
[26] *Sunday Pictorial*, 26 Jan. 1941, 3.   [27] *Daily Sketch*, 9 Jan. 1941, 5.
[28] Oswald Mosley, head of the British Union of Fascists (BUF) was imprisoned in 1940. Mosley was originally a member of the Labour Party, but dropped out and after flirting with left radical causes he eventually moved sharply to the right. Under his leadership in the 1930s, the BUF became increasingly violent and openly anti-Semitic.

release, were vigorously condemning the action and demanded that they be reimprisoned. Others reported hearing comments such as, 'one law for the rich and another for the poor', and described protest meetings held in factories. Unions passed resolutions of protest and the Belfast District of the National Union of Railwaymen also discussed the possibility of a general strike of transport workers.[29] In many regions anger was expressed at what people believed were the luxurious conditions of the Mosleys' life in prison.[30] The Mosleys in fact had been given a flat in Holloway Prison with permission to employ other prisoners as servants.[31] In one large London factory which the regional officer reported had not had a 'petition' drive in the past twenty-four years, workers organized one protesting Mosley's release.[32] Even the National Emergency Committee Chairman, George Hodkinson, was reported to have written, 'I want to impress upon you that the action of the Home Secretary is having a debilitating effect on the mind and enthusiasm for the war effort. If there was ever a case since the war broke out of creating "alarm and despondency" this is one and the Government is responsible for it.'[33] One of the regional officers reported miners saying, 'Why should pit lads be imprisoned for refusing to go underground if traitors like Mosley are set free?' And Home Intelligence worried about the 'thousands of hours' working time wasted in all the factories in discussing the subject and drawing up petitions.[34] Even when Herbert Morrison explained that Mosley was to report regularly to the police and was restricted to within a 7-mile radius of his home, protests persisted.[35]

With nearly every major demand for additional contribution to the war effort, the rhetoric of equality of sacrifice led to the expression of class antagonism. The call for women to register for war service provided such an opportunity. Again, Home Intelligence warned of the need for some kind of official statement about the 'universality of the call-up and its equalitarian application'. It noted that '[there] is a good deal of suspicion that "influence" will be used to get exemption and that part-time voluntary war work will be used as a loophole to avoid compulsory service'.[36] And again in August of 1941, after women were required to register, Home Intelligence reported that there were 'still suspicions that "women of the leisured classes" are "sheltering behind voluntary work of a semi-benevolent nature": in particular, some of the WVS [Women's Voluntary Services] offices are said to be very over staffed.'[37] In September, Home Intelligence warned of class feeling from a number of regions about the belief that 'well-to-do women and those of the upper classes tend to avoid war work altogether . . . It is suggested that the wives of those occupying leading positions should be either encouraged or enlisted into munitions

[29] HO 262/6 'Fascism General', 25 Nov. 1943.   [30] INF 1/292 Part 4, 16–23 Nov. 1943.
[31] Calder, The People's War, 133.   [32] HO 262/6, 'Fascism General', 25 Nov. 1943.
[33] Ibid.   [34] INF 1/292 Part 4, 23–30 Nov. 1943.   [35] Calder, The People's War, 551.
[36] Home Intelligence Weekly Report, dated 31 Mar. 1941. PRO/INF 1/292 1A.
[37] Home Intelligence Weekly Report, 6–13 Aug. 1941. PRO/INF 1/292 Part 2B.

2. Protest against the release of Oswald Mosley,
7 December 1943.
Hulton Archive

work.'[38] Even after women were conscripted into war-related activities, there were stories about wealthy women who were not 'doing their bit'. A Cardiff newspaper in the winter of 1942 maintained that 'There are still women who go to bridge and whist drives every day of every week. "What are the funds in aid of?" I asked one of them. "I don't know," she replied, "but I have been going for years".'[39]

When Bevin appealed to married women to work at least part-time, he raised a 'storm of disapproval and resentment', because 'privileged unmarried women are sheltering in inessential jobs at Government offices'.[40] And it is likely that the perceptions of class bias in the kinds of work that women of different classes were undertaking were accurate as the scholarship of Penny Summerfield has suggested.[41]

In the context of smouldering working-class suspicions of the rich that lingered on from the immediate pre-war years of unemployment (and indeed early wartime industrial dislocation), I am arguing that official injunctions to 'equality of sacrifice' provided both a language and a rationale for continuing expressions of class resentment. There were, moreover, special circumstances and debates throughout the war years that provided a context in which a discourse of class, class difference, and class conflict flourished. The remainder of the chapter will be devoted to a discussion of these particular arenas in which class awareness and antagonism were expressed.

Contestation between Capital and Labour

Open conflict between workers and employers continued throughout the wartime period. This conflict was expressed in two ways. First, there was recurrent mutual sniping by labour and capital as to whether it was workers or manufacturers who were responsible for the continuing productivity crisis. And second, in spite of efforts by the Churchill Government to bring the labour movement into the war effort by appointing Ernest Bevin to the post of Minister of Labour and National Security and by creating machinery to adjudicate disputes, continuing labour unrest led to repeated work stoppages.

Discussions concerning class divisions and expressions of class hostility were framed by rhetorics of patriotism and singular national purpose. This was evident in the way that Arthur Deakin, Acting General-Secretary of the Transport and General Workers' Union, who had taken over when Bevin was appointed to the Ministry of Labour, reported to the Union on Government efforts to develop the country's productive output. He began first by complimenting the workers for having responded so well to appeals to increase production.

[38] Home Intelligence Weekly Report, 29 Sept. to 6 Oct. 1941. PRO/INF 1/292 2B.
[39] *Western Mail & South Wales News*, 17 Feb. 1942, 4.
[40] Home Intelligence Weekly Reports, 17–24 Nov. 1941. PRO/INF 1/292 Part 2B.
[41] Penny Summerfield, *Women Workers in the Second World War: Production and Patriarchy in Conflict* (London: Croom Helm, 1984). For a comment on the presumed reluctance of an upper-class woman who 'spoke with a Girton accent', see Zelma Katin, *Clippie* (London: Gifford, 1944), 6.

Everywhere our members have been keen to eliminate wasteful effort and to give the maximum output possible . . . This has been so much in evidence that, almost daily, members and branches have called attention to the misuse and inefficient handling of the labour force. In some cases this has been purely due to ineffective workshop organisation, whilst in others it has been attributable to the hangover of price mechanism and profit motive so inherent in private capitalism.[42]

In either case, Deakin was implying that management had been the cause of production problems. Deakin went on to suggest that Socialist planning would be the only way to deal with the problems the nation faced and emphasized that there were opportunities in the wartime emergency 'for our people to develop that sense of responsibility and service for which our Movement has always stood'.[43]

Management, meanwhile, blamed workers for 'slacking' and causing production to slow up. According to Home Intelligence in a mid-February 1942 report, for example, managements complained 'the British workman isn't pulling his weight'; 'the workers don't care about the war'; 'you have to be chasing them all the time or they won't do a thing'; 'time is being wasted and lost to dodge income tax'.[44]

Throughout 1941 and 1942, workers and employers traded insults concerning who was at fault for the relatively slow rate of production.[45] In the column, 'From the Watchtower', in the Birmingham Labour-affiliated *Town Crier*, for example, Watchman wrote:

There are certain people in this country who are a greater menace to the national effort than the whole army of 'Fifth Columnists'. I refer to those who are uttering slanderous statements about the workers . . . Hardly a day passes without a speech or a newspaper article, uttered or written by a die-hard Tory M.P. or an employer who is still back in the 'good old days' when the 'Boss' had unrestricted power over the lives of his 'hands'. . . Let them have a few weeks unloading and loading ships at the blitzed docks, or in the coalpits, or at the bench in a munitions factory. Let them be paid no more than these men are being paid for the job, and let their wives have the same daily struggle to keep the family fed and clothed and housed on wages which have barely kept pace with the increased cost of living. Many a man who is shouting 'Slackers!' spends more on one meal at an hotel than a worker's wife can spend on several days' meals for a family.[46]

Watchman combined the language of class with the idioms of war and the national effort in expressing his response to the accusations against workmen that they were slacking in the war effort.

In mid-September 1941 Home Intelligence reported that while the workers

---

[42] Arthur Deakin, 'Our Testing Time', *T. & G. W. Record*, July 1940, 24. [43] Ibid. 25.
[44] Home Intelligence Special Reports, 13 Feb. 1942, Special Report No. 6. INF 1/293.
[45] For a thorough discussion of the production crisis, see James C. Hinton, *Shop Floor Citizens: Engineering Democracy in 1940s Britain* (Aldershot, Hants.: Edward Elgar, 1994), esp. chaps. 2 and 3.
[46] Watchman, 'From the Watchtower', *The Town Crier* (Birmingham), 21 June 1941, 3.

blamed managements for misusing manpower and materials, employers complained, citing Government regulations, that they 'cannot get authority to discipline men'.[47] Home Intelligence ominously reported at the beginning of the new year that workers are 'distinctly cynical about the necessity for putting their backs into things when they feel that much of their efforts will go for nothing through the bungling of managements'. Workers complained that they were kept idle day and night and that they were transferred to distant munitions factories only to discover that the factories were not working full time.[48] Employers accused workers in munitions factories and aerodrome sites of going to sleep and even of 'rabbiting during working hours', according to Home Intelligence.[49]

Grimly, Home Intelligence warned that workers in numerous regions were becoming disillusioned and blaming management for 'looking after their own interests', 'profiting from the war' and thinking about 'their own position after the war'. According to the Regional Intelligence Officer for the crucial Midland Region where much of the armaments industry was located, workers were discouraged— 'they do not feel called upon to "take off their shirts" when work is urgent.'[50] Home Security Regional Commissioners, concerned about defeatist attitudes, reported that some workers refused to exert themselves believing 'matters couldn't be much worse under whatever form of government, not even under Hitler, if Hitler should come here.' A Home Security informant, described as a member of the Home Guard and a trade union official said, 'this is a class of worker who, believing themselves to have little to lose, are not prepared in war or peace to exert themselves for anyone else's gain.'[51]

Although the production crisis lasted throughout the war, especially in coal mining, the debate about productivity was at its height in the winter of 1941–2. Responding, in part, to demands made by the unions, especially the Amalgamated Engineering Union (AEU) and the General and Municipal Workers, the Ministry of Supply signed an agreement with the unions to establish Joint Production Committees (JPCs). Government action followed the refusal by the Engineering Employers' Federation to agree with the AEU to establish such committees, fearing that they would be taken over by the militant shop stewards. As a consequence of the Government's action, the Engineering Employers' Federation and the AEU agreed to establish JPCs in engineering works with over one hundred and fifty employees. The committees were established to enable workers and employers, meeting together in

[47] INF 1/292 B, 17–24 Sept. 1941. See also INF 1/292 B, 20–27 Oct. 1941.
[48] INF 1/292 Part 2, 29 Dec. 1941–5 Jan. 1942.   [49] INF 1/292 Part 2, 19–26 Jan. 1942.
[50] INF 1/292 Part 2, 2–9 Mar. 1942.
[51] Monthly Regional Commissioners Report, Easter Region #4, 10 Feb. 1942. HO 199/417. Mass Observation's survey of the morale of industrial workers, *People in Production*, published in 1942, plainly revealed that antagonism between capital and labour continued despite the rhetoric of national unity being promulgated by propaganda organs of the Government, and by the media. *People in Production* (Harmondsworth: Penguin, 1942).

equal numbers, to work out production problems and other sources of tension between them.[52] By the end of 1943 there were 4,500 JPCs in existence in engineering and allied industries, JPCs in forty Royal Ordnance Factories, similar committees in nearly all the shipyards and more than one thousand pit committees. Their success, however, varied from one to the next, although the establishment of these committees was hailed by the militant sections of the labour movement as a victory.

Regardless of whether or not they increased productivity and enhanced wartime efficiency, the existence of JPCs did not significantly ease the tensions between workers and employers that continued unabated throughout the war. Strikes, labour stoppages, and organized 'go slow' protests occurred in numerous critical industries throughout the war. The immediate causes of the strikes ran the gamut from disputes over wages and piece rates, to protests over 'dilutees' and the breakdown of prior agreements, jurisdictional disputes between unions, and not infrequently, demonstrations against harsh shop-floor discipline.

Such strikes over wages, demarcational disputes, and protests over breaches of agreements were generally not well received by the public. Work stoppages were usually met by a barrage of letters to the editors of local newspapers complaining about workers' actions. Home Intelligence reported in the autumn of 1941, for example, that public response to strikes in Scotland and Northern Ireland aroused 'indignation and bitter comment' by the public.[53] Early in 1942 the Duke of Montrose wrote to the editor of the *Glasgow Herald* complaining of striking workers who allow others 'to sacrifice their lives for them'.[54] Labour supporters, however, could use the language of wartime national unity to respond to such pronouncements. C. H. Campbell, for example, wrote in response to Montrose, 'when an act of injustice is perpetuated of so gross a nature as to cause the spontaneous striking of a large company of the sufferer's fellows, then the perpetrator could reasonably be accused of an act of sabotage and proceeded against informally.'[55]

Fewer hours were lost to strikes in World War II than in World War I. This should not be surprising given the fact that all strikes in World War II were technically illegal because the Trades Union Congress had an agreement with the Government that unions would settle disputes through formal grievance procedures. Additionally, World War II and World War I were conducted under considerably different political arrangements. There was a Coalition Government, endorsed by the leadership of the unions, that incorporated the Labour Party. Also, there was more complete unionization in World War II than in World War I. These factors would be

---

[52] James C. Hinton discusses in some detail the complex politics involved in getting the employers to agree to setting up JPCs, and particularly focuses on the role of the Communist Party in pushing the issue of productivity and the advantages of JPCs (*Shop Floor Citizens*, chap. 3). For an official account, see Patricia Inman, *Labour in the Munitions Industries* (London: HMSO, 1957), esp. 371–92.

[53] Home Intelligence Weekly Reports, INF 1/292.   [54] *Glasgow Herald*, 18 Jan. 1942, 2.

[55] *Glasgow Herald*, 20 Jan. 1942, 2.

expected to have lessened the frequency as well as the duration and severity of strikes.[56] However, there were more numerous walk-outs in World War II than in World War I.[57] These numerous strikes were unofficial, locally organized work stoppages. Because the strikes that occurred were both unofficial and illegal, their persistence suggests that considerable discontent and discord rumbled beneath the surface of political calm.

A strike in Scotland by workers and apprentices at British Auxiliaries, at Govan, near Glasgow, in the autumn of 1940 is illustrative of the multiple tensions and divisions, as well as the shifting alliances that could be present in labour disputes throughout the war. The strike of workers at a firm which manufactured crucial parts for ship and airplane engines lasted two months before the workers and managers finally agreed on the terms under which the dispute would be negotiated and the workers returned to their jobs. The workmen walked off their jobs demanding reinstatement of the Convener of Shop Stewards who had been dismissed 'because of "interference with a woman worker"'.[58] The workmen were convinced that the Convener was actually fired for his trade-union activities. For their part, the employers insisted that the men return to work prior to calling a works conference to discuss the issues. But they also intimated that they would refuse to take the man back into the firm's employ under any condition.

Complicating matters considerably was the fact that the AEU opposed both the strike and the workers' demand that he be reinstated prior to an official proceeding to adjudicate the dispute. The Union's District Committee, however, endorsed the action of the strikers and granted them funds to further their protest.[59]

The conflict between the AEU Executive, on the one hand, and the striking workers and their District Committee, on the other hand, was undoubtedly exacerbated by the possibility that both members of the District Committee and some of the strikers (including the Shop Steward Convener) were either members of the Communist Party or sympathetic to 'left wing' approaches to industrial conflict.[60] The Shop Stewards Committee pressed the strikers' cause at other establishments, solicited financial support, and threatened to bring 80,000 workers out on strike if their Convener was not reinstated. The AEU Executive Committee and the Minister of Labour, Ernest Bevin, for their part, instructed the strikers to return to work and 'go through procedure'.

The strike was finally settled in the middle of November when both sides agreed to a compromise arbitrated by David Kirkwood MP on terms which both sides had

---

[56] For a similar argument, see Inman, *Labour in the Munitions Industries*, 395.

[57] See ibid. 394–5.

[58] Deputy Chief Industrial Commissioner Minute to Industrial Relations Division of the Ministry of Labour, 26 Sept. 1940. PRO/LAB 10/124.

[59] Minute of Deputy Chief Industrial Commissioner, 30 Sept. 1940. PRO/LAB 10/124.

[60] Weekly Report, Chief Conciliation Officer of Scotland, 14 Oct. 1939. PRO/LAB 10/360.

rejected previously. Kirkwood's success with the workers was probably due to his radical, left-wing credentials earned by his previous activities.[61]

Just prior to Kirkwood's intervention, the District Committee washed their hands of the affair and the settlement was arranged without their participation. Additionally, the AEU Executive and the Ministry of Labour representatives both in London and in Scotland were outraged that Kirkwood intervened, going around the AEU and working directly with the Shop Stewards Movement to settle the strike. Although the workers returned to their jobs, the dispute rumbled on for another three months.

The British Auxiliaries dispute involved relatively familiar conflicts between workers and employers—with workers claiming victimization because of union activity, and employers claiming the prerogatives of management to hire and fire. But overlaying this conflict in industrial relations was one between the union leaders, working closely with the Ministry of Labour, on the one hand, and, on the other, the rank and file supported, or perhaps strongly encouraged by 'left wing' or communist members of the Shop Stewards Movement and members of the District Council.

This conflict of ideologies and strategies was one that would be played out across the nation in a number of industries throughout the war as unofficial strikes and the Shop Stewards Movement continued to trouble union efforts to cooperate with the Government in the name of national unity. Less than a month after the official settlement in the British Auxiliaries dispute, 6,000 apprentices in the west of Scotland went on strike and refused to have anything to do with the union, claiming that the unions had done nothing for them and that they were capable of gaining more for themselves. The regional office of the Ministry of Labour in Glasgow believed that communists and radical shop stewards were behind it, but reported that 'managers have often been "club-footed" in the way they handled the workers'.[62]

Labour unrest persisted, especially in the country's mining industry, throughout the war. The industry had been hard-hit by the depression; young men were leaving the mining areas to seek employment elsewhere, and wages were generally depressed. Compared with the metal, engineering, aircraft and shipbuilding industries, coal mining was disproportionately affected by work stoppages. The industry accounted for nearly one-half of the total days lost through strikes in 1943; two-thirds in 1944; and one-fourth in 1945 compared with figures for engineering and shipbuilding combined.[63]

Relations between miners and owners in the major coalfields were fraught. In Scotland, managers complained about the 'obstructive attitude of the men' while 'miners and miners' leaders say that the owners, always arbitrary, have become even

[61] J. B. Galbraith, 'Memorandum. British Auxiliaries Limited', 15 Nov. 1940. LAB 10/124.
[62] Weekly Report, Chief Conciliation Officer for Scotland. LAB 10/362.
[63] Inman, *Labour in the Munitions Industries*, 393–4.

more arbitrary since the outbreak of war'.[64] The Government officially encouraged all workers to join the approved miners' union, but the owners refused to dismiss non-unionists from their employ, even though the men agreed not to strike if the employers had signed the agreement about unionization. Home Intelligence reported that as a result of bad feeling on both sides, especially in Lanarkshire, there were frequent 'short and apparently meaningless stoppages'.[65]

During the period when it was likely that the Allies would invade Europe, a strike in the coal-mining regions of South Wales and Yorkshire idled more than 200,000 men in the spring of 1944. Bevin became convinced that the strikes were fomented by Trotskyites. As a consequence, a new regulation, opposed by the unions, was passed in mid-April 1944, giving the Government the power to imprison or fine those responsible for 'inciting strikes and lockouts which interfere with essential services'. The law was never used, although its passage outraged the Left.

The persistent labour unrest affecting the major industries in the country was not only worrisome to the ministries responsible for producing the weapons of war, it articulated the fissures that underlay the image of a nation that had closed ranks in the face of the enemy. These particular divisions were primarily those of class in the classical Marxian sense of conflicts endemic within capitalist relations of production. But there also were political divisions within the industrial working class that, while putting a clamp on radicalism also provided a continuing reminder that although class hostility might be contained, it would not easily be stifled.

Heroic Russia

British Trotskyites, presumed to be behind some of the labour unrest, were few in number and generally ineffectual. But newspaper editors, as well as the newspaper letter-writing public, no doubt were puzzled by what appeared to be a continually rising level of worker discontent, given widespread working-class admiration from the summer of 1941 on for the part the USSR was playing in the war, and pressure from the Left for an even more vigorous war effort on the part of Britain.[66] Contestation over workplace conditions was one expression of class feeling. The enthusiastic support for the USSR and the Russian people that swept Britain, especially among members of the working classes, was yet another, and the two expressions were not always congruent. Like the rhetoric of unity such as equality of sacrifice or the more controversial Commonwealth Party's slogan of 'fair shares', marshalled to protest continuing economic and social disadvantage, images of the war effort in the Soviet Union were deployed as a somewhat veiled way of criticizing Britain.

---

[64] 'Scottish Miners and the Present Emergency', Report by Home Intelligence, 21 May 1941. INF 1/681.
[65] Ibid.
[66] See e.g. editorial blaming industrial unrest on Trotskyite agitators. *Glasgow Herald*, 7 Apr. 1944, 4; letter in response from H. W. Henderson, 11 Apr. 1944, 5.

Interest in the Soviet way of life abounded as Russia was increasingly portrayed as an industrialized workers' behemoth that had emerged only recently from its feudal past. Praising Russian effort and accomplishment served as a way to implicitly critique British society while remaining loyal to the war effort.

According to Mass Observation and British Institute of Public Opinion data, public opinion turned sharply against Russia when the Soviets attacked Finland in October 1939.[67] Before then, however, even after the Russians concluded the mutual non-aggression pact with Hitler, public opinion was not especially ill-disposed towards the Soviet Union. This was so despite extensive negative press coverage and Government propaganda that was unleashed with the Nazi–Soviet Pact and the subsequent Soviet invasion of Poland.[68] Such positive attitudes towards the Soviet Union were the product of reactions to the inter-war economic crisis in Britain coupled with the rise of Fascism on the Continent on the part of a broad segment of left-of-centre opinion. As Sidney Webb was quoted as saying, 'At the close of the year 1936, when nearly all the world seems staggering towards economic and social catastrophe, the USSR stands out from every other country as supremely the Land of Hope.'[69] Large numbers of workers and intellectuals began to look to the Soviet Union as a model for the future. As John Saville notes, 'The literature favourable to the Soviet Union was quite remarkable in its volume, and much of it emanated from non-Communist sources.'[70]

But after Russia invaded Finland, the heads of most unions and the leadership of the Trade Union Congress quickly joined the Government to condemn the Soviets. A short story published in the *A.E.U. Monthly Journal* in November 1939 illustrates well union efforts to construct a suitable sensibility about the USSR. The story concerns Peter, an ARP volunteer, who is introduced to the reader as he reflects on his socialist principles.

Principles! What were they? They had always seemed so clear cut hitherto . . . He was not prepared to describe himself as Communist, but he gloried in the achievements of the U.S.S.R., and acclaimed them as triumphs of the Socialist principle. The dictatorship was a phase that would pass . . . It had only been the building up of the mighty Red Army which had assured the inviolability of Russia's frontiers. But what was the position to-day? Peter almost groaned in mental anguish as he turned to his bookcase to search for enlightment [sic] upon the latest phase of the European complication.

---

[67] See Mass Observation Archive, File Report 848/849, article for *Political Quarterly*, 'Public Opinion about Russia', by Tom Harrisson (Microfilm), MOA, Sussex. On British Institute of Public Opinion data, see P. M. H. Bell, *John Bull and the Bear: British Public Opinion, Foreign Policy and the Soviet Union 1941–1945* (London: Edward Arnold, 1990), 34.

[68] See the data cited in Bell, *John Bull and the Bear*, 33–4.

[69] As quoted in Saville, 'May Day 1937', 260.

[70] Ibid. 261. For an interesting assessment of 1930s pro-Soviet opinion and reactions to Stalin's Purge Trials—1936–1938 in Britain see 260–70.

Peter pulled from his bookcase books and pamphlets by Marx and Lenin, 'but he could find nothing to appease his spirit'. He then brought his anxiety about principle to his District Secretary who advised him to 'just do his job' for now. 'What did it matter what Stalin or Molotov said a year ago, any more than it mattered what Gladstone said in '86? . . . the fact was that the Russian attitude, consciously or otherwise, had materially helped Hitler.' The story ended with Peter burning the books in his fireplace. 'What are you burning, Peter?' called his wife. 'Memories, just memories', said Peter.[71] The story effects a transformation in feeling by portraying the worker's ideals and his former admiration for the USSR sympathetically. But it suggests to its readers that they had been betrayed and now should shed their Marxist/Leninist ideals.

Then within days or even hours after Hitler's army marched onto Russian soil, official voices welcomed Russia into the war effort against Hitler. These voices followed the lead set by Churchill in his radio broadcast the evening of 22 June 1941 by constructing the Soviet Union and Britain as united in a joint effort to destroy Hitler, while at the same time distancing that unity of effort from any imaginable endorsement of communism.[72]

After being initially cautious, the trade union leadership ardently joined both the welcome and the arm's length stance towards communism. The July 1941 'editor's notes' in the *A.E.U. Monthly Journal* noted the profound change brought about by Russia's entry into the war on the side of Britain. The editor wrote, 'Among the working people of this country and of the United States we believe it is true to say that the Nazi attack on the Russian people brought a feeling of relief from a distressing strain. We hated to think that the Soviet Union had betrayed its Socialist ideals so far as to make friends with the enemy of freedom.'[73] The editorial also quickly distanced the labour movement from the British Communist Party by arguing that,

a main cause of friction, unrest, and conflict in the industrial sphere, as well as a source of political difficulty, has been removed . . . It is idle to pretend that since the war began the attitude of the Communists in this country has been helpful to the war effort . . . an active minority, numerically small but tireless in carrying on subversive propaganda, has been an element of discord, and a force working for disunity. That factor . . . at any rate has disappeared.[74]

It is difficult to say just how important the British communists had been in fomenting discord. As a number of Regional Intelligence Officers and regional labour officials had noted, they probably only had influence where there already were fraught industrial relations and workers had long-standing grievances.[75] In any case, for the

---

[71] E. Archbold, 'Manning the Post', *A.E.U. Monthly Journal*, Nov. 1939, 446–7.
[72] Churchill, *Second World War*, iii. 331–3, reprinted in Bell, *John Bull and the Bear*, 37.
[73] 'Editor's Notes', *A.E.U. Monthly Journal*, July 1941, 174.   [74] Ibid.
[75] See e.g. Weekly Report, Chief Conciliation Officer for Scotland. LAB 10/362.

rest of the war, the labour movement basically walked a clear line that supported popular enthusiasm for the Soviets while preserving their disapprobation for the British communists.[76] Birmingham's Labour weekly, *The Town Crier*, went so far as to say, 'If the Communist Party were voluntarily liquidated altogether, there would be a far better chance of real Anglo-Russian co-operation than there is now with the Communists, their acrobatics and dubious actions still fresh in the public mind, claiming to be the only voice that is authoritative in matters pertaining to Russia.'[77]

Undoubtedly outspoken British communists did not gain in popularity, at least immediately, from the turn of events in the summer of 1941. As the Labour press predicted, the British communists had to change their ideological line to accord with current events.[78] What had been an imperialist war once again became a war against Fascist tyranny as it had been defined prior to the non-aggression pact of August 1939.

F. P. Foster, a young man who was a devout communist, kept a diary during the war. As Britain began to prepare for war in the summer of 1939, he wrote, 'Have now established the correct line to take in the event of my being called up. This war is a war against Fascism and so it must be won. At the same time members of the Fifth Column are still in the Government. They must be fought also.'[79] Early in November, Foster began to write of the war as an 'Imperialist War'. For example, his diary entry for 15 November 1939, drawing upon both populist working-class sentiment and party ideology, reads, 'This damned war is just one big racket—there must be millions of pounds being made out of it—and after all it is only being stage managed so that the big imperialists can get their hands on more means of exploitation. Why should we fight their wars—it means that we would be killing people who are of the same class from which we come.'[80] Unfortunately, as far as is known, there is no diary for the period between November 1939 and December 1942. But it is clear that by the beginning of 1943, Foster's tone had changed again in line with the 'correct attitude' towards the war, and we find him castigating the British Government for not inspiring the British public to energetic participation in the war effort.[81]

The Government, too, had to establish its 'correct' line on the Soviet Union (or 'Russia' as was the preferred nomenclature), and was extremely concerned about how to manage public opinion after Hitler had invaded the country. The problem, as perceived by the Prime Minister and officials in relevant ministries was how to

[76] See e.g. editorial 'Russia, Cut Out the Can't-Face the Facts-Get On with the Job', *The Town Crier* (Birmingham's Labour weekly), 5 July 1941, 1, and 'Watchman', 'From the Watchtower: Comments on Communists and Russia', *The Town Crier*, 11 July 1941, 5.

[77] 'Russia's Real Friends', *The Town Crier*, 12 July 1941, 2.

[78] e.g. see 'From the Watchtower', *The Town Crier*, 28 June 1941, 5.

[79] F. P. Foster diary entry, 9 Aug. 1939. 88/37/1 at the Imperial War Museum. Every effort has been made to contact the copyright holder, but to no avail.

[80] Ibid., 15 Nov. 1939.   [81] See entry for ibid., 1 Feb. 1943.

control what they realized was likely to be an outpouring of interest in, and positive feeling about the Soviet Union, for Russians, and for things Russian. They were concerned, as was the labour movement leadership, that this enthusiasm would become support for communism under the auspices of the British Communist Party. As R. H. Parker, head of the Home Division of the Ministry of Information put it:

The great danger that lies before us at the moment is that the popularisation of Russia . . . must, if it is not interfered with, equally popularise Communism as a method of political living . . . The Russians are operating beyond expectation against the Germans, so that we cannot call Communism in itself inefficient. The control by Government in this country of the industry of the country; the levies made upon earnings and upon capital are all integral parts of the Bolshevik theory, and the combination of all these factors in my view is bound to educate the country into assuming that Communism, or crypto-communism, is either a reasonable alternative to the pre-war system of democratic theory, or is a logical sequence to the wartime system of social control.[82]

The eventual solution adopted by the Government was for the Ministry of Information to issue propaganda actively supporting Russia, but with as little mention of communism as possible, and to keep the Left from capitalizing on the situation.

As Ian McLaine has detailed, the Government's strategy about dealing with the evident popularity of Russia was to 'steal the thunder' of the Left, and especially of the British Communist Party, which they anticipated would 'cash in' on the surge of popular sentiment praising the Soviet Union.[83] The idea of 'stealing the thunder' of the Left involved 'outdoing them [the 'Left wing communists'] in pro-Russia propaganda on lines which may be suitably controlled'.[84] The Ministry of Information instructed its Regional Information Officers to 'capture' plans for celebrating the Soviets, such as 'Anglo-Russian Week'. One of the first had been planned by 'local Leftists' for Bristol in late November 1941 under the auspices of the Bristol Anglo-Russian Council. The Regional Information Officer for the Bristol area was instructed to 'capture this "Week" by putting our machinery at the disposal of a Managing Committee, including the Lord Mayor, or Sir C. Treveleyan, or the Bishop of Bristol'. They also thought to invite the Soviet Embassy to jointly sponsor the 'Week'.[85]

In addition to such directives, the Ministry of Information also made arrangements with Regional Security to inform Regional Information Officers about 'individuals who have a Communist history which may not be apparent on the surface',

---

[82] R. H. Parker to Director-General, 24 July 1941. INF 1/676.

[83] See Ian McLaine, *Ministry of Morale: Home Front Morale and the Ministry of Information in World War II* (London: George Allen & Unwin, 1979), esp. 197–216. Also see Addison, *The Road to 1945*, 134–41.

[84] Minute from Briggs to R. H. Parker dated 10 Oct. 1941 on the agreement between the Home Division and the Russian Division of the Ministry. PRO/INF 1/676. Also see 'Ministry of Information Policy on Communism and Russia', 14 Oct. 1941, INF 1/676; letter sent to RIOs, 15 Oct. 1941. INF 1/676.

[85] Nicolas Bentley, Home Intelligence to Smollett, Neutral Countries Division, 14 Oct. 1941.

as well as societies and groups which were communist or communist-affiliated.[86] This they did to avoid having such people and organizations prominently involved, which would have defeated the whole purpose of their plan.

By the end of October 1941, the Ministry's efforts at the regional level were well underway. Initiatives begun by such organizations as the Northampton Trades Council, the Huddersfield Trades Council, and 'people with left wing interests' in Manchester who formed an Anglo-Soviet Committee were co-opted by the ministry in cooperation with local and regional officials.[87] But Ministry efforts were not always met with open arms. In Bristol, for example, the Lord Mayor was described by the RIO as 'not too helpful', and the Regional Commissioner (of police) was 'unhelpful and even antagonist [sic]'.[88] Oddly, during this period when the policy of direct involvement of the Government in pro-Russia celebrations was being effected, the BBC refused to add the Soviet national anthem, the Internationale, to the national anthems of the allies that were broadcast every Sunday evening prior to the nine o'clock news. As a consequence the BBC was criticized in the press, and subsequently, rather than play the Internationale, they cancelled the programme.[89] It was not until nearly the end of January 1942 that Churchill finally permitted the Internationale to be played on official occasions, as well as on the BBC.[90]

In addition to various 'home-grown' celebrations, official visitors from the Soviet Union began to make tours of Britain in the late autumn of 1941. Such tours included a Russian Trade Union delegation to British factories and mines, and a tour by a Soviet Youth Delegation.

Their reception, especially by working-class people, was generally exuberant.[91] According to a Home Intelligence special report on the Soviet Youth Delegation that toured for ten days in mid-November 1942, they were met with 'enthusiasm . . . at all the works visited'. 'In Manchester the "Delegation was mobbed in the factories", and in the Midland Region the workers gave them a "rousing reception by banging on the benches." The manager of an Aircraft factory . . . said that "the workers have got so blase over distinguished visitors that even the King wouldn't raise a cheer— but the Russians did." '[92] The report indicated that while not all regions reported rousing welcomes, in Birmingham 'where they were presented to the Mayor,

---

[86] See draft of letter, marked 'very secret', to go to RIOs, no date. INF 1/676.

[87] See Memorandum by D. B. Briggs, 'Summary of the Present Position in Regard to the Home Division Policy Memorandum on Russia', 20 Oct. 1941. INF 1/676.

[88] Ibid.

[89] Addison, *The Road to 1945*, 134. For discussions of the role of the BBC, see Sian Nicholas, *The Echo of War: Home Front Propaganda and the Wartime BBC, 1939–45* (Manchester: Manchester University Press, 1996), 163–71; and Bell, *John Bull and the Bear*, 4–42; 71–3.

[90] Ibid. 135.

[91] Home Intelligence Special Report, 'The Soviet Youth Delegation', 9 Dec. 1942. PRO/INF 1/678.

[92] Ibid.

the Square was "practically filled"', and at a gathering of youths 'reported to be unusually large . . . the applause [was] "vociferous".'[93] In Bermondsey 'an enthusiastic crowd gathered—even the Police were enthusiastic'.[94]

Numerous celebrations across the country were organized throughout 1942 and 1943. There were, in addition to Anglo-Soviet weeks, International Woman's Day rallies, Red Army Day celebrations, and commemorations of the day the Nazis invaded the Soviet Union. In early January 1942, for example, Coventry staged an Anglo-Soviet week. It began on a Sunday at the Opera House, with the Mayor of Coventry presiding over the opening ceremonies. Sharing the platform with the Mayor was the Bishop of Coventry and the MPs for Coventry and nearby Nuneaton. A respected historian and the author of numerous books on Russia, Sir Bernard Pares, spoke. The programme was designed to 'appeal to every class of the community', according to the *Coventry Evening News* announcement of the week-long gala. Each day there were public functions scheduled featuring aspects of Russian life including the showing of numerous Russian films. The week-long festival included school programmes, lectures, and a concert by the London Philharmonic Orchestra conducted by Malcolm Sargent playing an Anglo-Russian programme of music; there was a woman's rally and an education rally. The week concluded with a parade of local organizations including civil defence workers, members of the National Fire Service, and a salute by the Mayor from the Council House steps. Opening during the week and on display for the month was an exhibition of Soviet life and books.[95] The exhibition was positioned behind a frontage that featured the British Lion and the Hammer and Sickle, surmounted by the flags of both nations. There were large photographs displaying aspects of life in the Soviet Union as well as charts and posters demonstrating, according to the press, the 'tremendous strides' made in the Soviet Union's Five-Year Plans.[96]

Such celebrations were held not only in 1942 and 1943 in the period following Russia's becoming a British ally, but throughout much of the war. In February 1944, for example, there were festivities across the country to pay tribute to the Red Army on its 26th anniversary. Salutes to the Red Army were held in Belfast, London (at Albert Hall), and in Edinburgh. At Belfast 'massed military bands' played 'the new Russian national anthem', as a newspaper report put it. The Internationale was also sung at London's Albert Hall, and the Poet Laureate's 'Ode to the Red Army' written to commemorate the anniversary was read. In Edinburgh, 2,500 people attended the celebration and a performance by the Scottish Orchestra.[97]

Along with praising the military exploits of Britain's new ally, its unified and patriotic citizenry, and its scientific and cultural achievements, speakers generally

[93] Home Intelligence Special Report, 'The Soviet Youth Delegation', 9 Dec. 1942. PRO/INF 1/678.
[94] Ibid.   [95] 'Anglo-Soviet Week in Coventry', *Coventry Evening Telegraph*, 8 Jan. 1942, 3.
[96] 'Coventry's Anglo-Soviet Exhibition', *Coventry Evening Telegraph*, 15 Jan. 1942, 3.
[97] 'Britain Salutes the Red Army', *Glasgow Herald*, 24 Feb. 1944, 6.

underscored one or another version of the Government's propaganda line about the Soviet Union. At the Coventry Anglo-Soviet week in January 1942, for example, Sir Bernard Pares who spoke at the opening ceremonies said about the USSR, 'officially the country to-day was not Communist but socialist. Neither was Stalin an internationalist. His programme had been solely one of patriotic construction.'[98] Captain Strickland, the MP for Coventry, prompted that in praising Russia, people should also acknowledge 'the Empire's achievements when we faced a mighty enemy alone'.[99] At the Albert Hall Rally to honour the Red Army in February 1944, Home Secretary Herbert Morrison, while paying tribute 'of profound respect and admiration to the Government, fighting forces and people of the Soviet Union', reminded the audience that 'mutual understanding between Britain and the Soviet Union was essential, but it must not turn into mere sentimental adulation or into any unthinking imitation of ideas and institutions'.[100]

Speakers, however, also could use the opportunity that talking about the Soviet Union gave them for expressions about class distinction in Britain. Far left-leaning MP D. N. Pritt, who addressed an audience in connection with Coventry's Anglo-Soviet Week ceremonies said of Russia, 'If Russia with her modest resources, can do all she has done in ten years' time, the whole of Europe could be changed beyond belief. We could have a Europe wherein not even a Balkan peasant can starve or even a banker can be rich.'[101] And the Bishop of Coventry proclaimed that after the war there would be a 'far greater measure of Socialism', but it would come about by 'persuasion not force'.[102] At a rally celebrating International Woman's Day, sponsored by Coventry's Anglo-Soviet Committee, Mrs M. Jordan, a cotton spinner who had lived and worked in the Soviet Union for eight years claimed not to have been at all surprised by feats of the Russian people. 'Always they have before them their vision of the new world in which there is equal opportunity for everyone, man and woman.'[103]

At the same time that the Soviet Union could serve as a foil for commentary about British class distinction, images of the Soviet Union also were used to stimulate commitment to the war effort. Images of Russia were deployed to inspire increased productivity on the part of workers, and to urge women to serve the country by working in factories or serving in the military. At a Midlands Trade Union conference in Birmingham in January 1942, attended by a delegation of Soviet Trade Unionists touring the country, the Labour weekly, *The Town Crier*, told of 'scenes of indescribable enthusiasm when L. N. Soloviev, Chairman of a Leningrad Factory

---

[98] *Coventry Evening Telegraph*, 19 Jan. 1942, 3.   [99] Ibid.

[100] *Glasgow Herald*, 24 Feb. 1944, 6.

[101] 'Coventry's Help Russia Week', *Coventry Evening Telegraph*, 12 Jan. 1942, 3. Pritt, who had been expelled from the Labour Party because of his radical activities, was a proponent of the People's Convention, organized by the Communists (attracting some 1,200 delegates in Jan. 1941). Pritt, however, was not a communist. See Calder, *The Peoples' War*, 244.

[102] *Coventry Evening Telegraph*, 19 Jan. 1942, 3.

[103] 'Women's Day Rally at Coventry', *Coventry Evening Telegraph*, 9 Mar. 1942, 3.

Committee, rose to address the conference bringing a "Flaming, fighting call" from the Leningrad Front'.[104] Soloviev was followed by E. M. Savkov, Chairman of the Donbas Miners, who gave 'astounding figures of production'. He described how in some pits they had increased their productivity by a thousand per cent, and in one, a miner who was 65, 'scorning to enjoy his adequate pension in ease, was producing 150 loads above the norm'.[105] The meeting passed a resolution pledging the organizations represented to 'an untiring effort to speed up and keep up war production'.[106] Even private diaries of workers recorded concern about British factory production and negatively compared Britain to the Soviet Union. Mrs L. White, whose husband was missing in action, worked at a local aircraft factory and wrote in late September 1943, 'had so little to do all night, that I actually read one book before I went home next morning. I can't understand why we are doing nothing at work, an aircraft factory—while the Russians are fighting like mad. Anyway, what can one expect with our Government.'[107] And Mrs M. Jordan, the cotton spinner who addressed the Coventry Women's Day Rally prodded, 'You women of Coventry, make a vow to-day that you will redouble your efforts to overcome every difficulty in the way of defeating Fascism.'[108] As these examples suggest, Soviet productivity was used both as a model and a reason to spur factory and mine output in Britain.

Images of Russian women were deployed as symbols both of proletarian womanhood and devoted national citizens. Symbolically, such images of women conveyed the idea that Russian citizens, both women and men, and therefore, the society itself were virile. In Chapter 4 of this book I will argue that undergirding depictions of femininity in Britain was the desire that women and family life should remain untransformed by the war. But the discourse about Russian women was very different. Russian women were depicted admiringly as masculine. This is perhaps best captured in the following example from the magazine of the left-leaning Fire Brigades Union. The article, on a TUC Conference for Women held in Manchester at the end of January 1942 began, 'Just how implacable, ruthless, and determined the women of Russia are was amply demonstrated by the two Russian Trade Union women delegates who addressed a meeting of hundreds of women.' It described

a middle-aged, stern-looking woman representing the garment workers of Russia . . . [who] promised just retribution for [their] sufferings. Blood for blood and the avenging of tears of all the women and children were phrases which, in the tones in which they were expressed, would have made the Germans shudder, and when Madame Nikolayeva later said that the Germans in Russia trembled at the name of Woman Partisan one could quite imagine that

---

[104] 'A Flaming, Fighting Call', *The Town Crier* (Birmingham), 10 Jan. 1942, 2.   [105] Ibid.
[106] Ibid.
[107] Diaries of Mrs L. White, entry for 23 Sept. 1943. 86/54/1 at the Imperial War Museum. Quoted with the permission of Louie Williams née White.
[108] *Coventry Evening Telegraph*, 9 Mar. 1942, 3.

this was correct if the two women at the conference were an example of the determination of the Russian women to be avenged.[109]

Even though Madames Malkova and Nikolayeva were actually existing people, they and their female compatriots were being portrayed iconographically in a manner reminiscent of Delacroix's famous painting, 'Liberty on the Barricades'. Like *Liberty*, Russian women represented 'the concentrated force of the invincible people', to quote Eric Hobsbawm.[110] In his essay on revolutionary images Hobsbawm suggests why such an image might have been of a female warrior. He writes, 'Since "the people" consists of a collection of different classes and occupations . . . a general symbol not identified with any of them is desirable'.[111]

In addition to serving as icons of a heroic people, the women of Russia were held up as models of determination for British women in numerous magazines and newspapers. *Sunday Pictorial*, in March 1942, for example, featured a picture of women working in a munitions factory with the identifying caption, 'wife of a steel worker admires the women of Russia; a mother of two who realizes that she can show more devotion to her country by getting into the munitions front lines—by copying the women of Russia'.[112] Russian women were depicted as models of self-sacrifice, and the images of them could be deployed as a popular defence of unpopular demands on British women, such as the proposal by the Ministry of Home Security that women should do fire-watching at night at their workplaces. In defending the Ministry's proposal at a raucous meeting in Coventry, Ellen Wilkinson who was jeeringly told that she 'ought to be in the WAAFS [Women's Auxiliary Air Force Service]', and 'was wasting good petrol riding up and down the country', earned a large ovation when she said, 'You're yelling, yet if you consider what the women of Stalingrad are going through'.[113]

Newspapers published excerpts of speeches by visiting Soviet women trade unionists exhorting the women of Britain to dedicate themselves to producing for the war effort. When the Soviet trade union delegation visited Cardiff in January 1942, a Cardiff newspaper quoted Mme Malkova, speaking at a gathering of trade unionists as saying, 'In the factories here we see that few women are working—not enough . . . Our people are working in the Soviet Union—sacrificing themselves without rest but here we have seen that not everything is being done . . . Over the oceans and mountains and steppes the call has come to the women of England. Our

---

[109] B. Harrison, 'And the Russians! T.U.C. Conference for Women', *The Firefighter*, Mar. 1942, no. 21, p. 2. MS 346/88 at the Modern Records Centre, Warwick.

[110] Eric Hobsbawm, 'Man and Woman: Images on the Left', *Worlds of Labour: Further Studies in the History of Labour* (London: Weidenfeld and Nicolson, 1984), 86.

[111] Ibid.; for analyses of women in Soviet poster art in the inter-war period, see Victoria E. Bonnell, 'The Representation of Women in Early Soviet Political Art', *Russian Review*, 50 (1991), 267–88; and 'The Peasant Woman in Stalinist Political Art of the 1930s', *American Historical Review*, 98 (Feb. 1993), 55–82.

[112] *Sunday Pictorial*, 1 Mar. 1942, 7.   [113] *Coventry Evening Telegraph*, 5 Oct. 1942, 5.

cause is common cause, our fight the common fight.'[114] One of the propaganda posters urging women to join the war effort published by the Ministry of Information uses imagery and words that echo Malkova's message. The poster (see Plate 3), in the style of Socialist Realism, could easily have been read at the time as depicting a Soviet woman issuing a call to the women of England 'over the oceans and mountains and steppes'.[115]

Such exhortations to increase effort and speed up production undoubtedly, for a time, did inspire and enhance dedication to the war effort by at least some workers at the shop level. It did not, however, necessarily cause British women to identify as *women* with the Soviets, except perhaps in further popularizing the idea that citizenship involved sacrifice for the national community. Neither did it increase the popularity of the British Communist Party among women or among workers generally. It did, however, provide yet another avenue for the expression of 'class feeling' or resentment about social inequality in Britain and to encourage support for some variant of socialism.

For example, the Reverend W. Bryn Thomas, a Welsh clergyman, wrote to the Cardiff newspaper asking rhetorically:

What is the truth about 'production'? It is that the Soviets have taken 'profit' as a motive out of industry, all output being for the good of the community and anything bordering on exploitation of human labour being looked upon and dealt with as the worst form of crime— worse, in fact, than the perpetration of an unpremeditated murder. In that setting the workers give of their very best, and at no time has it been found necessary to apply the penalty for loss of time in the mines.[116]

The Reverend went on to claim that Russian productivity was due to their shop stewards movements enabling workers to have a direct voice in production.[117]

A letter by M. Williams published in the *Leicester Evening Mail* in mid-August 1942 illustrates how rhetoric about the Soviet Union could be deployed to underscore the idea that class inequality was contrary to national unity. The letter argued that there should be no class distinction in Britain. In the USSR people,

having no ruling class or indeed any class distinction at all, are firmly convinced that each individual should develop his or her powers to the full and use them in willing co-operation for the good of their fellow workers in all lands . . . Should we not also aim at national unity for a common purpose . . . let us put aside class differences and combine in as intense an effort as those of our Soviet Allies or German enemies.[118]

As this letter and some of the other examples above suggest, the Soviet Union represented something of a utopia for some people during the war.

[114] 'Russian Woman Tells Welsh Women "Go into the Factories" ', *Western Mail & South Wales News*, 12 Jan. 1942, 8.

[115] INF 13/126/6.   [116] *Western Mail & South Wales News*, 3 Feb. 1942.

[117] Ibid.   [118] *Leicester Evening Mail*, 13 Aug. 1942, 3.

3. Poster: Women of Britain—
Come into the Factories.
Public Record Office

Utopian fantasies about life in Soviet Russia were not ideologically motivated, at least not in the sense of a formal political ideology, as the following example makes very clear. Learie Constantine, the Trinidadian cricket player, was subject to racial discrimination in wartime England despite his stature and popularity as an athlete. In December 1944 he wrote an enthusiastic letter describing his visit to a County Children's Home in Yorkshire where children were admitted by the County Public Assistance Committee. Extolling what he saw he wrote, 'the standard achieved and maintained is so high . . . that I concluded that almost a middle class was being created from children of such lowly origins . . . it seems to me that here, in the midst of capitalism and free enterprise exists a branch of Soviet Russia, of which few people have any knowledge.'[119]

The Evacuation

The official evacuation of children from the cities, disproportionately from the most impoverished families, produced a discourse concerning 'the social question' that underscored the dire consequences of urban poverty and brought national attention to its victims.[120] I deal with the evacuation both in this chapter and again in Chapter 6, 'Geographies of the Nation', as both anxieties about poverty and social welfare (the focus in this chapter), and urban–rural conflict (a main subject of Chapter 6) accompanied the exodus of these official evacuees from the cities where they were believed to be in immanent danger, to country areas where it was believed they would be relatively safe.[121]

As scholars of the nineteenth century have understood it, 'the social question' arose as a consequence of anxieties about pauperism and social disorder.[122] 'The social' in this sense refers to the arena of social problems and public concern about social disorder—to 'society' as an object of study and regulation. Although the

[119] Letter from Learie Constantine to Margaret Bucknall, Home Talks, BBC, 5 Dec. 1944. In file, 'Talks: Learie Constantine File 1, 1939–62', at the BBC Written Archives Centre, Caversham Park, Reading.

[120] See Angus Calder on why such a large percentage of evacuees were from the poorest reaches of urban society, *The People's War*, 40.

[121] More well-to-do families arranged privately to leave the cities for hotels and country houses, or to send their children abroad for the duration.

[122] For England, see Gareth Stedman Jones, *Outcast London: A Study in the Relationship between Classes in Victorian Society*, repr. (Harmondsworth, Middlesex: Penguin, 1984). While at the time that he wrote the book, Jones did not specifically name what it was he was discussing as 'the social', his focus on the problem of poverty and casual labour and the policies that were meant to deal with it may usefully be considered along with more recent literature as an analysis of the rise of the social. See also Eileen Yeo, *The Contest for Social Science: Relations and Representations of Gender and Class* (London: River Orams Press, 1996). For Germany, see George Steinmetz, *Regulating the Social: The Welfare State and Local Politics in Imperial Germany* (Princeton: Princeton University Press, 1993) and Kathleen Canning, *Languages of Labour and Gender: Female Factory Work in Germany, 1850–1914* (Ithaca, NY: Cornell University Press, 1996), esp. chap. 3. Also see the interesting theoretical essay by Giovanna Procacci, 'Social Economy and the Government of Poverty', in Graham Burchell, Colin Gordon, and Peter Miller (eds.), *The Foucault Effect: Studies in Governmentality* (Chicago: University of Chicago Press, 1991), 151–68.

growth of the professions of social research and social welfare that concerned themselves with the urban poor continued apace through the twentieth century, the evacuation focused a national spotlight on the lives of city children and their mothers. This attention consisted of a proliferating discourse about poverty, its causes and consequences, and what might be done about it. Moral condemnation of the poor for their behaviour mixed with outrage at such 'slanders on the working class'.[123] Public debates about the evacuation and the evacuees constituted a major site of discourse about social class.

There were three official evacuations from London and other metropolitan areas. The first occurred a few months prior to and immediately after war was declared in September 1939. It has been estimated that between June and the first week of September 1939, 2 million people about whom little is known, privately emigrated to the west of England and Wales.[124] Another untold number went abroad including about 5,000 persons who left the United Kingdom for the United States at the end of August 1939. These voluntary emigrants had both the funds and the connections to make arrangements for themselves. But it was the official evacuation from London and other urban areas in England and Scotland of nearly one and a half million people, largely mothers and their young children and children unaccompanied by a parent, around whom controversy swirled. By the beginning of 1940, nearly 700,000 evacuees in England and Wales had returned home. In Scotland by Christmas 1939 three-fourths of those evacuated from Clydeside had returned.[125]

A second and substantially smaller stream of around 300,000 evacuees left the cities during the spring of 1940 as Continental Europe was overrun by Nazi troops. With the beginning of the London Blitz in September 1940 around 1,250,000 emigrated to safer areas. The numbers of evacuees leaving particular urban areas depended upon the location of the air attacks. Evacuation slowed and by 1942 only a small number came into the reception areas. The last major evacuation which included about 1,000,000 in a two-month period, took place in the summer of 1944 as V-2 rockets exploded in London and south-eastern England.[126]

What had begun in the early autumn of 1939 as an emergency measure to save lives within a few months had come to be 'a social question of some magnitude and of uncertain duration'.[127] And it is how this 'social question' was constructed that

---

[123] Calder, *The People's War*, 42.

[124] Richard M. Titmuss, *Problems of Social Policy* (London: HMSO, 1950), 102. In spite of its significance to popular memory of the war years, and the numerous reminiscences and memoirs of evacuees that have been published, there is surprisingly little scholarly analysis of the process since 1950. Relying on Titmuss as well as other studies done during the war, Angus Calder provides a relatively comprehensive account in *The People's War*, 35–50.

[125] These figures are from Calder, *The People's War*, 39.

[126] The numbers involved in these evacuations are drawn from Titmuss, *Problems of Social Policy*, 355.

[127] F. Le Gros Clark and R. W. Toms, *Evacuation—Failure or Reform?* Fabian Tract 249, 1940, 2, as quoted in Calder, *The People's War*, 39.

concerns us here. Reactions to the initial resettlement of urban children and mothers, as well as those that followed, depicted a Britain not of national unity, but rather in the image of two nations created nearly a hundred years previously by Benjamin Disraeli. In place of Disraeli's industrial north and agricultural south, the two nations of the evacuation were the urban poor and country people. As Lily Boys, county organizer of the WVS (Women's Voluntary Services) put it, 'the dirt and low standard of living of the evacuees from big industrial cities of Leeds and Hull has been an eye-opener and an unpleasant shock to the inhabitants of an agricultural county like Lincolnshire, who had no idea that such terrible conditions existed.'[128]

The evacuation has sometimes been credited with having revealed to the country at large the depths of poverty in the urban centres in which some people had been living.[129] As the Women's Group on Public Welfare (WGPW) report on the evacuation, published in 1943 put it, 'The dreadful lesson of evacuation was the light it threw upon the home conditions of the lowest of the town dwellers.'[130] But the so-called 'lesson' was not uniform in its revelation.

Much of the commentary about the poor's 'standard of living' treated poverty in much the same language as pauperism had been viewed from the Victorian era onward. The newspapers at the time were full of letters rife with moral condemnation of the urban poor for their slovenly ways. The spotlight of concern was shown on 'problem families' and 'irresponsible women'. For example, a conference was planned by the Liverpool Council of Social Service in August 1945 to begin a 'concerted attack on the problem of the family whose standards of living and behaviour were so far below the minimum which could be tolerated in any civilised community as to make it a menace to society'. Although such families had been known for some time, the Report of the Conference suggested, it was more 'fully appreciated by the nation at large' when it was revealed by the large scale 1939 evacuation.[131]

As was the case in the nineteenth century, those in poverty were held morally responsible for their own plight, and mothers were to receive improved education and training for domesticity in order to make them efficient and responsible parents. For example, the Report of the Conference on Problem Families held in Liverpool claimed that poverty, bad housing, and overcrowding were not the

---

[128] Preliminary Report on Evacuation of Children and Others to Lindsey (Lincs.)', memorandum by Lily Boys, 13 Sept. 1939, HLG 7/74, PRO Kew, as quoted in Harold L. Smith (ed.), *Britain in the Second World War: A Social History* (Manchester and New York: Manchester University Press, 1996), 42.

[129] See e.g. Sian Nicholas, *The Echo of War* (Manchester: Manchester University Press, 1996), 75, 241. The idea that the evacuation 'aroused the conscience of the nation' and was a major inducement to enhanced welfare policies was articulated in Titmuss, *Problems of Social Policy*, esp. 507–8.

[130] Women's Group on Public Welfare, *Our Towns: A Close-Up* (London: Oxford University Press, 1943), p. xvi.

[131] Liverpool Council of Social Service, 'Problem Families, Report of Conference Convened on January 26 1946'.

cause of 'problem families'. Rather, according to the Deputy Medical Officer of Health of the City and Port of Liverpool, C. O. Stallybrass, 'inefficiency of the mother is an outstanding feature of these families'. Stallybrass asserted that, 'the initial discouragement of the mother reacts on the father's temper; the mother's further discouragement causes her to become increasingly sluttish and indifferent; the father takes his money and his affection elsewhere, or he falls into idleness and waste. The family life is in disintegration.'[132] As a solution Stallybrass recommended training for mothers and the establishment of marriage guidance clinics or, in severe cases, removal of children from the home to public guardianship.[133]

In Scotland in mid-September 1939 the letters to the editor pages of the *Glasgow Herald* were filled with controversy over the evacuation. Letter writers condemned the evacuation of 'disobedient and verminous children polluting' country homes.[134] Reading as though they were examples taken from the pages of Mary Douglas's book, *Purity and Danger*, letters and commentary describing working-class mothers and children often used the metaphor of 'pollution'. The metaphor was used not only by permanent residents of the reception areas. A social worker in Liverpool in a Wartime Bulletin of Information wrote of the 'poor ignorant, shiftless folk in Liverpool at Rest Centres who polluted Church Halls in two or three nights and whose children were learning to be City Savages'. Continuing her imperial metaphor, the writer remarked that a solution would require teachers of a 'missionary type' to reach the children of 'these seemingly irresponsive and irresponsible people'.[135]

In a column in the *Glasgow Herald* the Socialist Lord Provost of Glasgow, Lord Darling, countered those who would call the evacuee children 'polluters'. He retorted sarcastically,

These children may not have reached aristocratic standards of hygiene, but are more deserving of sympathy than censure. They come from houses which have been denied the amenities of modern civilisation, and are the victims of an environment that would have been impossible if in bygone years men had thought more of homes and families than of profits and dividends.[136]

The WGPW, itself, maintained that the 'slums are largely the result of low wages and insecurity, and it should no longer be open to private selfishness to perpetuate these evils'. And drawing upon the language of Christian socialism that contributed to the discourse of social transformation during the war, the WGPW argued, 'Trade and industry must take their place as servants, not masters of the community,

[132] Ibid. 9.   [133] Ibid. 10–11.
[134] Cited in letter by Lord Provost Darling, *Glasgow Herald*, 14 Sept. 1939, 5. Also see letter by 'Common Sense' who wondered 'what is to be done about those mothers and children of filthy habits who pollute the homes of the decent people on whom they are quartered?' 15 Sept. 1939, 5.
[135] Liverpool Council of Social Service, 'Wartime Bulletin of Information', vol. 2, No. 60, 6 Apr. 1942.
[136] *Glasgow Herald*, 14 Sept. 1939, 5.

recognising a duty not only economic but moral.'[137] But they coupled the required changes in social welfare policy with the necessity for a 'campaign for better education, academic, social and moral, [that] must be waged side by side with the battle against poverty and bad material conditions.'[138]

Stressing morality and education more than social conditions, the Scottish Women's Group on Public Welfare blamed the previous war for having disadvantaged adolescent girls who were now working-class mothers. 'What wonder that she failed to make good with her own little ones! What wonder that her dietary and shopping habits amazed the country hostess and the village shop! What wonder that she was heard in one recorded instance to say, "Johnnie, don't use the lady's carpet, use the surround!" '[139] The pamphlet concluded by maintaining that while '[i]mproved social conditions are necessary to make better human beings . . . [t]he touchstone of worth is . . . not wealth but righteousness, brotherhood, and friendship.'[140] And John Carruther replied to Lord Provost Darling's letter, 'sympathy for a woman who is too poor to procure proper food is admirable, but sympathy expressed for one who is too poor to keep a clean house and teach her children decent habits is mere sentimentality . . . Some slum dwellers do keep clean homes, others turn clean homes into slums.'[141] Observers seemed generally to agree that many working-class children were verminous, and that their households were unhygienic, although it is likely that their actual numbers were smaller than the outcry about them suggests.

Regardless, the public controversy over the impact of evacuation depicted a Britain riven in two rather than a unitary nation. This was further elaborated, albeit with a very different slant, in reports that circulated in the press painting wealthy householders who refused to take in evacuated children as villains of the evacuation. The Liverpool Council of Social Services commented in an issue of their *National Emergency Bulletin*, for instance, on a news report that a London County Council schoolmaster, serving as a billeting official in a small suburban town on the outskirts of Greater London, was unsuccessful in persuading householders to take some evacuated children. The *Bulletin* writer dramatically chastised such people saying it is

incredible that in a country that calls itself Christian there should exist such cruel selfishness that rather than put up with some dislocation of family life and some difficulties, there are people who prefer to send these helpless children back to the danger zone to be mutilated or murdered . . . [This is] not unique and it makes some of us wonder whether the war will

---

[137] Women's Group on Public Welfare, *Our Towns*, p. xix.   [138] Ibid., p. xviii.
[139] Scottish Women's Group on Public Welfare, *Our Scottish Towns: Evacuation and the Social Future* (Edinburgh: William Hodge, 1944), 2.
[140] Ibid. 45.   [141] *Glasgow Herald*, 16 Sept. 1939, 5.

come to an end until the destruction of material possessions makes such economic independence and selfishness impossible.[142]

Apparently, some local billeting officers were reluctant to insist that wealthy householders accept evacuees for fear of repercussions.[143]

Complaints about wealthier country home owners who refused to accept children from the cities were not the only ones to surface that reversed the direction of class criticism and focused disapproval on the upper classes. Householders in the reception areas complained that well-to-do parents sent their children into the country expecting them to be fed 'in the manner to which they are accustomed' without supplementing the 8s. 6d. per week state allowance. As 'Square the Fare' wrote to the *Glasgow Herald*, 'Why should parents of such well-dressed and well-nourished big lads expect me to draw on my resources to keep their offspring.'[144] Another letter complained that wealthy householders continued to get tax relief for their evacuated children who were living in simple country cottages. 'Victim of the Scheme' complained that the crowning blow was when the parents came to visit and expected to be entertained.'[145]

Although class resentments, especially complaints about the hygienic standards of poor urbanites, dominated popular discussion along with the occasional complaint that reversed the blame for evacuation difficulties, there was the odd published report by a 'foster parent' who enjoyed the experience of billeting urban children. Amy St Loe Strachey, for example, wrote, 'My six boys are making this dreary, lonely war not only tolerable, but often enjoyable.'[146] She refused to believe she was 'extraordinarily lucky' with the children she boarded, and included reception stories of two of her friends to substantiate her claim.[147] Strachey's account which echoed with the accents of her elevated class standing positioned the writer as beneficently providing a healthy environment that would transform her charges from badly behaved youngsters to respectable children. As she expressed it, 'the worst of these "bad boys" is now the most willing, responsive and altogether delightful of my delightful six.'[148] Such a posture was not unique to Strachey. The report of the National Federation of Women's Institutes on the evacuation, based on responses from 1,700 Institutes, commented, 'Many reports reveal how little home life some of the children had and how they responded to affection and discipline.'[149]

[142] 'National Emergency Bulletin', vol. 2., No. 48, Liverpool Council of Social Services, 27 Dec. 1940.

[143] Smith, *Britain in the Second World War*, 43. See also, 'Evacuation', Home Intelligence Report, 18–25 June 1941, INF 1/292, PRO Kew, as quoted in Smith above, 43–4.

[144] *Glasgow Herald*, 21 Sept. 1939, 5.   [145] Ibid.

[146] See Mrs (Amy) St Loe Strachey, *Borrowed Children: A Popular Account of Home Evacuation Problems and Their Remedies* (London: John Murray, 1940), 11.

[147] Ibid. 3–4.   [148] Ibid. 9.

[149] National Federation of Women's Institutes, *Town Children through Country Eyes* (Dorking, Surrey: National Federation of Women's Institutes, 1940).

Perhaps more than any other single 'event' or more accurately, series of events, the evacuation was represented in public discussions in ways that challenged the idea that British national identity was unitary. The first evacuation occurred before the war had been named as 'the People's War', a naming which most probably was coincident with the post-Dunkirk period, especially with the stories of comradeship during the Blitz. Thus, the initial responses to the evacuees could not be expected to have been inflected by the rhetorics of 'equality of sacrifice' or a populist-inspired levelling implied by the term 'People's War'. But subsequent evacuations and the reports assessing the experience that continued to be published at least into 1944 underscored the class divisions that continued to challenge the idea that Britain was a unitary entity through to 1945 and the war's end.

The Post-War Future

The evacuation made some of the problems associated with poverty painfully clear, and one response, as I suggested above, was to advocate post-war measures to alleviate economic disparities and their consequences. The social question raised anew by the evacuation fed, as did pro-Russia enthusiasm into discussions about the 'new Britain' that would emerge in the post-war world. Frank Foster, the Soviet-bedazzled, diary-writing British communist who printed on numerous blank pages, 'Long Live Comrade Stalin; Victory to the Red Army', expressed what is undoubtedly an extreme instance of this futuristic utopian sentiment. In early 1943 he wrote that the Soviet Union would lead the way when the war was over 'so that humanity will be able to step forward into what is only yet the future—tall white majestic cities will grace the earth, beautiful parks of rest, hygienic modern factories, majestic sweeping rivers, dredged and embanked with white concrete . . . Man what lies before you, freedom! Freedom!!'[150] While Foster's dedication to communism led him to focus his hopes for the future on the Soviet Union, expressions of 'class feeling' were commonly articulated through discussions about post-war Britain.

As early as 1939, and gathering strength as the war progressed, there was a growing almost millenarian belief that a new Britain would rise up from the ruins of war. This would be a Britain not only with rebuilt cities and towns, but a Britain that was socially transformed. This was certainly a theme of J. B. Priestley's enormously popular 1940 Sunday *Postscripts*, although Priestley's Left populism profoundly antagonized conservative listeners.

Mass Observation reported in November 1940 that there was a trend in public opinion 'towards uncertainty and questioning of the *status quo*'.[151] Until late in the

[150] Diaries of Frank Foster entry dated 14 Feb. 1943. Frank Foster box, 88/37/1, at the Imperial War Museum.

[151] Mass Observation, File Report #496, 'Popular Attitudes to Wartime Politics', 20 Nov. 1940.

summer of 1941 when Churchill and Roosevelt signed the Atlantic Charter, however, the Churchill Government was loathe to discuss post-war Britain or 'peace aims' and maintained vociferously when challenged that the appropriate 'war aim' was to defeat the enemy.[152] In the autumn of 1941 the BBC began a series of twelve talks entitled 'Making Plans' and designed other radio shows dealing with the issues of reconstruction for the winter. The Ministry of Information was contacted by Arthur Greenwood, head of the Government's Committee on Reconstruction, who wanted to see expanded discussion about post-war aims in order to discover 'what is in people's minds and educating them'.[153] But the future had been on the minds of 'the people' quite some time before this.

At the height of the Blitz, the people in bombed areas were understandably more concerned with the immediate future than with the long term. Yet Home Intelligence continued to report concern about 'what will happen when peace comes. Will there be more unemployment? Will everyone bear their fair share in the work of rehabilitation?'[154] By December 1940, Home Intelligence was reporting that both the press and the public were showing increased interest in peace aims. Working-class public opinion was reported to be focused especially on problems of 'unemployment and social reconstruction'.[155]

These concerns were featured in a special issue of *Picture Post*, 4 January 1941, devoted to 'A Plan for Britain'. The special issue opened with an essay by B. L. Coombes, a Welsh writer and an unemployed coal miner, who wrote cynically about both the present and what the future might hold. He commented that his 15-year-old son, who was a 'skilful mechanic' was unemployed, and apparently, 'the country doesn't want his skill or his labour'. He wondered if there would be 'any place for the grandsons, the youngest generation?'[156] He further articulated his conception of class difference by expounding upon 'the blunders of a government led by a class that was born to govern; and educated to believe that only the best was good enough for them . . . There are thousands—no, millions!—like me, who are willing to do hard and dangerous work as long as they get a fair reward for it. But this one thing angers us—the idea that a man is a dolt if he does work which dirties his hands or his clothes! The fact is that men like us have got to be efficient at our jobs—because we can't get promoted for muddling things!'[157] The articles in the special issue were designed to answer the miner's questions about whether or not there would be 'any place for the grandsons'. They included 'Work for All: The First Necessity in the New Britain' and 'Social Security' that would include a minimum wage, child

[152] For a discussion about the debate within the BBC and MOI about plans for radio talks and discussions of 'peace aims', see Nicholas, *The Echo of War*, 240–8.

[153] Letter from Office of the Minister Without Portfolio (Arthur Greenwood) to Brendan Bracken, 9 Oct. 1941. INF 1/862.

[154] Home Intelligence Weekly Report, 7 Oct. to 14 Oct. 1940. INF 1/292.

[155] Home Intelligence Weekly Report, 11–18 Dec. 1940. INF 1/292 Part 1A.

[156] B. L. Coombes, 'This is the Problem', *Picture Post*, vol. 10, No. 1, 4 Jan. 1941, 8.   [157] Ibid. 9.

allowances, a scheme of social insurance, and special forms of public assistance. The articles and the accompanying pictures contrasted the problems of pre-war Britain with transformed visions of the future to emphasize the necessity for reform. The editor received more than 2,000 letters in response to the special issue indicating the widespread interest in and concern about Britain's post-war future.[158]

For working-class people and for those higher up on the economic ladder who cared about 'the social question', concern about the future was linked to the pre-war past. The memory of the difficult immediate post–World War I years coupled with the depression that still haunted the country at the time of the outbreak of war when there were more than a million unemployed, made economic insecurity and class inequality central to wartime discourses about a future peacetime Britain. Two seemingly contradictory ideas about post-war Britain were prominent throughout the war years. One view portrayed a post-war Britain characterized by diminishing class distinction and a redistribution of wealth.[159] This was a view that projected the wartime slogans of 'equality of sacrifice' and 'fair shares' onto the years of peace that would follow. This conviction was challenged by those largely working-class people, the ones who had everything to gain from such a transformation, who expressed a much more cynical posture—one framed by pessimism which maintained that the war would change nothing—'vested interests' would see to that. And as an official in the Ministry of Information put it, based on postal censorship reports, 'these two opinions, though contradictory, are often held by the same people'.[160]

Public concern about the future continued to build during the winter and spring of 1942. Home Intelligence began reporting that many were demanding 'to be told what sort of a post-war society our rulers envisage as the result of victory'.[161] It was against such a background of apprehension and interest that Sir William Beveridge was drafting his Report on Social Insurance.

Even before it was published, the Press stirred interest in the impending Report by hinting at what it might propose. Beveridge himself was instrumental in this publicity. In the summer of 1942 he gave a speech in London to the Engineering Industries Association, an employers' association, which was covered in newspapers across the country. The *Leicester Evening Mail*, for example, featured an article that quoted from sections of the Beveridge speech. The headline, 'Plan Now Peacetime Job Security for All!', captured the two major points in Beveridge's talk. The first dealt with unemployment which Beveridge talked about as the 'evil' of 'idleness'; the second concerned the necessity for economic planning to prevent unemployment.[162] Such press coverage fuelled both a sense of hope that something would be done to solve the continuing problem of poverty and unemployment, and fear that nothing of the kind would happen.

---

[158] McLaine, *Ministry of Morale*, 175.   [159] See e.g. Weekly Report, 8–15 Jan. 1941. INF 1/292/1A.
[160] Note for the Minister (signature illegible), 17 Oct. 1941, INF 1/862.
[161] Weekly Report, 25 Mar. 1942. INF 1/292 Part 1.   [162] *Leicester Evening Mail*, 30 July 1942, 4.

The Beveridge Report, published on 1 December 1942 addressed what Sir William called 'the evil of want' by providing social security insurance to cover crises from the 'cradle to the grave'. Beveridge elaborated three guiding principles of the plan which, in the words of Angus Calder, 'married the doctrines of Liberal individualism to the revolutionary sentiments of the People's War'.[163] The plan, itself, provided that all wage earners would contribute equally in weekly installments and, in return, they would receive a uniform rate of benefit. Their contributions would be supplemented by increased employer and state subsidies. National public assistance would be available for people who were not covered by the plan. Proposals for a national minimum wage with child benefits provided as a supplement for wage earners with children and the formation of a national health service were central to the plan.

This is not the place to delve into an analysis of the Beveridge proposals, or in detail into the debates surrounding them.[164] Rather, I want to suggest that the Report became a site of discussion about class inequality and about what, if anything, was to be done about it.[165]

The Report generated enormous interest, attention, and commentary. All the major newspapers published summaries and a Gallup Poll conducted within two weeks of the Report's publication found that nineteen out of twenty people had heard of it, and nine out of ten believed its proposals should be adopted.[166]

As is well known, the Churchill Government was surprised and disquieted by the enthusiasm with which the public welcomed the Report. In mid-December an Army Bureau of Current Affairs (ABCA) pamphlet was published containing a synopsis of the plan written by Beveridge, but the War Office withdrew it two days later. The Minister of War apparently believed that the plan was so controversial that he could not permit what he believed would be politically geared discussions to take place under Army auspices. The withdrawal of the ABCA pamphlet prompted public hostility, press criticism, and class ridicule.[167] This is wonderfully illustrated by the Birmingham Labour Party newspaper's sarcastic comment:

Though civilians are discussing Beveridge the soldier must surrender his right to think to General Sir Maudlin Trite . . . and other nameless nitwits at the War Office, who probably arrived at their present positions via the . . . Hunt of Middle Wallop.

'By Gad, sir,' we can hear them saying. 'We must protect our men from this Bolshevism.'[168]

---

[163] Calder, *The People's War*, 528.

[164] For discussions, see Jose Harris, *William Beveridge: A Biography* (Oxford: Clarendon Press, 1977); Jose Harris, 'The Debate on State Welfare', in Harold L. Smith (ed.), *War and Social Change: British Society in the Second World War* (Manchester: Manchester University Press, 1986), 233–63; Addison, *The Road to 1945*, chap. 8.

[165] There were other issues during the war such as education reform that also sparked a debate over class and class privilege.

[166] Calder, *The People's War*, 527–8.

[167] For the public response immediately following the publication of the report, see Home Intelligence Weekly Report, 1–8 Dec. 1942, INF 1/292.

[168] *The Town Crier* (Birmingham), 'No Beveridge for the Troops', 23 Dec. 1942, 3.

In addition to withdrawing the ABCA pamphlet, the Government was reluctant to support or even comment on the plan. For several months the Government remained silent about what it planned to do with it. This silence and the Government's apparent hostility to the plan fed growing anxiety on the part of the public, especially the working-class public, that the provisions of the Report would never be enacted. Home Information, for example, reported in its Weekly Report for mid-December 1942 that people of the 'poor sections of the community' thought 'it is all too good to be true', and that there existed widespread 'scepticism as to the likelihood of the plan being accepted'. Home Information suggested that 'many people fear that it will be delayed or even wrecked' by the Insurance Companies and/or 'big business'.[169] Even as late as late January and early February 1943, Home Intelligence was reporting that the withdrawal of the ABCA pamphlet was 'still referred to with "disfavour"; it is even suggested that the ban is a "Government try-on" to see if they can "get away with" dropping the report.'[170] This fear was articulated in the form of the following doggerel, printed in the Birmingham Labour Party newspaper.

The New Cock Robin

Who'll kill Plan Bev'ridge?
I, said the Tory,
With axe large and gory,
I'll kill Plan Bev'ridge

Who'll see him die?
I, said Prudential
I think it essential,
I'll see him die.

Who'll drain his blood?
We, said the Lords
With our little swords,
We'll drain his blood.

Who'll make his shroud?
We, said the wealthy,
With action so stealthy,
We'll make his shroud.

. . .

And the men in the street
Fell a-sighing and a-sobbing,
When they heard that the sharks

---

[169] Home Intelligence Weekly Report, 15–22 Dec. 1942, INF 1/292 Part 3C.
[170] Home Intelligence Weekly Report, 26 Jan.–2 Feb. 1943. INF 1/2929 Part 3C.

> Would continue their robbing,
> When they heard that the sharks
> Would continue their robbing.

The debate over the Beveridge Plan which finally took place in the House of Commons in mid-February 1943 produced, according to Home Information, great controversy.[171] Its weekly report for 16–23 February 1943 noted that the majority, particularly

'workers' and 'the working class' . . . are disappointed, and in some cases 'frustrated' and 'angry', at what is believed to be:

i. *The Government's attitude to the Report*: It seems to be widely believed that the Beveridge plan is 'already dead', or that it will 'sooner or later be entirely squashed'. . .

ii. *The influence of vested interests*: The insurance companies are particularly 'blamed for the shelving of the plan' . . . In Scotland working people believe that the press is largely hostile and say: 'look at the big insurance advertisements appearing at the moment. This is how the press can be bribed.'[172]

The Government's White Paper on Social Insurance was published in September 1944. Although the plan was warmly welcomed, according to Home Information, 'a considerable number . . . among whom workers and left wing people are specified, are convinced it will never be implemented, or will be whittled away with excuses . . . Others, though not sceptical, are nevertheless depressed at the thought of the 'long time' it will take to put the provisions into practice. A few dismiss it as 'a political stunt to catch votes'.[173] The response to the Beveridge Plan the Government's White Paper, and anticipation of the future post-war Britain on the part of British people in the working classes continued throughout the war to demonstrate a peculiar blend of hope and cynicism.

'Class Feeling' was palpable during the war years, at least up through the June 1945 election which brought in a Labour Government. And labour activism in the autumn of 1945 suggests that workers were not altogether sanguine that 'equality of sacrifice' during the war years would be rewarded with a diminution of class difference once the conflict had ended.

In this chapter I have suggested that the issue of class inequality was central to the wartime nation. If the nation was one people, it was certainly a people who saw themselves as differentiated by social class. The call for equality of sacrifice, and the concern with social security in the post-war future publicized the possibility that class differences might be levelled as a result of the war. At the same time, the rhetorics of class difference that were part of and made use of this cultural construction undermined the very idea that the nation was unitary, and did so in ways that had tangible consequences. It is possible that it was precisely this tension

---

[171] Weekly Report, 16–23 Feb. 1943. INF 1/292 Part 3.   [172] Ibid. 3–4.
[173] Weekly Report, 26 Sept.–3 Oct. 1944. INF 1/292 Part 4.

67

between the fantasy of Britain as singular and the continued existence of and focus on class difference that generated both the palpable desire for some vague sort of utopian social transformation and the fear that nothing would change.

Those who loosely could be defined as working-class understood their worlds as profoundly affected by economic inequality. And public commentary generally recognized that class distinction scored the substance of British life. If anything the period of war that followed the unemployment crises of the 1930s sharpened those perceptions, and the 1945 election was one consequence as working-class voters shifted their allegiances to Labour.[174] The perception that Britain was divided by social class was articulated through several different languages. As I have shown, it surfaced in extensive labour conflict—even as the working class was divided between most of the union leadership and the leadership of the Labour Party, on the one hand, and many in the rank and file, on the other. Class was spoken through expressions of admiration for Russia. It recurred as a theme along with the revival of 'the social question' that accompanied the evacuation, and reverberated throughout the war in discussions about reconstruction and the post-war future. As Geoffrey Field has so perceptively noted, it both informed the language of patriotism, and was thoroughly imbricated with it.[175] Ironically, as this chapter has shown, the languages of nationhood, of a unitary Britain fighting 'the People's War', fed expressions of class antagonism subverting the very idea of a unitary British identity.

The historiography of whether or not the war actually produced social change, and whether or not it was a turning point towards a new left-leaning social and/or political consensus still reverberates with this tension. Ross McKibbin has written that England in the period 1918 to 1951 was a 'country of social classes into which the English freely categorized themselves'.[176] 'Despite the fact that the Second World War significantly recast social relationships', he suggests, it was a country in which those who had authority in 1951 were of the same social origins and social position as those who held it in 1918.[177] McKibbin maintains that there was a broad social democratic vision that permeated Britain generally during the war, animating the working class in particular. Yet he provocatively suggests that the very rhetoric about national unity that persisted through to the end of the war tempered radicalism.[178] The argument in this chapter is consonant with at least a part of McKibbin's

---

[174] On this point, see Ross McKibbin, 'Class and Conventional Wisdom: The Conservative Party and the "Public" in Inter-war Britain', in *The Ideologies of Class, Social Relations in Britain 1880–1950* (Oxford: Clarendon Press, 1994), 286–7.

[175] Geoffrey Field, 'Social Patriotism and the British Working Class: Appearance and Disappearance of a Tradition', *International Labor and Working-Class History*, 42 (Fall 1992), 20–39.

[176] Ross McKibbin, *Classes and Cultures: England 1918–1951* (Oxford: Oxford University Press, 1998), p. v. McKibbin speaks here of England, although I think his characterization applies to Britain as a whole in this time period.

[177] Ibid.   [178] Ibid. 533.

conclusions. It is arguable that the war 'recast social relations' generally. The evidence does not support such a sweeping claim either when it comes to gender or class relations. Yet McKibbin's contention that a 'broad social democratic vision' was pervasive during the war years seems, on balance, to be right. But it is exactly this conjecture—that there was a 'new consensus' that leaned left—that has been the subject of controversy among historians.[179] Arguments have raged over the hypothesis that there was a broad social and/or political consensus that emerged during the war. As Paul Addison has argued in the epilogue to the most recent edition of his landmark study, *The Road to 1945*, speaking primarily of the idea of political consensus, consensus is a *relative* term.[180] And, as Malcolm Smith has argued with regard to the British state, consensus and conflict can be, and were, coterminous.[181]

If there was a broad consensus, it was that the British nation was or must be an unadulterated whole. Whether or not the consensus about national unity was responsible for moderating radicalism, as McKibbin has suggested, is hard to judge. More likely, that moderation was complexly determined, but one major influence might well have been the 'broad social democratic vision' that pervaded public discourse.

Thus, my reading of the period suggests that those who argue that most of the British simply 'didn't care' about social reform—the 'apathy school', as James Hinton refers to such scholars—are wrong.[182] Instead of interpreting cynicism as a sign of apathy, I have argued that it was a symptom of the fear of unfulfilled desire. Rather than dismissing labour unrest as insignificant because strikes were short and local, I have argued that these were symptomatic of the degree of working-class resentment and hostility given that they were illegal and required workers to thwart the power of the union and the Government combined.

World War II, I would argue, witnessed a new 'structure of feeling', to use

---

[179] Participants in this debate include: Addison, *The Road to 1945*; Peter Hennessy, 'Never Again', in Brian Brivati and Harriet Jones (eds.), *What Difference Did the War Make?* (London and New York: Leicester University Press, 1993); Steven Fielding, 'What Did "The People" Want?: The Meaning of the 1945 General Election', *Historical Journal*, 35 (1992), 623–39; Tony Mason and Peter Thompson, ' "Reflections on a Revolution?" The Political Mood in Wartime Britain', in Nick Tiratsoo (ed.), *The Attlee Years* (London and New York: Pinter Publishers, 1991); S. Fielding, P. Thompson, and N. Tiratsoo, *'England Arise!': The Labour Party and Popular Politics in 1940s Britain* (Manchester: Manchester University Press, 1995); see also reviews by Sarah Benton, 'The 1945 "Republic" ', *History Workshop Journal*, 43 (Spring 1997), 249–57, John Marriott, 'Labour and the Popular', 258–65, and James Hinton, '1945 and the Apathy School', 266–72. Also see essays in Harold Smith (ed.), *War and Social Change: British Society in the Second World War* (Manchester: Manchester University Press, 1986).

[180] Addison, *The Road to 1945*, 287.

[181] Malcolm Smith, 'The Changing Nature of the British State, 1929–59: The Historiography of Consensus', in Brian Brivati and Harriet Jones (eds.), *What Difference Did the War Make?* (London and New York: Leicester University Press, 1993), 42–3.

[182] Hinton, '1945 and the Apathy School', 266–72.

Raymond Williams's insightful concept.[183] At the centre of this structure of feeling was concern about social and economic inequality and a renewed focus on 'the social question'. Surely, the proposition that 'social engineering' could transform society was part of the technocratic vision that long pre-dated the war. But, during the war years, that view became amplified. The culture of pro-Russian/Soviet sentiment that was fostered by the Government to co-opt left-wing propaganda contributed to this new 'structure of feeling'.

The concept of 'structure of feeling' suggests patterned indeterminacy. It signifies a shift in the centre of gravity of a political culture. But the precise working out of that shift over time in terms of changes in particular practices is not predetermined by the structure of feeling itself. Contained within a structure of feeling are simply new possibilities—possibilities, not a practical politics of social transformation.

[183] See Geoffrey Field who uses the same concept to depict the changed political climate in World War II ('Social Patriotism and the British Working Class: Appearance and Disappearance of a Tradition', *International Labor and Working-Class History*, 42 (Fall 1992), 24).

3

'Good-Time' Girls

AND QUINTESSENTIAL ALIENS

The nation was depicted as one in which 'the people' were sacrificing their private pleasures and individual interests and concerns and devoting themselves to the war effort. It is not surprising, then, that self-interestedness or selfishness came to be portrayed as antithetical to the wartime spirit. For some selfishness during the war became the epitome of sin. Canon A. Linwood Wright, Vicar of St Mark's, Leicester, wrote for example, 'We must root out all selfishness, for it is destructive of community life. The power to achieve victory does not lie primarily in money, men or machinery but in the enthusiasm and will to accept total responsibility with total sacrifice—to give and not to count the cost.'[1] Likening those who are selfish, wasteful, and irresponsible to the drugged 'lotus-eaters' of Tennyson's poem, Linwood Wright wrote of his pride in the great 'efforts of Britain and of the sacrifices of our young men. We can all, however, rise to even finer heights. But we can't do this until the lotus-eaters are converted or cast out from among us.'[2]

This passage importantly links the willingness to make sacrifices and put community needs ahead of personal ones with Britishness. Wright's published sermon suggests something else that is important to note. Britain contained within it 'lotus-eaters' who needed to be converted or cast out.

Crucially, national identity is constituted not only with regard to external enemies, but also to enemies within—to the 'lotus-eaters' inside of Britain to use Canon Wright's words. It is characteristic of nation-defining projects that they elide difference and mask divisions to create a common, overarching identity for the subjects of a nation state.[3] Yet, as Mary Poovey has suggested, 'the process by which

---

[1] A. Linwood Wright, 'Away With these Lotus-Eaters!' *Leicester Evening Mail*, 30 Sept. 1941, 3.

[2] Ibid.

[3] As Renata Salecl has put it, psychologically the nation is 'the fantasy structure through which society perceives itself as a homogeneous entity' ('The Fantasy Structure of Nationalist Discourse', *Praxis International*, 13 (Oct. 1993), 217). Or, as Katherine Verdery has written, the nation is an ideological construct; it does 'ideological work' ('Whither "Nation" and "Nationalism"?', *Daedalus*, 122 (Summer 1993), 39).

individuals or groups embrace the "nation" as the most meaningful context for self-definition necessarily involves temporarily marginalizing other rubrics that could also provide a sense of identity'.[4] If these identities cannot be submerged into the national community, they are excluded, and become a potent contrast against which the nation defines itself. Thus, the solidarity that supposedly binds the national community has been depicted in numerous societies by nationalist rhetoric and policy that celebrate versions of race, class, and ethnic homogeneity and promulgate norms of sexual purity and particular ideals of gender difference. As Jean Bethke Elshtain has commented, 'Historically war has crystallized and unified a nation's sense of self for, in and through war, diverse peoples have entered into relationships by pitting themselves *against* one another and, in so doing, distinguishing themselves for what they are by distancing themselves from what they are not.'[5] Wartime is an especially prime historical moment not only for demarcating the national self from that of the enemy, but also for identifying and excluding those who do not exemplify particular national virtues. It would not be surprising then, that moral discourses proliferate at such moments.

Scholars have traditionally thought about moral discourses in two ways: as statements of the sacred rules that dictate behaviour and as the evaluative and normative categories that organize perception and action.[6] In a fruitful shift of emphasis, philosopher Richard Rorty suggests that morality is 'the voice of ourselves as members of a community, speakers of a common language'.[7] This shift of emphasis focuses attention on the connections between morality and collective identities. Morality, Rorty proposes, is a matter of 'we-intentions', and the core meaning of 'immoral action' is 'the sort of thing *we* don't do . . . If done by one of us, or if done repeatedly by one of us, that person ceases to be one of us'.[8] This way of thinking about morality suggests that there is likely to be an outpouring of moral discourse in periods when the issue of community identity has become especially significant, times when questions about the nature and extent of community or national solidarity become highly charged, and when the bases of unity are feared to be fragmented.[9] Moral discourse becomes especially intensified, I am

---

[4] Mary Poovey, 'Curing the "Social Body" in 1832: James Phillips Kay and the Irish in Manchester', *Gender & History*, 5 (Summer 1993), 196.

[5] Jean Bethke Elshtain, *Women and War* (Chicago: University of Chicago Press, 1995), 256.

[6] See e.g. Arthur Stinchcombe, 'The Deep Structure of Moral Categories', in Jeffrey C. Alexander (ed.), *Durkheimian Sociology: Cultural Studies* (Cambridge and New York: Cambridge University Press, 1988), 68–9.

[7] Richard Rorty, *Contingency, Irony, and Solidarity* (Cambridge and New York: Cambridge University Press, 1989), 59.

[8] Ibid.

[9] In her study of the politics of censorship, Nicola Beisel suggests something similar when she argues that the 'cultural power' of moral appeals stems in part from how they 'construct group and individual identities'. See Beisel, 'Morals versus Art: Censorship, the Politics of Interpretation, and the Victorian Nude', *American Sociological Review*, 58 (Apr. 1993), 148.

suggesting, when perceptions of difference and the diversity within nations or communities become problematic; when national identity becomes a crucially powerful mode of identification. As I suggested in Chapter 1, this happens in wartime.

During a war, public attention is focused on questions such as who 'we' are and what it is that 'we' stand for. War, especially total war, transforms the everyday in unparalleled ways, as women and men face various new and untested opportunities with unforeseen consequences. Thus war's liberating potential threatens the very unity that the nation is imagined to represent. Under such conditions it should not be surprising that internal enemies might be identified and singled out as 'anti-citizens' or as 'unBritish'. While a variety of 'others' were distinguished from the moral participants of the wartime national community at some point during the period (for example, conscientious objectors come to mind), accusations of selfishness particularly swirled around two figures who are the focus of this chapter.

The first and longer section concerning the 'lotus-eaters' in the nation of self-sacrificing citizens centres on girls and young women who associated with GIs. They were portrayed as self-absorbed pleasure-seekers. The second section deals with the depiction of Jews in public discourse as both rapacious and as persistently putting their own self-interest above those of society.

Sex and Citizenship

As war became increasingly imminent in 1939, the National Council of Women and representatives of various moral welfare and social purity organizations began to express their concern about young girls hanging around military encampments. During World War I, as Philippa Levine has detailed, their predecessors had advocated hiring women to control the women and girls who were seen consorting with soldiers.[10] Led by the National Council of Women, these groups took as a special mission the promotion of women's unique capacities for police work, and they continued to advocate the hiring of women police in the inter-war period. Then too there was some concern about the sexual immorality of young women.[11] With the onset of World War II, they stepped up their campaign, lobbying the Home Office to pressure local constabularies to hire policewomen who would deal with the

[10] Philippa Levine, ' "Walking the Streets in a Way No Decent Woman Should": Women Police in World War I', *Journal of Modern History*, 66 (Mar. 1994), 34–78. Also see Lucy Bland, 'In the Name of Protection: The Policing of Women in the First World War', in Julia Brophy and Carol Smart (eds.), *Women-in-Law: Explorations in Law, Family and Sexuality* (London: Routledge, 1985); and Angela Woollacott, ' "Khaki Fever" and Its Control: Gender, Class, Age and Sexual Morality on the British Homefront in the First World War', *Journal of Contemporary History*, 29 (Apr. 1994), 325–47.

[11] See Marek Kohn, *Dope Girls: The Birth of the British Drug Underground* (London: Lawrence and Wishart, 1992).

women and girls whose behaviour they deemed questionable.[12] While the Home Office made funds available for the purpose of adding women as auxiliary police personnel, it exerted no pressure on the constabularies. Local women's groups, such as the Women's Citizens Association of Preston, campaigned to persuade their chief constables and the Watch Committee to hire women police.[13] But at least in Preston and possibly in other communities as well, they were not successful until or after the autumn of 1942.

Beginning in late 1942, a greater and more diverse public commented on and denounced the romantic escapades of women and girls, intensifying both official and unofficial scrutiny of their behaviour. Participants included not only social purity and moral welfare workers and the National Council of Women, but private citizens, social workers and probation officers, clergymen, a variety of national and local government officials, the military, and the press. Newspapers in geographically dispersed rural and urban districts increased widespread anxiety by printing lurid headlines, feature articles, a proliferation of letters to the editor, and editorials that dissected the causes and consequences of teenage girls 'running wild' or going out 'for a good time'.[14] Routine reports often went into excruciating detail describing their 'indiscretions', fuelling the panic by exciting both outrage and prurient attention.[15]

The public commentary about the behaviour of women and girls was clearly stimulated by the growing presence of American GIs in British towns and cities.[16] The Americans began arriving in the late winter of 1942 and the numbers of Americans on British soil began to grow rapidly during that year and early in 1943.[17]

---

[12] Church of England Moral Welfare Council, *Quarterly Leaflet*, 5 (Feb. 1940), 3. In Feb. 1939, the National Council of Women sent a deputation to the Home Office to ask that they enlist women as special police constables, a request that was refused. Memo to Mrs E. Wood, 25 Sept. 1942, Box 3, National Council of Women Papers, Police Federation, Surbiton, England.

[13] Women Police Sectional Committee Minutes, Dec. 1941, National Council of Women Papers, Miscellaneous Documents, Police Federation, Surbiton.

[14] See e.g. *Daily Herald*, 23 Mar. 1943, 5; *Chard and Ilminster News*, 13 Feb. 1943, 4; *Bath and Wiltshire Chronicle and Herald*, 1 July 1943, 8; *Leicester Evening Mail*, 16 Jan. 1943, 3; *Liverpool Daily Post*, 2 July 1943, 4.

[15] The work of Judith Walkowitz demonstrates the role of the media in fashioning audiences for sexual scandal and discourses of sexual danger, *City of Dreadful Delight: Narratives of Sexual Danger in Late-Victorian London* (Chicago: University of Chicago Press, 1992). On the role of contemporary media in focusing public attention on issues of sexual morality, see Simon Watney, *Policing Desire: Pornography, AIDS, and the Media*, 2nd edn. (Minneapolis: University of Minnesota Press, 1989).

[16] This happened, as well, in the autumn of 1918 with the arrival of American troops in London. See Susan R. Grayzel, *Women's Identities at War: Gender, Motherhood, and Politics and Britain and France during the First World War* (Chapel Hill and London: University of North Carolina Press, 1999), 136–40.

[17] For works devoted to the American presence in Britain during World War II, see David Reynolds, *Rich Relations: The American Occupation of Britain, 1942–1945* (New York: Random House, 1995); Juliet Gardiner, *'Over Here': The GIs in Wartime Britain* (London: Collins & Brown, 1992); Graham Smith, *When Jim Crow Met John Bull: Black American Soldiers in World War II Britain* (New York: St Martin's Press, 1988). For a more extensive discussion of the issues produced by the interaction of American men

By D-Day there were around a million American soldiers in Britain. American soldiers were most often the ones who appeared in reports as the objects of desire of these young women, and it was their presence that triggered the widespread perception that a wave of 'moral laxity' was engulfing the country. The Americans, however, did not cause a dramatic change in young women's sexual behaviours to the extent that the public uproar suggested. What had changed was that they, rather than local British men and boys, became the objects of women's desires. The arrival of these foreign troops made visible what might have occurred with much less comment had there not been a war.[18] The fact that they were not British, and that they often represented themselves as coming to Britain's rescue, undoubtedly threatened national pride and potentially the morale of British soldiers fighting overseas. Additionally, the presence of the Americans added the issue of race to apprehensions that wartime conditions were causing women and girls to lose their self-control and were putting the moral fabric of the nation in jeopardy.

While I will deal specifically with the issue of race in Chapter 6, here I focus attention on public responses to the girls and young women seen in the company of African-American soldiers. It was the policy of the US government that 10 per cent of the soldiers sent to the United Kingdom were to be African-American. The fact that the US army was segregated and African-American soldiers were in all-black battalions (with the usual exception that their officers were white) made African-American troops a visible presence in Britain, especially as most troops were stationed in rural areas of the country. Popular and official reactions to British women's associations with American soldiers clearly were transformed by race. The racial inflection of the construction of the problem is illustrated by an extensive article detailing the behaviour of women and black men in the *Huddersfield Daily*

---

and British women than presented here, see Sonya O. Rose, 'Girls and GIs: Race, Sex, and Diplomacy in Second World War Britain', *International History Review*, 19 (Feb. 1997), 146–60. For the presence of GIs in wartime Australia, see Marilyn Lake, 'The Desire for a Yank: Sexual Relations between Australian Women and American Servicemen during World War II', *Journal of the History of Sexuality*, 2 (Nov. 1992), 621–33; John Hammond Moore, *Over-Sexed, Over-Paid and Over Here: Americans in Australia, 1941–1945* (St Lucia: University of Queensland Press, 1981); Michael Sturma, 'Public Health and Sexual Morality: Venereal Disease in World War II Australia', *Signs*, 13 (1988), 725–40. For research specifically on African-American soldiers in Australia, see Kay Saunders, 'In a Cloud of Lust: Black GIs and Sex in World War II,' in Joy Damousi and Marilyn Lake (eds.), *Gender and War: Australians at War in the Twentieth Century* (Cambridge: Cambridge University Press, 1995), 178–90.

[18] See e.g. the description by Stephen Humphries of 'larking about between the sexes' by adolescents in the years prior to the war. *Hooligans or Rebels?* (Oxford: Basil Blackwell, 1981), 135–40. For a description of the interaction of inter-war Preston youth, see Derek Thompson, 'Courtship and Marriage between the Wars', *Oral History*, 3/2 (1975), 42–3. David Reynolds also suggests that wartime behaviour was not radically different (*Rich Relations*, 276). For a discussion of the significance of the 'visibility' of behaviour deemed immoral for the transformation of a moral problem from being a matter of individual sin or indiscretion to being a public problem, see Constance Nathanson, *Dangerous Passage: The Social Control of Sexuality in Women's Adolescence* (Philadephia: Temple University Press, 1991), chap. 1.

Examiner in the summer of 1943.[19] The report, which initiated an extensive series of letters to the editor, contained considerable details of the writer's investigative reporting, and included depictions with clear erotic overtones.[20]

> Two of the officers suddenly flashed their torches into the road. There stood a negro and a girl with their arms round each other. Titters and subdued American voices came from the other side of the road where the lorries were drawn up. Girls were inside one of the lorries with the men. As the engine was being started the girls got out. The lorry moved slowly away and in the darkness of the night a female voice cried out, 'Goodnight, my darkie boy. I'll see you at eight tomorrow night.' The girl and one of her friends then walked a few yards and joined men who were going by another lorry. Men's and women's voices came from neighbouring doorways. Once when an officer flashed his lamp I saw two negroes and two girls in fond embraces.[21]

The problem of British women and girls engaging in immoral behaviour with Americans was redefined here as a problem of interracial sex.

While white American soldiers ('Americans') were represented as a 'presence' tempting young girls along the 'road to ruin', which the white British women were supposed to resist, the positioning of black soldiers ('coloured Americans') in public discussions was somewhat different. The Huddersfield reporter made it clear that the race of the soldiers was absolutely critical to the problem of young women's sexual morality, and that restricting the access that black men had to white British women might well be necessary. She wrote, 'some people who wish a certain course to be adopted . . . are perhaps attaching blame to those who, if not altogether blameless, are victims of circumstances which might even be too much for some white men similarly situated.'[22] The statement hinting that black men were less capable of self-control than white men drew upon long-standing ideas that unbridled sexuality and lack of self-control were racial traits that made non-whites both morally inferior and more childlike than whites—ideas that legitimated the subordination of black men to white control.[23]

Racial ideology led not only to differing symbolic representations of the issue; it also produced and was reflected in the deployment by British officials of various techniques of surveillance and control to cope with the problem of white British

---

[19] *Huddersfield Daily Examiner*, 10 July 1943, 3.

[20] The correspondence lasted two weeks and ended with a notice to correspondents that, although the newspaper had received a number of further letters about 'Girls who Prey on Negroes', the editor decided that the question had been 'sufficiently ventilated, and the correspondence must be regarded as closed' (*Huddersfield Daily Examiner*, 4 Oct. 1943, 3). This series of letters has been reprinted, in part, and discussed by Elbert L. Harris, 'Social Activities of the Negro Soldier in England', *Negro History Bulletin*, 11/7 (Apr. 1948), 152–6.

[21] Ibid.   [22] Ibid.

[23] These racialized depictions of unbridled sexuality had been applied earlier to the Irish and also to the British poor. See Poovey, 'Curing the "Social Body" in 1832'.

4. *Picture Post* photograph,
'Inside London's Coloured Clubs', 17 July 1944.
Hulton Archive

women fraternizing with black American men.[24] These efforts to manage and control the situation were aimed primarily at the girls and young women, not at the African-American soldiers. While the presence of black soldiers was constructed as a generic problem, racial identification in news reports often was used to suggest that the young girls who associated with 'coloured Americans' were especially immoral or degraded. In other words, the race of the men with whom young white British women and girls were consorting affected the *extent* to which the behaviour of these young women and girls was seen to be immoral. Interracial sex, was understood as a kind of sexual perversion; a construction that described the patrons of a club in Soho as consisting of 'women in male attire, effeminate men and coloured men accompanied by white women'.[25] The reports of interracial sex in World War II, then, may be understood to have further magnified the apprehension about women's sexual morality that had been provoked by the presence of large numbers of foreign troops on British soil. Young white British women and girls were not only having illicit sex, but many were having it with black men.

By examining the language used to articulate the nature of the problem posed by the behaviour of women and girls, we can better understand why their morals became an intense focus of public discussion during the war. It exposes the larger cultural context that both contributed to and was informed by discussions about them.

I have suggested that numerous portraits of the British at war portrayed the nation as a unified community of ordinary people unstintingly contributing to the war effort. How do images of sexually active, pleasure-seeking young women and girls fit with a nation being characterized as unified around self-sacrifice?

Numerous scholars have suggested that sexual morality has been crucial to delineating the boundaries of the nation. In his provocative work on nationalism and sexuality, George Mosse argued that the control of sexual desire, deeply constitutive of bourgeois notions of respectability, was integral to developing nationalisms.[26] And recently Ann Stoler has written:

Discourses of sexuality do more than define the distinctions of the bourgeois self; in identifying marginal members of the body politic, they have mapped the moral parameters of European nations. These deeply sedimented discourses on sexual morality could redraw the

---

[24] For discussions of official responses to the problem of black Americans consorting with white British women, see Smith, *When Jim Crow Met John Bull*, 177–8, 192–6; Reynolds, *Rich Relations*, 224–30; Rose, 'Girls and GIs', 148–60. See also Mica Nava's analysis of the involvement of young British women and African-American soldiers in, Mica Nava, 'Wider Horizons and Modern Desire: The Contradictions of America and Racial Difference in London, 1935–45', *New Formations*, 37 (1996), 71–91.

[25] Howard M. Tyrer, 'My Fight Against Vice', *Sunday Pictorial*, 28 Apr. 1940, 21.

[26] George L. Mosse, *Nationalism and Sexuality: Middle-Class Morality and Sexual Norms in Modern Europe* (Madison: University of Wisconsin Press, 1985).

'interior frontiers' of national communities, frontiers that were secured through—and sometimes in collision with—the boundaries of race.[27]

This literature suggests, then, that sexual propriety and control often have been central to nation-building. And so it was in Britain during World War II.

Two major themes characterized the nation during the war and were implicit in the passages by Priestley and Orwell quoted in Chapter 1.[28] The first was the nation as a brave and quietly (rather than bombastically) heroic people. This portrait distinguished the British from the Nazi enemy who were characterized as vauntingly militaristic. The second was a nation of quintessentially reasonable citizens who willingly and with good humour sacrificed their private and personal interests and desires for the collective good. As I will argue in Chapter 4, these themes combining heroism and good-humoured reasonableness were those that especially were attached to the ideal of the manly wartime citizen and figured the nation, in contrast to Germany, as both masculine and temperate. J. B. Priestley articulated the nation as both temperate and heroic in his depiction of how the little pleasure steamers put aside their frivolous ways in the service of the nation.

They were usually paddle steamers, making a great deal more fuss with all their churning than they made speed; and they weren't proud, for they let you see their works going round. They liked to call themselves 'Queens' and 'Belles' . . . But they were called out of that world . . . Yes, these 'Brighton Belles' and 'Brighton Queens' left that innocent foolish world of theirs—to sail into the inferno, to defy bombs, shells, magnetic mines, torpedoes, machine-gun fire—to rescue our soldiers.[29]

This was a nation that could not incorporate within it pleasure-seeking, fun-loving, and sexually expressive women and girls. The women and girls who could not or would not put aside their 'foolish world' to rescue the nation were being constructed as anti-citizens—in contrast to those who were self-sacrificing and would put themselves in harm's way.

The term 'moral laxity' was repeated over and over again in letters, editorials, and official documents. As the Bishop of Norwich put it in his proclamation on 'Moral Laxity', 'nothing is more alarming than the decay of personal standards of sexual morality . . . nothing threatens more the future of our race. When men and women

[27] Ann Laura Stoler, *Race and the Education of Desire: Foucault's History of Sexuality and the Colonial Order of Things* (Durham, NC and London: Duke University Press, 1995), 7.

[28] There were other themes that constituted the imagined community. For example, Simon Featherstone has pointed to the significance of rural life, in wartime literature. (Featherstone, 'The Nation as Pastoral in British Literature of the Second World War', 155–68). And Geoffrey Field has pointed to the social patriotism, the 'new "structure of feeling" ' that 'emerged, one that fused bitter memories of the interwar past, hostility to the traditional class structure, and expectations of social change. The new vocabulary was both unifying and levelling.' See his 'Social Patriotism and the British Working Class: Appearance and Disappearance of a Tradition', *International Labor and Working-Class History*, 42 (Fall 1992), 20–39.

[29] J. B. Priestley, Broadcast from 5 June 1940, in Priestley, *Postscripts* (London, 1940), 3.

grow loose in personal morality they endanger their own eternal salvation and they endanger too the England of to-morrow [*sic*].'[30]

The Bishop chastised the 'women and especially young girls in town and village alike' for their 'casual acquaintances' with soldiers, warning, 'We are in danger of our national character rotting at the root.'[31] 'Moral laxity' was a phrase that connoted weakness and a lack of will, and the prelate figured it as a threat to Britishness. His use of the trope 'rotting at the root' to describe the threat that young women's sexual encounters posed to the nation deployed a gardening expression that contrasted an Edenic, pastoral England with one threatened by young girls who willingly succumbed to their sexual desires.

The women and young girls who were perceived to be straying from convention and who were overtly seeking entertainment and pleasure were given the ironic label of 'good-time girls' or 'good timers'. The term 'good-time girl' was omnipresent in the language of moral alarm and was used to describe women who were irresponsible—who failed to consider their commitments to others.[32]

'Good-time girls' often were associated with venereal disease in official documents as well as in public discussion. Blame for venereal disease often was placed on the so-called 'amateur prostitute' as it was in World War I.[33] At a meeting of the Joint Committee on Venereal Disease, at which representatives of both the Canadian and US military were represented along with delegates from the War Office, the Ministry of Health, the Home Office, and the Metropolitan Police, the representative of the Metropolitan Police argued that the greatest source of infection 'was to be found among young, irresponsible "good-time" girls and young women', rather than among the regular 'professional type'.[34] At another meeting the committee expressed the shared belief that the most dangerous sources of infection were 'good-time girls' who were 'in search of excitement' and young persons 'who have no moral background and who are out of control'.[35] While the debates and discussions about venereal disease were focused on disease control, and anxiety about the spread of VD was heightened to a large extent because of the potential impact it had on Britain's relations with allied forces, the problem was understood in moral terms

---

[30] *Norfolk News and Weekly Press*, 9 Oct. 1943, 4. The Reverand A. Lynch, Rector of Desford, similarly asked, 'what kind of a Britain can be made out of this debauchery?' (*Leicester Evening Mail*, 1 Feb. 1944, 5).

[31] Ibid.

[32] On the links between a medical discourse of responsibility, national health, and the behaviour of women, see Lucy Bland and Frank Mort, 'Look Out for the "Good Time" Girl: Dangerous Sexualities as a Threat to National Health', in Bill Schwarz (ed.), *Formations of Nation and People* (London and Boston: Routledge and Kegan Paul, 1984), 131–51.

[33] Woollacott, 'Khaki Fever'; Bland, 'In the Name of Protection'; Frank Mort, *Dangerous Sexualities: Medico-Moral Politics in England since 1830* (London and New York: Routledge and Kegan Paul, 1987).

[34] Minutes of the Joint Committee on Venereal Disease, 2nd meeting, 10 July 1943. MH 55/2325, at the PRO, Kew.

[35] Minutes of the Joint Committee on Venereal Disease, 3rd meeting, 1 Oct. 1943. MH 55/2325, at the PRO, Kew.

to be caused by 'good-time' girls who were described as 'out of control' and 'irresponsible'. Fears about the rising rates of venereal disease contributed to the larger discourse about the 'moral laxity' of women and girls rather than producing it, while the language of moral outrage concerning the behaviour of women and girls shaped official as well as popular discussion about the medical problem.[36]

In addition to being an epithet to describe the behaviour of girls and young unmarried women and its connections to apprehensions about VD, the term 'good-time girl' also was used to describe irresponsible married women and mothers. Government officials and social welfare agencies were as concerned about the behaviour of married women as they were with the activities of single women and young girls. They were apprehensive about the problems of morale that would occur if women pursued extramarital relationships.[37] Additionally, social service agencies increasingly had to deal with cases of married women bearing children fathered by men other than their husbands.[38]

Open public discussion in newspapers about married women and mothers, however, rarely if ever dealt directly with these issues. Rather, disapprobation of adult women was framed in the language of irresponsible, pleasure-seeking behaviour and child neglect. For example, the *Leicester Evening Mail* featured a report in the summer of 1943 with the headline, 'City Woman Out for "Good Time", Neglects Child'.[39] The article concerned a young mother whose husband was away in the service who was sent to prison for three months for neglecting her 2-year-old. A probation officer said that 'the woman's one desire seemed to be to have a good time', and the report went on to state that the court had learned from neighbours that men visited her at various times of the night. The police inspector who made the arrest described observing a soldier entering the house around midnight, and later hearing 'voices and the distinct drawl of an American'.[40]

Geoffrey Field has persuasively argued that such disapprobation about motherhood and apprehension about family life was directed specifically at the working class.[41] The rhetoric about 'good-time girls' drew upon a long-standing implicit

---

[36] It was, in Frank Mort's terms, a medico-moral discourse. See Mort, *Dangerous Sexualities*. US representatives, in contrast to British commentators on the question of venereal disease, blamed British prostitutes for the spread of venereal disease and wanted the British Government to enact laws or change police procedures so that prostitutes would be swept off the streets—something the British Government refused to do. See Reynolds, *Rich Relations*, chap. 13.

[37] 'Morale Report', Feb.–May 1942; 'Draft Morale Report', May–July 1942; 'Morale Report', Aug.–Oct. 1942; 'Morale Reports', Aug.–Oct. 1943; 'Morale Report', Nov. 1943–Jan. 1944. All in War Office files, WO 32 15772 at the PRO, Kew.

[38] Lettice Fisher, *Twenty-one Years and After, 1918–1946* (London: Council for the Unmarried Woman and Her Child, 1946), 19. The National Council for the Unmarried Woman and Her Child, *23rd Report*, July 1941–Sept. 1942, 15–16; *24th Report*, Oct. 1942–1943, 8; *26th Report*, Oct. 1944–Apr. 1946, 15.

[39] *Leicester Evening Mail*, 7 July 1943, 5.   [40] Ibid.

[41] Geoffrey Field, 'Perspectives on the Working-Class Family in Wartime Britain, 1939–1945', *International Labor and Working-Class History*, 38 (Fall 1990), 3–28.

association between working-class women and promiscuity and prostitution. During the inter-war period, with changing understandings of female sexuality and a growing emphasis on sex as an expression of marital love, the term 'gold-digger' came into common parlance referring to women who accepted gifts for sex or who married out of their class for the sake of money. As Judy Giles has suggested, the term 'gold-digger' had both gender and class connotations.[42] The growth of consumerism and the attraction of adolescents and single working-class women to cosmetics, fashion, department stores, and the cinema in the 1930s led to public denigration and suspicion, and often to contempt, as historian Sally Alexander has suggested.[43] Thus, anxieties about irresponsible women drew upon and were, at least in part, framed within the context of a newly recharged apprehensiveness about working-class family life on the part of bourgeois and elite moralizers that had a long history. Clearly, police surveillance and action as well as programmes and policy considerations by social welfare organizations targeted working-class women and girls.

Letter-writer L. Boyd, who participated in the letters-to-the-editor exchange in Leicester about the behaviour of young women, however, altered the class meanings of the language of moral outrage to make a statement about class privilege. She wrote, 'many in the middle class are doing little . . . We all know the type—those who sit back and watch others work, playing bridge to excess and having as comfortable a time as possible. These good-timers should be rooted out and sent to dirty their dainty fingers in war factories.'[44] As this letter suggests, the gendered language of irresponsible pleasure-seeking and selfishness lent itself to a number of possible interpretations. While it often resonated with a discredited working-class morality, it also could be used by working-class women to critique privileged women for not contributing to the war effort. Thus, while the objects of moral purity rhetoric might well have been working-class girls and women, it was framed in a universal language that could take on different class inflections. Moral purity rhetoric, then, echoed the construction of the national 'we' as a society in which class was less important than virtuous behaviour in defining the members of the national community.

One strand of the construction of 'good-time girls' harkened back to the late 1920s 'flapper' panic that coincided with anxiety about the possibility of extending the suffrage to young women and arose in the aftermath of World War I.[45] The 1920s

[42] Judy Giles, ' "Playing Hard to Get": Working-Class Women, Sexuality and Respectability in Britain, 1918–40', *Women's History Review*, 1/2 (1992), 247.

[43] Sally Alexander, 'Becoming a Woman in London in the 1920s and 1930s', in her *Becoming a Woman and Other Essays in 19ᵗʰ and 20ᵗʰ Century Feminist History* (New York: New York University Press, 1995), 204–7, 219–24.

[44] *Leicester Evening Mail*, 8 July 1943, 3.

[45] Billie Melman, *Women and the Popular Imagination in the Twenties: Flappers and Nymphs* (London: MacMillan Press, 1988).

witnessed an unprecedented explosion of writings about 'the contemporary young female', writings that blurred rather than emphasized class distinction, especially in a shared 'motif of the young female as androgyne'.[46] Furthermore, the persistent discussion about population decline both during the inter-war period and throughout the war, which especially fixed on middle-class and elite family size, often decried the selfishness of such bourgeois women and married couples who put their own material desires and selfish pleasures above their responsibilities for reproducing the next generation of fit Britons.[47] The wartime discussion about young women's morality, therefore, fashioned a class-neutral, normative female moral subject who would exhibit both sexual restraint and social responsibility. This was a female subject whose behaviour would reinforce rather than disturb the myth of a heroic Britain emerging victoriously from the throes of war due to the heroic efforts and sacrifices of the 'ordinary people'.

In the morality tales published in newspapers and in the depictions by social purity organizations, social workers, and clergy, women and girls wearing bright make-up, drinking in pubs, and on or in the arms of soldiers, were implicitly being contrasted with the images of self-restraint, moral fortitude, and cheerful altruism that were being touted as characterizing the British people in this time of adversity. This was made explicit in a War Office memo that expressed concern about the 'depressing effect on those British women who are working hard, sacrificing much and cheerfully embracing austerity, when they see so many young women allowed to evade their National Responsibilities, wasting money on drink, trafficking in clothing coupons, getting more than their share of smart clothes, encouraging the black market and escaping Income Tax'.[48] The Liverpool Youth Organizations Committee Annual Report for 1944[49] contrasted the heroism, endurance, and cheerfulness that the British displayed at Dunkirk and at Arnheim, during the Battle of Britain and in the blitzed cities with the 'lamentable outbreak of hooliganism, theft, sexual immorality and various forms of anti-social behavior that make social welfare workers wonder for a moment whether all their labours have not been in vain'.[50]

The persistent expressions of concern about sexual morality were peppered with key references to the importance of 'good citizenship'. For example, a Mrs Foster

[46] Ibid. 149.

[47] On pro-natalism, see Denise Riley, '"The Free Mothers": Pronatalism and Working Women in Industry at the End of the Last War in Britain', *History Workshop Journal*, 11 (1981), 59–118.

[48] This document concerned prostitution, but uses some of the same language, including the term, 'moral laxity' to describe how Americans must view Britain when they see prostitution flourishing in the country. See 'Accosting in City Streets', Memo written by Col. Rowe of the War Office and sent to the Foreign Office, dated 2 Feb. 1943. FO 371/34124 at the PRO, Kew.

[49] Liverpool Youth Organizations Committee Annual Report, in Liverpool Council of Social Services Annual Report for 1944, 10.

[50] *Leicester Evening Mail*, 'Loose Morals: Blame Men as Well as Girls', 10 July 1943, 4.

who spoke for the Association for Moral and Social Hygiene called on the govern-ment to 'make it known that all who engage in sexual promiscuity might not only be responsible for spreading V.D., but were lacking in good citizenship'.[51] The report on venereal diseases by the Medical Advisory Committee of Scotland maintained that 'to eradicate venereal diseases completely from civilized communities will require . . . a high standard of enlightened citizenship'.[52] Urging legal measures to deal with the problem of 'safeguarding young girls who cheerfully risk wrecking their lives', an editorial in the *Leicester Evening Mail* said that public conscience should be aroused, and more needed to be done by parents 'that will ensure their [young girls] attaining a standard of decent citizenship'.[53] The repeated references to 'citizenship' warrant attention. Why was there such an emphasis on the citizenship of young women and girls during the 1940s?

Citizenship as a subject of discourse was important during World War II for two reasons. In the first place truly universal suffrage was granted only eleven years prior to the start of the war when women under the age of 30 were granted the right to vote in national elections on the same basis as men. The 1918 Representation of the People Act had granted virtual universal manhood suffrage, but it restricted the women's vote by age. This restriction entrusted the vote to women likely to be mature wives and mothers, not to young and possibly frivolous single women. The 1928 Act, which gave the vote to women on the same basis as men was called 'the flapper vote', signifying that the flapper, symbol of the modern young woman, depicted as both androgynous and libidinous, could now vote.[54] Resistance to women's participation in politics persisted during the inter-war period. Women were slow to be adopted as candidates for the House of Commons. And they were excluded from the House of Lords until the late 1950s. In the debate over that issue, the Earl of Glasgow claimed that women 'are not . . . suited to politics . . . They are often moved by their hearts more than they are by their heads.'[55] Discussion in the 1930s and 1940s about education for citizenship, there-fore, responded in part to apprehension that those who were newly enfranchised could not be trusted with the political rights of citizenship without instruction and control.

A second reason that citizenship was an important discursive focus during the war concerned what it meant to be a 'good citizen' in a People's War. As I suggested in Chapter 1, one dimension of the discursive framework of citizenship is con-cerned with moral practice. It delimits how persons should conduct themselves as

---

[51] Medical Advisory Committee (Scotland), *Report on Venereal Diseases*, cmd. 6518 (Edinburgh: HMSO, 1944), 8.
[52] Ibid.   [53] *Leicester Evening Mail*, 27 Oct. 1943, 3.
[54] Melman, *Women and the Popular Imagination*, 149.
[55] As quoted in Brian Harrison, *Separate Spheres: The Opposition to Women's Suffrage in Britain* (London: Croom Helm, 1978), 235.

members of the national community. And this was how it was being used in the rhetoric about female sexuality during the war. 'Good citizenship' was the mid-twentieth-century version of the much older notion of 'civic virtue'. 'Virtue' signified the capacity of persons to participate in the polity because they were capable of self-discipline and could be trusted to put aside their private interests for the public good.

The idiom of citizenship in World War II discussions in Britain referred to the obligations that national subjects have to their communities and envisioned citizens as active contributors to a democratic society. The ideal of the citizen who actively expresses a 'public spirit' was being articulated in a variety of very different discursive arenas in the 1940s and was especially consonant with the image of the nation as a unified community whose members elevated the common good over their personal desires and interests.[56] The notion of 'public spiritedness' or what is now called 'active citizenship' could have various meanings including the voluntarist ideal that politicians of various stripes who have touted it as antithetical to the supposedly 'passive citizen' created by the welfare state—an ideal of citizenship resonating with liberal political thought.[57]

The ideal of citizenship that was emerging during the war, however, bore a decided family resemblance to notions of citizenship in the tradition of civic republicanism or civic humanism rather than of liberal individualism. Ideals of civic humanism made their way into British thought from the classical world of Greece and Rome and their development by Machiavelli to James Harrington and John

[56] For a discussion of the active citizen taken up by the British Left that emerged in response to war, see Miles Taylor, 'Patriotism, History and the Left in Twentieth-Century Britain', *Historical Journal*, 33 (Sept. 1990), 980–3. This view of citizenship, which certainly was populist and fit neatly with a collectivist spirit, was not limited only to the Left. For a general discussion of citizenship as it was understood in World War II, see David Morgan and Mary Evans, *The Battle for Britain: Citizenship and Ideology in the Second World War* (London and New York: Routledge, 1993). For a discussion of working-class patriotism that drew upon the heroism of the Blitz, see Field, 'Social Patriotism and the British Working Class', 20–39. For a discussion of the research organization, Political and Economic Planning (PEP) and its 'active democracy' group, formed to encourage the continuation of a participatory democracy after the war, see Abigail Beach, 'Forging a "Nation of Participants": Political and Economic Planning in Labour's Britain', in Richard Weight and Abigail Beach (eds.), *The Right to Belong: Citizenship and National Identity in Britain, 1930–1960* (London: I. B. Tauris, 1998), 89–115.

[57] For a discussion of late 20th-century Conservative ideas about 'active citizenship', see Michael Ignatieff, 'Citizenship and Moral Narcissism', in Geoff Andrews (ed.), *Citizenship* (London: Lawrence and Wishart, 1991), 26–36; Morgan and Evans, *The Battle for Britain*, chap. 7. On voluntarism during the period, see William Beveridge, *Voluntary Action: A Report on the Methods of Social Advance* (London: G. Allen & Unwin, 1948). For a discussion of voluntarism during the first half of the 20th century, see Geoffrey Finlayson, 'A Moving Frontier: Voluntarism and the State in British Social Welfare 1911–1949', *Twentieth Century British History*, 1/2 (1990), 183–206. Also see Jose Harris's discussion of British idealism, 'Political Thought and the Welfare State 1870–1940', *Past and Present*, 135 (1992), 116–41, and Andrew Vincent and Raymond Plant, *Philosophy, Politics and Citizenship: The Life and Thought of the British Idealists* (Oxford: Basil Blackwell, 1984).

Milton and other seventeenth-century radicals.[58] Some of these ideals were incorporated in British idealist thought of the late nineteenth and early twentieth century.[59] The New Liberalism of this same period had also incorporated and revitalized political symbols and issues that stressed the importance of citizenship, communal responsibility, and social welfare.[60]

In the past, civic republicanism had emphasized property as the basis for citizenship. Landed property was believed to enable individuals to exercise their political judgement independently. Independence and rational self-control thus were the keys to virtue. The virtue of civic-minded men who would sacrifice self for the general good was associated with both. Women were not. While this is not the place to chart the changing historical meanings of the concept of 'virtue', it is important to note that in the era of universal suffrage and in the hands of those on the Left who particularly promoted ideas about active citizenship and the common good, it assumed a more egalitarian and democratic cast. Nonetheless, 'good citizenship' and the older meanings of 'virtue' both were defined in opposition to 'passion'. Self-control would enable political persons to rule their passions, subordinating their private concerns and appetites to the public good.

Ideals of republicanism, expressed in contemporary language, worked particularly well in the late 1930s and 1940s as a way of articulating a vision of the nation and its patriotic citizenry that contrasted with Fascism. The tradition of civic republicanism emphasizes both the notion of a common good that is prior to or takes precedence over individual desires and interests *and* the idea that it is only by the active involvement of citizens in the affairs of the community that individual liberty can be preserved in the face of tyranny.

During the 1940s the principles of republican citizenship were not only being

---

[58] There is a huge literature on civic republicanism. For discussions of particular aspects of these ideas, see Quentin Skinner, 'On Justice, the Common Good and the Priority of Liberty', in Chantal Mouffe (ed.), *Dimensions of Radical Democracy* (London: Verso, 1992), 211–24; J. G. A. Pocock, *Machiavellian Moment: Florentine Political Thought and the Atlantic Republican Tradition* (Princeton: Princeton University Press, 1975); J. G. A. Pocock, 'Virtue and Commerce in the Eighteenth Century', *Journal of Interdisciplinary History*, 3 (1972), 119–34; Adrian Oldfield, *Citizenship and Community: Civic Republicanism and the Modern World* (London and New York: Routledge, 1990); Hanna Pitkin, *Fortune Is a Woman: Gender and Politics in the Thought of Nicolo Machiavelli* (Berkeley and Los Angeles: University of California Press, 1984).

[59] Vincent and Plant, *Philosophy, Politics and Citizenship*, esp. chap. 9.

[60] For discussions of the New Liberalism, see Michael Freedan, *The New Liberalism: An Ideology of Social Reform* (Oxford: Clarendon Press, 1978); Peter Weiler, *The New Liberalism: Liberal Social Theory in Great Britain 1889–1914* (New York and London: Garland Publishing, 1982); Stefan Collini, *Liberalism and Sociology: L. T. Hobhouse and Political Argument in England, 1880–1915* (Cambridge: Cambridge University Press, 1979). The lineage of many of the ideas espoused during the late 1930s and 1940s about social reform, the creation of ethical institutions, the importance of community and the common good undergirding the premises of the welfare state can be traced to the New Liberalism of L. T. Hobhouse and J. A. Hobson. Yet the rhetoric of citizenship and the nation during the war was framed by the classic republican notion that 'good citizenship' was embodied in the capacity of (rational) persons to put aside their individual interests for the public good.

constructed in relation to the wartime nation, but they were fostered and elaborated in the exploding public discussion about reconstruction that actively imagined the kind of society that could be built after the war. Architects, town and city planners, educational reformers, and advocates of expanding state social provision attempted to imagine how the country could be rebuilt and its institutions reformed to foster the continuation of that community spirit and sense of active citizenship so widely depicted as characterizing the British at war. While the rhetorics of planning and architecture, for example, were multi-vocal with varying degrees of emphasis on rationality, orderliness, particular aesthetic values, and differing social values, a major theme in these literatures was constructing *communities*—places of sociability that would maximize the spirit of citizenship.[61] Planner-architect C. B. Purdom, for example, articulated the values of civic republicanism in his discussion of what ought to be the right size for a city:

The mass-mind makes democracy impossible, for it disintegrates human personality . . . If civilization has any object it must be to prevent the existence of the mass-mind, which is its greatest danger. Human values are realized in personalities, who take responsibility and are capable of self-government. To develop personalities is the highest function of civic existence. Education, economic and political responsibility, co-operation in the conduct of affairs, and, above all, personal knowledge of other people through which criticism can be brought to bear upon social affairs, are the means through which personality is developed and citizenship raised to a high level.[62]

Purdom further suggested, 'A new architecture is needed for the cities of tomorrow, not that of the aggressive le Corbusier school, but an architecture that has a true community spirit.'[63] A. Trystan Edwards, advocating the plan proposed in the mid-1930s for building '100 New Towns', maintained that one kind of 'vulgarity in architecture' is when 'buildings show bad manners' by expressing 'unsociability'.[64] The eminent architect Ralph Tubbs, remarking on his sketch for a town centre, maintained that it should be the 'architectural interpretation of the fact that we are, each of us, in the words of John Donne, "involved in Mankinde" '.[65]

One of the most elaborate plans to maximize community spirit and to minimize an ethos of individualism and self-oriented behaviour was the Reilly Plan published

[61] Morgan and Evans suggest that in contrast to the pre-war years when the idea of planning had been resisted by advocates of laissez-faire, in the context of the political and social climate of World War II it reached its apotheosis (see *Battle for Britain*, 32). On planning during the war, see John Stevenson, 'Planners' Moon? The Second World War and the Planning Movement', in Harold L. Smith (ed.), *War and Social Change: British Society in the Second World War* (Manchester: Manchester University Press, 1986), 58–77.

[62] C. B. Purdom, *Britain's Cities Tomorrow: Notes for Everyman on a Great Theme* (London: King, Littlewood & King, 1942), 24.

[63] Ibid. 27–8.

[64] A. Trystan Edwards, *A Hundred New Towns?* (London: J. M. Dent & Sons, 1944), 26.

[65] Ralph Tubbs, *The Englishman Builds* (Harmondsworth: Penguin Books, 1945), 57.

in *Picture Post* in 1944. The plan was adopted by Labour who were attracted to it because of its emphasis on community at their 1944 party conference.[66] As Lawrence Wolfe, who promoted the plan in *Picture Post* put it, the scheme is 'community planning *not* suburb planning'. The Reilly Plan addressed the problem of designing a small community to stimulate a cooperative spirit amongst its residents that would nurture the wartime collective spirit in the post-war future. To do this Wolfe suggested it was necessary to 'create conditions under which the selfish impulses of our selfish fellow-men will quite naturally manifest themselves in a way that constitutes cooperation'.[67] Wolfe tied the issue of sexual morality to the nature of community provision and community spirit.[68] To cure the proclivities of young people from engaging in sexual immorality and juvenile delinquency, he argued, communities need to provide 'sufficient legitimate occupation for their hands as well as their minds'.[69] More generally, when the idiom of citizenship was deployed in discussions of sexual morality during the war it referred to the question of how to fashion responsible, self-disciplined, and self-denying subjects who would be capable of actively participating in a democratic society.

Young people especially (and particularly young women) were the objects of the exhortations expressed in the language of citizenship. The YWCA's newsletter, whose intended audience was teenage girls, carried a regularly appearing special section 'News for Citizens'. A surprising range of topics was considered by the editors as inspiring good citizenship. The column in December 1941 urged young women doing war work to 'Join Your Trade Union' proclaiming, 'We British have great democratic traditions of which we can justly be proud; for it was *our* country which was the pioneer in organising trade unions and co-operatives.' The remainder of the article was devoted to the importance of being a patriotic unionist, working for the future.[70]

Issues of 'News for Citizens' in 1943 informed readers about the content of the Government's White Paper on education and the importance of the Beveridge Report that set out plans for the creation of Britain's welfare state.[71] While these topics generally encouraged a political civic awareness in young people, the June 1943 'News for Citizens' column dealt with sex education. It encouraged readers to think of sex as 'the creative energy and, rightly directed, it exists for marriage:

---

[66] For a brief discussion of the Reilly Plan, and an analysis of Labour's policies on the built environment, see Nick Tiratsoo, ' "New Vistas": The Labour Party, Citizenship and the Built Environment in the 1940s,' in Richard Weight and Abigail Beach (eds.), *The Right to Belong: Citizenship and National Identity in Britain, 1930–1960* (London: I. B. Tauris, 1998), 136–56.

[67] Lawrence Wolfe, *The Reilly Plan—A New Way of Life* (London: Nicholson & Watson, 1945), 35–6. Rather than seeing 'the spirit of the Blitz' as inherent in 'British Character', he argued it was a product of 'external circumstances', 42.

[68] Ibid. 56–78.   [69] Ibid. 63.   [70] YWCA, *The Blue Triangle*, Dec. 1941.

[71] On the Beveridge Report, see *News for Citizens*, Mar. 1943; 'Education for Tomorrow', *News for Citizens*, Dec. 1943.

marriage exists for the family, the family for the Church and the Church for God'. The article then proceeded 'Any action or thought that may cheapen sex or use it lightly and carelessly may be described as the wrong attitude. It is only too easy to slip into this, especially in war-time.' It went on to ask rhetorically how this happens to respectable and well-meaning girls.

A pretty girl has a nice time dancing with someone she has just met. She becomes a little alarmed at his 'freshness.' Her conscience warns her that it is time to stop. However, the Devil is in on this too, and he whispers that, after all, she is not a kid and everyone else seems to like this sort of thing, anyway. So she gives in . . . and there may be several sad endings to the story . . . the real bitterness is in fact that 'having a good time,' as it is so wrongly called, affects the whole community.[72]

The YWCA treatise on sexuality made use of the wartime language of community spirit to associate sex and citizenship. It suggests the importance of self-control and self-discipline to the 'ethic of responsibility' that was key to the symbolic meaning of citizenship in wartime discourse.

Youth groups and organizations were seen as routes to educating young people for citizenship. Welfare workers, educators, and government officials campaigned actively to have teenagers participate in youth organizations and in the newly established Youth Service. The idea that organized leisure activities and clubs for youth instilled a sense of duty and commitment to self-discipline and responsible behaviour increasingly became an article of faith during the inter-war period.[73] During World War I, the Girl Guides was started, partly in response to the 'epidemic' of 'khaki fever' that was thought to be sweeping the country.[74] During World War II participation in youth groups was seen as a preventative and cure for 'moral laxity', as well as a vehicle for citizenship training. Youth workers referred to morally recalcitrant teenagers as 'unclubbable'.[75]

In December 1941 young people aged 16 and 17 were required to register with local education authorities. As the White Paper 'Youth Registration in 1942' declared, 'The purpose of the registration was to enable Local Education Authorities to make contact with all young people of the ages concerned and to encourage them to find the best way of fitting themselves to do their duty as citizens and of assisting the present national effort.'[76] The main purpose was to reach 'those who had left school and who were no longer under educational supervision and discipline'. The young

---

[72] YWCA, *The Blue Triangle*, June 1943.

[73] See e.g. 'The Purpose and Content of Youth Service' Report of Youth Advisory Council to Minister of Education in 1943 (London: HMSO, 1945), 10.

[74] Richard A. Voeltz, 'The Antidote to "Khaki Fever"? The Expansion of the British Girl Guides during the First World War', *Journal of Contemporary History*, 27 (1992), 627–38.

[75] 'Adolescence and Sex Problems', Report of Sheffield Probation Officer, 1945 in Reports of Principal Probation Officers. HO 45/20730 at the PRO, Kew.

[76] *Youth Registration in 1942*, cmd. 6446 (HMSO, May 1943), 2.

registrants were asked at the time of registration to list the clubs and organizations to which they belonged. If they were 'non-participating', they were 'invited to an interview' where they would be urged to join. The idea was to encourage young people to make good use of organized leisure activities rather than spending their time in unsupervised activities such as 'hanging about' and going to the cinema and dance halls.[77] The emphasis of youth organizations was teaching young people to use their leisure time properly and 'to make the right choices'.[78] In other words, the youth movement as it was called was created to fashion self-disciplined and responsible moral subjects.[79] The World War II obsession with the morality of girls and young women in Britain was thus articulated in terms that constructed moral subjects as responsible citizens. How are we to understand this particular articulation?

To answer this question, it is useful to consider again the tradition of civic republicanism that was echoed in wartime reimaginings of the nation and citizenship. This tradition, as I have suggested, emphasizes both the ideal of 'active citizenship' and the notion that a common good exists 'prior to and independent of individual desires and interests'.[80] As Chantal Mouffe has argued, such ideas are antithetical to pluralism (and to true democracy) when they emphasize a *particular* notion of the common good and shared moral values.[81] While in World War II, ideals of citizenship required what historian Raphael Samuel called 'a secular altruism', they also as he suggested 'stigmatized anyone who stepped out of line as "anti-social" '.[82]

If the nation was being imagined as a unified community of people capable of putting the national interest above their own needs and desires, then fun-loving, sexually expressive women and girls threatened that sense of unity that was imagined to be the essence of Britishness in wartime. This was a temperate but heroic nation, one exemplifying not only self-sacrifice but also 'impartial reason', that defined itself against the feminine.[83] The discourses of moral purity thus figured

[77] The primary objects of the White Paper discussion were the approximately 50 per cent of boys and the 65 to 75 per cent of girls who were 'unattached'.

[78] See 'The Purpose and Content of the Youth Service', Report of Youth Advisory Council to the Minister of Education in 1943 (HMSO, 1945), and 'The Youth Services after the War', Report of Youth Advisory Council to the Board of Education (HMSO, 1943).

[79] As Mariana Valverde has suggested, discourses of moral purity in general construct moral subjects. See Mariana Valverde, 'The Rhetoric of Reform: Tropes and the Moral Subject', *International Journal of the Sociology of Law*, 18 (1990), 61–73; Mariana Valverde, *'The Age of Light, Soap, and Water': Moral Reform in Turn of the Century English Canada* (Toronto: McClelland and Stewart, 1991).

[80] Chantal Mouffe, 'Feminism, Citizenship and Radical Democratic Politics', in Judith Butler and Joan W. Scott (eds.), *Feminists Theorize the Political* (New York and London: Routledge, 1992), 377.

[81] Ibid. 378. Also see her analysis comparing liberal citizenship and civic republican citizenship in 'Democratic Citizenship and the Political Community', in Chantal Mouffe (ed.), *Dimensions of Radical Democracy* (London: Verso, 1992), 225–39.

[82] Raphael Samuel, 'Introduction: Exciting to be English', in Raphael Samuel (ed.), *Patriotism: The Making and Unmaking of British National Identity*, i (London and New York: Routledge, 1989), xxi.

[83] For an analysis of the Revolutionary period in American history that suggests very similar processes, see Carroll Smith-Rosenberg, 'Beyond Roles, Beyond Spheres: Thinking about Gender in the Early Republic', *William and Mary Quarterly*, 3rd ser., 46 (1989), 565–81.

duty and sexuality, bravery and pleasure, and sacrifice and desire as oppositional human characteristics.

Although narratives about the moral laxity of 'good-time' girls and the various techniques of social control employed to police women's behaviour aimed both to construct moral citizens and to limit their associations with soldiers, ironically they also advertised the adventures and pleasures of wartime life. Moreover neither the rhetoric of moral purity nor the efforts to police young women's behaviour were uncontested. Occasional letters to the editors of newspapers ridiculed the moral purity advocates as being old-fashioned or simply old and having forgotten what it was like to be young. Others defended Britain's youth or simply rejected the outrage as overblown. Still others maintained that it was necessary for hard-working young people to have time for themselves and to have fun.

Many of the young women and girls continued to seek pleasure and adventure with soldiers throughout the war. Enmeshed in a popular culture that linked sex and love and valorized romance, they resisted a definition of citizenship that excluded carnal pleasure and passionate desire.[84] The following front page story appeared in the *Sunday Pictorial* at the end of August 1945: 'The scene was Bristol, most English of all English cities. The time was 2 A.M. yesterday. The actors were a mob of screaming girls aged between 17 and 25.' The cause of the 'hysteria' according to the report was that four companies of 'American Negro soldiers in the city were leaving for home.' 'The girls besieged the barracks where the soldiers were and began singing, "Don't Fence Me In." This was too much for the coloured men who began to break down the barbed wire. In a few minutes hundreds of girls and U.S. soldiers were kissing and embracing.'[85]

While the obsessive expressions of concern with the moral behaviour of women and girls continued throughout the war to construct moral subjects as responsible citizens who would refrain from such behaviour, many young women drew their moral lessons from other sources. The cautionary morality tales that were published in newspapers across the country suggest more about a fantasy of moral purity complexly linked to a utopian longing for a new Britain whose citizens would be responsible community participants than about the romantic fantasies and sexual desires of the young women who were their primary objects.

In constructing this national fantasy, the rhetorics of moral disapprobation depicted some women and girls as antithetical to the nation, especially those women whose amorous escapades were so perverse as to jeopardize the nation's presumed racial homogeneity. It simultaneously incorporated virtuous women

---

[84] For work on the articulation of female sexual desire in World War II Australia, see Lake, 'The Desire for a Yank', and Marilyn Lake, 'Female Desires: The Meaning of World War II', in Joy Damousi and Marilyn Lake (eds.), *Gender and War: Australians at War in the Twentieth Century* (Cambridge: Cambridge University Press, 1995), 60–80.

[85] *Sunday Pictorial*, 26 Aug. 1995, 1.

and all men as comrades in struggle. Although class differentiated which women were made the targets of overt policies of social control, public expressions of apprehension about women and girls who frolicked with soldiers emphasized the desirability of creating female moral citizens appropriate to fighting a 'People's War', and building a 'new Britain' when it was over. Sexually expressive women and girls were a danger to the virtuous nation. Such women displayed what might be termed 'libidinal femininity'. Libidinal women were an 'internal other' against which the nation was defining itself. The construction of pleasure-seeking women as villainous and contemptuous 'anti-citizens' was part and parcel of the process by which the nation was imagined as a 'deep horizontal comradeship' of virtuous citizens.

Wartime Anti-Semitism

Considering wartime anti-Semitic rhetoric and expressions of anxiety about young women as sexually desiring subjects in the same chapter, as part of a common theme, may at first glance seem odd. There is, however, an uncanny similarity in the way that the public discussions about such young women and Jews were framed. Both 'good-time girls' and Jews were depicted in terms that contrasted them with the 'ordinary' people of Britain who were self-sacrificing, community-oriented, and conscientious. Sexually adventuresome girls and Jews both were accused of engaging in activities that demonstrated that they were selfish.

Women and girls exhibiting libidinal femininity were castigated as 'failed citizens' who jeopardized the long-term future of the nation. Jews, however, were accused of engaging in selfish actions or were suspected of being avaricious because they were Jews whose very nature demonstrated them to be 'unEnglish' or 'unBritish'.

Just as anxieties about the sexual behaviour of young women and girls are a recurrent theme in British history, escalating at some times and dying down at others, so too anti-Semitism has been articulated and rearticulated throughout the history of early modern and modern Britain. Each time there is a new articulation, the terms of the discourse change as they become interwoven with and modified by new cultural themes and concerns.[86]

From a post-Holocaust perspective it might be difficult to comprehend how and why anti-Semitism should have been as prominent as it was in public culture during the years of World War II. In fact, as Harold Smith has suggested based on a British Institute of Public Opinion survey conducted in late February 1943, anti-

---

[86] For a more extended discussion of the continuities and transformations of cultural discourses, see Sonya O. Rose, 'Cultural Analysis and Moral Discourses: Episodes, Continuities, and Transformations', in Victoria E. Bonnell and Lynn Hunt (eds.), *Beyond the Cultural Turn* (Berkeley and Los Angeles: University of California Press, 1999), 217–38.

Semitism may well have increased in Britain during the war.[87] As Tony Kushner explains, anti-Semitism was 'not alien to the British experience, or simply unrespectable'.[88] It had been on the rise during the inter-war years and persisted into the 1940s generated not only by Fascist and pro-Fascist sympathizers, but as part of 'daily discourse, literature and the press', as Kushner has put it.[89] Pro-Fascist groups existed throughout the war, and virulent anti-Semitic publications continued to be printed.[90] While these groups and publications were important to the problem of anti-Semitism in British society, more relevant to this study is the portrayal of Jews in 'ordinary' public culture—in the press and in popular public opinion that was unlikely to have been directly under the influence of extreme right-wing groups.[91]

From the last decades of the nineteenth century through the inter-war period, Jews had faced various forms of social discrimination and were the brunt of jokes, of the music hall variety and of quips in more 'cultured' conversation.[92] Scholars have noted a rise in anti-Semitic sentiment especially during periods of immigration—late in the nineteenth and in the early years of the twentieth century, for example, when anti-alien and anti-Jewish attitudes merged and flourished.

A clear feature of modern British anti-Semitism is that Jews are perceived as a 'foreign group', as 'alien'. Anti-alien sentiment more generally persisted throughout the twentieth century, focusing at times on Jews, on the Chinese, and on blacks.[93] As Kushner suggests, while the characterization of Jews as aliens may have been aimed at recent immigrants in particular, even 'anglicized Jewry . . . could not escape the alien tag'.[94] Further, David Cesarani argues that anti-alien discourse may be understood as a 'fusion of all those elements of political, cultural and social thought where the Other is constructed as part of the process of self-definition', and thus he

---

[87] Harold L. Smith (ed.), *Britain in the Second World War: A Social History* (Manchester and New York: Manchester University Press, 1996), 59–60.

[88] Tony Kushner, *The Persistence of Prejudice, Antisemitism in British Society during the Second World War* (Manchester: Manchester University Press, 1989), 11.

[89] Ibid. 12. For a historical analysis that contests the extent of anti-Semitism in British history and its significance for the Jews of Britain, see W. D. Rubinstein, *A History of the Jews in the English-Speaking World: Great Britain* (London: MacMillan, 1996).

[90] Kushner, *Persistence*, 36.

[91] For studies of Fascist and anti-Semitic organizations and actors during the war, see Kushner, *Persistence*, 14–77; Richard Griffiths, *Patriotism Perverted: Captain Ramsay, the Right Club and British Anti-Semitism, 1939–40* (London: Constable, 1998).

[92] Griffiths, *Patriotism Perverted*, 12–13; Kushner, *Persistence*, 131–3.

[93] David Cesarani, 'An Alien Concept? The Continuity of Anti-Alienism in British Society before 1940', in David Cesarani and Tony Kushner (eds.), *The Internment of Aliens in Twentieth Century Britain* (London: Frank Cass, 1993), 25–52.

[94] Kushner, *Persistence*, 9. Kushner perceptively notes that the 'alien Jew stereotype . . . proved to be both persistent and malleable', 115.

maintains that it is at the heart of British political culture.[95] And so it was during World War II, even as the Nazis embarked on their campaign of extermination.

As Hitler's troops overran Western Europe, fears about 'fifth column' traitors led the Government to intern all Italian, German, and Austrian men during the perilous weeks of late spring and early summer of 1940. Those Germans and Austrians residing in the United Kingdom who had been classified as 'enemy aliens' had already been interned by the middle of May. Mass Observation noted the heightened anxiety sweeping the country and remarked:

The always latent antagonism to the alien and foreigner began to flare up. Nearly everyone, as previous research has shown, is latently somewhat antisemitic and somewhat anti-alien. But ordinarily it is not the done thing to express such sentiments publicly. The news from Holland made it the done thing all of a sudden . . . Sir John Anderson's new restrictions on aliens corresponded with this feeling and were therefore widely welcomed.[96]

As a consequence of the decision to intern non-enemy alien Germans and Austrians, some 30,000 people were rounded up and were detained in various parts of the country, most notably on the Isle of Man. The majority of those interned during that spring and summer were Jewish refugees.[97] Eventually, there was a public reaction against the internment and deportation policies, and the Government reversed its position. But the episode must certainly have reinforced the association of Jews as a distinct foreign element within a Britain portrayed in public culture as increasingly unified. Jews were represented as 'other' to the British. Their presumed negative character traits and the perception of them as inherently and intractably different made them less than wanted guests. As historian Colin Holmes has argued, the policy of internment itself stemmed from a long-standing hostility towards aliens, a hostility which was reinforced during the war.[98]

Historically long-lived stereotypes of Jews were fused with the wartime discourse that denigrated selfishness and the elevation of self-interest over the interests of the larger community. In the early days of the war, during the mass evacuations from the cities, for example, Mass Observation reports suggested that Jews were widely believed to be cowards whose first thought was to save themselves.[99] Such images persisted through the Blitz, as Jews were accused of crowding into shelters, getting into shelters early in the day to secure the best places and otherwise monopolizing shelter space.[100] Home Intelligence reported in early September 1940 that anti-

[95] Cesarani, 'An Alien Concept?', 27.

[96] As quoted in Bernard Wasserstein, *Britain and the Jews of Europe, 1939–1945*, 2nd edn. (London and New York: Leicester University Press, 1999), 81. Mass Observation, which began in 1937, recorded aspects of everyday life and public opinion about a variety of issues, and during the war years focused heavily on morale and attitudes related to morale.

[97] Ibid. 82–3.

[98] Colin Holmes, *John Bull's Island: Immigration and British Society, 1871–1971* (London: Macmillan, 1988), 191–2.

[99] See Kushner, *Persistence*, 65.   [100] Ibid. 54–5.

Semitism was growing in districts heavily populated by Jews who 'are said to show too great a keenness to save their own skins and too little consideration for other people', and simultaneously there were reports of persistent anti-Semitism in evacuation reception areas.[101] Suggesting that Jews were both cowardly and selfish, they were described as flocking to safe areas. Windsor, for example, was reported to be 'packed with Jews'; 'hundreds . . . arrived in Swindon'; and 'Llandudno has been referred to as "Jerusalem by the sea".'[102] As the demand for civilian labour grew, young Jewish women were accused of finding the means to avoid doing war work. Regarding the latter, Home Intelligence reported that in some areas there was a 'good deal of feeling that Jewish girls are finding some method of escaping war work, and caustic references are made to the "number of frail Jewish mothers who need to keep their daughters at home to look after them"'.[103]

Underscoring the centrality of self-sacrifice and of unselfishly working towards the common good as core wartime British values, the most prominent accusation against Jews concerned their alleged black market activities. The identification of Jews with illegal marketing practices reworked the Shylock image that paired Jews with the sin of usury, just as in World War I they were charged with war profiteering.[104] In the 1920s and 1930s there were numerous complaints from grocers' associations about cut-priced goods that targeted Jewish merchants and led to a movement for fair pricing.[105]

During the war, attacks against Jews for their presumed participation in the black market appeared in numerous newspapers with diverse political orientations and readerships including *Time and Tide*, the *Daily Mirror*, and the *Spectator*. The image of the Jewish black marketeer also was portrayed in radio plays, popular literature, comics, the House of Commons, and 'even in a "brainteaser", where contestants had to work out the prison sentences of Messrs Abrams, Brody and Cohen'.[106] As a Home Intelligence report suggested, in several regions of the country people were blaming Jews as both merchants and customers of the black market—customers who were willing to pay any price.[107] The public discussions concerning Jews making money out of wartime shortages drew upon and was articulated with a more general popular sentiment vilifying materialism and ostentatious display of wealth. General statements such as the following were commonplace during the war:

---

[101] Daily Report on Morale, Home Intelligence, 9 Sept. 1940. HO 199/436. Weekly Report by Home Intelligence, 7–21 Oct. 1940; 21–28 Oct. 1940; 4–11 Nov. 1940. INF 1/292 Part IA.

[102] Weekly Report by Home Intelligence, 21–28 Oct. 1940. INF 1/292 Part 1a.

[103] Home Intelligence Weekly Reports, 10–17 Nov. 1941. PRO/INF 1/292 Part 2.

[104] Kushner, *Persistence*, 119. For an alternative interpretation of the Shylock image, see Rubinstein, *A History of the Jews*, 40–1.

[105] Personal communication from Todd Endelman.

[106] See Kushner, *Persistence*, 120 and citations in note 47, p. 225.

[107] Home Intelligence Reports, 22–29 Sept. 1941. PRO/INF 1/292 2b.

It is not, of course, suggested that privilege has ceased to exist or that selfishness has disappeared . . . but, if it exists, explained and even apologized for; that ostentation is frowned upon, luxury dare not come out in the open, sacrifice is expected, danger is shared. At a time when all are exposed to the same peril there is no tolerance for those who would seek security at the expense of their neighbors.[108]

This was a class-inflected statement in the course of which the writer called for 'equality of opportunity for all and a tolerable life for the humblest citizen', arguing that it was essential to plan for a 'new Britain' to take shape after the war had ended. It is a restatement of wartime civic virtue that focuses both on shared responsibility and on restraint in the pursuit of monetary gain and its display. Selfishness in such renditions focused attention on the pursuit of material wealth.

In addressing the Bolton Rotary Club the Vicar of Bolton, went further, drawing upon a long history of Christian Socialism by remarking that 'the root cause of our disasters, national and economic, is the predominance of the profit motive in industry and commerce . . . profit is not the real aim or the first purpose of production'.[109]

While these particular statements were not directed at Jews, they framed and made especially potent accusations that Jews were primarily responsible for extracting money through black market activities. Disapproval of materialism and the ostentatious display of wealth certainly were expressions of the 'class feeling' that I considered in Chapter 2. But as Kushner suggests, blaming Jews for being obsessed with wealth was a way to shift the focus of attention from the British wealthy elite, to an alien presence that could be rooted out.[110] Once it was eliminated the British nation would then be inherently moral, its denizens infused with the patriotic spirit of sacrifice for the common good. Blaming Jews also was a way to deflect criticism away from the black market as a distorted outgrowth of capitalist practices by focusing on Jews as its perpetrators. If there were wealth-obsessed, selfish people in Britain, it was not because the British themselves were that way, or that the capitalist economy was organized around individual profit-making. Rather, money-mad selfishness was alien to true Britishness, and it was the alien presence that tainted the national community.[111]

As a corollary to the belief that Jews took advantage of the war to accrue personal gain, they also were accused of squandering money and engaging in ostentatious displays of wealth. A masseuse wrote to Victor Gollancz in July 1945, responding to his pamphlet, *'Nowhere to Lay their Heads'—The Jewish Tragedy in Europe and Its Solution,*

---

[108] Janet Adam Smith, 'The Quickening', *Britain To-Day*, 19 Sept. 1941, 3.
[109] (Bolton) *Journal and Guardian*, 21 Feb. 1941, 4.   [110] Kushner, *Persistence*, 115.
[111] For an interesting parallel in the discourse about Jews and marketing practices in 20th-century Peru, see David Nugent, *Modernity at the Edge of Empire: State, Individual and Nation in the Northern Peruvian Andes, 1885–1935* (Stanford, Calif.: Stanford University Press, 1997), 1–5.

since being masseuse in a very expensive hydro and finding that 70% of the patients were rich Jews who lived too well during 10 months of the year, and then came to fast off superfluous fat for the remainder, and finding that the other 25% were usually English people who were genuinely ill and had saved for years in order to spend a few weeks during which to receive a cure, while the other 5% were rich mucks from the aristocracy who were coming for a tone-up, I began to wonder why it was that so much wealth seemed to be in Jewish hands, when we were hearing of the terrible suffering abroad. It was nothing for £15 to be passed across the card table in the evening, and they dripped diamonds and material wealth.[112]

More generally, flaunting objects of adornment, or other material displays of consumption during the war were considered to be bad manners and were often read as acts of self-indulgence. As 'Thrifty' wrote to the *Leicester Evening Mail*:

Some people will buy anything that looks showy. This extravagance will not do, if we are to pay for war. We are told that young wage earners are objecting to having to pay income-tax and are staying away from their jobs. Yet these selfish persons would be the first to spend their money on dress and finery. To be neatly shabby today is the hallmark of patriotism.[113]

Consternation about spending money for 'dress and finery' was usually directed at young working-class girls and had been historically since at least the nineteenth century. And in the 1940s, 'good-time girls' often were accused of exchanging sex for gifts bought for them by GIs.

Ostentation also had long been associated with Jews. This association suggested that Jews lacked good taste, a characteristic that contributed to marking them as marginal to the British class system regardless of their wealth. It revealed them as poor mimics of their British 'social betters' further accenting their perpetual status as aliens. As the masseuse commented in her letter, 'they were common! On the whole they were extremely so, and they would try to bribe me to give an extra long massage, with promises of silk stockings or boxes of chocolates . . . It seemed to be in their blood to diddle people for their own benefit.'[114]

The connection between the selfishness of sexually active girls and Jews was made more or less explicitly by the masseuse in her letter to Gollancz. She wrote, 'Go into the Jewish-owned cinema restaurant in Maidenhead or the ladies' rooms in Oxford St. restaurants and see the thickly lipsticked faces and the characteristic bushed out hair. Why is it they give such an impression of selfishness? And why are the girls so intensely sexy?'[115]

If Jews were feminized by descriptions of them as ostentatious, charges that Jews were cowardly and that they were incapable of stoically coping with the stress of war also portrayed Jews as an unmanly people. Virulent anti-Semitism arose in early

---

[112] Quoted in Todd M. Endelman, 'Anti-Semitism in War-time Britain: Evidence from the Victor Gollancz Collection', *Michael*, 10 (1986), 84. I am grateful to Todd Endelman for calling my attention to this article published by the Diaspora Research Institute, Tel-Aviv University. The letter is in the Gollancz Papers at the Modern Records Centre, Warwick University, MS 157/3/LI/NT/1/202.
[113] *Leicester Evening Mail*, 2 Jan. 1942, 5.   [114] Ibid.   [115] Ibid.

March 1943, for example, with the news that there had been a panic at the entrance of the Bethnal Green tube shelter leading to the deaths of 173 people.[116] A similar disaster in the East End in 1918 had been blamed on Jews.[117] Once again rumours that Jews had been responsible for the Bethnal Green disaster spread quickly across London, and as far away as the West Country and the Midlands. According to Kushner, however, the entrance to the shelter was in a largely non-Jewish area of the East End. Apparently, it was also believed at the time that the reason so few Jews had been killed in the panic was because they had already packed the shelter before the disaster occurred. But as Kushner has argued, very few Jews used that particular shelter because they had been made to feel unwelcome there.[118]

In spite of government denials that Jews had been responsible for the panic, rumours of their culpability persisted, framed by stereotypic images of the cowardly and overly emotional and, therefore, inherently unmanly Jew.[119] These feminizing conceptions of Jews reinforced their inherent alienness as it reaffirmed the idea of the British as a manly nation, facing the enemy bravely and with a 'stiff upper lip', a subject about which I will have more to say in Chapter 5.

I have been suggesting that anti-Semitic claims that Jews panicked in the Blitz, avoided national service, monopolized shelters, participated in the black market, and were ostentatious in dress and manner identified the people who did such things—those who were cowardly and self-serving—as inherently not British. What Angus Calder has called the 'myth of the Blitz', the legend that the British endured Nazi bombs with their heads held high, and dealt with food and other shortages with stoicism, was in part constructed by identifying those who did not behave according to the moral scripts of wartime citizenship as Jews—as aliens who were innately 'unBritish'. Anti-Semitism and wartime rhetoric cooperated in making the Jews' status as British problematic regardless of their legal status as British citizens and they underscored the Britishness of 'the people' who 'naturally' belonged to the national community.

Anti-Semitic rhetoric increased across the country from late in 1942 through 1943 and especially during the winter and spring of 1943. Ironically, this wave of anti-Semitism accompanied the increasing publicity given to Nazi atrocities against Polish Jews, and grew especially after the Government acknowledged to Parliament in mid-December 1942 that Hitler was massacring the Jews of Poland. Certainly there were numerous and widespread expressions of revulsion produced by the revelations, but statements critical of the behaviour of Jews during this period mounted as well. Members of the clergy, public officials, and many, many others, clamoured for the Government to give European Jews sanctuary in Britain. In

---

[116] This is discussed in Kushner, *Persistence*, 60–1, 125–6.   [117] Ibid. 126.   [118] Ibid.

[119] For a discussion of the response of some European Jews to the stereotype of the unmanly Jew earlier in the century, see George L. Mosse, *The Image of Man: The Creation of Modern Masculinity* (New York: Oxford University Press, 1996), 152–3.

February 1943, Canon A. Linwood Wright, for example, worried publicly about the 'crocodile tears' shed by the British about Hitler's Jewish victims and urged the country to open its doors and give refuge to them.[120] In turn his article in the *Leicester Evening Mail* unleashed a flood of anti-Semitic commentary over the next few weeks in the letters column. Two days after his article was printed, for example, L. Morgan of Leicester wondered why Britain should accept the burden, arguing that the Jews should be sent to Africa, Asia, or America. Morgan commented that the Home Secretary who had said that Jewish children from Vichy France would not be allowed into the country because an 'outburst of antisemitism might follow' gave a sound reason. 'He knows the feeling in this country better than the zealots who are actuated by purely humanitarian motives.' To clarify, Morgan remarked, 'There is not the slightest doubt that a certain type of Jew is very unpopular in Britain. It is unnecessary to explain why. The Jews have many qualities that one can admire, but we do not see the best side.'[121] Another letter writer, 'V', said, 'I feel that the Jews have asked for a lot of what has come to them . . . We already have far too many Jews—and Irish too.'[122] In March 1943 Home Security recorded that while there were reports in several regions of sympathy for Jews in Europe, 'it is often added, "we don't want any more in this country".'[123] Even as sophisticated a person as the writer Naomi Mitchison said in 1943 that she had 'a certain suspicion of Jews, and when one reads of what is happening [to the Jews of Europe] one has a tendency to think it serves them right before one can catch oneself up'.[124]

During this period anti-Semitism was openly expressed in Glasgow in a series of letters-to-the-editor of the relatively staid *Glasgow Herald*. The exchange of letters was in response to news of Nazi massacres of Jews and began in mid-December 1942. For the first few weeks letter writers engaged in a dispassionate and intellectually framed discussion about the causes of anti-Semitism. They debated the degree to which the German people were viciously anti-Semitic and could be held morally responsible for their government's policies. Letters questioned whether or not all Germans were responsible, whether such virulent anti-Semitism was to be found just among Germans, or whether people from other countries might do the same; letters discussed Jewish repression by Poles and Russian Cossacks. Then on 14 January 1943 a letter written by 'W.H.S.W.' was printed that opened the floodgates to a wave of anti-Semitic commentary as well as vehement responses by members of the Jewish community and their supporters.

---

[120] Canon A. Linwood Wright, *Leicester Evening Mail*, 16 Feb. 1943, 3.

[121] L. Morgan, letter, *Leicester Evening Mail*, 18 Feb. 1943, 3.

[122] 23 Feb. 1943, 3. A few days later, a letter was printed complaining that 'V' had 'no right to put the Irish in the same category as the Jews' (*Leicester Evening Mail*, 26 Feb. 1943, 3).

[123] Home Security Report, 16–23 Mar. 1943. INF 1/292 Part 3c.

[124] Mass Observation Archive (MOA): DR M1534, Mar. 1943, as quoted in Tony Kushner, 'Remembering to Forget: Racism and Anti-Racism in Postwar Britain', in Bryan Cheyette and Laura Marcus (eds.), *Modernity, Culture and 'the Jew'* (Cambridge: Polity Press, 1998), 227.

The letter laid out some of the main themes of wartime anti-Semitism. The writer expressed surprise that up to now there had been

no mention of the dilemma existing in the minds of multitudes in this country. The dilemma is occasioned on the one side by our natural hatred of cruelty and injustice, and on the other by the fact, represented repeatedly in your news columns, that a very great many of the cases of convictions of acts prejudicial to the prosecution of the war—black marketing, exceeding quotas, avoidance of national service, etc.—are of persons of Jewish name . . .

. . . In any nation people of another race have to walk circumspectly. Unfortunately there are more indifferent Jews than there are of the sort we respect, or the indifferent ones are more blatant. In the public mind they are all regarded as being alike—ruthlessly selfish.[125]

W.H.S.W. underscored the virtuousness of the British who by their 'nature' hated cruelty and injustice thus emphasizing the 'otherness' of Jews.

In addition to the accusation of selfishness the writer stressed the inability of the Jews to become inconspicuous—that is, they remained forever alien, forever conspicuously different. As L.C.S. wrote in a letter to Victor Gollancz in June 1945,

Now although it is true to say that there are as many people, or more in proportion to their respective numbers, who are not Jews who are guilty of these practices [bribery to get the goods they want, pushing in shops], it is the fact that these Jews . . . [do not] wish to be assimilated to the population of the country in which they live, which draws upon themselves the unwelcome light of publicity for offenses which *otherwise would not attract such attention.*[126]

In order to fit in, to assimilate, they had to 'walk circumspectly'. But was this possible, if they were conspicuously different? Could Jews become inconspicuous? Could they become invisible? Good Jews were those who *always* walked circumspectly—who did not 'act Jewish'—but they were always in danger of making a misstep; of calling attention to their 'racial condition'. Their very circumspection itself might signal their difference; they would be 'almost but not quite' British, to borrow Homi Babha's conceptualization of colonial mimicry.[127] Such statements as the Glasgow letter writer's about circumspection and conspicuousness suggest that the 'condition of being a Jew' was, in part, a bodily one. It was a condition that was diagnosed visually.

There was, of course, a long history of visual depictions of Jews as dark-skinned or swarthy (and in the nineteenth century, as either part African, or closer to Africans than whites) with particular anatomical features, especially the shape of the nose. Such depictions suggested that otherness was marked upon the Jew's body

---

[125] *Glasgow Herald*, 14 Jan. 1943, 4.

[126] Quoted in Endelman, 'Anti-Semitism in War-Time Britain', 91. From MS 157/3/LI/NT/1/20 at the Modern Records Centre. Emphasis in the original.

[127] Homi Babha, 'Of Mimicry and Man: The Ambivalence of Colonial Discourse', in Homi Babha (ed.), *The Location of Culture* (London and New York: Routledge, 1994), 85–92.

and was an outward sign of inherent racial difference.[128] As Sander Gilman has put it, 'The Jew remains a Jew even when disguised . . . One cannot hide—nose job or no nose job—from the lessons of race.'[129]

Home Intelligence reports and the nationally distributed newspaper *Jewish Chronicle* concurred that indeed there had been an increase in anti-Semitic feeling in Britain during the winter of 1943, as the letters to the editor in cities such as Leicester and Glasgow suggest.[130] Even the *New Statesman and the Nation* printed a letter (one of several the editor indicated had been received) complaining of the 'ill-mannered and unsocial behavior of a percentage of foreign Jews'.[131] The *Jewish Chronicle*, while blaming pro-Nazi groups for instigating the growing problem and claiming, as did the Government, that it was an organized effort, asked 'can there be a surprise if some even ordinarily sensible and decent people succumb to this fiendish plan, if, tired and fretful beneath years of wartime strain, they suspend their normal sanity so far as to think that "there must be something in it", if a certain malaise spreads and becomes the breeding ground of suspicion developing into downright anti-Jewish hostility?'[132]

Government avoidance of the issue of anti-Semitism, coupled with the fairly widespread construction of Jews as perpetual aliens, probably magnified politically motivated, organized, anti-Semitic efforts, leading 'ordinary people' to be open to the idea that there must be a problem with Jews themselves for them to earn such treatment by Hitler and his minions. Even J. L. Hodson who in January 1943 wrote to Herbert Morrison urging that the country accept Jewish refugee children, had several months earlier recorded in his diary that he had heard about the behaviour of Jews who are 'creating a problem and making themselves unpopular . . . We shouldn't hesitate to criticise British folk if they behaved thus, and the Jews ought not to be immune.' Jewish 'otherness' to Hodson made them distinct from 'British folk'.[133]

Like many others who expressed hostility to Jews, W.H.S.W., the Glasgow letter writer, blamed the Jews themselves for anti-Semitism. Another letter writer who wrote in support of W.H.S.W. said that there 'is no doubt that the cause [of

---

[128] For discussions about the significance of Jewish bodies for anti-Semitism and Jewish self-identity, see Sander L. Gilman's many works on the subject including, *The Jew's Body* (New York: Routledge, 1991); *Making the Body Beautiful: A Cultural History of Aesthetic Surgery* (Princeton: Princeton University Press, 1999); '"I'm Down on Whores": Race and Gender in Victorian London', in David Theo Goldberg (ed.), *Anatomy of Racism* (Minneapolis and London: University of Minnesota Press, 1990), 146–70.

[129] Sander L. Gilman, 'The Visibility of the Jew in the Diaspora: Body Imagery and Its Cultural Context', The B. G. Rudolph Lecture in Judaic Studies, Syracuse University, May 1992, 27.

[130] See Wasserstein, *Britain and the Jews*, 105; see e.g. Home Security Regional Commissioners' Reports, 12–19 Jan. 1943, 19–26 Jan., 26 Jan. to 2 Feb. 1943; 16–23 Mar. 1943. PRO/INF 1/292 Part 3C. *Jewish Chronicle*, 26 Feb. 1943, 8.

[131] As reported in the *Jewish Chronicle*, 5 Mar. 1943, 10.   [132] *Jewish Chronicle*, 26 Feb. 1943, 8.

[133] J. L. Hodson, *Home Front* (London: Victor Gollancz, 1944), diary entry for 17 May 1942, 32–3; also see entry for 24 Jan. 1943, 282.

anti-Semitism] lies in the Jews themselves . . . it is unfortunately too true that far too many are unscrupulous in their methods and generally arrogant in their manner and behaviour.'[134]

Although there were many readers of the *Glasgow Herald* who wrote to condemn these viewpoints and claimed that such anti-Semitic sentiments were 'playing into Hitler's game', the outbreak of anti-Semitic commentary across the country that occurred as Hitler's murderous policy became known in Britain calls out for explanation. Was this confirmation of the Government's fear that any explicit mention of the suffering of Jews, or attention paid to anti-Semitism would increase anti-Semitism?

Throughout the war, the Government was preoccupied with the issue of anti-Semitism, and its first priority regarding anti-Semitism was to avoid stimulating it.[135] Purportedly because of this fear, the Government refused to directly address the problem of British anti-Semitism or to allow any official discussion of or attacks on it. The Government's Palestine policy was another possible motive for this reluctance.[136] Additionally, government officials repeatedly explained that 'fear of domestic anti-Semitism was at the bottom of the government's refusal to allow anything other than a trickle of refugees into the country'.[137] Herbert Morrison in particular maintained that the Home Office was reluctant to admit Jewish refugees because of anti-Semitism, even during 1942 and 1943 when the Nazi policy of systematic extermination of European Jews was becoming accepted as reality in British Government circles.[138] Morrison warned that 'there was considerable anti-Semitism under the surface in this country'.[139]

Jewish 'alienness' was a subject in private correspondence during the period when there was widespread publicity about the Nazi mass murders of Jews. A young woman wrote in a letter to her officer fiancee who was serving abroad that she found the West End to be virtually awash with overweight, oily-looking Jewish men and overly made-up women with dyed hair and cheap-looking clothes. In her judgement, they somehow managed to avoid being called up for wartime service, and she expressed the opinion that they should be forced to leave the country when the war was over.[140] This young woman invoked a variety of anti-Semitic stereotypes to justify her sense that Jews simply did not belong in Britain.

As the letter from Glasgow's W.H.S.W. indicated, accusations that Jews were heavily involved in black market activities justified purported British ambivalence about Nazi treatment of Jews. Several letters joining the debate about the behaviour of Jews in the *Glasgow Herald* focused exclusively on this issue. Professor C. A.

---

[134] Letter by A.G.M., *Glasgow Herald*, 19 Jan. 1943, 3. [135] Kushner, *Persistence*, 137–8.
[136] Personal communication from Todd Endelman. [137] Kushner, *Persistence*, 155.
[138] For a discussion, see Wasserstein, *Britain and the Jews*, 98–119. [139] Quoted in ibid. 105.
[140] Paraphrased from Miss E. M. Bolster, letters (Con Shelf), letter dated 28 Mar. 1943. At the Imperial War Museum.

Campbell of Glasgow University tried to provide evidence to the effect that news-paper coverage of prosecutions for such law violations as black marketeering was biased against Jews. Jewish names, he said, are more likely to be reported in the press than the names of non-Jews who had been convicted.[141] But arguments such as this, backed up with data, did little to quell the criticism. The widely held presumption by people in Glasgow that Jews were heavily involved in the black market was sup-ported by a rumour, believed by at least some of them, that Jews were changing their names and adopting Scottish clan names.[142] Thus these contributors to the dis-course of anti-Semitic sentiment proposed that even those with 'non-Jewish names' who were convicted were really Jews in disguise; Jews were Jews and black marke-teers were Jews. But why the increase in anti-Semitism when Nazi atrocities against European Jews were discussed openly in Britain?

The proliferating expressions of anti-Semitism were not reactions to news of Nazi atrocities in Poland in 1942 per se, but rather they were reactions to the wide-spread humanitarian appeals to open the gates to massive Jewish immigration into Britain. As Louise London has put it with regard to the policy-makers, 'In Britain . . . profound tension existed between a genuine aspiration to adhere to humanitar-ian principles and self-protectiveness against foreigners whose ethnicity was perceived as alien. British observers found Nazi Germany's goal of homogenising its population much less of an affront than the inhumane methods used to implement it. The British, too, placed a value on homogeneity.'[143] According to London, it was the belief that Jews were inherently 'other', that they were unassimilable, that led the British Government to temper humanitarian sentiment and refuse to loosen refugee immigration and visa restrictions even when confronted with the facts of the Holocaust.[144] Jews threatened British national identity, for however the British may have differed from one another, and this book explores some of these differ-ences, at least they shared one thing in common in addition to being at war with Germany. Whatever other identities they might have, and whatever diverse social and geographical locations they might occupy, they shared the fact that they were not Jews. As Kathleen Paul has suggested in the case of the response to the large-scale post-war immigration to the United Kingdom on the part of non-white people from the colonies, formal citizenship mattered less than national identity. As she put it, 'migrating citizens of colour were rejected as members of British society because they had never been and could never become "really" British.'[145] In World War II

---

[141] *Glasgow Herald*, 26 Jan. 1943, 2.   [142] Ibid.

[143] Louise London, *Whitehall and the Jews, 1933–1948: British Immigration Policy, Jewish Refugees and the Holocaust* (Cambridge: Cambridge University Press, 2000), 281.

[144] Ibid. esp. 279–84.

[145] Kathleen Paul, *Whitewashing Britain: Race and Citizenship in the Postwar Era* (Ithaca, NY: Cornell University Press, 1997), p. xv. It is instructive to note that anti non-white immigrant sentiment became increasingly pronounced as the numbers of non-white immigrants who were likely to be long-term res-idents within the United Kingdom increased. This is parallel to the increasing expression of anti-

Jews, regardless of their status as citizens or refugees, were alien. At least during this period of British history, race signalled by visual signs meant unalterable, unassimilable cultural difference.

Zygmunt Bauman has argued that it is not just *anti*-Semitism that needs to be explained, but *philo*-Semitism as well, or what he has termed, following the Polish-Jewish literary historian and critic Artur Sandauer, '*allosemitism*'.[146] He argues that it is the extreme 'othering' of the Jew—containing the seeds of both positive and negative attitudes and feelings—that needs to be understood. Bauman argues provocatively that modern Europe developed as an order of nation-states and the 'myth of national self-sameness' became a legitimizing framework for political power. 'Into this Europe of nations, states, and nation-states, only Jews did not fit, having only gypsies for company . . . They were the epitome of incongruity: a non-national nation, and so cast a shadow on the fundamental principle of modern European order: that nationhood is the essence of human destiny.'[147] Modern anti-Semitism, he proposes, developed out of the post-Enlightenment frenzy for order. Jews were figures of ambivalence, unclassifiable, and always out of place.[148]

While there is much to debate in Bauman's formulation, it anticipates and accords with the argument about anti-Semitism in this chapter. Jews threatened whatever homogeneity could be imagined as characterizing the British as a nation. The figure of the Jew, exercising masculine aggression in the pursuit of wealth as well as feminine-like cowardice, whose very body was envisioned as not quite white, and who even when trying to assimilate and fit in to British life, was 'almost but not quite' British, was the epitome of ambivalence—of being uncategorizable and a threat to order.

What Kathleen Wilson has argued about 'the others within' the eighteenth-century nation applies equally to Britain in the twentieth century. She writes,

the presence and resistances of those whose Englishness or Britishness could not be taken as self-evident demonstrated that the continual reinventions of the nation and of the terms of national belonging could not be capacious or elastic enough to accommodate all of 'the others' within . . . Jews . . . were among the groups targeted for denigration, harassment, physical segregation, or forced exile during . . . various political crises . . . As such, even if their members could act like citizens in the public sphere of association, voice opinions, and

Semitic sentiment as the possibility that Great Britain would play host to Jewish refugees was being debated publicly. In both cases, racism was fundamentally about the desire for homogeneity, on the one hand, and the perception that particular others were quintessentially unassimilable—were unalterably 'other', on the other.

[146] Zygmunt Bauman, 'Allosemitism: Premodern, Modern, Postmodern', in Bryan Cheyette and Laura Marcus (eds.), *Modernity, Culture and 'the Jew'* (Cambridge: Polity Press, 1998), 143.

[147] Ibid. 153.

[148] Bauman's ideas about Jews being ambivalent, uncategorizable others is similar to Mary Douglas's ideas about pollution. See Mary Douglas, *Purity and Danger: An Analysis of Concepts of Pollution and Taboo* (New York: Praeger, 1966).

promote their own versions of the public interest, their membership in the nation was tenta-tive and unstable, revealing the fictive nature of a 'national identity'.[149]

In this chapter I have argued that a rhetoric about self-sacrifice and dedication to the common good was central to the wartime conception of moral citizenship and that it provided a language to distinguish those who were 'unBritish' from the British who were, by definition, patriotically self-sacrificing. 'Good citizenship' was a term that was ubiquitous in discussions about the girls and young women who sought romance and sexual pleasure in the company of soldiers, but it was con-spicuously absent in the public denigration of Jews for their presumed selfish behaviour.[150] I have suggested that this was so because Jews were thought to be aliens *whether or not they were citizens*.

The distinction between those whose behaviour signaled that they were 'good' or 'bad' citizens and those who were judged to be essentially unBritish suggests what is at stake in awarding the status of citizen to those who are born outside of the bor-ders of the nation state to non-citizen parents. At stake is the construction of, the populating of, 'the nation' as an imagined community of 'the people'. It is in part for this reason that the distinctions between who are and who are not citizens, who are or are not *full* citizens with the same obligations and entitlements as everyone else, have been the objects of struggle. And it is not only those who have been excluded, constrained, or marginalized who have engaged in contestation. So also those in control of maintaining the boundaries of belonging, entitlement, and participation have been politically engaged around these issues. As political scientist Rogers Smith suggests in the case of the United States,

Citizenship laws . . . are among the most fundamental of political creations. They distribute power, assign status and define political purposes. They create the most recognized political identity of the individuals they embrace, one displayed on passports scrutinized at every contested border. They also assign negative identities to the 'aliens' they fence out . . . Citizenship laws also literally constitute—they create with legal words—a collective civic identity. They proclaim the existence of a political 'people' and designate who those persons are as a people, in ways that often become integral to individuals' senses of personal identity as well.[151]

Smith argues that the exclusionary tendencies in the construction of citizenship laws stem from the ascriptive civic myths or ideologies that define 'the people'. The appeal of these ascriptive civic myths assure that,

---

[149] Kathleen Wilson, 'Citizenship, Empire, and Modernity in the English Provinces, c.1720–90', in Catherine Hall (ed.), *Cultures of Empire* (New York: Routledge, 2000), 169.

[150] At least in the material that I read, I saw no discussion that specifically stated that Jews lacked 'good citizenship' or that they were not 'good citizens'.

[151] Rogers M. Smith, *Civic Ideals: Conflicting Visions of Citizenship in U.S. History* (New Haven and London: Yale University Press, 1997), 30–1.

regardless of their personal achievements or economic status, their inborn characteristics make them part of a special community . . . which is thanks to some combination of nature, history, and God, distinctively and permanently worthy . . . Those assurances have helped millions . . . to feel proud and confident about who they are and about their futures, both as individuals and as a national community.[152]

The connection Smith makes between ascriptive civic myths and definitions of the boundaries of citizenship suggests that who is granted and *acknowledged* to be a citizen is intimately associated with, in the case of Britain, Britishness. I have argued that in contrast to wayward girls who were considered to be failed citizens, Jews were considered alien—that is not citizens at all—regardless of their legal status in the country. As Enoch Powell so bluntly argued regarding non-white immigrants in the post-war period, 'The West Indian or Indian does not, by being born in England, become an Englishman. In law he becomes a United Kingdom citizen by birth; in fact he is a West Indian or an Asian still.'[153] And I have maintained that such sentiments about Jews were implicit in wartime anti-Semitism as well. As a Mass Observer overheard someone remark, 'the Jews are different, they're like foreigners; in fact you might say they are foreigners.'[154]

Selfishness was antithetical to the spirit of the People's War. Both girls who were believed to be flaunting sexual mores and Jews who were imagined as quintessentially self-serving were internal threats to the British moral community. Sexually expressive young women who selfishly and irresponsibly pursued romantic desire were other to the virtuous citizens of the home front. They were anti-citizens in a society of responsible, community-oriented citizens. The supposed selfishness of the Jews manifested itself in an unstoppable desire for material wealth, and their presumed cowardice led them to disregard the needs of anyone but themselves, making them 'other' to the heroic and manly British nation at war. While British girls might possibly be taught how to be sexually responsible citizens, Jews would always be Jews.

---

[152] Rogers M. Smith, *Civic Ideals: Conflicting Visions of Citizenship in U.S. History* (New Haven and London: Yale University Press, 1997), 38.

[153] Quoted in Paul, *Whitewashing*, 178.　　[154] Mass Observation File Report 1648, F45C, 2.

4

'Be Truly Feminine'

CONTRADICTORY OBLIGATIONS AND
AMBIVALENT REPRESENTATIONS

As the previous chapter suggested commentary about citizenship focused primarily on obligations. It restated ideas associated with the much older republican or civic humanist tradition—one stressing sacrifice and civic virtue in contrast to liberal citizenship's emphasis on individual rights. But as I will explain in the first part of this chapter, when women fulfilled their wartime duties of citizenship, conflict was generated over both traditional gender norms and women's civil and social rights. Additionally, as I have suggested previously, diverse public conversations and widely disseminated representations depicted the British people as belonging to a unified national community that shared a common national identity. In important ways, this unified national community sharing a common national identity was imagined to be a family. But as I show in the second part of this chapter, specific understandings of wartime femininity while crucial to this familial construction, also destabilized it.

Citizenship

Women's citizenship during World War II, involving both rights and a variety of different kinds of obligations, had complex and often contradictory meanings and consequences. Although women had the same formal political rights as men, in practice they were politically disadvantaged relative to men, and they were denied significant civil and social rights. Lower wages, property rights, the possibility of loss of both British nationality and access to employment upon marriage, and restricted occupational opportunities were among the disabilities that women suffered relative to men at the time of the outbreak of war in 1939.

During the war the duties of citizenship generally consisted of participating in a wide variety of activities relating to national defence. More extensively than in World War I, the Government in World War II enlisted civilians of all ages as volunteers and conscripts to support the war effort in the military, in civil defence, by producing the necessary goods and services for military battle, and survival at home.[1] As in World War I, this process of engaging civilians directly in the war effort was gendered. Generally the responsibilities of citizens were differently allocated to men and women. But what Angela Woollacott has termed 'patriotic involvement' could also result in the blurring of gendered responsibilities.[2]

In the 1940s, in the specific context of war, especially one following close on the heels of an economic depression, there was a dramatic shift away from valorizing individual interest and preserving individual liberty to emphasizing the common good. It was within this framework that Government, the press, and members of the public stressed the obligations of citizenship—obligations or responsibilities that included upholding moral standards, actively demonstrating loyalty and national commitment by volunteer efforts and fulfilling those state-enforced obligations concerned with military defence.

This republican or communitarian-like citizenship that was being elaborated during the war co-existed with liberal citizenship. While recently a number of political theorists have attempted to construct normative theories that reconcile liberal citizenship with its stress on individual rights, and republican or communitarian citizenship with its stress on the common good, in wartime Britain, especially as these constituting features of citizenship were applied to women, they produced contradictions and tensions.[3]

As awareness of their unequal status as citizens relative to men became heightened, their unequal rights as members of a liberal political state became subject to contestation—contestation that disrupted the idea that there was a national *common* good. Furthermore, fulfilling the obligations of citizenship by undertaking some of the *same* wartime duties as men provoked protest both by men who felt their masculine prerogatives threatened and by women, who argued that equal obligations should be matched by equal rights. Such protests unsettled the conception of Britain as an inclusive and unitary community.

Additionally as the last chapter suggested, regardless of their patriotic involve-

[1] On women's work and involvement in World War I in Britain, see Angela Woollacott, '*On Her Their Lives Depend': Munitions Workers in the Great War* (Berkeley and London: University of California Press, 1994); Gail Braybon, *Women Workers in the First World War: The British Experience*, repr. (London: Routledge, 1990); Gail Braybon and Penny Summerfield, *Out of the Cage: Women's Experiences in Two World Wars* (London: Pandora, 1987); Laura Lee Downs, *Manufacturing Inequality: Gender Division in the French and British Metalworking Industries, 1914–1939* (Ithaca, NY and London: Cornell University Press, 1995); Deborah Thom, *Nice Girls and Rude Girls: Women Workers in World War I* (London: I. B. Tauris, 1998); Susan R. Grayzel, *Women's Identities at War: Gender, Motherhood and Politics in Britain and France* (Chapel Hill: University of North Carolina Press, 1999).

[2] Angela Woollacott, 'Women Munitions Makers, War and Citizenship', *Peace Review*, 8 (Sept. 1996), 373.

[3] See e.g. Richard Dagger, *Civic Virtues, Rights, Citizenship, and Republican Liberalism* (New York and Oxford: Oxford University Press, 1997). Also see Charles Taylor, 'Cross-Purposes: The Liberal–Communitarian Debate', in Nancy Rosenblum (ed.), *Liberalism and the Moral Life* (Cambridge, Mass. and London: Harvard University Press, 1989), 159–82.

ment or their performance of the duties of wartime citizenship, women and girls were subject to censure for lacking 'good citizenship' if they were perceived to be sexually immoral. Ironically, undertaking some of the specific duties of wartime citizenship exposed women to the charge of being immoral and/or irresponsible—in other words of not being good citizens.

In April 1941, abandoning its earlier policy that women would be asked to participate in the war effort on a volunteer basis, the Government began registering women for war service so that they could be directed into war work, by conscription if necessary—increasing the numbers of women available for factory and agricultural employment and for the Forces. In December of 1941, Parliament authorized the call-up of women aged 20 to 30 for service in the military or in industry. By the middle of the war, the large majority of adult women were directly participating in the war effort in full- or part-time employment, and/or they were engaged in voluntary civil defence and other war-related activities. While the registration of women at first included women up to the age of 45, after 1943 women aged 45 to 50 had to register. Although as Penny Summerfield has argued, class by and large determined the activities performed by different women, most women thus were engaged in some manner in the war effort.[4]

Not surprisingly gender distinguished the nature of the activities in which men and women were engaged. Although women were supposed to have shorter hours of civil defence duty than men, women often voluntarily served the same number of hours of duty as the men, but they received a lower weekly wage. Generally women in civil defence were given indoor jobs such as routine office work. Work on rescue teams, demolition squads, and stretcher parties was reserved for men.[5]

For the most part, the War Office attempted to keep women out of the direct line of fire and did not permit them to carry firearms. Many women resented the idea that the War Office believed that men fought to 'protect their womenfolk'. According to one report, for instance, 'country women' in Scotland conjured up images of heroic Russian women fighting to defend their homeland in justifying their desire to take an active part in the event of an invasion of Britain. The Scottish women remarked that 'a basket of hand grenades is no heavier than a basket of turnips'.[6]

But as men were called up for the Armed Forces, the need for increasing numbers of workers in all economic sectors and in civil defence resulted in significant blurring of gender differentiation in wartime work of various kinds, including women's

---

[4] Penny Summerfield, *Women Workers in the Second World War: Production and Patriarchy in Conflict* (London: Croom Helm, 1984). For a study of how women reacted to their wartime work based on oral histories, see Sue Bruley, ' "A Very Happy Crowd': Women in Industry in South London in World War Two', *History Workshop Journal*, 44 (Autumn 1997), 58–76.

[5] 'Women's Work in Civil Defense', Memo by W.V.S. for Civil Defence, n.d. PRO/HO 199/401.

[6] Weekly Reports, 23–30 Mar. 1942. INF 1/292 Part 2.

deployment at anti-aircraft batteries. As Ernest Bevin, Minister of Labour and National Security, said regarding women in a June 1941 speech at Wimbledon, 'We want you in radio and technical work and all kinds of occupations. It is wrong to assume all we want you for is washing up dishes.'[7]

As women moved into employment that previously had been done by men, or when policy was actively contemplated that would require women to perform certain civil defence duties along with men, controversy followed. Just as in peacetime industry, male workers frequently resented the women who were hired to do work that formerly had been their sole preserve, and employers often were reluctant to hire women in part as a result of the men's opposition. In agriculture, many farmers dragged their feet about employing members of the Women's Land Army, and before the agricultural workers' unions began recruiting the women to membership, male agricultural workers ridiculed the Land Army in their publications. The *Land Worker*, magazine of the Agricultural Workers' Union, noted in January 1940, for example, that women were not rushing to join the Women's Land Army suggesting that, 'soil rhymes with toil, and hoes have never been as attractive as hose. And country life is not all "the blackbird's tune, the beanflower's boon, and May and June".'[8] Dripping with sarcasm, the reporter revealed his 'damned if you do, damned if you don't' attitude, writing of recently having seen a woman landworker 'who was tackling her work in what her employer described as a manly way. "No one can say," he remarked to us "that yon girl is womanish".'[9]

Some male workers acted in ways that made it hard for women to master the work assigned to them and others behaved in ways that reminded the women workers that they were female first and workers second.[10] That the women were known as 'dilutees', just as they had been in World War I, reinforced their secondary status, and often their low pay relative to men. The engineering unions worked out a plan with the Government whereby after a probationary training period, women doing the same work as men would receive the same wages. But these agreements covered only a small proportion of the women working during the war especially as most women were employed doing work defined (or redefined for the 'duration') as women's work.

In spite of the drastic need for personnel, the possibility that women would engage in particular civil defence tasks on the same basis as men provoked loud and sometimes quite successful protest. Even in the face of significant protest, for example, the Home Guard and the War Office successfully resisted women becoming regular, uniform-wearing members of the Home Guard.[11]

---

[7] *Daily Express*, 7 June 1941, 1.   [8] *Land Worker* 21/248, Jan. 1940, 3.   [9] Ibid.
[10] Summerfield, *Women Workers*, 153–7.
[11] For a discussion, see Penny Summerfield and Corinna Penniston-Bird, 'Women in the Firing Line: The Home Guard and the Defense of Gender Boundaries in Britain in the Second World War', *Women's History Review*, 9 (2000), 231–55.

Significant controversy also flared over compulsory fire prevention duty for women in a number of cities in the late summer and autumn of 1942. City officials and some members of the public at large loudly argued against a proposed call-up of women to serve as fireguards in their places of employment at night. In Liverpool, for example, the Liverpool Civil Defence Emergency Committee, the City Council, the Liverpool Provisions and Trade Association, and the Lord Mayor officially protested the 'Fire Prevention (Business Premises) (No. 3) Order', under which women would be compelled to fire-watch at their places of employment in vulnerable areas of the city. For weeks letter-writing readers of the press voiced their opposition to the Order. Dudley Windel, for example, wrote, 'Such a proposal is to me—and probably to others of my sex a very serious reflection on my manhood.'[12] James Blair, admiring Windel's letter, asked, 'Will any British man deny that in introducing it [the Fire-watching Order] the Minister of Home Security is forcing us to sacrifice the last shred of our manhood?' Linking national pride with masculinity, he continued, 'we have led the world in chivalry and respect for our women and to place them in position for mass-murder . . . is an act against which all men worthy of the name will revolt.'[13]

Some men not only objected to requiring women to be in the line of fire, a place of both danger and valour reserved for men, they also expressed the desire to protect young women from the immorality they might encounter or engage in while observing the night skies. The Liverpool Chamber of Commerce maintained that 'the duties to be undertaken by fireguards in the city area in black-out hours were not those that women, particularly young women should be called upon to face . . . they should not be exposed to the moral laxity which exists in some cities during air raids.'[14] Herbert Morrison, Minister of Home Security, replied to such Liverpool critics saying, 'the most foolish talk of all was that there was extreme and substantial moral danger to women to being asked to stay at their place of work and firewatch . . . I do not know what kind of label it is that some of these critics are trying to hang around the necks of the men and women of their own areas.'[15]

Ellen Wilkinson, Parliamentary Secretary to the Ministry of Home Security defended the policy arguing that women were generally in favour of the plan.[16] A British Institute of Public Opinion Survey conducted in September 1942, however, found that nationally 53 per cent of men and 52 per cent of women did not think women should be compelled to do fire-watching at night on business premises.[17] But at least some of the women who objected to the call-up did so because they were already burdened with heavy domestic and public responsibilities, not because they

---

[12] *Liverpool Daily Post*, 11 Aug. 1942, 2.   [13] *Liverpool Daily Post*, 15 Aug. 1942, 2.
[14] *Liverpool Daily Post*, 26 Aug. 1942, 3.   [15] *Leicester Evening Mail*, 24 Sept. 1942, 1.
[16] *Liverpool Daily Post*, 21 Sept. 1942, 2.
[17] 'Results of a British Institute of Public Opinion Survey completed on Sept. 20. 1942'. INF 1/292 Part 3.

feared physical or moral danger. In Leicester, where there was substantial support for the fire-watching order, 'Full-Timer', for example, protested the addition of fire-watching duties to her already full schedule. She explained that she was married, kept up a family allotment, had a day-time job and, as she put it, 'of course [did] the housework'. Rather than oppose outright the call-up of women for fire-watching, she suggested requiring the duty of 'married and single girls with no domestic responsibilities'.[18] A single woman wrote in response that she had an aged mother at home; she worked full-time, did all the shopping and housework, had other evening duties and fire-watched in her residential area. She simply could not take on additional fire-watching duties.[19] Women's 'double day' of caregiving and war work already was especially difficult under the straightened circumstances of wartime.

Other women, however, opposed the idea that they should receive differential treatment because they were women. Rona Seymour-Brown, who had been a volunteer fire-watcher in Liverpool since the raids had begun, maintained that since there was so rarely a 'real raid', the volunteers spent their time knitting and mending. She commented, '[U]ntil I read the recent correspondence I always felt guilty that I was only a fireguard.' She continued,

When the war is over, I for one will be delighted to be entirely feminine, if not entirely helpless . . . What most of us desire is to have possession of a gun, but if we must remain non-combatants and even civilians, at least let us be citizens to the best of our abilities.[20]

The gendering of the opportunities for patriotic involvement in the war was clearly an issue of equity for some women, as Rona Seymour-Brown's sarcasm suggests. They wanted to be granted the possibility to perform the *same* duties of citizenship as men 'to the best of their ability'. But as the letters concerning chivalry and protection against moral danger suggest, there were those who were anxious to preserve full citizenship as a masculine prerogative.

Although some cities such as Leicester supported the fire-watching order, Liverpool and Coventry were joined by Sheffield and Birmingham in opposing it. In the summer of 1943 the Ministry of Home Security compromised and issued another order regarding Fire Guard duties. Women would only be asked to fire-watch at their places of employment outside of business hours when sufficient numbers of men were not available. The Minister also directed that in particular areas designated as especially dangerous by local authorities, women would not be required (or permitted) to undertake fire-guard duty.[21]

[18] *Leicester Evening Mail*, 14 Aug. 1941, 3.

[19] Penny Summerfield suggests that shopping for food was an esp. burdensome task, particularly for women who worked full time. See *Women Workers*, 99–122.

[20] *Liverpool Daily Post*, 21 Apr. 1942, 2.

[21] Report of Liverpool Civil Defence Emergency Committee, 26 Aug. 1943 to 29 Sept. 1943. 352 MIN/WAT/1/67 at the Liverpool City Records Office.

The debate over fire-watching not only provoked the ire of those who were concerned to maintain the masculinity of certain duties of citizenship, the original order also served to justify a stepped-up campaign for equal rights for women. The years between the wars had been a time of progressive decline in feminist activities and the movement itself had splintered as both class and ideological differences came to the fore. The inter-war period also witnessed powerful anti-feminist reaction attended by the imposition of marriage bars in employment and restrictions on women's opportunities in the civil services.[22]

In sharp contrast to World War I, which abruptly halted feminist political agitation, World War II stimulated and reinvigorated feminist activism. Various feminist groups and women members of Parliament joined forces to insist that women be given significant opportunities to make wartime contributions and to be compensated satisfactorily for doing so.[23] They battled for equal pay, equal opportunity to participate in the war effort, for greater say in important political decisions and, in their one successful effort, for equal compensation in the event of injury sustained as a result of enemy action, of particular concern here.

The Personal Injuries Act of 1939 had mandated a differential rate of compensation of 7/- a week between unmarried men and unmarried women who had suffered war injuries as civilians. The Government maintained that the inequality followed from the average difference in rates of pay for women and men. The women protesting the lower compensation rate for women countered that the cost of living was the same for men and women and that compensation rates generally were based on the cost of living.

Women members of Parliament vociferously argued for repeal of the provision that made women's compensation lower than men's. Both Mavis Tate and Edith Summerskill were active in parliamentary contestation about the issue. Mavis Tate's motion in the House of Commons on 1 May 1941 to annul the Personal Injuries Act stimulated substantial debate. Seconding the motion, Edith Summerskill reminded the House that the issue was particularly pressing because 'we had on 19th April something that was historic. For the first time in the history of the country women were registered for war work, and there is now the threat that women will be compulsorily removed to do essential war work.'[24] Women's changed position as citizens was offered by Dr Summerskill as a basis for rethinking the issue of equal

[22] For a discussion of the anti-feminist backlash, see Susan Kingsley Kent, *Making Peace: The Reconstruction of Gender in Interwar Britain* (Princeton: Princeton University Press, 1993). For discussions of inter-war feminism, see Martin Pugh, *Women and the Women's Movement in Britain, 1914–1959* (London: Macmillan, 1992); Harold L. Smith (ed.), *British Feminism in the Twentieth Century* (Aldershot, Hants.: Edward Elgar, 1990); Barbara Caine, *English Feminism, 1780–1980* (Oxford: Oxford University Press, 1997), chap. 5.

[23] On post-1918 feminism, see Pugh, *Women and the Women's Movement*; Caine, *English Feminism*; and essays in Smith (ed.), *British Feminism in the Twentieth Century*.

[24] *Parliamentary Debates*, 5th ser., vol. 371 (1 May 1941), cols. 639–40.

compensation. For, like men, women were now subject to being called up for war service and possibly moved about the country as their labour was needed.[25] The MP for Glasgow, Mrs Hardie, concurred with Summerskill, contending that 'the woman who takes up the same duties as a man should be in the same position as the man'.[26]

Numerous women's and feminist organizations including the Women's Publicity Planning Association, the National Council of Women, and the British Federation of Business and Professional Women (BFBPW) had joined in protesting the inequality in compensation. The BFBPW were instrumental in establishing the Equal Compensation Campaign chaired by Mavis Tate. The group concentrated on increasing support for equal compensation in Parliament.[27] Across the country mass rallies, petition campaigns, and deputations were organized to press the issue. In April 1942 Mrs Tate, in spite of the Minister of Pension's opposition, successfully moved a resolution for equal compensation at a meeting of the Conservative Association. And the 1942 annual Labour Party Conference also supported equal compensation. Edith Summerskill and Mavis Tate presented various petitions to Parliament during the spring and early summer. When the possibility that women would be compelled to do fire-watching at night was discussed that summer, they questioned the Minister of Home Security about the equal compensation issue. In their minds the two were inextricably linked.

In the context of the heralded call for 'equality of sacrifice', the possibility that fire-watching would be made obligatory for women as well as for men significantly energized the protest about equal compensation for war-related injuries. An editorial in the *Leicester Evening Mail* in early August 1942 applauding compulsory fire-watching, for example, supported equal compensation in the event of injury 'if women are to share equally in the duties of civilians'.[28] In a letter 'Feminist' urged women in Leicester to 'get a petition ready now before we take up our new duties', to urge equal compensation for war injuries since their services to the nation once more will be required.[29] The Liverpool Civil Defence Emergency Committee in its resolution concerning the fire-watching order maintained that if women are to be compelled, they should be given equal compensation to men if they are injured.[30] Speaking for the General Council of the Trades Union Congress at its meeting in Blackpool early in September 1942, J. Hallsworth argued that 'fire-watching was an

[25] See Antonia Lant, 'Prologue: Mobile Femininity', in Christine Gledhill and Gillian Swanson (eds.), *Nationalising Femininity: Culture, Sexuality and British Cinema in the Second World War* (Manchester: Manchester University Press, 1996), 13–34.

[26] *Parliamentary Debates*, 1 May 1941, col. 649.

[27] See the description of the campaign for equal compensation by Harold L. Smith, 'The Problem of "Equal Pay for Equal Work" in Great Britain during World War II', *Journal of Modern History*, 53 (Dec. 1981), esp. 661–3.

[28] *Leicester Evening Mail*, 3 Aug. 1942, 3.   [29] *Leicester Evening Mail*, 14 Aug. 1942, 3.

[30] Minutes of Liverpool Civil Defence Emergency Committee, 1 Sept. 1942. 352/MIN/WAT/1/67 at the Liverpool City Records Office.

imposed service with men and women alike facing a common peril', and it seemed to him that the Government's attitude in not providing equal compensation for injury 'was absolutely inconsistent'.[31] The link between equal obligations and equal compensation was clear to the public at large.

The Government too recognized that the increased political activity around the issue of equal compensation was connected to the ruling about compulsory fire prevention duties for women.[32] After a debate in the House of Commons in late November 1942, the Government established a Select Committee to consider appropriate compensation levels for war injuries sustained by civilians. The Committee's report published 16 February 1943, found in favour of equal compensation for women and men and in April the Government announced that it was prepared to comply with the finding. This was the only major victory that feminists could claim for gender equity during the war.

The Government reasoned that there was an essential difference between compensation for injuries during wartime and any permanent scheme of compensation which would be based on wages.[33] Dissociating the issue of equal compensation for injuries sustained during the war and pay rates was important to the Government because of the earlier connection between the two issues made by both the Government and those who supported equal pay. In his memorandum to the War Cabinet discussing the Select Committee's findings, the Minister of Pensions expressed his fear that the issues still would be closely linked in the public's mind, and it would not be many months before the proposals on equal compensation were used as 'a basis for fresh claims'.[34] Indeed, as historian Harold Smith points out, it was not long after, in 1943, that a militant movement for equal pay developed among women industrial workers.[35]

As might be expected women raised the question of equal pay when they moved into jobs that formerly had been done by men or did work in industries that had been dominated by men. The issue of equal pay for equal work had been an important one for feminists in the 1920s as organizations such as the Six Point Group, the Open Door Council, and the London Society for Women's Service demanded that women teachers, professional women, and civil servants receive

---

[31] *Coventry Evening Telegraph*, 9 Sept. 1942, 3.

[32] 'Differentiation of Rates of Civilian War Injury Compensation as between Men and Women', Memorandum by Sir Walter Womersley, 25 Sept. 1942. PRO/CAB 71/10, LP (42) 214, as quoted in Harold L. Smith (ed.), *Britain in the Second World War: A Social History* (Manchester and New York: Manchester University Press, 1996), 65.

[33] This summary is based on the *Women's Bulletin* (organ of the Women's Freedom League), No. 295, 25 June 1943, 1–5.

[34] 'Personal Injuries (Civilians) Scheme, Equal Compensation for Men and Women', Memorandum by the Minister of Pensions, 4 Mar. 1943. PRO/PIN 15/2800.

[35] Smith (ed.), *Britain in the Second World War*, 664. For a discussion of the major strike on the issue of equal pay, see Smith, 'The Problem of "Equal Pay for Equal Work"', 664–5.

pay equal to their male counterparts.[36] But in 1936 after a parliamentary campaign that resulted in the House of Commons voting in favour of granting women civil servants equal pay, followed by its reversal when Prime Minister Stanley Baldwin forced a vote of confidence on the issue, the campaign became relatively quiescent.[37]

Equal pay became, during the war, a significant trade union question and feminist issue reactivated by wartime circumstances. Male trade unionists advocated equal pay or 'the rate for the job' to insure that they would not be undercut by women in the labour market. One of the most frequent causes of women's labour activism during the war involved protests over being paid less than men.[38] It was an especially crucial issue for women's rights campaigners both inside and outside Parliament; a matter that had support from groups that varied across the feminist spectrum. The Equal Pay Campaign Committee, chaired by Mavis Tate, with around one hundred affiliated women's organizations, was established in 1943 and represented some four million women.[39] The major hold-out in joining the Committee was the Standing Committee of Working Women's Organizations, a Labour Party advisory group, which had traditionally been chary of middle-class feminism.[40] The women's civil service and teachers' unions, however, began campaigns on their own. The upshot of these campaigns was that an amendment to the Education Bill requiring equal pay for women teachers, opposed by the Government, was approved by Commons 117 to 116. But Churchill forced a vote of confidence on the issue, as Stanley Baldwin had done, and the amendment went down to defeat. The Government then established a Royal Commission to study the issue of equal pay (but not to make specific recommendations) predicting correctly that this would derail the parliamentary campaign.[41] Like the campaign for equal compensation, equal pay for women was invigorated in large measure by the demands on women for 'equality of sacrifice'.

The issue of equal pay for women was a topic of conversation among the 'ordinary people' of the country, in addition to being a volatile concern in Parliament.[42] The subject was discussed, for example, by Corrado Ruffoni and Pamela in their private correspondence.

[36] Caine, *English Feminism*, 231. For an assessment of the role of women teachers in the feminist movement, see Alison Oram, *Women Teachers and Feminist Politics 1900–1939* (Manchester: Manchester University Press, 1996).

[37] Smith, 'The Problem of "Equal Pay for Equal Work"'.

[38] According to Penny Summerfield, the strike of working women at the Hillington factory over equal pay in 1943 was one of the first of such battles that women workers fought through their unions. See Summerfield, *Women Workers in the Second World War*, 171–3. See also Smith, 'The problem of "Equal Pay for Equal Work"'.

[39] Ibid. 667.   [40] Ibid.   [41] For discussion, see ibid. 670–1; Caine, *English Feminism*, 232–3.

[42] The *Glasgow Herald* received letters on the issue of equal pay for teachers specifically, and equal pay more generally in the summer of 1944. See letters dated 14 July 1944, 4; 18 July 1944, 2; 19 July 1944, 4; 24 July 1944, 2; 24 July 1944, 2; 4 Aug. 1944, 2.

Corrado Ruffoni was a Conscientious Objector (CO) of Italian descent who joined other COs doing alternative service by working in agriculture. Pamela, his fiancée, joined the Women's Land Army. In April 1944 she initiated an exchange of letters about the question of equal pay. Replying to her query about his thoughts on the issue he wrote,

well, in one sense I am all for it, but I am inclined to be against it. You see if they pay women equally to men, employers will exploit them in this way, and employ a woman cheaper than he can a man, a most obvious fact, if this equal pay comes, [sic] men will not be able to keep a home . . . in time that is what would definitely happen. Women would feel more independent of men, which would lower the moral standards of the country, which unfortunately are low enough, birth rates would fall drastically.[43]

Pamela replied that the trade union wanted equal pay so that men will have their jobs back after the war, and so women would not be able to undercut them. She agreed that the question raised 'a lot of other questions. In theory, I certainly think a woman doing the same job as any single man should be entitled to the same wages.' She contested his view that equal pay would lower moral standards. She said, 'it would amuse me to see women independent of men, and as far as a lower birthrate, I think there's quite enough people knocking about, and what with the prospect of wars . . . well.'[44] Generally, the tone of her letters suggests that she was a woman who did not shrink from asserting herself and enjoyed exercising her own capabilities. She often wrote proudly about the work she was doing, which she noted required 'arm strength' and stamina.[45] At the same time she agreed with the prevailing sentiment that married men, because they were breadwinners, deserved higher rates of pay than women.

While war service could create the conditions and opportunity for feminists to energize equal rights protests, certain types of war service had quite different effects, putting women in jeopardy of being charged with immorality. Rumours about the sexually 'loose' conduct of Service women, especially women in the Auxiliary Territorial Service (ATS), proliferated in the early 1940s. According to Violet Markham, the head of a ministerial committee on Women's Welfare in the Services, there were husbands in uniform who accompanied their wives to the recruitment office saying, 'On no account shall she go into the ATS . . . we have consistently tried to get some explanation. We haven't been able to get to the bottom of it. The

[43] Letter dated 20 Apr. 1944, 'Letters to Pamela', in C. Ruffoni, 88/35/1, at the Imperial War Museum, London. Every effort has been made to contact the copyright holder for permission to quote, but to no avail.

[44] Letter dated 23 Apr. 1944. 'Pamela's letters to Corrado', in C. Ruffino, 88/35/2, at the Imperial War Museum.

[45] See e.g. letters dated 4 Nov. 1943 and 2 Mar. 1944, 'Pamela's letters to Corrado', in C. Ruffino, 88/35/2, at the Imperial War Museum.

only reply has been, "No she shall not go into the ATS; my wife shall not go". [46] When women ventured into particular kinds of war service, or they left their homes and communities to work in war factories in far away cities, or as members of the Women's Land Army they went to work on the land in communities where the women were outsiders, they were subject to accusations of being immoral. [47] The Agricultural Council of Glamorgan (Wales), for example, discussed the possibility of placing a curfew on the Land Girls because of their activities with male soldiers on the streets at night. [48]

By fulfilling their wartime obligations women put themselves in the position of being accused of bad citizenship. In World War II Britain women and men could enact good citizenship in numerous ways, but for women, sexuality and mother-hood were fundamental. Even if she were an excellent machinist working on air-planes, or a cooperative and loyal member of the ATS, or an efficient tractor-driver in the Women's Land Army, a woman would not be a 'good citizen' if she was thought to be sexually promiscuous. Her capacity for good citizenship also was questioned if she was thought to be neglecting her children, even if she was duti-fully working in an ordnance factory.

Women's liability to the charge of sexual promiscuity associated with their being in the armed services was made clear in hearings conducted by the Women's Ser-vices Welfare and Amenities Committee with recruitment officers of the Ministry of Labour. The Chair, Violet Markham, asked how the ministry dealt with girls who were 'quite unsuitable material'. A ministry official reported, 'Women were directed into the services under the National Service Acts who were totally unsuitable and it was discovered after a few months, and they were with infinite difficulty dis-charged.' [49] Unlike the Women's Royal Navy (WRNS) where the young women who enlisted needed to provide three references, references were not obtained from con-scripts. They were called up like male conscripts, sent for medical examination, and enrolled. Consideration had been given as to whether or not the interviewing offi-cer at the Medical Board could go 'into this question of character or try to form an impression of character', but ATS and Ministry of Labour personnel agreed that the 'interviewer wouldn't be able to take that on—the only thing to do was to risk some

---

[46] Women's Services (Welfare and Amenities Committee), Minutes of Evidence, 29 May 1942. PRO/LAB 26/63.

[47] The furore led to the formation of an investigatory committee. The 'Report of the Committee on Amenities and Welfare Conditions in the Three Women's Services' concluded, 'in the opinion of those most competent to form a judgment, promiscuous conduct in the Women's Services is confined to a small proportion of the whole.' 'Report of the Committee on Amenities and Welfare Conditions in the Three Women's Services', *Parliamentary Papers 1941–42*, vol. 4, Cmd 6384 (London, 1942), 51, quoted in Smith (ed.), *Britain in the Second World War*, 264.

[48] *Weekly Mail and Cardiff Times*, 7 Oct. 1939, 8; 14 Oct. 1939, 2.

[49] 'Women's Services (Welfare and Amenities Committee)', Minutes of Evidence, 29 May 1942. PRO/LAB 26/63.

of them getting posted'. Violet Markham commented that the 'ATS must be free to discharge them quickly when they arrived and were found to be misbehaving themselves.'[50] Clearly, serving in the ATS was not enough. Members of the ATS had to demonstrate that they were sexually respectable. In contrast sexual promiscuity among male recruits to the Forces was not a moral concern for the War Office or the Admiralty. In fact, they were provided with condoms when they left Britain for overseas duty.[51]

As the previous chapter has detailed, young civilian women and girls also were held to a high standard of sexual propriety. But, along with the letters and feature articles about the immorality of young women and girls in the press, there were occasional letters that contested this rush to moral judgement. While many of the letter writers ridiculed equating 'youthful high spirits' with bad citizenship, others protested the focus on girls instead of women. 'Bathonian', for example, wondered why there was such a 'fuss about the behaviour of young Bath girls during the black-out'. The real culprits were the married women who 'find time to go to public houses with other men. No doubt the probation officer could surprise the public with the number of homes already broken up, with tragic consequences for the children.'[52]

Apprehension about married women's sexual morality was often connected to a second discourse on women's civic virtue—one that stressed their abilities as mothers. This wartime theme drew upon a long history of commentary on the subject stretching back at least as far as the mid- and late nineteenth century when, as many scholars have noted, working-class women in particular were accused by members of the middle classes of doing a disservice to society by being bad mothers.[53] A letter written by L. K. Gordon of Leicester is an example of the wartime anxiety concerning irresponsible mothers:

the war has caused a search for pleasure among selfish people who neglect their first obligation—to their children . . . I suggest that rigorous prosecution of those who fail in their duty should be tried, to teach unnatural parents that it does not pay to be cruel.[54]

Echoing these sentiments, the Reverend A. E. Kimpton of Leicester, who was concerned about the fact that children in the city were not attending Sunday School,

---

[50] Ibid.

[51] See my 'The "Sex Question" in Anglo-American Relations in the Second World War', *International History Review*, 20 (Dec. 1998), 884–903.

[52] *Bath and Wiltshire Chronicle*, 14 Oct. 1943, 5. See also the letter to the editor in this newspaper from 'under eighteen', 23 Oct. 1943, 5.

[53] See e.g. Jane Lewis, *The Politics of Motherhood: Child and Maternal Welfare in England, 1900–1939* (London: Croom Helm, 1980); Ellen Ross, *Love and Toil: Motherhood in Outcast London, 1870–1918* (New York: Oxford University Press, 1993).

[54] For the councillor's statement, see, 'More Neglected Children', *Leicester Evening Mail*, 15 May 1943. Letter by L. K. Gordon, *Leicester Evening Mail*, 16 May 1943.

remarked to the Leicester Diocesan Conference, 'We deplore the decay of home life, and the shocking irresponsibility of mothers for their children.'[55]

By fulfilling their wartime obligations and engaging in war work, British women jeopardized their 'civic virtue' if they appeared in any way to be neglecting their maternal duties. For example, the matron of a day nursery in Tottenham reported to a Ministry of Information officer that the mothers left their children at the nursery from 7.00 in the morning until 5.00 or 5.30 in the afternoon. She said, '[S]ome mothers are very glad to shed their responsibility.'[56] *Women's Own* featured an article 'Hand Over the Babies!' in March 1944.' "If only there were a nursery near-by, where I could put my baby, I could take up some sort of job . . ." It's a fairly common wish nowadays, and one cannot help wondering why so many mothers appeared only too anxious to "hand over the babies".'[57] Preying upon maternal guilt, and castigating women for having 'impure' motives for going to work, the article's author continued, 'I do not criticize mothers as a whole; I only point out that such mothers exist. And I wonder if the war isn't making things extremely simple for these so-called mothers. How will they settle their lives afterwards?'[58] Such pronouncements whose audience undoubtedly was assumed to be middle-class, made invisible the 10 per cent of married working-class women who continued their necessity-driven pre-war wage earning during the war.

Even when economic and/or national necessity was acknowledged as a reason for married women's employment outside of the home, such employment was frowned upon. The British Council of Churches in its pamphlet *Home and Family Life*, commented upon 'wartime disturbances of women's disposition for family life'. The statement maintained that the conscription of unmarried women did not change their basic natures as did the employment of married women. 'Necessary though such employment may be, it is impoverishing the home-life of the community, especially as it affects women with very young children and children of school age.'[59] The pamphlet expressed concern that married women's wartime employment led them to desire an 'equal standard for men and women'. Linking the desire for equality bred of being a working mother to sexual promiscuity, the British Council of Churches statement maintained,

The throwing off of sex restraint by women is but one aspect of the whole problem of the relationship of the sexes and affects family life at many points. Moral standards are influenced by the desire of the woman . . . for a recognition that she is on equal ground [with men].[60]

---

[55] 'Decay of Home Life', *Leicester Evening Mail*, 2 June 1943, 1.
[56] 'Raw Material for London Report', n.d. (probably spring 1941). PRO/HO 199/436.
[57] 'Hand Over the Babies!', *Woman's Own*, 24 Mar. 1944, 7.   [58] Ibid.
[59] British Council of Churches, *Home and Family Life* (London, 1943), 61.   [60] Ibid.

The Church was not alone in its concern about the negative impact on family life of women's employment. This was also a theme that was recurrent in discussions about population decline.

One such discussion was the House of Commons debate on population held in mid-July 1943. In the debate Sir Francis Fremantle, for example, maintained that 'the family instinct is gradually being suffocated by the love of comfort and pleasure. Primarily women in the industries and professions want to earn money'.[61] He went on to argue,

this war has given us a wrong turn. There is a great temptation because women have discovered means of making money and of being better off than is compatible with family life . . . The women's movement has become an anti-population movement, very largely because there is a wrong division of the male and female shares in national life.[62]

Although a few legislators such as Fremantle blamed parents and/or women for putting material interests ahead of more spiritual ones, most of those engaging in the debate stressed the idea that social welfare programmes such as family allowances and various forms of social security would stimulate the desire on the part of women and men to raise larger families than they had in the recent past.

But the debate also included discussion about the possibility that women might want to work or have careers AND raise families. Legislators such as Fremantle, the ILP (Independent Labour Party) Member for Glasgow, Andrew Maxton, and Edith Summerskill argued from different points of view that women could and should not do this. The Welshman James Griffiths, however, proposed that profound social changes were needed so that women would not have to 'choose between a career and motherhood'.[63] He argued that plans for reconstruction must be based on the fact that some women will want both.

Believing that it was impossible for women to have both a career and motherhood, Edith Summerskill suggested that women would choose jobs over children because of the low status of the housewife. She argued that it was the 'woman in the home who decides the size of the family, and you cannot emancipate women outside the home and expect the woman in the home to remain unaffected by the change'.[64] In particular Summerskill pointed to women's economic dependency within the household and proposed that the relative economic and social standing of husband and wife should be equalized in order to raise the birth rate. She favoured children's allowances and proposed that the wife and mother be given a legal right to a share of the family income, a right that wives did not then possess.[65]

Griffiths and Summerskill made use of the public concern about women's moral obligation to mother to suggest that fundamental change in the gender order was

---

[61] *Parliamentary Debates*, 5th ser., vol. 391 (16 July 1943), col. 606.   [62] Ibid., col. 607.
[63] Ibid., cols. 621, 599, 569.   [64] Ibid., col. 597.   [65] Ibid., cols. 599–600.

necessary in order to make it possible for women to perform this national duty. Their arguments about equal rights, motherhood, and employment blurred the line between 'difference feminism' and 'equal rights feminism'.[66] Although Summerskill seems to have believed that motherhood excluded employment outside the home, Griffiths presumed it would be possible to organize society in such a way that women would not have to choose between motherhood and equal rights in the workplace.

In practice, as these examples have suggested, fulfilling the obligations of wartime citizenship had contradictory effects both for women and for the nation understood as a unitary community. On the one hand, the war opened up new opportunities for women to exercise their obligations as citizens and to demand equal rights. On the other hand, however, gender difference continued to be a fundamental principle of wartime policies and their application, reinforcing the centrality of gender difference to the nation.[67] The war also created circumstances under which women's virtues as members of the nation could be called into question as they enacted the duties of citizenship.

In addition to the contradictions in the practices of citizenship and the consequences of these practices, there were anomalies articulated in public appeals to women's patriotism and depictions of their wartime service. Contrary points of view were available in public discourse that suggested different interpretations of the meanings of women's wartime roles. Some depictions on their own could produce contradictory meanings—meanings that potentially opened the way for transformations in conceptions of femininity and female citizenship, while simultaneously underscoring the idea that national identity was and should remain differentiated by gender. The next section of this chapter addresses these ambivalent representations of femininity.

Representations of Femininity

'Be truly feminine', Sonnie Hale, the variety actor, told women. 'This does not mean to say that you must be fluffy in looks or mind. But to-day there is a danger of too much back-slapping and loud voices among the fair sex—and how I hate it.'[68]

Hale was one of 'six famous men' whose ideas about 'the ideal woman' were recounted to readers of *Woman's Own*, one of the most widely read women's maga-

---

[66] See esp. Alison Oram, who suggests that feminists during the war attempted to bridge the political gaps between those committed to concerns with equality and those who opposed equal rights feminism. Alison Oram, ' "Bombs Don't Discriminate!": Women's Political Activism in the Second World War', in Christine Gledhill and Gillian Swanson (eds.), *Nationalising Femininity: Culture, Sexuality and British Cinema in the Second World War* (Manchester: Manchester University Press, 1996), 54–5, 60–1.

[67] This is a major theme in Philomena Goodman's *Women, Sexuality and War* (Basingstoke, Hants.: Palgrave, 2002).

[68] *Woman's Own*, 16 Mar. 1940, 13.

zines in the country.[69] After warning women to be wary of adopting too masculine a demeanour, Hale reinforced his concern specifically with reference to women in the services. 'You may be in one of the women's services and therefore in uniform. If you are, remember there is no need to strut and shout around. There is no need to ape men.' But in order both to caution women about the possibility of becoming too masculine and at the same time not to dissuade them from joining the services, Hale asserted that it was possible for women to wear a uniform and remain feminine. 'I have seen women look the epitome of feminine smartness in a riding habit which is as severe as any uniform,' he remarked.[70] Hale was telling women that they could join in the war effort, but they must not, as a result, become 'men'.

In this section of the chapter I am concerned with how the public culture of wartime Britain characterized women and femininity. As we shall see, representations of wartime womanhood underscored the expectations that women should preserve a conventional feminine persona and continue to cultivate the desire for marriage and motherhood. But at the same time, they were to contribute heroically to the war effort in factories, on the land, in the services, or in civil defence. They should participate, yes, but not become transformed by that participation. As numerous scholars have noted, such contributions were to be made 'for the duration' only. Women were to do their wartime jobs, engage in acts of heroism, and be considered by others and consider themselves to be crucial to the war effort, all without changing their feminine ways of being. But many of these representations made conceivable the worrisome possibility that the 'duration' would not leave women and the gender order unaltered. This anxiety figured particularly in how the future post-war Britain was imagined during the war years. What follows explores the ambivalent meanings of wartime femininity circulating in the public culture of the home front.

Sonnie Hale, the variety show actor, was not alone in worrying that women might adopt too 'mannish' a deportment. Antoine, 'world-famous hairdresser with salons in Paris and London', wrote patronizingly about his ideal woman:

Possessing more knowledge now than at any other stage of your development, I look for your wisdom in applying it and I frown on you flaunting it. You must be like an accomplished actor whose art conceals his art.

You know better than to attempt an artificial equality with your menfolk nowadays. You are not ashamed any more to be a woman, knowing where your own power lies. You are still amusingly vain. That is good, because with your age-old vanity and your new courage you are ready for anything—even for the continuance of your coiffure in an air-raid shelter whilst a battle royal is raging overhead.[71]

[69] For a discussion of *Woman's Own* and its advice to women about 'managing the self' in wartime, see Janice Winship, 'Women's Magazines: Times of War and Management of the Self in *Woman's Own*', in Christine Gledhill and Gillian Swanson (eds.), *Nationalising Femininity: Culture, Sexuality and British Cinema in the Second World War* (Manchester: Manchester University Press, 1996), 127–39.
[70] Ibid.　　[71] Ibid.

Such advice to women early in the war, even before women were required to register for and were conscripted into wartime service, suggests there was significant public apprehension (at least on the part of some men) that women's wartime responsibilities and opportunities would permanently transform the gender order. There was, however, one female role that women could assume without endangering established norms of gender difference. They could be nurses.

Nurses symbolically epitomized the qualities that all women should emulate in performing their patriotic duty—they were quintessentially both caring and heroic. As political theorist Jean Bethke Elshtain has argued, 'field nursing places women near the arena of danger but not in the thick of things, locating them figuratively in a familiar (family) way in relation to the dead and dying: women succor, soothe, heal, tend, offer solace.'[72] Nurses in the services went abroad in the earliest detachments to the Continent and later in the invasions of Africa, Italy, and France, long before service women generally were required to join their male colleagues on the front.[73] Because they were doing stereotypically female work, they could be exposed to danger—after all, it was their job, one with a classically feminine job description.

Beverley Nichols, the author and feature writer for the *Sunday Chronicle* expressed just such sentiments. He wrote, '[N]urses represent all I love and cherish in Womanhood [*sic*].' He elaborated, 'A British nurse . . . Those two words tell a tale of bravery, charity, sweetness and good humour.'[74] And Crystal Pudney, writing in *Britain To-Day*, the publication of the British Council advertising the British way of life, particularly for an American audience wrote,

Everyone has read of the heroic behaviour of British nurses in last year's raids. Guy's Hospital was hit at least nine times; and here is what the Matron said: 'I've walked through the wards when the bombs were falling all round us and I've seen nurses—young probationers of eighteen—carrying on with their usual tasks as though nothing had happened . . . chatting and laughing with their patients, not a sign of fear however scared they may have felt . . . Time after time nurses put out incendiaries in the grounds.[75]

In contrast to this applause for nurses putting out incendiaries, members of the Coventry Emergency Committee told the press that Coventry would not follow the

---

[72] Jean Bethke Elshtain, *Women and War* (Chicago and London: University of Chicago Press, 1995), 183. See, however, Sandra Gilbert's discussion of the differences between men's and women's literary representations of nurses in World War I. Sandra Gilbert, 'Soldier's Heart: Literary Men, Literary Women, and the Great War', in Margaret Randolph Higonnet et al. (ed.), *Behind the Lines: Gender and the Two World Wars* (New Haven and London: Yale University Press, 1987), 67–8.

[73] For a study of World War II nurses, see Penny Stains, *Nurses at War: Women on the Frontline, 1939–45* (Stroud, Glos.: Sutton, 2000).

[74] *Sunday Chronicle*, 15 Sept. 1940, 2.

[75] Crystal Pudney, 'Nursing in War-Time', *Britain To-Day*, 78 (Oct. 1942), 13–14. Also see Theodora Benson, *Sweethearts and Wives: Their Part in War* (London: Faber and Faber, 1942), 69. She described the 'gentleness of their duty . . . as something Christlike'.

Menders of Men . . .

After the smoke and flame
of Blitz,
after the crash and shock
of fighting convoy,
after the strain and roar
and thirst of battle—
Quiet . . .
and those white caps
moving silently, efficiently
about the ward.
A kind face
leaning over—
" How are you feeling ?
Eh—more comfortable ?
You'll be all right."
In the long night watches
the shaded lamp
of the night nurse
is like a star
in the dark.
A pillow eased . . .
a glass of water.
Dawn breaks—at last.
Pain grows less—hope
returns with a joke.
Day follows day
in kindness—then,
You can get up tomorrow
"Oh gosh—that's great!"

*   *   *   *

Into the wheel-chair
into the sunshine,
White caps of healing
well in attendance—
I say Nurse—
Plenty of laughs . . .
broken lives
repaired !

*   *   *   *

Let us remember all they are doing when we
consider our work and our saving. Let our
saving reflect the measure of our gratitude to
them. Save more.

. . . — Save for Victory

5. National Savings celebrates
nurses' contribution to the war
effort.
Public Record Office

example of Plymouth where, while on a visit to inspect bomb-damaged towns, they found a squad of 'girls' doing demolition work. 'We would not ask girls to do that sort of work in Coventry. There would be a public outcry if we did.'[76] While nurses could enact femininity while performing dangerous work because they were nurses, there was a good deal more public apprehension about the blurring or breakdown in the gender order if women and girls in less explicitly feminine roles were asked to engage in activities traditionally coded as male, as we have seen in the protests over women being compelled to be fire guards at night.

Feminist groups contributed to discussions about the possibility of a permanent transformation of the gender order. For example, in its first issue of 1942, the journal of the Women's Freedom League, *The Bulletin*, proclaimed, 'The woman of the future is taking shape within the crucible of this war. She will not be passive but active. She will take the lead everywhere.'[77] Seeing the war as making possible long-term gains in the position of women in economic life and in politics, women MPs began to insist in public meetings and in deputations to the Ministry of Labour that women could and should make a vital impact on the war effort by providing both their labour power and their administrative and leadership capacities. They were joined in these efforts by groups such as the BFBPW.

The BFBPW was composed of predominantly upper-middle and upper-class women, with the MP Viscountess Astor as President and the indomitable Caroline Haslett, representing the Women's Engineering Society, as chair.[78] In the first issue of its quarterly bulletin, *Women at Work*, the aims of the organization were stated as 'protecting the economic status of women and their inclusion in all branches of Industry, in newly formed Government Departments, and the Service on the same basis as men where the qualifications are equal'.[79]

The BFBPW worked closely with, and had overlapping membership on, the Woman Power Committee, the committee of women MPs formed by Conservative MP Irene Ward primarily to urge that the Government employ women in skilled positions and especially to give 'educated' women the opportunity to move into supervisory positions in factories.[80] Yet in spite of their demands that the Government better utilize the services women could offer, many of its members maintained that married women and mothers should not be required to participate

[76] 'Girls Help in Clearing Bomb sites—An Example Coventry Will Not Follow', *Coventry Evening Telegraph*, 30 Jan. 1943, 5.

[77] 'The Woman of the Future', *The Bulletin*, #260, 2 Jan. 1942, 1.

[78] Caroline Haslett was among the vanguard of women in the broad field of engineering. She was President of the Women's Gas Council in addition to being the President of the Women's Engineering Society which she helped to found. She also served as an adviser to the Ministry of Labour and National Security during the war.

[79] *Women at Work*, 1/1 (Nov. 1940), 1.

[80] For a historical account of the formation and functioning of the Woman Power Committee, see Harold L. Smith, 'The Womanpower Problem in Britain during the Second World War', *Historical Journal*, 27 (1984), 928–31.

in the war effort. Some of the women MPs were only willing to support compulsory registration of women when they were assured that sufficient measures were in place to protect domestic arrangements.[81] Their messages to and about women often were ambiguous about the nature of women's responsibilities to the nation.

Historian Alison Oram's analysis of the Women's Publicity and Planning Association publication, *International Women's News*, suggests that this group, too, was unclear as to whether they spoke for the woman worker or for the housewife.[82] Thus feminists were ambivalent about how the nation should establish its priorities for women's responsibilities during the war.[83]

Their ambivalence is evident in various issues of the BFBPW's *Women at Work*. For example, the BFBPW printed for the benefit of its members a talk given by the anthropologist Margaret Mead in the September 1943 issue of *Women at Work*. Mead wrote, '[t]he comparative study of human society suggests that women are less in need of socially recognised achievement other than the achievement of bringing a human life safely from conception to birth.'[84] She suggested,

Until science has developed methods for eliminating gestation entirely so that women no longer have to expend their energies in either the periodic or protracted or the climactic aspects of child bearing, men and women of the same natural gifts will compete unequally and therefore destructively for the happiness of the woman, if asked to perform identical tasks and no others.[85]

Thus, according to Mead, women are on unequal footing relative to men throughout the course of their lives because of their 'specialized' physiology. Furthermore, their happiness is dependent upon doing tasks appropriate to their sex.

Earlier that year in a speech to the BFBPW and published in *Women at Work*, Sir Stafford Cripps, the enormously popular Leader of the House of Commons with a seat on the War Cabinet, gave his opinion that 'equality of capacity' exists between men and women. But, '[T]here is, of course, one essential difference which even the most fervent champion of equality will admit—women have an added responsibility in society which they would not wish to ignore—the responsibility of rearing and bringing up children.'[86] Unlike Mead, Cripps maintained, 'The incidents of life will always make a difference between the sexes, but this relates primarily to the young mother and should not persist throughout adult life and certainly should not lead to any general discrimination.'[87] Cripps held up as models Russian women, widely esteemed throughout Britain for the heroic contributions that they made to Russia's war effort. He reminded his audience that in Russia 'men and women alike

---

[81] See ibid.; Caine, *English Feminism*, 231. [82] Oram, 'Bombs Don't Discriminate!', 55.
[83] Ibid.
[84] Margaret Mead, 'Science, Women and the Problem of Power', Extract of a talk under BFBPW auspices, in *Women at Work*, Sept. 1943, 1/12 (1943), 5.
[85] Ibid. [86] *Women at Work*, 1/10 (Mar. 1943), 5. [87] Ibid. 6–7.

are looked upon as full citizens . . . yet Russian women have not in any way given up their essential function of motherhood'.[88] Alison Oram correctly, I think, points out that rather than being constructed oppositionally, 'difference feminism' and 'equality feminism' were articulated together during the war.[89] But this ambivalent pairing of different feminisms also may well have reflected profound uncertainty about just how women would be changed by the war. Public pronouncements from people such as Stafford Cripps and Margaret Mead, and the MPs James Griffith and Edith Summerskill, as well as from the different feminist organizations and the Church contributed to an extensive public debate about the dangers that beset women, their families, and ultimately, the nation at large as a result of women's contributions to the war.

There were numerous other participants in these anxiety-ridden discussions about the potential that women and the gender order would be transformed including military service recruitment campaign materials, advertisements, and a variety of different print media. They produced representations that were designed to instil patriotic commitment while at the same time reassuring both women *and* men that, regardless of what it was women were doing during the war, their femininity would survive.

Drawing upon a familiar melodramatic narrative, one frequently deployed theme promised that love and marriage would follow wartime service and sacrifice. The National Savings Committee, for example, featured a patriotic advertisement in newspapers in April 1944, 'Salute the Soldier'. The reader's eye (see Plate 6) is caught by a drawing of a man and a woman, both in the Services, sharing a quiet moment of intimate conversation over a cup of tea. He is looking at her intently as she gazes into the distance as if contemplating the future. Below the drawing are verses describing how their lives in the military kept them apart. In the end, though, she is rewarded by a promotion—a promotion that fulfils her desire for marriage, not one that gives her an advancement in the services or enhanced status in public life.

This theme was elaborated more explicitly by the MP Edith Summerskill in an article she wrote for *Sunday Pictorial* in the early autumn of 1942. Summerskill reassured women in the services that men would want to marry them. She reported on her 'discoveries' as a member of the government committee inquiring into the welfare of women in the services (the committee organized to investigate the accusations of immorality against service women on which Summerskill was one of the two women members). Summerskill expressed her admiration for women in the services, applauded women's capabilities and remarked that 'the war . . . has been responsible for a change in sex relations that would have taken fifty years to effect in peace time'. But she immediately modified this observation by writing,

---

[88] *Women at Work*, 1/10 (Mar. 1943), 6.   [89] Oram, 'Bombs Don't Discriminate!', 65–6.

6. National Savings advertisement, 'The Corporal and the Sarge'. Public Record Office

The Corporal and the Sarge

They only find to lose again,
They only meet to part,
They've little time to linger
With the language of the heart.

She to her radio station,
He for the road to Rome,
There's much to do and far to go
Before they both come home.

And he must march full many a mile,
And fight through change and charge,
Ere he promotes his Corporal
And makes her Mrs. Sarge.

SALUTE THE SOLDIER

The soldier is giving up all he holds most dear.
What can we do to show our gratitude? We can Salute
the Soldier by saving more and yet more — every day
and every week — not only in your special "Salute
the Soldier" Week, but all the time.

Issued by the National Savings Committee

I found that not only have men finally come to accept women as equals, but even to acknowledge them quite often as superiors. And having discovered that, the men, far from loathing these intelligent and capable women, actually fall in love with them—and marry them. Now that is sex equality with a vengeance, and I believe it is one of the most hopeful signs of our times.[90]

To bolster her claim that men find 'clever women' in the services attractive, she said that the 'marriage rate in the women's services is very high indeed. A woman in uniform with the old soldier's courage, an independent viewpoint and a quick brain does not appear to repel the opposite sex. The reverse, in fact, is the case.'[91] Summerskill promoted the idea that 'sex equality' would come from the war but that capable women need not fear that as a result they would become unlovable. While promising that women could fully express their intelligence and competence in the military, such proclamations also reinforced the idea that heterosexual marriage was necessary to women's happiness. And, by adopting a reassuring tone, they confirmed the possibility that successful women could well be threatening or even repugnant to potential suitors. If this idea had not been firmly entrenched in popular thought, the reassurance hardly would have been necessary.

In addition to the representations championing the idea that women could be competent and patriotic and still find a husband, various publications stressed the compatibility of women's wartime service with glamour.[92] A Ministry of Information pamphlet, for example, intending to show women's contributions to the war effort, maintained that their sometimes heroic efforts never detracted from their physical charms. *Eve in Overalls* described the variety of jobs women were undertaking during the war. One section was entitled 'Beauty and the Blimps', and depicted the work of a crew of women engaged in balloon barrage defence. The author proclaimed,

The girls carry out all this work with strict military discipline, and it is all done with perfect good humour . . . Yet feminine coquetry will never give up all its claims. Whether under a cap or a steel helmet their hair—and this is generally very beautiful in England—is arranged to show the permanent waves to the very best advantage.[93]

But after recounting that the girls were wearing the same uniform as their male comrades while still retaining 'the allure of their sex', he reported that one of them asked him 'with feigned anxiety',

'Don't you think that we are becoming a little too mannish?' . . . She knew very well that there was no question of gallantry conflicting with truth, for she had magnificent eyes, lovely hair

---

[90] *Sunday Pictorial*, 6 Sept. 1942, 4.   [91] Ibid.

[92] For an insightful essay on the contradictions involved in and produced by constructions of 'patriotic femininity' see, ' "Patrotic Femininity": Women's Morals and Men's Moral During the Second World War', *Gender and History* 10 (Aug. 1998), 278–293.

[93] Arthur Waters, *Eve in Overalls* (London: Ministry of Information, 1942), 14.

and a delightful mouth, and, what was more, she was aware of this, and was even more aware that no one could long resist her bewitching smile.[94]

Like Summerskill, the author of the pamphlet attempted to reassure his audience that traditional femininity and war service were compatible. This was a common theme in the print media during the war.

The Ministry of Information pamphlet on women's contributions to the war effort, *Eve in Overalls*, described women in factories as having 'well-cared for hands and hair and they wear, whenever possible, pretty shoes. They have not given up their necklaces nor their bracelets nor their lipsticks'.[95]

Such an approach was not universally appreciated. Mary Sutherland, editor of *Labour Woman*, the magazine for women in the Labour Party, wrote in her monthly commentary of the 'realities' of the hard, dirty, noisy, and unpleasant work in the factories and contrasted these realities with 'the pictures of young women in immaculate overalls in well-lit, spacious and airy factories'. She urged the Government to approach 'our young women as if they were adults who are more concerned to play their part . . . than about keeping their hands clean and their nails polished.'[96]

More commonly, however, women throughout the country repeatedly heard reminders of how femininity was constructed in 'normal times', and the significance of glamour to that construction. Even the War Office attended to the problem of women's physical appearance. It had an undergarment manufacturer design a special corset—one that would be practical under a uniform but would also 'safe-guard women's femininity for the duration'.[97] And, as Antonia Lant has suggested, the baroque nature of wartime cosmetics legislation testifies to the important cultural place of make-up in British life, even as the 'stereotype of the painted lady as lethal for fighting men persisted in official posters and films'.[98] Plate 7 is an example of such a poster that uses the image of a 'painted lady' to represent a potentially dangerous woman.

Housewives were not exempted from being targets of fashion and self-care advice. For example, they were prompted to take care of their personal appearance in *Fanfare*, a magazine for homemakers published by the Women's Gas Council. In an article entitled 'Take a Chance on Being Beautiful', Anna Bella wrote that while she doubted that many women were neglecting their household tasks, 'I . . . believe that some are neglecting their personal appearance.'[99] The author gave her readers

---

[94] Ibid. 17.   [95] Ibid. 36.   [96] *Labour Woman*, 29 (Nov. 1941), 115.

[97] As quoted in Pat Kirkham, 'Fashioning the Feminine: Dress, Appearance and Femininity in Wartime Britain', in Gledhill and Swanson (eds.), *Nationalising Femininity*, 156.

[98] Lant, 'Prologue: Mobile Femininity', 24. On cosmetics in the USA during the war, see Page Dougherty Delano, 'Making Up for War: Sexuality and Citizenship in Wartime Culture', *Feminist Studies*, 26 (2000), 33–69.

[99] Anna Bella, 'Take a Chance on Being Beautiful', *Fanfare*, 3 (Winter 1940), 8.

7. Poster of glamorous and dangerous woman.
Public Record Office

beauty tips so that they could 'keep young and beautiful'. Even mothers and house-wives were not securely feminine unless they made a concerted effort to beautify themselves.

In an early March 1940 issue of the *Sunday Pictorial*, a writer identified as 'our Psychologist' observed that during the war, 'when men wear uniforms and go forth to battle, the clothes of women swing to the ultra-feminine'. Then, he said, there is a swing in the other direction. After World War I there was a trend to the 'masculine in clothes. And in women, themselves, too, for that matter!' After reminiscing about those 'queer days', he went on:

But in wartime the position and relationship of the sexes finds its old level. Man is once more the warrior. Woman is his mate, his home-maker, his solace. Woman expresses this attitude in her clothes and hair fashions, as she is doing today.[100]

But this sharp gender differentiation was increasingly difficult to maintain as the war progressed, even as more effort was expended to maintain it.

As more and more women were called up to work in factories, women workers were encouraged to pay attention to their physical appearance. Constance Waller wrote a letter published in the feminist-leaning newspaper *Time and Tide* respond-ing to an article and earlier correspondence about the problem of head lice in the long hair worn by women in the ATS. She made a 'suggestion in the form of a parallel'.

Early in the war half a dozen girls from London went to work in a Midlands munitions factory . . . The factory workers didn't care how they looked while they were at work. They wore down-at-heel shoes, shabby old clothes and their hair either rat-tailed or full of curling pins ready for the evening's metamorphosis. The London girls had been mannequins and photographic models. They arrived at the factory in well-cut slacks and sweaters, beau-tifully shod, coiffured and made up . . . By the end of a fortnight the whole factory had smartened up—men as well as women. The quality and smartness of their work improved in proportion.[101]

As this quote suggests, the discourse on wartime glamour was inscribed by the lan-guage of class—a language which positioned elite women as the 'social mothers' of working-class women by stressing cleanliness and orderliness. As Pat Kirkham has suggested, the 'wide-spread emphasis on smartness, neatness and cleanliness dur-ing the war . . . can be viewed as part of a much longer and complex process of the "improvement" of working-class appearances'.[102] Waller's letter partakes of the idea that 'smartness' was associated with improved behaviour as glamour could be a tool to raise productivity.

The link between increasing production and women's physical appearance was a

---

[100] *Sunday Pictorial*, 3 Mar. 1940, 13.   [101] *Time and Tide*, 14 Mar. 1942, 215.
[102] Kirkham, 'Fashioning the Feminine', 156.

major theme in a two-page feature article written by Norah Alexander for the *Sunday Pictorial* in August of 1943. A picture of the 'vital, red headed revue star, Zoe Gail', posing pin-up fashion in a bathing suit appeared on the left-hand page of the two-page spread along with her beauty tips. The article itself stressed how important it was that women look their best while working in a factory, and featured the story of how beauty experts transformed Elsie Forrest, a machine operator in a factory 'not far from London'. She was described as a 'typical war-factory girl' who 'looked tired, grimy and rather cross'. The newspaper arranged for her to be given a beauty treatment in a 'famous West End shop'.

The right-hand page of the article displayed Elsie's before and after pictures. Alexander reported that Elsie 'took a day off from her factory—with the management's full blessing and consent'. To emphasize the fact that despite Government's all-out, nationwide effort to increase production, the management agreed to giving Elsie a day off, Alexander wrote:

I'd like you to read those last seven words again, please because they alone will help to prove my point. People in charge of factories can't afford to indulge in gestures like that just for sentiment. They gave Elsie a whole day off from war-work because THEY KNEW what I've been telling you for months. A girl who looks good works well. Her appearance has an important bearing on production every time—quite apart from the obvious deduction that the owner of a tidy face will have a tidy pair of hands and mind.[103]

As these examples suggest, glamour, beauty, clothes, and personal appearance were being used strategically to recruit women into factories, to boost productivity by raising morale, and to promote orderliness. What sense are we to make of these uses of glamour?

They suggest that being physically attractive and focusing on self-adornment were necessary preoccupations for women even in wartime. Such deployments of glamour contributed to the construction of what I will call 'sexualized femininity'. Sexualized femininity was a crucial component in the construction of gender difference, under threat by the movement of women away from their families and into work and service that previously had been the preserve of men, even if those movements were 'just for the duration'. The stress on glamour, however, emphasized caring for the self by attending to one's body—a vision which, at least on its face, contrasted with the demand for selflessness and stoicism. Pushed too vigorously, the vision of the glamorous woman conflicted with the impetus to austerity. Home-front films depicted glamorous women as causing consternation to film characters, as Antonia Lant has argued.[104] Glamorous women also were depicted

---

[103] *Sunday Pictorial*, 22 Aug. 1943, 14–15.

[104] Lant, 'Prologue: Mobile Femininity', 22–4. Her discussion of the contradictory status of feminine glamour is very insightful (see pp. 22–8).

as potentially dangerous to the nation as I suggested earlier and as illustrated in Plate 7.

Although riddled with contradictions, the discourse fabricated caring for the self as a national duty. Thus, sexualized femininity, with its focus on the female body, was marshalled to make acceptable the 'gender-bending' obligations of citizenship for women. Gender difference was so marked upon the body that it would be visible in spite of such masculine attire as uniforms and overalls.

This deployment had the following interpretive possibilities. First, it reinforced the idea that femininity for women was fundamentally dependent upon physical appearance. Second, it might well convince women that they could retain their feminine good looks AND be competent workers and professionals. Doing work that formerly had been done by men or exploiting new work and civic opportunities would not make them 'mannish'; women might continue to be feminine even as the gender order was being transformed in profound ways. Furthermore, if taken too far, sexualized femininity might become 'libidinal femininity'—the 'other' to good citizenship as discussed in Chapter 3. Libidinal femininity endangered the fundamental core of the nation by threatening radical social transformation.

The idea that 'sexualized femininity' might jeopardize the 'traditional' gender order was not lost on some observers. Despite his reassuring remarks that the girls doing hard and dangerous work had lost none of their physical attractiveness, the author of *Eve in Overalls* expressed his concern that all was not well:

But as I left them, I could not help wondering about the future of these young things, spending their time in the hubbub of camp life . . . freed from all normal restraint. And I thought of my grandmother, a charming and tender wraith! 'Where, oh where, Grandmama, are your jars of preserves and your press full of scented linen?'

While these 'Eves' still retained their physical attractiveness, the author expressed his fear that *maternal* femininity might be sacrificed as a result of the war and its loosening of the constraints on women.[105] Thus, the very attempts to picture women at war as being glamorous and marriageable, as exemplifying sexualized femininity, could also reinforce anxieties that the equally traditional version of mature femininity constructed around motherhood and family would not survive the war.

In addition to insisting that women engage in beauty practices, as a number of scholars have suggested, wartime cultural representations associated women and

---

[105] The same sentiments were expressed in an article contrasting Land Girls who used cosmetics and 'wears breeches on a figure that shows them off to an advantage not common in country working clothes', and a 'womanly woman', a widowed mother of eight children who supported herself by being a farmworker. See J. R. Allan, 'Immemorial Land Girl, "The Merry Widow"', *Glasgow Herald*, 25 May 1940, 3.

home, femininity and maternity with boring regularity.[106] As Jenny Hartley has astutely observed, the war made home visible.[107] The iconic value of 'home', as she has noted, was broadcast by the BBC's radio programme 'The Home Front', and it was advertised in its 'Home Service', which began broadcasting three days prior to the declaration of war.[108] Early in the war people were told of women's significance to the home on the home front. Throughout the war women were reminded that their primary roles were as mothers and wives, and at war's end, there was an intensified focus on women as mothers and housewives and on what they would want in their future homes.

Although the home front was peopled by men as well as women—men too old or too young to be called up for duty and young men in reserved occupations doing essential work—women symbolically represented the 'home front'. In early June 1940 *Sunday Pictorial* featured a two-page spread, 'When a Man Goes Away to the War'. 'As Britain's war machine swings into top gear, the women step up to take their places in the Second Line. While the men are away they are keeping the home front going'.[109] Although the article featured stories about four women who were employed in wartime work while their husbands were away, it emphasized that women were responsible for the 'second line', just as they were ordinarily responsible for their homes. The text of the article began, 'Britain's second line of defence is your house, my house, and the house next door. As the call-up is speeded more and more women are being left behind to hold that second line of defence.'[110] And it ended, 'four women of the home front, cheerful, capable, energetic and courageous. There will never be a break though on Britain's Second Line.'[111] Regardless of what else women might do during wartime, they were almost universally understood to be wives and mothers first. And their service as wives and mothers was rearticulated as a contribution to the nation.

Sunday Pictorial emphasized women's fundamental place as companions to their husbands and the mothers of the next generation by printing what was purported to be the 'private diary of a wartime bride', providing a month-by-month account of the bride's first year of marriage. Written as a melodrama, the newly married woman records how her desire for excitement and friendship led eventually to her being 'propositioned' by her boss, the subsequent loss of her job, and the near break-up of her marriage. But on her first anniversary she was redeemed,

---

[106] See e.g. Lucy Noakes, *War and the British: Gender, Memory and National Identity* (London: I. B. Tauris, 1998), 51, 71–2.

[107] Jenny Hartley, *Millions Like Us: British Women's Fiction of the Second World War* (London: Virago Press, 1997), 54.

[108] Ibid. See also Antonia Lant's discussion of the iconic value of 'home' as actual homes were disintegrating in her 'Prologue', 15–17.

[109] *Sunday Pictorial*, 8 June 1940, 10–11.   [110] Ibid. 10.   [111] Ibid. 11.

I wanted a sign—and I got it. The baby that's coming to us in seven months' time was the guiding light that pointed my way. I knew then that one can serve one's country and oneself just as well, if not better, by being a wife and mother as by driving an army lorry.[112]

The idea that a woman's obligation to her family was also an obligation to the nation was a frequently rehearsed theme that reinforced the conception that women's 'true' position was in the private sphere of the household performing their roles as mothers.

Pro-natalism continued unrelentingly throughout the war years culminating in the Royal Commission on Population which was formed in 1943 by the Churchill Government in response to a motion signed by almost ninety MPs who feared a further decline in the population.[113] Although the birth rate actually rose during the war, at the time there was enormous apprehension that Great Britain, because it was not growing in size, would lose its place as a world power and would not have the labour supply necessary for post-war reconstruction.

Numerous articles in the press appeared over the course of the war that urged childless married women to have babies. One pro-natalist advocate was Mrs Rose Buchner, whose series of articles on the rewards of motherhood and women's obligations to be mothers was published in *Sunday Pictorial*. Even in the post-Dunkirk months of the Blitz, Mrs Buchner wrote articles promoting childbearing, authenticating her advice by referring to her own life experience. In December 1940 she 'confessed' that she had waited a long time before beginning her family, but that eventually she came to realize her 'selfish ignorance' when she 'discovered the magic of keeping a home; the thrill of eating one's own apple-pie'.[114] Drawing on the language of 'patriotic involvement', Buchner, identified as 'mother of three', posed a 'Challenge to Selfish Wives'. She wrote, 'If a man is worth his salt he wants children of his own, but he needs a partner who will give him those children—not a woman who will shirk her duty.'[115] The article went on to blame women for the decline in the birth rate because of their selfishness, arguing that 'men are too chivalrous to demand their rights from their businesslike wives'.[116]

What did these conflicting and oftentimes contradictory constructions of wartime womanhood say about how the nation was imagined as a community? They suggest that the national community was envisioned as a family, just as George Orwell had proposed. It was a family with a gendered structure of authority relations, and a sexual division of labour. As Anne McClintock has noted, 'the family' as

[112] *Sunday Pictorial*, 9 Mar. 1941, 11.
[113] On pro-natalism in this period, see Denise Riley, ' "The Free Mothers": Pronatalism and Working Women in Industry at the End of the Last War in Britain', *History Workshop Journal*, 11 (1981), 59–118 and Denise Riley, *War in the Nursery: Theories of the Child and Mother* (London: Virago, 1983).
[114] Rose Buchner, 'I Must Confess', *Sunday Pictorial*, 1 Dec. 1940, 8.
[115] Rose Buchner, '—And Here's a Challenge to Selfish Wives', *Sunday Pictorial*, 23 Feb. 1941, 19.
[116] Ibid.

a figure of speech is 'indispensable . . . for sanctioning social hierarchy within a putative organic unity of interests'.[117] The British national family was one in which a sharply constrained but clearly evident sexualized femininity was crucial to its formation and maintenance, and it was one that assigned to adult women the role of securing and shoring up the home(front). Home and family powerfully symbolized stability and safety. In spite of the fact that there was much made by Ministry of Information publicity about the crucial importance of home front morale in the face of nightly bombing when the home front became a front line of battle, the home front was seen as a necessary but secondary space. Generally, women were only acceptable in positions of danger in which, like children, they were victims. They were tolerable in roles that required them to be more proactive in coping with combat when they were in jobs like nursing that were clearly and unquestioningly identified with femininity.

But while these may have been the dominant conceptions of the nation-as-family at war and women's roles within it, as I have suggested, the discourse was riddled with ambiguity, opening up interpretive possibilities that undercut its dominant message. These ambiguities and instabilities were evident as well in public discussions about the future.

The symbolic equation of home and family with stability and order suggests why there was so much attention to femininity and the roles of women during the war.[118] Not surprisingly, as we already have seen, there was significant apprehension during the war years that the family, and especially women's place in and commitment to it, would be altered as a consequence of the war. The question of whether or not women actually were changed by the war also has been the topic of lively scholarly debate since the war. The war years themselves produced a variegated view of whether or not there was or would be a transformation in women's consciousness and position.

Margaret Goldsmith, the author of historical biographies as well as other popular literature, wrote during the war that there has been a 'revolution in the position of women in England since the outbreak of war . . . and their great contribution to the war effort has accelerated this change in their relationship to the community'.[119] Acknowledging that many women and men considered these changes a 'passing phase', she commented that this was 'wishful thinking by those who hate change and

---

[117] Anne McClintock, *Imperial Leather: Race, Gender and Sexuality in the Colonial Context* (New York and London: Routledge, 1995), 45.

[118] On the significance of a rhetoric of domesticity during the war, see Margaret Allen, 'The Domestic Ideal and the Mobilization of Woman Power', *Women's Studies International Forum*, 6 (1983), 401–12. The concern that women return to domesticity after the war also was articulated in US propaganda, see Leila Rupp, *Mobilizing Women for War* (Princeton: Princeton University Press, 1978) and Maureen Honey, *Creating Rosie the Riveter: Class, Gender, and Propaganda during World War II* (Amherst: University of Massachusetts Press, 1984).

[119] Margaret Goldsmith, *Women and the Future* (London: Lindsay Drummond, 1946), 9.

. . . fear any changes which may affect family life'.[120] Goldsmith predicted that the women who now want to return to domesticity would find themselves restless and would experience their domestic duties as narrow.[121] For Goldsmith, then, the war would indeed leave a lasting impact on women's lives that would become increasingly evident with time.

Writing in *Woman's Own*, Norah James, convinced especially of the war's impact on married women as well as on their husbands, maintained that as the war was winding down, women needed to prepare themselves to deal with these changes. They would need to cope with changes in their husbands who had 'passed through experiences so gigantic that they are bound to have left their mark on them'.[122] Writing for a more popular audience than Goldsmith, James warned that there would likely be a 'change in the women themselves which they must learn how to control'.

Quite possibly, they have become more independent since their husbands went away. They have had to shoulder responsibilities that would not have been theirs in normal times. Some women may even have learned to enjoy the independence of salaries of their own. Giving these up may not be too easy.[123]

For James, change was something women would have to manage in their husbands and suppress in themselves.

And an article in the *International Women's News*, the newsletter of the International Alliance for Suffrage and Equal Citizenship, published in Britain and sponsored by the Women's Publicity Planning Association during the war, proposed that 'women will emerge from this war with an advance in personal status'.[124] In particular the writer suggested that women had become more independent than before the war but that a wife and mother's independence was healthy for the family unit in the long run. She warned, however, that the serviceman abroad would probably not like the idea that his wife had changed because he would have an idealized 'picture of home, wife, and family, and their priority peace aim will be to return to the physical and emotional security of their home and find it exactly as it was when they went away'.[125] In order to cope with their return she advised women to compromise. 'When men have had time to settle down, when they feel at home again, the time will come for women to bring up their new independence, capabilities, readiness for equality.'[126] Yet, the same newsletter printed an article, 'The Heritage of the Home', on how the war had produced what amounted to the disintegration of family life, with tragic consequences for children. The writer, Dorothy Paterson, extolled

[120] Ibid.   [121] Ibid. 17.

[122] Norah C. James, 'Back to Real Life', *Woman's Own*, 25 Apr. 1944, 15.

[123] Ibid.

[124] Anonymous, 'Soldier's Return', *International Women's News*, 39/5 (Feb. 1945), 54. For a discussion of the attempt by the publication and the WPPA itself to represent both 'difference feminism' and 'equal rights feminism', see Oram, 'Bombs Don't Discriminate!'.

[125] Ibid. 55.   [126] Ibid.

motherhood and argued, 'Woman's spiritual and moral significance as a worker in the home and among her young, is an enduring family bond. More will be achieved by woman in choosing this plan for living than by eager and acquisitive competition with man.'[127] These quite different positions are representative of the range of points of view about the likelihood that the war would have a long-lasting impact on women's lives and their aspirations and whether the outcome would be positive or negative.

Regardless of whether or not they were aware that they or their families might have been transfigured to some extent by the war, almost all of the reports of what women themselves at the time were saying (either to researchers or more informally) suggest that the large majority looked forward to returning home to a life of domesticity.

Mass Observation, as well as local and national newspapers, the Wartime Social Survey, and feminist publications suggested that women 'desire to return to domestic life as soon as it is reasonably possible'.[128] Of course, men too wanted to return to 'domesticity'—that is to life centred around their families and households.[129] Penny Summerfield has shown, however, that the actual figures belied the idea that everything would be the way it had been before the war for those couples in male breadwinner households. In fact, it was the minority of married and single women who did *not* want to continue in paid employment after the war. Only 36 per cent of married women and 7 per cent of single women stated unambiguously that they intended not to remain in paid work after 'the duration'.[130] The photograph in Plate 8 of London aircraft construction workers demonstrating against redundancies suggests that at least some women were quite vociferous about wanting to keep their jobs.

Yet Mass Observation's report in March 1944 supported the idea that there would not be a significant change in household arrangements by concluding, 'Both men and women agree . . . that men should be the breadwinners, and there is little sign of sex antagonism. It is on this foundation of goodwill that the future must be built.'[131] And strangely, in reporting on a conference of the Transport and General Workers' Union in Coventry held to demand the rate for the job for women in *civil-*

---

[127] Dorothy Paterson, 'The Heritage and . . . of the Home', *International Women's News*, 37/9 (July 1943), 134.

[128] See e.g. Mass Observation, 'Will the Factory Girls Want to Stay Put or Go Home?', 8 Mar. 1944, F-R 2059, Mass Observation Archive. M. M. Nutall, 'Back in Civvy Street, What do Service Women Want?', *International Women's News*, 38/1 (Oct. 1943), 5.

[129] Joanna Bourke argues that World War I soldiers had looked forward to a life of domesticity on their return from the battle fields. See her *Dismembering the Male: Men's Bodies, Britain and the Great War* (London: Reaktion Books, 1996), 162–70.

[130] See Penny Summerfield, ' "The Girl that Makes the Thing that Drills the Hole that Holds the Spring . . .": Discourses of Women and Work in the Second World War', in Gledhill and Swanson (eds.), *Nationalising Femininity*, 47–8.

[131] Mass Observation, F-R 2509, 2, 8.

8. Demonstration against redundancies,
1 November 1944.
Hulton Archive

ian life, the *Coventry Evening Telegraph* editorialized by inserting the observation that 'most women . . . look forward to the time when they can leave the factories for the home'.[132]

Given such reports, it is not surprising that a spate of programmes were offered to help prepare women to return to a life of domesticity. Rosita Forbes, a feature writer for *Woman's Own* wrote early in 1941, a time when the outcome and duration of the war were anything but certain, that women should start planning immediately for the post-war years by learning how to 'better' themselves at housekeeping. Writing prior to the call-up of women but during the period of extensive countrywide bombing, she proposed that after the war 'most of us women will be flung—out of uniform and lorries or transport planes or the drivers' seats of official cars—back into home life. But the men who fought for us will be quite justified in asking for a higher standard of housewifery.'[133] She advised women not in essential war work to take a 'self-bettering course' on housewifery.

Forbes was certainly not alone in her concern about standards of domesticity. There were numerous programmes offered for women and girls during the war to teach them the skills of home-making. The Women's Land Army offered its recruits, free of charge, training in 'Homecraft'.[134] The files of the Women's Forum, a sub-committee of the Women's Group on Public Welfare, contains a syllabus for those 'preparing themselves for home-making' dating from the spring or summer of 1945. The syllabus extolled the 'vocation of home-making, [which] for all that it has been belittled in the past, calls for a breadth of knowledge, a depth of self-discipline and a height of idealism hardly to be equaled in any other profession'.[135] The writers referred to some of the same qualities that were presumed to have been nurtured by the war in praising housewifery as a post-war occupation.

In Scotland as elsewhere in Britain local education authorities and youth social services offered classes in housewifery for girls. Members of the Education Committee of Lanarkshire lamented the fact that of a total of 5,006 eligible girls only 147 were attending cookery classes and 90 were in sick nursing classes, while 940 attended classes in country and ballroom dancing. Mrs Shaw who presented the figures said 'that as educationists they must have some thought for the homes of the future and asked if pressure could not be brought to bear on these young women 'for the sake of the new world that is promised to us'.[136]

---

[132] *Coventry Evening Telegraph*, 4 Aug. 1943, 4.

[133] Rosita Forbes, 'Be a Success', *Woman's Own*, 1 Feb. 1941, 23.

[134] Minutes of the Buckingham County Committee of the Women's Land Army, 5 Feb. 1944. MAF 59/32, at the Public Records Office.

[135] WF/B 11, 1942–46. At the Fawcett Library—now the Women's Library, London Guildhall University.

[136] *Glasgow Herald*, 8 Feb. 1945, 2.

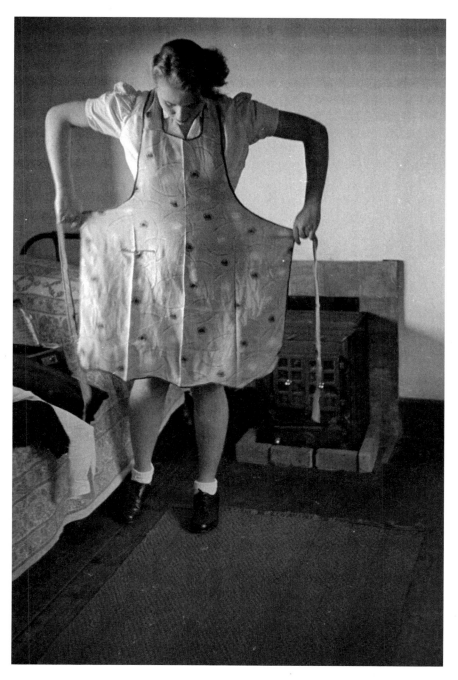

9. *Picture Post* photograph showing women on a
home training course, 8 December 1945.
Hulton Archive

This fervent focus on domesticity repositioned women as housewives and mothers, but it also provoked discussion about social and political reform that could potentially have changed what it meant to be a wife and mother. The war years saw a renaissance of active interest on the part of women's groups in improving the status of the housewife and mother.

Drawing upon the sentiments of those who were concerned that women's domestic labours would be short-changed in favour of war work and of those who were anxious to make sure that women war workers and service personnel return to the home after the war was over, the Women's Institutes' publication *Home and Country*, for example, published an essay by Renee Haynes. She gave it the title 'The Nation's Cinderella' and dealt with women 'doing their own traditional and specific job of running a household and bringing up a family'.[137] She said that one strand of feminism had been to assert that such women 'should be considered as important, as responsible and as much worthy of respect as women doing the kind of job that can be done equally well by either sex; and that their work is just as vital as the other kind, if not more so'.[138] She then spelled out how much in this area remains to be done: 'the married woman working in her own house at "unpaid domestic labour" tends to be the national Cinderella'. Haynes discussed the range of areas in which wives who work at home are the 'national Cinderellas'. She proposed that housewives and mothers provide free of charge what others do as paid work and used as an example the household labour involved in housing evacuees. Her statement presaged what in the 1970s would be at the centre of the 'domestic labour debate' among marxist and socialist feminists.

Concern about women's rights as mothers and wives, as well as about the status of motherhood, motivated the activities of the Married Women's Association, known as the 'housewives' trade union'. Edith Summerskill, MP, was president of the association which gave evidence to the Beveridge Committee—the 'Inter-departmental Committee on Social Reconstruction'. The Association protested the fact that legally any money housewives saved from their housekeeping allowance belonged not to them, but to their husbands, and that wives had no insurance equivalent to unemployment insurance or any right to a pension. The Association presented a seven-point charter to the Committee to redress these inequalities and to elevate the status of the housewife to that of a worker rather than a dependant.[139] As the Honourable Secretary of the Association put it in a letter to newspapers,

We women must take a far more intelligent interest in matters of international relationships, education, financial systems, house planning & etc., not working against men but with them—sharing responsibilities, helping to solve problems as they arise, insisting on our voic-

---

[137] *Home and Country*, 24/7 (July 1942), 115.   [138] Ibid.
[139] *Coventry Evening Telegraph*, 3 Oct. 1942, 3.

144

es being heard and our wishes attended to in matters which concern our own lives and the lives of our children. In most things that we do we must have an equal amount of power and responsibility, and must be capable of making right use of both.[140]

Thus, the emphasis on domesticity and motherhood for women in the post-war years was accompanied by a resurgence of activism on behalf of women's rights as wives and mothers.

Supporting the idea that women would/should return to domesticity, there were wide-ranging discussions about the homes of the future. The return to domesticity was re-articulated during the war years as a move into modernity via household technology. Advertisements prepared women to be household consumers by emphasizing technological efficiency and linked household technology with scientific progress made during wartime. For example, in August 1944 the Prestcold Refrigeration Company published an advertisement proclaiming that 'Refrigeration will gain from Experience in War'. The fine print in the advertisement claimed that air photography, vital to the war effort, 'owes much to Prestcold Refrigeration'. And in bold the company proudly proclaimed, 'Experience gained in aerial warfare will be used by Prestcold engineers to the great benefit of the kitchen of the future when their experience will enable them to take the lead in making refrigerators at low cost for every class of home.'[141] Women were told that they would need to learn how to use the technology of the 'new domestic science as against the old "housework"'.[142] A newspaper article discussing the new science suggested that 'every bride-to-be should be compelled to obtain a certificate of domestic science proficiency'.[143]

At a conference on 'The Work and Status of the Housewife', sponsored by the Standing Committee of Working Women's Organisations, Mrs Marthe Louis Levy, whose talk was published in the May 1943 issue of *Labour Woman*, discussed the necessity for the 'rationalisation of housework'.[144] She was particularly concerned that the technology to lighten household work be made available to working-class women and suggested the possibility of buying cooperatives.

Levy's conception of how to rationalize housework involved more than electrical and mechanical gadgetry. She argued that 'a true rationalisation of housework will only be attained by as wide an extension as possible of collective services and specialisation of tasks'. Espousing socialist ideas and linking them to the wartime ideals of community, Levy argued that buying cooperatives would only be 'the cells out of which will grow a collective society'.[145]

Her image of the future for women involved collectivizing household services in

---

[140] Letter by (Mrs) Howard Sully published in *Western Mail and South Wales News*, 3 Apr. 1944, 3.
[141] *Glasgow Herald*, 3 Aug. 1944, 3.   [142] *Coventry Evening Telegraph*, 1 May 1943, 3.
[143] Ibid.
[144] Marthe Louis Levy, 'Rationalisation of Housework', *Labour Woman*, May 1943, 50.
[145] Ibid. 51.

the interests of freeing women to be involved in a broad range of extra-household activities.

In other words is it a trade in itself to be a married woman? At present with the comfortless houses it is one, and a hard and little appreciated one at that. But if we employ ourselves in making the task lighter . . . by collective service—is it in order that married women may spend their time in gossip? No, as household duties are simplified by rationalisation, woman will become available for other social tasks: salaried industrial, agricultural or professional work; salaried work in collective domestic services; perhaps also, simply, for bringing up her children. It will also be for cultivating their minds, taking an active part in the organisation of the country, in the distribution of goods.[146]

This vision of the future for women was a socialist modernity rather than a capitalist one. But even those who did not advocate collectivizing household services or who were opposed to the state or community taking on any of the 'traditional' functions of the mother and wife in peacetime were concerned about women's civic participation in the future.

For example, the Press Association lobby correspondent, according to the *Coventry Evening Telegraph* hypothesized in the spring of 1943 that women who experienced communal life in the service, Land Army, or factory may undergo a psychological shift in outlook. The correspondent suggested that the 'new wife . . . will be much less house-tied, much more anxious to play her part in social and civic activities, opposed to domestic drudgery, in favour, through war experience, of using a central restaurant attached to the estate or block of flats in which she lives, and even requiring such conveniences as a bar'.[147]

Other observers, however, were far less sanguine about the possibility that women would be more concerned with social and community affairs in the future than they had been prior to the war. M. M. Nutall, for example, argued that women wanted to return to the intimacy of their private domestic dwellings because they had had enough of community life in the war.

That this attitude is prevalent among all branches of the Services is an undoubted fact; and it is not only a mood of reaction against the communal existence that Service life entails, but an urgent feminine need . . . For a woman to sink her individuality in a common pool, and to be unable to express her personality either through her home, her clothes, or her intimate personal interests, is to deprive herself of an essential requisite to her natural development.[148]

She went on to state that very few servicewomen were interested in and aware of the wider issues of politics—including the kinds of houses and cities that would be available after the war. Thus, even a return to domesticity had its costs.

Prior to the war the lack of civic engagement by housewives had been a major concern of the Women's Institutes and the Townswomen's Guilds, who saw as their

---

[146] Marthe Louis Levy, 'Rationalisation of Housework', *Labour Woman*, May 1943, 50.
[147] *Coventry Evening Telegraph*, 1 May 1943, 3.   [148] Nutall, 'Back in Civvy Street', 5

missions, to provide housewives and mothers with education for citizenship and to widen their horizons through cultural and social activities. Similarly M. M. Nutall maintained that through education women might learn to 'direct their thoughts through and beyond their domestic interests to encompass such issues as housing, town planning, education and health, all well within the scope of their knowledge and imagination'.[149]

Some commentators, then, worried that women's return to domesticity spelled the end of women's active citizenship. Still others, and *Woman's Own* writer Norah James was one, believed that women were changed by the war to have a wider social consciousness. At the same time, James maintained, 'for those who have understood the comradeship of a community life, it is essential, if the family is to retain its importance—and it must—that a new community life must be developed from the family unit'.[150]

These myriad reflections on women's post-war future were infused with the nagging question of how the war would change women. The most prevalent opinion was that women would 'return' to home and motherhood. But this prediction also occasioned commentary suggesting that the boundaries around and meanings of domesticity itself would be transformed, raising once again the possibility that the imagined pre-war stable gender order could not be reconstructed.

Additionally, although much of the discussion about women in the post-war world focused on domesticity as contrasted with formal employment, there was also attention given to the issue of post-war economic opportunities for women. *Woman's Own* put it this way, 'for many, Mr. Right may never turn up. In any case, a woman has an equal right to a job as a man.'[151] As Antonia Fugger wrote in the feminist *Catholic Citizen*, the newsletter of the former Catholic women's suffrage society, the St Joan's Social and Political Alliance:

Most of the nations of the Continent have a larger female than male population even in peace-time. The last war destroyed millions of male lives, thus depriving large numbers of women of all chance of marriage and family . . . After this war there will again probably be insufficient men to husband every woman. And then what will those suggest who claim marriage and motherhood as the only true vocation for women? Will they suggest polygamy, perhaps?[152]

She both stressed that women's labour urgently will be needed for reconstruction and raised the possibility of there being unhappy consequences for the country if 'woman's faculties, hopes and ambitions . . . continue to be thwarted'.[153]

In Scotland, the need for women's labour to continue in engineering in the post-war years was the subject of an analysis by the *Glasgow Herald* in the winter of 1944.

---

[149] Ibid. 6.   [150] Norah C. James, 'Back to Real Life', *Woman's Own*, 24 Mar. 1944, 15.
[151] *Woman's Own*, 22 Sept. 1944, 7.
[152] Antonia Fugger, 'Women and Society', *Catholic Citizen*, 28/3 (15 Mar. 1942), 1.   [153] Ibid.

The 'special correspondent' who wrote the article suggested that it was now accepted that women had a niche in engineering and they were 'regarded as an asset for the availability of suitable women's work in the mass production of thousands of small parts is one of the factors in securing the hoped-for establishment of these newer industries in Scotland. To this extent women would be helping to provide new work for men.'[154] The correspondent indicated that many engineering operations had been simplified so that they can be done by women or other previously unskilled labour. 'Women have . . . added their own qualities of dexterity and capacity for application to repetitive work.'[155] The primary thrust of the article was to argue that because of the modernizing of industrial methods and personnel management, women would play a greater part than before the war in industrializing Scotland and would 'add to, and not detract from, the amenities and best features of Scottish life'. As long as women did not threaten men's jobs, and were a 'draw' for industry from the South, they would be welcome as workers.

Clearly, hostility towards women doing 'men's work' was not dissipated by the war. Indeed, there was a generally recognized presumption that because men were understood to be family breadwinners by 'nature', they should have jobs in preference to women, who were considered to be dependants like children.[156] As the 'Special Correspondent' for the *Glasgow Herald* put it,

the position of men in . . . industry must be safeguarded, and the problem will be that of determining where 'women's work' ends and 'men's work' begins. Certain processes have been recognised all along as being women's work, but the line of demarcation has tended to become difficult to define at certain stages.[157]

And the fear of a 'sex war' to follow with the peace remained in the minds of the public throughout World War II.[158]

Hoping to avoid such conflict as well as other dire possibilities, an editorial in the *Western Mail and South Wales News*, published in Cardiff, trusted that the pre-war gender order would re-emerge when the war was over. The editorial was written in response to the BFBPW chairwoman's statement to a House of Commons Committee that 'women engaged in professional occupations in Britain exceeded the number of men by 35,930'.[159] Not realizing that this 'excess' was likely due to the expansion of the 'women's professions' of social work, nursing, etc., the writer proposed that 'men who were for so long in sole occupation of these sheltered fields of

---

[154] *Glasgow Herald*, 29 Feb. 1944, 2.   [155] Ibid.

[156] See the quotation from Mass Observation cited above. And, in an editorial in the *Glasgow Herald*, the writer linked the issue of equal pay for men and women (and the presumption that men and women would be paid a 'bachelor's wage' if there was pay equality) to the argument that 'men have families to feed'. See *Glasgow Herald*, 20 Apr. 1944, 4.

[157] 'Women's Place in Industry', 2.

[158] For the post–World War I anxieties about women and gender, see Kent, *Making Peace*.

[159] *Western Mail and South Wales News*, 9 Jan. 1943, 2.

activity have generously opened the gates so wide for women as to be submerged into a minority!'[160] The editorial then alarmingly informed readers that the displacement of men from such jobs in the inter-war period in countries like India, Germany, and Italy because of the worldwide depression, resulted in 'a reservoir of intellectual energy being perverted into revolutionary ends'. Such post-war problems may be solved in Britain after this war, the editorial writer suggested, if 'we continue to regard the home as the basis of our society and strive to consolidate that basis—the natural division of labour and services as between the sexes'.[161] But feminist activists, revived by the patriotic fervour of the war, were determined to see an eventual transformation in that 'natural' division of labour as it affected women as British citizens.

In conclusion, although the nation was imagined as a community of equally sacrificing citizens, and Britishness was understood as a singular enduring identity, this chapter has shown that women's status, their activities of citizenship, and wartime participation blurred the seamlessness of this picture. While in the abstract the idea of the nation could be elaborated so as to encompass all who were 'pulling their weight' by actively supporting the nation in its years of trial, when it was peopled with female figures it lost its coherence. The very category 'woman' in the context of the 'People's War' was full of contradictions. Regardless of the nature of her patriotic contribution or how she enacted femininity, she was problematic. Gender difference was both essential to the nation and disruptive of its imagined unity.

I have argued that citizenship had contradictory and contested meanings for women during World War II. Citizenship was not a single, unitary status, relationship, or practice. It was, rather, a complex of contested rights, contradictory gendered duties, and ideals of civic virtue. Regardless of women's overt contributions to the war effort, they could be accused of lacking good citizenship if they did not demonstrate feminine virtue by being sexually 'responsible' and by being good mothers. Fulfilling the obligations of citizenship by undertaking certain kinds of wartime service actually exposed young women to the charge of lacking the essential virtues of citizenship, particularly if they were away from home and family. Many of the opportunities for women to fulfil their obligations as wartime citizens were highly gendered. But, as the gender differentiation of wartime service began to break down with the need for an expanding labour supply, the movement of women into jobs and activities formerly associated exclusively with men laid bare the fact that women lacked civil and social rights equal to men's. Finally, the pressure for women to have children as a national duty opened an emotionally powerful avenue for them to claim particular social rights. And it contributed to the demands for social security that were central to the widespread desire for a new Britain to emerge from post-war reconstruction.

[160] Ibid.   [161] Ibid.

I have also considered how wartime femininity was constructed in popular discourses. I suggested that pervasive depictions of British womanhood during the war stressed two often contradictory characteristics. Women were to retain their traditional commitment to motherhood while exhibiting a carefully modulated form of sexualized femininity. But the media emphasis on glamour, when coupled with the possibility that women could become the equal of men in the public sphere, could threaten the coherence of the nation constructed on a foundation of gender difference. Women could remain female while assuming a public status equal to that of men. The very requirement that women take up new responsibilities, frequently removing them from the 'secure' boundaries of family life, provoked continual anxiety that women and family life thereby would be changed. As Jenny Hartley has noted, 'an icon of the war, the home represented what must be defended and protected; but at the same time it was changing its constituent elements and altering its behaviour patterns.'[162]

If women and family life represented stability—an unmovable anchor for the nation in the raging storm of war—somehow they were to remain unchanged as a new Britain was formed in its aftermath. The imperatives of civic virtue—the moral aspects of female citizenship—coincided with the wartime understanding of what it meant to be a woman. These imperatives, restrained sexualized femininity and commitment to motherhood, were to be the materials out of which that anchor was fashioned. These models of femininity, however, were unstable. Pushed too far in one direction, women manifesting sexualized femininity could become licentious painted ladies—they would exhibit libidinal femininity that marked women as bad citizens. If the commitment to domesticity became too pronounced, women failed to practise the arts of citizenship. But the requirements of citizenship also were contradictory, and as these contradictions were articulated in wartime practices, the imagined unity of the nation envisaged as a familial community that would last into the peace was threatened even as it was proclaimed to be everlasting.

[162] Hartley, *Millions Like Us*, 54.

5

Temperate Heroes

MASCULINITY ON THE HOME FRONT

In contrast to the persistent public expressions of anxiety about femininity and how women might change as a result of their wartime experiences, only rarely was 'manliness' or 'manhood'—masculinity, as such—the focus of debate and scrutiny. Public attention was directed to the cultural meanings of manhood only when something happened that challenged deeply held and taken-for-granted ideas about male–female differences.[1]

As sociologist R. W. Connell has proposed, masculinity is a hegemonic project by which he means that it is constructed through cultural practices that legitimate men's power vis-à-vis women in the gender order.[2] It is through these cultural practices that individuals come to identify themselves and others as members of the social category 'men'; this involves an ideology about manhood or manliness embodying a historically shifting field of dominant or preferred meanings that creates the appearance that its performance and perquisites are 'natural'.[3]

The relative invisibility of masculinity is a central feature of this cultural project. Masculinity is invisible for three reasons. In the first place, masculinity represents symbolic authority in a system of gendered cultural meanings in which mascu-

---

[1] For the difficulty in studying masculinity, see David H. J. Morgan, *Discovering Men* (London and New York: Routledge, 1992), esp. chaps. 2 and 3. For a discussion of civilian masculinities in World War II, see Penny Summerfield, *Reconstructing Women's Wartime Lives: Discourse and Subjectivity in Oral Histories of the Second World War* (Manchester: Manchester University Press, 1998), chap. 4.

[2] R. W. Connell, *Masculinities* (Berkeley and Los Angeles: University of California Press, 1995), esp. 71–81.

[3] I am adopting Gail Bederman's definition of gender as an ideological process 'whereby concrete individuals are constituted as members of a preexisting social category—as men or as women'. (*Manliness & Civilization: A Cultural History of Gender and Race in the United States, 1880–1917* (Chicago and London: University of Chicago Press, 1995, 71). The term 'dominant and preferred meanings' is from Stuart Hall's conceptualization of a hegemonic viewpoint as a discursive domain of '*dominant* or *preferred meanings*'. (Stuart Hall, 'Encoding, Decoding', in Simon During (ed.), *The Cultural Studies Reader* (London: Routledge, 1993), 90–103, esp. 98–102).

linity is understood as 'not femininity'.[4] It is an unmarked category; it is defined, that is, by what it is not.

Secondly, the meanings of masculinity—the ideals of manhood—are those that define personhood in the abstract. Thus, the question of what it meant to be a good person or a good human being at a particular moment in modern European history was answered with a list of characteristics associated with the ideals of masculinity. And, as we shall see in this chapter, there was a rough equivalence between the strictures of wartime masculinity and the World War II constructions of Englishness and Britishness. 'Good citizenship' and masculinity were virtually the mirror images of one another. Masculinity, in other words, was normative personhood.

Finally because masculinity is a hegemonic project, the power of men as men and the association between ideal masculinity and exemplary personhood are simply perceived in a society as 'normal' or as common sense. For example, since the Enlightenment, rationality has been a supreme virtue but its association with masculinity in contrast to femininity generally goes unnoticed. Further as Connell proposes, 'Given that heterosexual men socially selected for hegemonic masculinity run the corporations and the state, the routine maintenance of these institutions will normally do the job'.[5]

An explicit politics of masculinity only emerges when men perceive a challenge to their ordinarily assumed place of authority and power. And, as I shall discuss later in this chapter, when this happens it reveals aspects of male privilege or common-sense notions of masculinity that ordinarily remain in the background.

While a politics of masculinity was infrequently overt in World War II Britain, the meanings of manliness were everywhere. Masculinity was portrayed in the iconography of workers and their work, in armed services recruitment posters and in wartime advertisements aimed at men and at women. It was evident, as well, on wartime radio, in documentary and feature films, and in novels and stories.

What was new in the 1940s was the particular multidimensional and loose configuration of attributes associated with manliness that coalesced relatively early in the war—with Dunkirk and the Blitz—informing what Angus Calder has suggested was a mythical national sensibility.[6] The specific characteristics of the exemplary man or citizen were not in themselves brand new in World War II. Some had been in existence since at least the mid-nineteenth century, and some had a much longer lineage. Others were the product of new articulations from the inter-war period that were strengthened as they became enmeshed in newer wartime discourses.[7] This chapter will suggest that hegemonic masculinity was

---

[4] See Connell, *Masculinities*, 70, for a brief discussion of this semiotic definition of masculinity.

[5] Ibid. 212.   [6] Angus Calder, *The Myth of the Blitz* (London: Jonathan Cape, 1991).

[7] This formulation draws theoretically on ideas that I developed more fully in 'Cultural Analysis and Moral Discourses: Episodes, Continuities, and Transformations', in Victoria E. Bonnell and Lynn Hunt

comprised of elements both from the inter-war construction of an 'anti-heroic' masculinity and those long associated with the soldier-hero—traits most clearly exemplified by combat soldiers. These seemingly opposed ideals depicted not only hegemonic masculinity, but also the nation—especially as it was imagined to be fighting a 'People's War'. On a more abstract or theoretical level, this chapter suggests that masculinity is a field of gender meanings, the composition of which changes historically as does the particular constellation of meanings that predominate at a given historical conjuncture. It is precisely because masculinity is a field of different meanings that may be contradictory in practice and in performance that masculinity is fragile.[8] In World War II hegemonic masculinity was unstable, not in small measure because its successful enactment, as I will show, depended upon being visibly a member of the fighting forces.

A Masculine Nation

Alison Light has argued that during the inter-war period, representations of the nation became less stereotypically masculine than they had been before World War I.[9] Home, 'the little man' and ordinariness replaced adventure in far away places, great heroes, and challenging circumstances in the construction of Englishness. If the nation, identified as bearing these characteristics, was a more domestic and feminine nation in the 1930s than the pre-war aggressive, heroic, and belligerent one, very early in World War II the virtues of a domestic, conservative, and middle-class nation were those that came to define manhood and 'good citizenship' as well. In World War II, the virility of the 'good citizen', and masculinity itself, were tempered. What accounts for such a restrained version of exemplary masculinity in World War II (restrained at least in contrast to representations of masculinity in World War I)?

If both national identity and masculinity are constructed in opposition to an 'other', there was no more 'hyper-masculine' other than the Nazis against whom to fashion nationhood and masculinity.[10] In his second Sunday Postscript the week

(eds.), *Beyond the Cultural Turn* (Berkeley and Los Angeles: University of California Press, 1999), 217–42. It also bears a close resemblance, to Graham Dawson's useful concept of 'cultural imaginary'. See Graham Dawson, *Soldier Heroes: British Adventure, Empire and the Imagining of Masculinities* (London and New York: Routledge, 1994), 50–3.

[8] Lynn Segal suggests that masculinity is 'structured through contradiction: the more it asserts itself, the more it calls itself into question' (*Slow Motion* (London: Virago, 1991), 123). For an interesting analysis of the varying performances of masculinity by Indian colonial men in London at the end of the 19th century, see Antoinette Burton, 'A "Pilgrim Reformer" at the Heart of the Empire: Behramji Malabari in Late-Victorian London', *Gender & History*, 8 (Aug. 1996), 175–96.

[9] Alison Light, *Forever England: Femininity, Literature, and Conservatism between the Wars* (London and New York: Routledge, 1991).

[10] On masculinity and Nazism, see Klaus Thelweleit, *Male Fantasies*, i and ii (Minneapolis: University of Minnesota Press, 1989).

following Dunkirk in June 1940, J. B. Priestley explicitly compared representations of the German military and the British military:

Yesterday morning I saw the Nazi film, 'Baptism of Fire,' which deals with the invasion and attempted destruction of Poland. Now this is the film that has been used as a 'bogy-man' to frighten neutrals who are about to be 'protected' by the Reich . . . What is it really like? It's the opposite of 'the Lion Has Wings'—and I mean by that, that it presents all the contrary quali-ties.[11] Our film didn't take itself too solemnly; showed our airmen as likeable human beings, cracking jokes with their wives and sweethearts. But this Nazi picture is all 'drums and trom-bones'—gloom and threats. A loud German voice bullies you through it all. There's a lot about destruction and death, and not a glimmer of humour, or fun, or ordinary human rela-tionships. It's all machines and robot stuff. The key-word throughout is 'Bomb'.[12]

These same themes were reproduced in an advertisement promoting saving by the National Savings Committee published in newspapers across the country in early February 1944, 'Time off for a Conqueror' (Plate 10). Showing a British soldier playing with a child, the legend contrasts 'Jerry' who shoots and smashes everything with 'men' who would rather 'try to talk to Ma—or mend things for the kid'.

The connection between the nation and a tempered British masculinity was evident in numerous other representations. Just as in the Priestley quote above, the following advertisement lauded British sense of humour and camaraderie as a national and masculine characteristic, one which was popularized in the wartime song lyrics that advised those having a difficult time to 'keep smiling through'. The advertisement, obviously aimed at men, was for Worthington Beer and appeared in *Picture Post* in late March 1940.

It is the custom of the English when there is serious trouble to be faced, to lift their voices in loud and rollicking song. They will command all within earshot to smile, to pack up their troubles, to give up worrying . . . it is part of the English strength to deny all fore-boding when the hour is grave. Let your smile shine out then, undimmed by worries that are not yours alone. And if the waiting be hard, seek fortitude and clear, calm thought over a Worthington—the golden brew that has nurtured generations of the yeomen of England.[13]

The accompanying illustration was of a glass of beer with a man's smiling face con-tained within it. The advertisement connected this relatively carefree attitude with a long history of English yeomen. Recommending that men seek 'clear, calm

---

[11]   *The Lion Has Wings* was the first feature-length British film of the war. It was produced by Alexan-der Korda, made expressly for its propaganda value, and released to the public on 3 Nov. 1939. For a discussion of the film's production and reception, see Anthony Aldgate and Jeffrey Richards, *Britain Can Take It: The British Cinema in the Second World War* (Oxford: Basil Blackwell, 1986), 21–5.

[12]   J. B. Priestley, ' "Postscript", Sunday, 9th June, 1940', in J. B. Priestley, *All England Listened: The Wartime Broadcasts of J. B. Priestley* (New York: Chilmark Press, 1967), 11–12.

[13]   *Picture Post*, 23 Mar. 1940, 55. The use of 'England' for nation as a problem for national unity will be discussed in Chapter 6.

10. National Savings advertisement, 'Time off for a Conqueror'. Public Record Office

Time off for a Conqueror

Now Jerry is a "Conqueror"—and mostly very cross;
He arrests 'em and he shoots 'em
                    just to show 'em who is boss.
But the British Tommy's different
                    —he can't do what Jerry did,
Instead of shooting father he goes playing with the kid.
Now Jerry smashes everything—to show he doesn't care,
He steals their poor belongings
                    —then warns them "If they dare . . ."
But the Men who beat the "Conqueror"
                    (*that's our Harry, Bert and Syd*)
They'd rather try to talk to Ma
                    —or mend things for the kid!

How can we show our gratitude

to these men? The best, the most practical
tribute we can offer them is to give them
our complete support—by saving more.
Let that be your salute to the soldier.
SAVE MORE.

Issued by the National Savings Committee

thought' referenced other presumed national and masculine characteristics such as rationality and emotional reserve that had a long history.

In a BBC broadcast in the series 'Living Opinion' in July 1942 the participants discussed the question 'What is an Englishman?'. One of the participants, a Czech national residing in London, commented:

Every country has a contribution to make, and I think the English contribution is this calmness, this levelness, this sense of being above the battle. We fall to quarreling much too easily. The Englishman has a very balanced temper and a sense of fair play which people who lose their tempers easily can't have. In a sense I think you know, that a discussion like this is very typically English.[14]

As I mentioned in Chapter 3, 'reason' had long been associated with both masculinity and good citizenship, or civic virtue. But the quintessential 'emotional reserve' of the respectable British man also has a long history, which was rearticulated in the wartime version of the 'stiff upper lip' represented by the Blitz expression and propaganda film, *London (or Britain) Can Take It.*[15] John Tosh has suggested that the 'stiff upper lip' characteristic of middle-class British men at the turn of the twentieth century, had its roots at least in part, in the Victorian dissociation of gender attributes in which 'affection and tenderness' were associated with mothers, while fathers were supposed to be 'stern and undemonstrative'.[16] He proposes that this was an outcome of the association of men and domesticity that Leonore Davidoff and Catherine Hall have so convincingly argued was forged during the early Victorian years.[17] Tosh suggests that eventually this 'splitting' produced a masculine 'flight from domesticity' expressed in imperial adventure and military heroism in the years prior to 1918.[18]

One reaction to the horrors of World War I was the 'anti-heroic mood' of the inter-war years. Alison Light maintains that in the period 1920–40 there was a distaste for and an embarrassment about the 'romantic languages of national pride' that produced a realignment of sexual identities and a redefinition of Englishness.[19] As men became more 'homely', and the private, domestic sphere became the heart

---

[14] 'What is an Englishman?' 'Living Opinion', 17 July 1942, Home Service, in Radio Talks Scripts Film T 615, p. 4, at the BBC Written Archives Centre, Caversham Park, Reading (BBC).

[15] The film *London Can Take It*, was first produced to be shown to US audiences to arouse sympathy and support for Britain. A shorter version shown within the country was retitled *Britain Can Take It*. For a discussion of the film, see Aldgate and Richards, *Britain Can Take It*, 120–2.

[16] John Tosh, 'Domesticity and Manliness', in Michael Roper and John Tosh (eds.), *Manful Assertions: Masculinities in Britain since 1800* (London and New York: Routledge, 1991), 65.

[17] Leonore Davidoff and Catherine Hall, *Family Fortunes: Men and Women of the English Middle Class, 1780–1850*, 2nd edn. (forthcoming).

[18] Tosh, "Domesticity", 65–8.

[19] Light, *Forever England*, 8. Joanna Bourke, however, seems to imply that at least in the late 1920s, in the context of industrial unrest and economic turmoil, the figure of Kitchener became emblematic of the truly masculine warrior. See *Dismembering the Male: Men's Bodies, Britain and the Great War* (London: Reaktion Books, 1996), 242–50, esp. 244.

of the nation, middle-class femininity took on what had previously been 'regarded as distinctly masculine qualities: in particular the ethics or code of self-control and a language of reticence'.[20] I agree with Light that women were expected to be emotionally reserved, and during World War II, to be good citizens by maintaining a cheerful demeanour and a 'stiff upper lip'. The well-publicized stoicism of British women in World War II, however, highlighted the manly vigour of the British nation as a whole.

'Emotional reticence' remained, I would argue, a quintessentially masculine characteristic—one that men were required to manifest, but that British women too were represented as possessing. The difference is, however, that if women did not maintain their good cheer and calm reserve they were not being good citizens; they were being silly girls or foolish women. In contrast, if a man lost control of his emotions, he was not being manly. Such a distinction was expressed graphically by the popular journalist and writer, Beverley Nichols:

How many grown men, achieving heroism . . . realise that their toughness and their endurance stretch back . . . back into the mists of childhood, when they ran crying to mother with a cut finger and she said . . . 'Brave little boys don't cry!' How many women keeping a stiff upper lip during . . . danger and difficulty, carrying on calmly during a raid when they feel much more like bursting into tears, realise that their behaviour was determined for them long ago by a quiet voice saying, during some childish tantrum, 'That's not a pretty face to make, darling . . . and if the wind were to change it might stay like that.'[21]

This difference also was vividly expressed in a wartime memoir of a boy entitled 'Growing Up in Wartime London'. John Sweetland wrote his memoir in the summer of 1945 when he was 18 on the basis of notes and diaries he had written throughout the war. He repeatedly described his mother as being 'terrified' during the Blitz, while he worked to calm his own fears by listening to classical music and reading *Picture Post*.[22] He wrote that in 1942 his mother was required to register and participate in civil defence, but that her 'debut was not a success, and to the amusement of father', she found a job as far as possible from civil defence or factory work.[23] Sweetland's description of the difference between his mother's reaction and his own to the Blitz suggests how significant the national 'stiff upper lip' was to being a man. And his patronizing depiction of his mother's discomfort with war work and the amusement of his father with whom Sweetland clearly identifies underscore the connections between masculine subjectivity and good wartime citizenship.

Additionally, as Light suggests, the anti-heroic mood of the post–World War I era, was also the source of the construction of the 'little men' as representatives of

---

[20] Light, *Forever England*, 210.

[21] Beverley Nichols, 'Is Your Child Your Own or the State's?', *Sunday Chronicle*, 23 Mar. 1941, 2.

[22] John L. Sweetland, 'Growing Up in Wartime London, 1939–45'. 97/21/1, at the Imperial War Museum.

[23] Ibid. 21.

the British nation, those who in World War II were to become the 'ordinary people' of the home front.[24] Such 'little men' were depicted on a BBC radio programme, part of the 'Living Opinion' discussion series, by the participants, identified as 'working men', who discussed the topic 'What is a Good Man?'. One of them proposed to the others:

We've all been giving examples of men we've admired . . . all the men we've singled out have been quiet men. I won't say soft, but quiet, stay-at-home, good, ideal husbands, good neighbours, but not forceful and not leaders. It isn't as if we hadn't been fighters ourselves. I used to fancy myself, in my younger days with the gloves a bit, and so did Walt, and Harry started life taking on all comers—there's nothing wrong in a fight, is there?[25]

One of the others, Walt, answered him, 'No, there's nowt at all.' Walt went on to talk about a fighter who is a church-goer, 'and I don't think he drinks, he enjoys life, he doesn't knock people about unnecessary'.[26] And another participant, Harry, defended the idea that a man who drank could still be a good man, and then reminded the others 'some people say . . . our "live and let live" and our staying at home, has let the Japs and the Germans go abroad and make themselves strong. Is it because we've lost a sense of the goodness we'd be prepared to impose on the world?'[27] After some discussion the men agreed that they should not be imposing by force, but rather by influence, 'forceful influence'. One of them illustrated this idea by describing a football centre-half who used to say,' "Come on, lads, come on lads", and they used to get their final goal from his forceful influence'.[28]

This exchange, constructed by the BBC as the 'voice of the people', dramatizes how the home-loving, quiet reticence, which as Light suggests was a conservative and middle-class vision, could be rearticulated under the new wartime circumstance. It became a masculine construction, and by bringing into the discussion the distinctively masculine sports of boxing and football, one with which working-class men might identify. This vision, as it was reclaimed for masculinity, contributed to how 'the people' in the People's War were imagined. It could be fitted to the wartime mood that opposed Chamberlainite appeasement and non-involvement by the participants' discussion of 'forceful influence'.

Echoing the construction of the new anti-heroic masculine national identity, the editor of the monthly publication of the Iron and Steel Trades Federation, *Man and Metal*, wrote at the end of 1942 of Britain's special 'contribution to civilization'.

It is not that we consider ourselves to be God's chosen people. We no longer echo Kipling's claims or read without a blush Cecil Rhodes' contention that 'we are the first race of the World

[24] Light, *Forever England*, 106, 211.
[25] 'What is a Good Man', 'Living Opinion', 24 Apr. 1941, Home Service in Radio Talks Scripts Film T 405, p. 8, at the BBC WAC.
[26] Ibid.   [27] Ibid.   [28] Ibid. 9.

and the more of the world we inhabit the better it is for the human race.' . . . We recognise now that our arms alone are not sufficient to secure the weak from aggression, and we are even ready to admit that the foreign tag about British hypocrisy was not without some justification . . .

Perhaps we have been too modest . . . [W]e have let our cause go by default, so that it was possible before the blitz for Americans to call us supine, and for Germans to believe us decadent, and for Frenchmen to think us perfidious.[29]

Britain's special contributions, 'without which the world would be recognisably the poorer' were, according to the author, good humour and decency. By 'good humour' he meant being 'good tempered'. This was the national characteristic that the Czech participant in the BBC programme 'What is an Englishman' had mentioned as a major contribution of the British. The editorial writer for *Man and Metal* wrote that decency

is a baffling quality to analyse; bound up with it are the conceptions of fair play and consideration for others . . . There are elements of our capitalism and in our imperialism that are the opposite of decent. But I believe that most foreigners would admit that Britain has shown the quality of decency, the sense of fair play and kindliness, more consistently than any other great nation in the contemporary world.[30]

Fair play, tolerance, and kindliness have roots in ancient notions of chivalry, and in the more modern idea of 'character'—the manly code of behaviour taught to boys at public school.[31] As George Mosse has suggested, the concept of chivalry from the feudal past became generalized; 'it meant a certain attitude and behavior linked, for example in England, where it was strong, to compassion, straightforwardness, and patriotism.'[32] Mosse argues that the ideals of chivalry were rearticulated as middle-class manners and morals—what was to become respectable behaviour.[33] Thus, the masculinity of the 'good citizen' combined elements of an idealized lower and upper middle-class manliness, and one with which working-class men could identify.

But it was not just moral toughness, and what we might identify, from the earlier discussion of the British 'stiff upper lip', as 'emotional toughness' that was central to modern and especially wartime masculinity and nationhood. As Mosse has suggested, manliness meant, as well, 'physical toughness'.[34]

---

[29] 'Britain's Contribution', *Man and Metal*, Dec. 1942, 136. MS 36, at the Modern Records Centre, Warwick.

[30] Ibid.

[31] George L. Mosse, *The Image of Man: The Creation of Modern Masculinity* (New York: Oxford University Press, 1996), 23. For a critique of Mosse's work on the grounds that he portrays masculinity as historically unchanging, once it is formed early in the modern era, see Stefan Dudink, 'The Trouble with Men: Problems in the History of "Masculinity"', *European Journal of Cultural Studies*, 1–3 (Sept. 1998), 419–31.

[32] Mosse, *The Image of Man*, 23.   [33] Ibid.   [34] Ibid.

Manly Heroism

The centrality of physical toughness to masculinity, especially in wartime, focuses our attention on some of the ideals of the soldier-hero—the construction of a military masculinity with its emphasis on bravery, courage, physical strength and endurance, and male bonding. As Graham Dawson has argued, narratives about soldier-heroes have been crucial to the constructions of masculinity and the nation as unchanging essences.[35] Wars have been among the most gendered of events. Classically, and even more pointedly in the period under discussion with mass conscription of 'able-bodied' young men for the fighting services, soldiering was quintessentially a male civic responsibility. It was an obligation—both legal and moral—of male citizenship.

Dawson's argument is basically that stories about male heroism in battle or in other arenas that test men's courage, strength, and fortitude are training manuals for masculine identity more generally.[36] There is ample evidence that young boys during World War II were fascinated by stories of battle and its machinery, incorporating them in fantasies about being fighting participants in the war.

For example, John Sweetland's memoir recalls that in the summer of 1940 after Dunkirk (Sweetland would have been about 13 years old) 'we boys discussed with some excitement what we could do to the first German soldiers to enter our street'.[37] He recalled that the boys traded pieces of shrapnel and used them as a 'form of currency'.

Mass Observation quite regularly reported on children's reactions to the war. In an account in July 1940, an observer, noting the differences in the reactions of boys and girls to the war, recorded the following exchange between the observer and children in Stepney that had taken place at the end of April when British troops were still fighting on the Continent. The observer asked Betty if she would like it if she had a chance to go and fight.

Betty: Coo, no, I never could. Coo, I couldn't go up in an aeroplane. It would make my tummy go all funny like it does in a train only worse.
Obs: What about you, Albert, would you like to join up?
Albert: Would I? Oh boy, I'd like to take a crack at some of them jerries [sic].
Obs: What would you join? Army, Navy or Air Force?
Albert: Air Force. I'd just pull the catch and down they'd all drop, all the bombs (he demonstrates) Pop, pop, pop, pop. My brother is a lorry driver. He has to drive with one hand and shoot with the other. Coo, he must have eyes all over his head. Drive with one hand

---

[35] Dawson, *Soldier Heroes*, 11–13.

[36] Also see David H. J. Morgan, 'Theater of War: Combat, the Military, and Masculinities', in Harry Brod and Michael Kaufman (eds.), *Theorizing Masculinities* (London: Sage Publications, 1994), 165–6.

[37] Sweetland, 'Growing up', 4.

and shoot with the other, he does. I'd like to be in a tank. Zoom, zoom, up and down, knocking down everything in your way. I'd like to knock some of them jerries' houses down.[38]

Such an exchange suggests, not surprisingly, that boys and girls had acquired or at least were rehearsing gender differentiated wartime subjectivities.

Heroic narratives featuring feats in battle were regularly reported in the press. For example, a Cardiff newspaper published a story depicting the heroism of Squadron Sgt.-major Thomas who earned a medal for his bravery and initiative. The story portrays the Sgt.-major as being bold and adventurous, intelligent and efficient, courageous and patriotic. It also makes the point that Thomas had been a railway worker in peacetime (one of the ordinary men), and he was able to use his knowledge of trains in his heroic actions. Thomas came up with a plan for destroying a large portion of the railway rolling stock of Greece during the period when Britain was attempting to stop the German onslaught there. After being assisted in organizing the plan by members of the squad, Thomas, acting alone and despite enemy gunfire, destroyed the trains. In later fighting, he was taken prisoner and sent to Italy, but he and a comrade escaped to the Allied lines 400 miles to the south. This heroic narrative underscored another important dimension of the soldier-hero. He was a team-player with strong bonds to his mates, yet distinguished himself as an individual. Individuality, not individualism was key to wartime masculinity. This code of masculine conduct, as historian Robert Nye suggests, resembles Norbert Elias's depiction of Old Regime court society. 'Court society represents itself, each individual being distinguished from every other, all together distinguishing themselves from non-members, so that each individual and the group as a whole confirm their existence as a value in itself.'[39] Elias's depiction of court society also resembles the sportsman-like ideal so important as training for middle-class masculinity in nineteenth-century British public schools and middle-class corporate masculinity in the contemporary period.[40]

Epic heroic tales also were told about those who were not in the fighting forces,

[38] 'Children and the War', File Report 299, July 1940, p. 9. Mass Observation Archive (Microfilm). For similar evidence from Mass Observation at a date later in the war, see 'What Your Child Thinks of the War', Mass Observation, File Report 662–3, Apr. 1943.

[39] Norbert Elias, *The Civilizing Process*, iii. *The Court Society*, trans. Edmund Jephcott (New York: Pantheon, 1983), 103, as quoted by Robert Nye, *Masculinity and Male Codes of Honor in Modern France* (Berkeley and Los Angeles: University of California, 1998), 8.

[40] For a discussion of the links between military life and post-war corporate executives, see Michael Roper, *Masculinity and the British Organization Man since 1945* (Oxford and New York: Oxford University Press, 1994), 111–17. For discussions about the 19th-century British public schools, and the cult of sport, see J. A. Mangan, 'Social Darwinism and Upper-Class Education in Late Victorian and Edwardian England', in J. A. Mangan and James Walvin (eds.), *Manliness and Morality: Middle-Class Masculinity in Britain and America, 1800–1940* (Manchester: Manchester University Press, 1987), 135–59, and James Walvin, 'Symbols of Moral Superiority: Slavery, Sport and the Changing World Order, 1800–1950', in Mangan and Walvin (eds.), *Manliness*, 242–60.

but who had dangerous jobs on the home front. One of the most successful documentary films of the war, Humphrey Jennings's *Fires Were Started*, featured 'ordinary men', auxiliary firemen, one of whom, the newcomer to the group, was portrayed as solidly middle class and not used to heavy physical labour. The film starkly shows these ordinary men courageously, but calmly fighting a blazing inferno to save the docks during the London Blitz. One of them died saving one of his mates. *Fires Were Started* was both enormously popular and critically acclaimed. John Sweetland, the 18-year-old memoirist, recalled having seen it seven times.

Soldier-like heroism on the part of 'ordinary men' also was celebrated in feature films like *The Foreman Went to France*. Released in April 1942, the film takes place in 1940 when the Nazis were invading France. The hero, Fred (played by Clifford Evans) travels to France to keep some important equipment from falling into enemy hands. After a perilous journey he succeeds in getting the machinery back to England.[41] All of the media participated in celebrating masculine feats of heroism.

One of the most successful of the Sunday Postscript broadcasters after J. B. Priestley had left the BBC was Frank Laskier, a sailor in the Merchant Navy. During a broadcast he told a long story about a sailor, who despite being gravely injured and in a life boat, 'never shirked his watch; he'd baled, he'd steered, he'd kept a lookout and he never complained'.[42] After two days adrift they returned to the blazing ship they had abandoned, and the man

crawled up the ladder . . . and he went down into the engine-room and he watched for 2 days and for 2 nights without rest or respite or sleep, and he never complained. And in the evening of the second day, Paddy went up aloft to his room and laid down on his bunk and died . . . They buried him at sea, under the Union Jack . . . All over the world you see the letter 'V'; all over occupied Europe, all over England is that 'V'; but for *us* the 'V' stands for Victory—and for Vengeance.[43]

By also stressing the idea that this man was an ordinary man, who could have been living on his listeners' street, he encouraged other men to be self-sacrificing and subject themselves to great risk—to seek victory and vengeance.

Laskier's challenge was a theme used by the Admiralty in a campaign to spur shipyard workers to greater effort. An issue of *Warwork News*, produced by the Admiralty for war workers, featured a picture of a group of men identified as members of the Merchant Navy. The caption reads 'These men went through Hell for You.' They had been in an open boat for 23 days after their ship had been sunk by the Germans somewhere in the Atlantic. 'The men of the Royal Navy and Merchant Navy ask you

[41] Ealing Studios, *The Foreman Went to France* [1942], directed by Charles Frend, and associate producer Alberto Cavalcanti, based on a story by J. B. Priestley.

[42] Frank Laskier, Sunday Postscript, 26 Oct. 1941, Home Service in Radio Talks Scripts Films T 277/278, p. 5, at the BBC WAC.

[43] Ibid. 5–6.

to give every ounce of effort to speed up production.'[44] In this portrait the heroes, whose trials the readers were asked to imagine and with whom they were expected to identify, were those who faced enemy fire in battle.

Another Admiralty poster, however, rather than distinguishing 'industry' from 'courage', equated them. One poster showed a shipyard worker's hands meeting the hands of a member of the Royal Navy with a u-boat/shark being squeezed between them. The caption read, 'Put it there'.[45] In another poster issued by the Admiralty bearing the caption, 'Give 'Em Both Barrels', a photograph of a young sailor manning guns on board ship appears at the top of the image. Below, a sketch of a worker (wearing a worker's cap) was drawn showing him holding a riveter as though it were a gun with one hand on the 'trigger', and the other holding the 'barrel'.[46] Male heroism on the battle front, and its rough equivalent on the home front were common representations that iconographically connected masculinity with heroic conduct.

The many visual images of male heroism in posters suggest the significance of the male body for the construction of masculinity.[47] George Mosse has commented at length on the significance of the male body to conceptions of manliness in the modern period.[48] Its significance lay, he argues, in the tendency of moderns since the Enlightenment to associate physical attributes with inner qualities.[49] During the French Revolution, the male body became 'a symbol of a healthy nation and society. Indeed . . . the male body continued to perform this function until it became in the twentieth century one of the most powerful means of national and even socialist self-representation.'[50]

Mosse proposes that the masculine ideal of beauty was drawn from Classical Greek images.[51] The ideal masculine body projected both 'strength and restraint'.[52] An advertisement that used an idealized classical figure, reproduced in Plate 11, pictured a mythical Roman rather than a classical Greek male figure, and showed him along with a realistic/modern one. One male form projected beauty and imperial

---

[44] *Warwork News*, issue 5, 1941, p. 3a., 'Industry Publicity'. PRO/INF 2/72.

[45] 'Industrial Publicity', p. 8 (no date). INF 2/72.   [46] Ibid. 6.

[47] As Robert Nye has written, the 'profound connections between sexuality and identity encourage' men to aspire to become men of honour; threats to men's sexual capacity were threats to manhood. Because of this, 'masculinity is exceedingly fragile, is open to constant challenge, and produces keen feelings of vulnerability in men' (Nye, *Masculinity*, 10). Although Nye's study concerns the role of honour in France from 1890 to 1914, his observation about the fragility of masculinity produced by the significance of male sexuality to constructions of manliness continues to be valid for a number of western societies to this day. For a discussion of the fragility of masculinity at the psychic level, see Michael Roper and John Tosh (eds.), *Manful Assertions: Masculinities in Britain Since 1800* (London and New York: Routledge, 1991), 15.

[48] Mosse, *The Image of Man*, 24–50.   [49] Ibid. 24.   [50] Ibid. 27.

[51] Ibid., esp. 28–40. His discussion is almost solely about the 18th- and 19th-century German intellectual fascination with Greek sculpture.

[52] Ibid. 29.

FOR PERFECT SHEETS
AND TINPLATE

Richard Thomas

The cities men must build....

will be the work of artists, architects, engineers,
and skilled craftsmen using steel, concrete and
all the latest resources to shape the new
dwellings. These beautiful and gracious cities
must be lasting and strong so that future
generations may become brave and kindly, as
well as industrious and wise.

THE UNITED STEEL COMPANIES LIMITED

Steel, Peech & Tozer, Sheffield | Appleby-Frodingham Steel Co. Ltd., Scunthorpe | The Rothervale Collieries, Treeton
Samuel Fox & Co. Ltd., Sheffield | Workington Iron & Steel Co., Workington | United Coke & Chemicals Co. Ltd.
United Strip & Bar Mills, Sheffield | The Sheffield Coal Co. Ltd. | Thos. Butlin & Co., Wellingborough

U.S.P. 10

11. Advertising for the United Steel Companies appearing in
Man and Metal, October 1942,
p. 119 of MS 38,
Modern Records Centre, Warwick

authority, while the other exhibited strength and determination. Sponsored by The United Steel Companies it spoke of the future and portrayed a man in a worker's cap, shirt sleeves rolled up, arms folded, and jaw set, shaded in dark tones standing in front of a towering stark, white, statuesque male figure of a Roman. Both figures were drawn with their faces in profile view, their bodies facing the viewer. One of the Roman's arms was on the worker's shoulder; the other was outstretched as if to show the way to the future represented as an ultra modern city in the distance. The legend explicitly coupled the ideals of bravery and kindliness.[53]

Regardless of the particular style of artistic representation, British viewers of the iconography suggesting endurance, effort, and/or strength, would probably have associated these images with the physically fit male body. Physical fitness as an ideal and a set of practices had been growing in importance throughout the century.[54]

The emphasis on male physical fitness can be traced back to the late nineteenth century, when several all-male organizations began practising what has been called 'muscular Christianity'.[55] The Boys' Brigade (the youth organization of the Church of England) and the YMCA both attempted to join manliness and Christianity by offering fighting and games that stressed strength and discipline.[56] In contrast, the Salvation Army, although it attempted to emphasize manliness by emulating the military with its uniforms, was accused of effeminacy by newspaper critics and youth gangs. It stressed empowerment by religion over the power of physical strength.[57] These were competing forms of working-class masculinity. However, the emphasis on health and fitness grew with secular organizations such as the Boy Scouts founded in 1908 and the Health and Strength League, a working-class and lower middle-class men's organization whose motto was, 'Sacred thy body even as the soul', established in 1906.[58] In 1910 the organization's manual was circulated to

---

[53] *Man and Metal*, Oct. 1942, 119. MS 36, at the Modern Records Centre, Warwick.

[54] For discussions of fitness at the end of the 19th century, see John Springhall, 'Building Character in the British Boy: The Attempt to Extend Christian Manliness to Working-Class Adolescents, 1880–1914', in Mangan and Walvin (eds.), *Manliness and Morality*; Norman Vance, *Sinews of the Spirit: The Ideal of Christian Manliness in Victorian Literature and Religious Thought* (Cambridge: Cambridge University Press, 1985). For the 20th century and the inter-war period, see Joanna Bourke, *Working-Class Cultures in Britain, 1890–1960: Gender, Class and Ethnicity* (London and New York: Routledge, 1994), and Robert Graves and Alan Hodge, *The Long Week-End: A Social History of Great Britain, 1918–1939*, 2nd edn. (New York: W. W. Norton, 1994 [1940]), 369. Also see Bourke's very interesting discussion of the extension of the military obsession with fitness in World War I to civilians (Bourke, *Dismembering the Male*, 180–92).

[55] For discussions, see Springhall, 'Building Character', 52–74; Vance, *Sinews of the Spirit*. On physical culture in this period, see Michael Anton Budd, *The Sculpture Machine* (New York: New York University Press, 1997).

[56] On the Boy's Brigade, see Springhall, 'Building Character', 52–61.

[57] For a discussion of masculinity and the Salvation Army, see Pamela J. Walker, ' "I Live but Not yet I for Christ Liveth in Me": Men and Masculinity in the Salvation Army, 1865–90', in Roper and Tosh (eds.), *Manful Assertions*, 92–112, esp. 106–7.

[58] Quoted in Mosse, *The Image of Man*, 137. For a discussion of the Health and Strength League, see Bourke, *Working-Class Cultures*, 42–5.

90,000 boys a week; its membership in 1911 was 13,000 young men and by 1935 124,000 belonged.[59] In addition to learning moral values and being schooled to respect 'brotherhood', members were required to pledge themselves to 'forward the cause of physical culture, to take "judicious exercise" daily, and to encourage fitness'.[60] Booklets on physical improvement aimed at working-class men and youth were popular throughout the period.[61] There was a woman's counterpart organization emphasizing health and fitness, but it was called the League of Health and Beauty (in contrast to Strength) and it organized classes in physical exercise.[62] As the writers Robert Graves and Alan Hodge, who discussed the fitness movement in their *The Long Week-End*, published early in the war years, wrote, 'No special classes were provided for men, it being assumed that most of them did take exercise.'[63] In the mid-1930s *The Times* had urged 'a great national effort to improve the physique of the nation' should be undertaken. King Edward VIII was cited as an example of a truly 'fit' man. To help working-class boys to keep fit a fund was started in the memory of King George V to provide them with playing fields.[64] Keeping fit had an aesthetic dimension as well as one concerned with health and morality. As George Mosse commented, male beauty was 'confounded with strength and the developing of one's muscles'.[65]

It should not be surprising, then, that the importance of male physical fitness and muscular beauty continued into, and was reinforced by, the militarization of the home front. Advertisements for Charles Atlas and the fitness programme of 'The World's Most Perfectly Developed Man' appeared throughout the war.[66] Health products for men promised slimming and energy, such as Linia Belt to tone weak muscles and lift 'sagging organs to their correct position'.[67] In August 1940, *Picture Post* featured an article illustrated exclusively with numerous images of male civilians, 'Citizens Get Fit'. The theme of the article was 'the civilian [man] is no longer behind the front. He is the front. So everywhere he is getting himself fit.'[68] Such advertisements and articles addressed an anxiety about the male body, rooted perhaps, in concerns about the manliness of the administrative, managerial, and professional activities of middle-class and elite men.

A Low cartoon, published while the Chamberlain Government was still in power, reproduced in Plate 12, links fitness (or lack of it) and the war effort. In the background untitled but representing Germany, loomed a massive male figure, drawn like a wrestler or a cave man (perhaps Attila the Hun), whose biceps and chest

---

[59] Quoted in Mosse, 42.   [60] Ibid. 43.

[61] In the 1940s, for example, Charles T. Trevor authored pamphlets entitled: *How to Develop a Powerful Abdomen* (1943); *How to Develop Powerful Arms* (1944); anonymously published were *The Muscles of the Body and How to Develop Them* (1942), and Edward Aston, *How to Develop a Powerful Grip* (1946). These references are from Bourke, *Working-Class Cultures*, 219 n. 96.

[62] Graves and Hodge, *The Long Week-End*.   [63] Ibid. 369–70.   [64] Ibid. 369.

[65] Mosse, *The Image of Man*, 137.   [66] See e.g. *Picture Post*, 8 July 1939, 6.

[67] See e.g. *Picture Post*, 30 Sept. 1939, 29.   [68] *Picture Post*, 14 Aug. 1940, 20.

12. Low cartoon, *Picture Post*,
27 January 1940

muscles bulge as he flexes his arm muscles. In the foreground is a balding middle-aged, paunchy man (labelled 'Allies' Potential Superiority') shown holding weights and wearing shorts made of the Union Jack. Behind him stands an older frail-looking man labelled 'Simon' (referring to John Simon, Chancellor of the Exchequer), with a bit of thin white hair, holding a weight in one hand and pointing anxiously to the muscular figure behind him. A third figure, a small, balding man labelled Reynaud (referring to the French Prime Minister), lifts weights and grins, seemingly unaware of the dangerous figure behind him. Low's cartoon connected the physically fit male body with the military might and leadership necessary to win the war.[69]

This emphasis on male beauty and physical fitness had a corollary; the hegemonic male was young. Hegemonic masculinity was constructed, in part that is, in opposition to old men. Fitness and health advertisements promised, 'takes years off age!', as did Litesome, an undergarment that braced stomach muscles.[70] Generally older men, who were not eligible for active duty, were represented in the media as doing something trivial. The Home Guard, for example, was not infrequently represented in a way that portrayed its members as having a lesser role in the war effort than younger men.[71] An advertisement for Four Square Tobacco began, 'Old soldiers never die! We just fade into the Home Guard, where we can still teach the youngsters a thing or two—how to smoke a pipe, for instance.'[72]

Letters to the press worried about the physical capacity of the old men in civil defence to do their jobs. 'I do not wish to be unduly critical of the A.R.P. personnel, but after seeing some of the specimens who are wearing the uniform of the Auxiliary Police Force, I do suggest that a medical test of all prospective members should be enforced.'[73] Another letter criticized giving 'men of a certain age' responsibility for others. 'We all welcome the decision to appoint a "Mr. Sensible" for each street . . . We would like men somewhat younger than the fashionable age of three score years and ten, and some what more agile than a cripple.'[74] And yet another letter writer stated that he would prefer to take orders from the Boy Scouts than from 'once retired generals' who behave with 'conspicuous gallantry'.[75]

Not long after Chamberlain had resigned and Churchill had formed his Coalition Government, Edward Hulton, editor of *Picture Post*, wrote about the turn the war had taken, and the importance of leadership on the home front as a consequence. His criticism of the previous government was unapologetic. 'Above all the leaders must be *men* [emphasis in the original]. For the last twenty years they have

---

[69] *Picture Post*, 27 Jan. 1940, 39.   [70] See e.g. *Picture Post*, 6 July 1940, 38.

[71] This point is also made by Penny Summerfield and Corinna Penniston-Bird, 'Women in the Firing Line: The Home Guard and the Defense of Gender Boundaries in Britain in the Second World War', *Women's History Review*, 9 (2000), 231–55.

[72] *Picture Post*, 30 Nov. 1940, 4.   [73] *Picture Post*, 28 Oct. 1939.

[74] *Picture Post*, 15 June 1940, 36.   [75] 'From the Mouths of Babes', *Picture Post*, 29 June 1940, 34.

been a lot of old women. The Old Woman Democracy of Neville Chamberlain, John Simon and Samuel Hoare has got to give way to the Leader Democracy of such men as Churchill, Duff Cooper, Bevin, Morrison and Amery.'[76] Hulton's language makes clear the links between fitness and age, on the one hand, and masculinity, on the other, that were integral to the construction of the nation. He not only demeaned the former leadership for being old, but also for being womanish—feminizing those whose views and policies were outmoded and weak.

Older men, especially those who were given some official responsibility were often portrayed as comedic objects. An issue of the *Radio Times*, for example, contained a humorous picture of 'Granfer, a new recruit to the Home Guard . . . proudly showing off his uniform', illustrating an article about civil defence recruits, 'Granfer Joins Up'.[77]

But of course, such negative attitudes about older men were out of keeping with the wartime mood of citizenship in which everyone was encouraged to 'do their bit' and to actively participate in the war effort. Not surprisingly then, 'old men' fought back with their letters to the editor.[78] And there were efforts by officials and the media to recruit older men and to reassure the country that the 'old brigade'—what was to become the Home Guard—could in fact be counted upon in the event of an invasion.[79]

The common sense of the time was that men naturally wanted to fight to defend their countries, while women naturally wanted to bear children. As Barbara Hedworth, a regular feature writer for *Woman's Own* put it,

in the heart of every man there throbs that . . . passion for his own country . . . that deep-rooted desire to serve *her* the moment *she* is in trouble . . . a man's patriotism is an emotion which doesn't admit logic or arguments; it is part of his very existence and seldom is it satisfied by any passive task which may come his way. Just as it is born in the heart of every normal women [*sic*] to have children, so it is born in the heart of every man to defend that which rightfully belongs to him, his wife, his children, his home, *his country*. (Emphasis in the original)[80]

This interesting and very gendered depiction not only suggests that men naturally hunger to serve their countries; it also suggests something important about masculinity—a characteristic with a long history of articulation. Men defend and protect women and children.

The contestation over fire-watching, discussed in Chapter 4, provoked a politics of masculinity that focused in particular on this usually taken-for-granted perquisite of men. After the Home Secretary hinted in the House of Commons that

---

[76] *Picture Post*, 29 June 1940, 33.   [77] *Radio Times*, 30 Aug. 1940, 19.

[78] 'Crabbed Age and Youth', *Picture Post*, 22 June 1940, 33.

[79] e.g., *Picture Post*, 21 Sept. 1940, 9; 'We Also Serve', *Radio Times*, 28 Feb. 1941, 32.

[80] Barbara Hedworth, 'Would You Try to Keep Him Back?', *Woman's Own*, 4 May 1940, 37. My emphasis.

fire-watching would be made compulsory for women, the *Coventry Evening Telegraph* editorialized,

On reflection it seems a little surprising that no male Member considered this a suitable opportunity for an expression of masculine disquiet at the prospect of extending compulsory fire-watching to women. Surely this is a job our men-folk can tackle . . . Women fire-watchers . . . can only relieve male fire-watchers of a part of their danger and discomfort. To all honest masculine sentiment this must be a distasteful expedient.[81]

Not long after, Kane Gerard of Coventry wrote a letter to the editor to complain.

What a spineless lot we men are to-day allowing the Government to get away with such blatant immorality—there was a time when we British prided ourselves that we treated our women as women and that as men we must do all the soldiering to protect them . . . I am sure that the average decent citizen would gladly suffer two duties instead of one that our womenfolk could remain in the home or in some safety.[82]

The 'decent citizen' was obviously male, and the idea that men would not want to protect women was anathema to this man. Such a view of masculinity was founded upon a fundamental construction of femininity— it was seen as weak and vulnerable, and thus need in of protection.

Men's prerogative to be the protectors of the nation was jealously guarded and underlined the 'sex distinction' that gave men the ability to bear arms. The right to weapons also was reserved for men in the Forces and for those in the Home Guard (not even the police, of course, had the prerogative of carrying firearms).[83] Given both this sex and military distinction, it is not surprising that the existence of a fair number of conscientious objectors (COs) during World War II challenged hegemonic masculinity.

Conscientious Objectors

The Military Service Bill, passed by Parliament in 1939, contained a 'conscience clause' allowing individuals to be given 'conscientious objector status' and releasing them from combat duties. Applicants' appeals for such exemption were subject to rulings by tribunals established for the purposes of judging the validity of their claims that conscience prohibited them from combat or active participation in a war. Unlike in World War I there would be no involvement by the War Office in the

[81] 'Women Fire-watchers', *Coventry Evening Telegraph*, 7 Aug. 1942, 4.
[82] *Coventry Evening Telegraph*, 11 Aug. 1942, 4.
[83] Penny Summerfield has discussed the jealousy with which men in the Home Guard preserved their masculine prerogative to carry weapons. See her, ' "My Dress for an Army Uniform": Gender Instabilities in the Two World Wars', Inaugural Lecture, University of Lancaster, 30 Apr. 1997, 15–23; and Penny Summerfield, ' "She Wants a Gun Not a Dishcloth!": Gender, Service and Citizenship in Britain in the Second World War', in G. J. DeGroot and C. Penniston-Bird (eds.), *A Soldier and a Woman: Sexual Integration in the Military* (Harlow, England: Pearson Education Ltd., 2000), 119–34.

tribunals. The tribunals themselves were set up to provide some representation by people of differing political views, labour unions, and observers including representatives of pacifist organizations. All told, there was an increase over World War I in the numbers of people granted exemption on the basis of having a conscientious objection to war. In World War II there were 59,000 registered conscientious objectors, or roughly 1.2 per cent of the 5 million who were conscripted. In World War I, 16,000 of the 6 million men who were conscripted or 0.125 per cent were so registered.[84] But as Martin Ceadel points out, more men were refused CO status in the 1940s. Thus, he suggests, the effect of the Government's reforms in dealing with COs was primarily 'psychological'.[85]

Allowing claims of conscience to override the obligations of military service was justified as a practice demonstrating British tolerance as contrasted with Nazi persecution of pacifists, aligning the policy with the construction of wartime hegemonic masculinity proper. For example, during one of the numerous letters-to-the-editor exchanges about conscientious objectors in one of the many newspapers in the country where they were published, 'Lawyer' wrote, in response to a correspondent who had suggested branding COs, 'we must be careful our patriotism does not turn us into persecutors and purgers'. While some conscientious objectors might endure branding, he continued, 'it would reflect on the impartiality of the branders . . . and remind the public that it is a German method to brand those they disagree with.'[86] But as we shall see, 'Lawyer's' defence of conscientious objection as grounds for exemption was a minority response at least as it was represented in the popular press. Popular reactions to conscientious objectors underscored the central importance of military service for enacting masculinity.

There was a variety of grounds on which pacifists argued their case, but religion was the most common, and most commonly effective. Jehovah's Witnesses, however, were frequently subject to abuse in tribunals. The group was not generally publicly accepted as an established religious denomination, and thus their claims to conscience were vigorously challenged. At a tribunal at Bristol in May 1943, Judge Wethered, the chair, for example, regarded them as doing 'very mischievous work; it was assisting the forces of evil. He could not understand how people accepted the nonsense.' Furthermore, he accused the group of 'going round undermining the confidence of people in their government at the present time'.[87]

---

[84] Rachel Barker, *Conscience, Government and War: Conscientious Objection in Great Britain, 1939–45* (London: Routledge, 1982), 121.

[85] Martin Ceadel, *Pacifism in Britain 1914–1945: The Defining of a Faith* (Oxford: Clarendon Press, 1980), 302. For a discussion of the internal politics among those who advocated pacifism of one form or another, see chap. 16. For an account of wartime conscientious objectors, see Denis Hayes, *Challenge of Conscience: The Story of the Conscientious Objectors of 1939–49* (London: Allen and Unwin, 1949).

[86] *Evesham Journal and Four Shires Advertiser*, 13 Feb. 1943, 5.

[87] *Bridgewater Mercury*, 2 Mar. 1943. 'Cuttings 1941–1947', Temp MS 914/11/2/1, at the Religious Society of Friends Library, London (FL).

The men who claimed exemption on the basis of conscience articulated alternative versions of masculine citizenship to the hegemonic one that required men to defend the country. The Witnesses, for example, claimed an allegiance to a higher authority than the state. They routinely said, 'I am not of this world; my citizenship is in heaven.'[88]

Tribunal members often greeted this statement with scorn. At one such hearing, for example, after the applicant admitted that he worked because it was necessary, as he put it, to 'keep myself and my family', the chair retorted, 'Exactly—you are in this world and you have to entangle yourself in its affairs. But when it comes to defending your country which enables you to live, you are not prepared to do so.'[89]

One of the more celebrated instances of harassment by the military of a Jehovah's Witness who had been denied exemption involved Stanley Hilton. By the summer of 1943 and his fourth court martial, he had spent nearly three years in custody under remand, detention, or imprisonment.[90] After many pleas on his behalf and substantial criticism of the War Department for its 'cat and mouse' treatment of Hilton, he was released from prison at the end of 1943 to work as a coal miner.

If tribunals and the military were intolerant of Jehovah's Witnesses, some vocal members of the British public were even more so. According to a news report, for example, agricultural workers in Essex had complained that after working for a full week, they were required to do Home Guard duty on Sundays, while 'these Witnesses, mostly young fellows with "Americany" voices are free to tour the countryside, holding open-air services, playing records and selling pamphlets.'[91] Mentioning the 'Americany' accents was undoubtedly a reference to the fact that the sect originated in the United States and members of the Witnesses had come to Britain to proselytize. It also was a way of identifying the Witnesses as not truly English.

The response both by the tribunals and the public at large to the Witnesses is reminiscent of the reception by many members of the working class and city officials to the Salvation Army in the late nineteenth century. Some of the practices of the two groups were similar, if not identical. As historian Pamela Walker describes the Salvationists, they too 'spent most of their leisure hours evangelizing and attending meetings'.[92] They too distributed pamphlets and periodicals across the country. For their efforts, they had to withstand ridicule and assault.[93] And, like the Salvationists, who Walker argues offered a spiritual manliness, one devoted to their own and others' salvation, so too did the Witnesses.

Not all conscientious objectors were the recipients of public disapprobation.

[88] *Lincolnshire Standard*, 8 Oct. 1942. Clippings file, Temp MS 914/11/1, at the FL.
[89] *Aldershot News*, 18 Sept. 1942. Clippings file, Temp MS 914/11/2, at the FL.
[90] *Baptist Times*, 19 Aug. 1943, in 'Press Cuttings on Stanley Hilton', MS 914/11/3/4, at the FL.
[91] *Essex Chronicle*, 25 Sept. 1942 (no page indicated). Clippings file, Temp MS 914/11/2 (1941–1947), at the FL.
[92] Walker, 'Men and Masculinity', 93.   [93] Ibid. 93–5.

Those who, through alternative service, risked their lives to serve others, were 'good objectors'. Even though they refused combat, they were exemplifying one of the strictures of wartime masculinity, confronting risk and offering self-sacrifice. For example, in January 1943 at Bootle, the Rotary Club lunchtime speaker spoke about the Friends Ambulance Unit. He was quoted as saying, 'all the men engaged in this work are Conscientious Objectors, but they are objectors of the right sort because although they do not believe in taking lives, they risk their own to save others.'[94] A *Sunday Pictorial* article of September 1942 underscores the distinction sometimes made between COs, drawing on the language of wartime heroic masculinity. The headline read, 'They Wouldn't Fight but, Would You Call Them Cowards?'

This was a story about Nik Anderson who was shot while driving an ambulance in Tobruck in the North Africa campaign. The journalist used the incident to make a statement about 'other' COs—the 'wrong sort'. He wrote that Anderson could have found himself

a job on the farm of some rich, easy-going pacifist—a nice funkhole somewhere in the country, miles away from bomb threatened cities. But Nik Anderson knew that a conscience can work two ways. His conscience would not have allowed him to skulk in the country—like so many other pacifists—while his fellow-countrymen suffered.

. . . In this country there are about 40,000 registered Conscientious Objectors . . . We know how they laze about their silly 'peace' farms and adopt an omnipotent and superior attitude to war-troubled Britain. We have seen them strolling in the quiet, peaceful lanes of England in their coloured corduroy trousers and shimmering silk shirts. These slackers have not escaped our notice.[95]

The reference to 'coloured corduroy trousers and shimmering silk shirts' suggests effeminacy and intellectual eccentricity, as a contrast to the self-sacrificing, heroic Anderson. The men who wore such gaudy clothes clashed with the Englishness of the country lanes on which they strolled.

Understandably criticism of conscientious objectors increased in the spring and early summer of 1940 as the rest of Europe was occupied by Germany and fears mounted about a possible invasion of the United Kingdom. While the tribunals supposedly tested 'conscience' by assessing the grounds for a self-proclaimed pacifist's belief, the public were largely unaware of the basis for an applicant's appeal for exemption on the grounds of conscience. And although some few Quakers and others were known in their communities to be doing important alternative service, mostly the general public had no idea what the objector was doing. The most common response to conscientious objection was to distrust the grounds of conscience and to claim that the CO was a coward. The Mayor of Warrington, for example, proclaimed, 'What was good enough for the present Mayor in 1914, when his brother

[94] *Bootle Times*, 8 Jan. 1943. Clippings file, Temp MS 914/11/2, at the FL.
[95] *Sunday Pictorial*, 6 Sept. 1942. Clippings file, MS 619/11/2, at the FL.

was killed beside him, and what is good enough for my eldest son, is good enough for anyone who has any British manhood in his blood.'[96]

Members of the public and tribunal judges implied that conscientious objectors were so unmasculine or unmanly that either they would not protect women—even those to whom they were close—or that they sought the protection of women for themselves.[97] For example, a Chorley schoolteacher who was also a Methodist preacher was denied exemption after he was asked at the tribunal what he would do if he had a girlfriend and she was attacked. The man replied, 'I'd investigate'. Interrupting, the Chair said:

No girl I know would think of having anything to do with a young man unless she felt sure he would be prepared to defend her. If a girl were assaulted would you not be prepared to defend her?

I cannot answer.

Chair: What! Do you mean to state you cannot say? I should not think there was any man in this country who would not be ready to defend his wife or any girl if she was being attacked.[98]

And conscientious objectors were accused of being protected by women in the protests over Home Secretary and Minister of Home Security Herbert Morrison's proposal that women be compelled to do fire-watching in their places of business at night.

When Ellen Wilkinson, Parliamentary Secretary to the Minister of Home Security, talked to the Liverpool business community in October 1942, she said:

'all the women I have spoken to would be perfectly willing to come along if it were not for—'

A voice and loud applause: "For the conchies."

Miss Wilkinson: 'No. They consider far too many men are not doing firewatching.' (Loud and prolonged applause)

A woman then remarked: "Bring the conchies out and then we'll do it." More applause

Miss Wilkinson: 'The Government recognizes no conscientious objection to firewatching.'

A man shouted: "What about Morrison? He is hiding behind a woman. Let *him* come up."[99]

This exchange suggests both that conscientious objectors were not doing their citizenly duty, and that because Wilkinson was there defending the Government's case, Morrison, who had been a pacifist in World War I, was 'hiding behind a woman'.

[96] *Liverpool Daily Post and Mercury*, 26 Apr. 1940, 6.

[97] For an excellent discussion of the hostility against conscientious objectors in World War I see Nicoletta F. Gullace, '*The Blood of Our Sons': Men, Women, and the Renegotiation of British Citizenship During the Great War* (New York and Houndsmill: Palgrave Macmillan, 2002) esp. Part II.

[98] 27 Apr. 1940. Album of press cuttings from the Lancashire Tribunal, Manchester, p. 15. MS 914/11/1, at the FL.

[99] *Manchester Evening News*, 6 Oct. 1942. Clippings file, Temp MS 914/11/2, at the FL.

At about the same time the *Nottingham Guardian* reported on a talk given by the president of the Nottingham Scouts Squadron of the Air Training Corps. The speaker wondered 'how much longer we were going to obey the dictates of Mr. Bevin and Mr. Morrison while 50 or 60 thousand COs refused to raise a finger in defence of their country, but had to be protected by women.'[100] And a letter from a 'Nottingham mother' maintained that conscientious objectors rather than married women should be called on to do fire-watching. 'It is not fair to the nation that certain c.o.s should be more sheltered from danger than mothers of today and potential mothers of the future.'[101] These examples underscore the idea discussed earlier that one of the taken-for-granted masculine responsibilities, challenged both by the fire-watching order and by men who refused to fight, was to serve as the protectors of women.

Frequently conscientious objectors were publicly shamed by being labelled 'sissies', 'pansies', and other terms denoting effeminacy and hinting that their sexuality was suspect. Just prior to Dunkirk the *Leicester Evening Mail* featured an editorial with headlines that screamed, 'Scrap These C.O. Tribunals!'. It argued that given the threat to Great Britain posed by the Nazis, the country should not be granting exemption to men on the basis of a conscientious objection to fighting.

Hitler and his gangsters have never lacked scathing things to say about the democracies: that they are effete, in the German view, is only a mild form of condemnation. The Fuehrer, who already regards himself as Divine, obviously thinks people living under such a system are not as other men, certainly not the equal of his young Germans who have been schooled in Nazi nationalism and trained like the warriors of old for battle.[102]

If COs were not quite men, then the nation by tolerating them was, itself, effete.

The weekend of the escape from Dunkirk, *Sunday Pictorial* declared 'war on the nauseating young men who pretend that they believe in "peace"'.[103] The editorial proclaimed, 'We don't like the elegant sissies who fester the restaurants of London, gossiping like girls about their "hearts" and "inner souls". They've got more scent than sense.'[104] And a scathing two-page article condemning pacifists appeared in *Sunday Pictorial* the week after Dunkirk headlined, 'PACIFISTS AND PANSIES'.

After proclaiming that the men who escaped from Flanders had risked their lives for days and nights on end for the British empire, the author suggested putting COs in a labour camp with a military guard. Perhaps then 'they'd gradually become men under this kind of treatment'. The article included outrageous statements purport-

---

[100] *Nottingham Guardian*, 5 Oct. 1942. Clippings file, 916/11/2, at the FL.
[101] *Nottingham Guardian*, 3 Oct. 1942. Clippings file, 916/11/2, at the FL.
[102] *Leicester Evening Mail*, 29 May 1940, 4.   [103] 'Pacifists', *Sunday Pictorial*, 2 June 1940, 8.
[104] Ibid.

edly made by pacifists at tribunals, and described the applicants for exemption as 'pale lilies', 'long-haired, mental perverts with no chins, no character, and no spirit', and 'national pansies', in contrast to a 'man who was a man, not a pansy'.[105]

It is, perhaps, understandable that in reaction to a devastating military defeat when the 'war heroes' were returning to Britain, there might be expressions of extreme intolerance for those who refused to fight on the basis of conscience. But the language of outrage focused less on patriotism and more on male sexuality. Like the young girls discussed in Chapter 3 who were labelled 'amateur prostitutes' for having sexual adventures with soldiers, pacifists often were constructed as feminized anti-citizens.[106] Even after the outlook for eventual victory appeared more positive, the Duke of Bedford, who argued the pacifist cause regularly in the House of Lords throughout the war, was lambasted in a cartoon claiming that when ordinary citizens get into trouble with the authorities for almost 'blooming' anything, the Duke 'can get away without a fine for his attempt to get a bunch of *pansies* off the firewatching roster'.[107] Bedford's pacifism, it should be noted, was widely assumed to have been related to his being an aristocratic Fascist sympathizer. The cartoon, then, also may be read as a swipe at upper-class men.

Men whose commitment to the war effort was suspect, even if they were neither COs nor accused of being pacifists, also were tarred with the brush of effeminacy or were considered sexually suspect. In lambasting Oxford University youth for their disinterest in the war, popular writer Beverley Nichols commented, for example:

I am more and more amazed by the weirdly dressed youths . . .

Nobody expects, or desires, the young men of Oxford to abandon their ancient right to make themselves sartorially ridiculous . . . It's simply a matter of proportion. When I saw, emerging from a high-powered car, a youth wearing pale yellow corduroy trousers, Riviera sandals over bare feet, and a pale pink silk blouse and hair that needed not only cutting but bobbing, I felt that the proportion was a little distorted.[108]

The suggestion that the youth's hair needed 'bobbing' plus the pale pink silk blouse, project the judgement of 'effeminacy' of the young intellectuals of Balliol College who seemed to Nichols to be much more interested in meetings of the Arts Club, English Club, and Music Society than in the war. Here again upper-class masculinity was the subject of ridicule with the young men of Balliol portrayed as sexually suspect shirkers.

The stridently hostile article, 'Pacifists and Pansies', mentioned above com-

---

[105] Bernard Gray, 'Pacifists and Pansies', *Sunday Pictorial*, 9 June 1940, 8–9.
[106] On the girls and young women, see Chapter 2, and my 'Sex, Citizenship and the Nation in World War II Britain', *American Historical Review*, 103 (Oct. 1998), 1147–76.
[107] J. C. Walker, 'What a Blooming War', cartoon in *Western Mail & South Wales News*, 15 Mar. 1943, 3.
[108] *Sunday Chronicle*, 2 June 1940, 5.

plained that the 'paternal, well-meaning Tribunal exempts the school-master on condition that he goes back to his job of spreading poison in the minds of the nation's children'.[109] Across the country there were numerous city and town councils that dismissed COs from their teaching positions, some claiming that they were doing so at the urging of parents. The Manchester and York city councils fired COs from city employment;[110] Cardiff dismissed its teachers.[111] Canon A. R. Lee, at a meeting of the North Riding Education Committee that voted to suspend a teacher without pay, wondered, 'What would be thought if a C.O. were to stand in front of a class of children whose relatives had gone to fight for their King and country? What influence would such a person have on the morale and courage of young children, and what would be the effect on the parents of the children?'[112] Dismissals continued throughout the war. Late in the war, for example, the Leeds Education Committee dismissed a CO who was a woodwork teacher for refusing to show boys how to make toy models of battleships.[113] In the winter of 1945 Reverend James at Carmarthenshire Education Committee proposed rescinding the earlier ban on appointing COs as teachers. The proposal was defeated although James told the committee that he knew of a conscientious objector who had served in the Royal Army Medical Corps and had been recommended by his commanding officer for a medal. He asked if such a man was 'to be debarred after having served his country with distinction?'

City and town councils also were under pressure to dismiss workers who were registered as conscientious objectors. City councils that refused to fire COs were not infrequently attacked in the press. After the Leicester City Council agreed not to fire the pacifists in its employ, 'Again a Soldier' wrote to the *Leicester Evening Mail*: 'Am I suffering the loss of all I had expected to scrape out of my Army pay in order to help to maintain these C.O.s in Corporation jobs?'[114]

Although applicants for exemption from combat often were required to remain in their current positions, work on farms or in the mines, and/or take an active role in the Air Raid Patrol, the fire guards, or the Royal Army Medical Corps, their attempts to fulfil these requirements often met with hostility. While parents may have objected to COs teaching their children, and taxpayers resented tax money being spent to support pacifists in city or county government, would-be fellow workers or members of civil defence units resented their presence. For them having COs in their midst was polluting. Some of the language used to describe or resist their presence suggests that they were experienced as tainting their workmates. Journalist H. W. Seaman complaining about COs being paid a war bonus if they were employed by the town of Norwich, for example, reported

[109] Gray, 'Pacifists', 8.   [110] *Education*, 85 (24 May 1940), 433.
[111] *Education*, 85 (7 June 1940), 507.   [112] *Education*, 85 (22 Nov. 1940), 359.
[113] *News Chronicle* (London). Clippings file (1943–1946), MS 914/11/2/9, at the FL.
[114] *Leicester Evening Mail*, 25 June 1940, 4.

that Council offices in the Norwich Town Hall 'are infested by Conscientious Objectors'.[115]

A major controversy erupted at Stafford when it was learned that a 24-year-old conscientious objector had been appointed to the post of ARP organizer for the borough. After a month of protest from civil defence personnel who had threatened to resign their rank rather than be instructed by or work with the man, the Stafford Town Council asked the CO to relinquish his appointment. Thus, although COs were publicly damned if they did not take on positions that put them at some risk, or at least could garner some respect if they did, their doing so could also elicit hostility. But the hostility reserved for those men who had registered and been granted conscientious objector status could also be a threat to any young man not in military dress.

Uniformed Masculinity

In April 1940 *Sunday Chronicle* carried an article by a regular feature writer calling himself 'Yorick'. It was written as a tongue-in-cheek commentary about COs.

As most of you know, or have guessed, I am an out-and-out Pacifist with a horror of war and physical violence . . . I was walking along the street the other day when a girl in khaki . . . came up and handed me a white feather.

Slapping her smartly across the face, I inquired politely, 'What's this for?'

'To clean your pipe, of course,' she said hastily, and hurried away.

The following day, I was walking down the same street when another girl in navy blue slacks . . . came up and handed me another white feather.

Knocking her silly sailor hat, I said, 'What's this for?'

'I thought I'd like to tickle your ear,' she said hastily, and slunk off.

The third day I was walking along the same street when a shy young man came up and handed me a white feather.

'It dwopped out of my new hat,' he explained very sweetly. 'Would you mind vewy much fixing it for me? It's a fwightful nuisance leaving my mirror at home.'

Well, customers, I did warn you that I was an out-and-out Pacifist. Or did I?[116]

Although this essay demeaned conscientious objectors with satire, it also had another meaning. Any male out of uniform (unless he was obviously too old to be in the military), regardless of what it was he was doing for the war effort, could be given a white feather to mark him as a pacifist and an unmanly coward. Being visibly a member of the fighting services was necessary to the performance of wartime masculinity.

Throughout the war years, at least until the military began extensive demobilization, men out of uniform were subjects of 'white feather campaigns' throughout the

---

[115] H. W. Seaman, 'City's "Conchies" Get War Bonus', *Sunday Chronicle*, 21 Apr. 1940, 5.
[116] Yorick, 'Over the Garden Wall', *Sunday Chronicle*, 14 Apr. 1940, 7.

country. It is difficult to know, however, just how extensive was the practice, borrowed from World War I, of people—mainly women—handing white feathers to those they suspected of being pacifists.[117] In 1943, for example, the *Coventry Evening Telegraph* carried an article, 'Another war hero gets "white feather".' The man reporting the incident said he was wearing the King's Badge awarded to him along with his 100 per cent disability pension; he had just been discharged from hospital and had only recently begun walking again. He commented, 'I have for all time sacrificed my health and strength to defend such people as this woman who handed me the "white feather".'[118] As historian Nicoletta Gulace suggests, after the Great War returning soldiers told such stories, expressing their resentment. As she put it, 'the ironic contrast between the authentic bravery of men who fought and women's sartorial reading of male courage thus fills narrative accounts of the white feather campaign, endowing this descriptive medium with rich retributive possibilities.'[119]

Most of the white feather incidents the Press commented upon were those involving servicemen or ex-servicemen out of uniform. This public shaming ceremony was not officially sponsored, and in fact was officially criticized. But its existence and what appears to have been the media coverage primarily of those cases involving military heroes underlines, in the context of the prosecution of the People's War, the importance of combat service to wartime hegemonic masculinity. 'The signs of manhood relied on that external emblem of courage—the military uniform,' to quote Gullace.[120]

Although the hostility against men who were in civilian clothing did not reach the pitch of World War I, ill-will certainly was widespread. After a letter writer complained to the Coventry newspaper about the men who remained in war factories to evade military service, another protested that he was 'literally throwing "white feathers" at hundreds of patriotic workmen in order to give vent to his feelings concerning a minority who seek to evade military service . . . Surely it is not yet a crime for a young, fit, man to be seen out of khaki. They are condemned without fair consideration of their circumstances.'[121]

But the antagonism in Coventry, a centre for the manufacture of ammunition, continued. A letter writer wrote about a month later wondering how COs and 'army dodgers' felt about the first ATS girl to be killed in action. 'I think it is time that the managements came to the conclusion that they are shielding these people no longer, and that their place is behind guns and not women's skirts.'[122] Here men out of

---

[117] For an insightful discussion of the World War I 'white feather' campaign and its post-war aftermath, see Nicoletta F. Gullace, 'White Feathers and Wounded Men: Female Patriotism and the Memory of the Great War', *Journal of British Studies*, 36 (Apr. 1997), 178–206.

[118] *Coventry Evening Telegraph*, 15 Apr. 1943, 6.   [119] Gullace, 'White Feathers', 199–200.

[120] Ibid. 199.   [121] *Coventry Evening Telegraph*, 31 Mar. 1942, 2.

[122] *Coventry Evening Telegraph*, 24 Apr. 1942, 4.

uniform, perceived as being either COs or 'army dodgers', are castigated as emasculated cowards who fail to protect 'their womenfolk'.

The connections between being in the fighting services and masculinity were articulated in a variety of different representations. For example, a vignette published in the *Police Review*, a 'trade journal' for policemen, told the story of a youth, 'little more than a boy', who had gone AWOL, and was brought to the Police Station. An 'elderly Sergeant' dealt with him. Rather than calling him 'soft', the sergeant told the story of his own experience in the 'last war' with a young student at theological college—a 'lad something like you', who was uncomfortable with the rough life of army camp. But he was not only brave in battle, he helped calm his comrades under fire with his words of faith. The sergeant claimed that he was not religious, but that this man had convinced him that 'good will always overcome evil'. 'There was a new light in the boy's eyes as he somewhat timidly offered his hand to the man who was, perhaps, more religious than he thought. "I understand, officer," he said. "I'm afraid my ideas got a bit mixed up. I'll stick it." '[123] This brief story was about many things—about the kindly old policeman, and, perhaps, about a now discredited pacifism that in the 1920s and 1930s had grown in response to World War I. But it is also a story of a 'lad' doing what he needed to do to become a man.

The message about the centrality of soldiering to masculinity was made also through contrasts with women. Beverley Nichols, a popular writer of the period, wrote an article condemning the wives of RAF members who followed their husbands to live nearby the airbase. Nichols commented, 'Cannot women realise that flying and fighting and everything that goes with it is a hundred per cent masculine business—a business from which they should isolate themselves.'[124]

One way that serving in the military was made to appear quintessentially masculine was by associating soldiers with 'rough ways'. In the vignette about the young deserter, another theme of the story was that the boy had been somewhat sheltered, and was unused to the coarse ways of many of the men he had encountered in his week in the army. He was to become a 'man' by being able to tolerate crudeness in his comrades even if he himself did not emulate them. Such stereotypically 'rough' male practices as swearing and drinking were expected of men in the Forces.

In the autumn of 1942 the National Council of Women in London passed a resolution calling for a 'No-Treating' Order hoping to discourage men in the military from spending their small salaries on 'rounds' at pubs. An editorial in the *Kelso Chronicle and Border Pioneer* expressed outrage.

Wars are fought by men, not children in a nursery; and men don't wish to be tied to apron strings and told how they may spend their pocket money. War isn't a Sunday School outing, with children in nice clean suits doing as teacher tells them; but a terrible, harsh, and bloody

---

[123] 'Ellbee', 'The Deserter', *Police Review*, 8 Mar. 1940, 185.
[124] Beverley Nichols, 'Wives of the RAF', *Daily Sketch*, 2 Jan. 1941, 11.

struggle for survival, in which only those who can themselves be terrible, harsh, and bloody can hope to win. The Hitlerite monster can be grappled only by men with hearts of steel.[125]

This depiction of masculinity was quite the opposite of the temperate masculinity that was the focus earlier in the chapter. The 'tempering' of masculinity had limits. By threatening to interfere with pub ritual through which men performed masculinity for the benefit of other men, the National Council of Women had crossed the line.

Such incidents, including the hostility towards men who were obviously too old for service, those who claimed exemption on the basis of conscience, or indeed on any other ground even that they were in essential war work, points to the instability of hegemonic masculinity cobbled together as it was from aspects of both anti-heroic and heroic forms of masculinity. Its merger could only be enacted successfully if the man in question was in military dress. It is no wonder, then, that many young men who served on the home front in a civilian capacity joined the Home Guard in order to have a military uniform.[126] The characteristics of masculinity that combined the qualities of temperate masculinity with those of the soldier-hero coexisted uneasily during the war. The masculine subject, on the one hand, could slide towards pacifism, and, on the other, could approach hyper-masculinity, the 'other' of World War II temperate masculinity.

The slide towards hyper-masculinity seemed to be most often suggested in discussions about training young men and boys to be masculine citizens. The *Glasgow Herald*, for example, reported on a fund to open clubs for sport and recreation for boys to use in their spare time as part of training for 'citizenship'. The paper editorialized, 'If post-war Britain does not succeed in breeding a manhood equal in spirit and brawn to any that has made our country great in the past, it will not be the fault of the many organisations which are taking an interest in youth welfare.'[127] Such sentiments were nowhere more dramatically evident than in the Conservative Party's proposals for youth training. As the Education Sub-Committee of the Conservative Party put it,

The educational approach to the training of character has tended to forget that character must be 'tough' as well as 'good'. It has aimed mainly at the timid ideal of the well-behaved citizen, fitting . . . into a neatly patterned community . . . and hardly at all at the qualities without which the community itself must fall to pieces—the bold qualities of adventurousness, initiative, enjoyment of difficulty and danger, the fighting spirit—in a word, grit.[128]

---

[125] *Kelso Chronicle and Border Pioneer*, 6 Nov. 1942, 4.

[126] As reported by Penny Summerfield and Corinna Penniston-Bird, *Contesting Home Defence: Women, Men and the Home Guard in the Second World War* (Manchester: Manchester University Press, forthcoming).

[127] 'Clubs for A.C.F.', *Glasgow Herald*, 18 May 1944, 5.

[128] 'Aims of a System of National Education', First Interim Report, Educational Sub-Committee of the Conservative, Unionists. Final Revised Draft, 8 July 1942. PRO/ED 136/280.

In the Education files of the Public Records Office where this version of Conservative proposals is archived, there is also an unsigned and undated typescript commentary on the proposals. It accuses the Conservative proposal of extreme nationalism. The writer critiques specific points by comparing them to Nazi proclamations.

The Fire Brigades Union, although far on the other side of the political spectrum from the Conservatives, also adopted a version of militant but class-based masculinity which would have been at odds with one that valorized temperate sensibilities. Their pro-Russia stance was evident in the issues of their newsletter *Firefighter*, once Russia had been attacked by the Nazis. At their Annual Conference in July 1942, the membership debated a motion proposed by the Executive Committee to support the opening of a Second Front in Eastern Europe. In his argument for the motion, a member of the Management Committee said, countering an argument against it on the grounds that Britain had only recently been recovering from the blitzes,

When you are prepared to burn your homes, when you are prepared to see your children and your women tortured and put to death in the most barbarous manner, when you are prepared to do this and still fight, then you can say that you have gone through something . . . but please do not compare what this country has gone through with what the people of the Soviet Union have gone through.[129]

In effect, the man was praising the Soviets for being willing to continue to fight for the nation when, like Abraham, their loved ones had been sacrificed. This sentiment fed upon and turned on its side the taken-for-granted male duty to defend women and children. Enduring their brutalization at the hands of the enemy and continuing to fight was a supreme test of masculinity.

Given the dependence on actual participation in the fighting services for the amalgamation of the anti-heroic rhetoric of the inter-war period and the soldier-hero at war to be successful, what of those men who remained on the home front because they were in essential jobs? How were workers represented in public culture, both in Government propaganda, and by their own spokesmen?

Working Men on the Home Front

Certainly the Government made an effort to convince the public as well as workers of the importance of industrial and agricultural labour to the overall war effort. Not surprisingly, given the centrality of the soldier-hero and ultimately military service to hegemonic masculinity, a frequent linkage made visually and by written messages was that between soldiering and working. An industrial recruitment poster for the Ministry of Labour and National Security, 'Train to Win', for example,

---

[129] *Firefighter*, July 1942, p. 69. MS 346/1/6/5, at the MRC.

displayed a middle-aged man with a large wrench, lifted to his shoulder as if it were a rifle.[130] The connection was more explicit in the series of posters issued by the Ministry of Production, 'Every Rivet a Bullet'. In one version, 'Speed the Ships', a battleship was drawn so that it nearly filled the page. It was an imposing image dwarfing the working men below it who were portrayed standing with their backs to the viewer, while the figures on board ship were facing the viewer. It is unclear if the men on board were in uniform or in workers' overalls.

But the significance of workers in the war effort was also portrayed with some ambivalence. For example, a series of propaganda posters in the Ministry of Information's Industrial Publicity campaign featured a drawing of a uniformed member of the military pointing to the viewer—in one was a sailor, in another a soldier wearing a helmet, and in another a pilot. They were represented as saying, respectively, 'You can help to build me a ship; to build me a gun; to build me a plane.' They all carried the legend, 'you can learn quickly and you will be WORKING TO WIN.'[131] In another poster, a smiling pilot was shown stepping out of his plane to shake the hand of a worker drawn as a middle-aged man in an open shirt wearing a cap.[132] These posters emphasize the 'helping' role of the worker rather than a co-equal effort between industry and the military.

Generally workers in posters were sketched in a stylized, realistic manner, as had been the fashion in graphic design since the 1930s, with shirt sleeves rolled up or dressed in a sleeveless undershirt, revealing them to have muscular, fit, and strong bodies.[133] One advertisement by the National Savings Committee to encourage workers to buy savings certificates and defence bonds was headed 'All together now!' It linked national identity and working-class muscular masculinity. The advertisement, presented in Plate 13, depicted a line of muscular men lifting an obviously heavy railway tie with a legend urging civilians to 'lend a hand'.[134]

Both the Press and propaganda experts presented verbal portraits of various home front occupations that were crucial to the war effort. Beverley Nichols wrote about shipyard workers after having toured Clydeside shipyards.

If you made a composite picture of the average Clydeside worker it would show firstly, a man of fiery independence. A man to whom freedom is as necessary as fresh air. And for this very reason, it would show also a man of rock-hard patriotism. Not a flag-waver, not a ceremonialist . . . He'll grouse, he'll curse, he'll threaten . . . But the Clydeside worker will get on with the job.[135]

---

[130] INF 13/126(2) (n.d.).   [131] 'Industrial Publicity', p. 22. INF 2/72.   [132] Ibid. 41.

[133] For an analysis of the changing cultural politics of Soviet poster art, see Victoria E. Bonnell, *Iconography of Power: Soviet Political Posters under Lenin and Stalin* (Berkeley and Los Angeles: University of California Press, 1997), esp. chap. 1. Also see Eric Hobsbawm, 'Man and Woman: Images on the Left', in *Worlds of Labour: Further Studies in the History of Labour* (London: Weidenfeld and Nicolson, 1984), 83–102.

[134] *A.E.U. Monthly Journal*, June 1940, 195. MS 259/4/14/54, at the MRC.

[135] *Sunday Chronicle*, 26 Jan. 1941, 2. MS 259/4/14/55, at the MRC.

When there's a big job of work to be done it's a British instinct to "lend a hand." Today Britain is faced with the biggest job of work in all history — to defeat the evil forces of Nazidom once and for all — and in the shortest possible time.

All together now!

We can't all fight with weapons in our hands but *everyone*—men, women and children, too—can give direct, continuous and personal help by saving as much as they can every week and lending it to the Nation.

Join a Savings Group

Here's the simplest method—join a War Savings Group (or help to form one in your workshop, office or school). Your weekly savings will, all put together, make up a great and ever-growing volume of money to back up our fighting forces with ample supplies and equipment.

And remember, too, all the time you are putting by this money you are saving for your own and your children's future.

• • •

Apply to your local Savings Committee, The National Savings Commissioner for your Region, or to the National Savings Committee, London, S.W.1.

SAVE to WIN the WAR

SAVINGS CERTIFICATES   DEFENCE BONDS : POST OFFICE AND TRUSTEE SAVINGS BANK

13. Muscular men 'Lend a Hand'
for National Savings.
Public Record Office

Nichols made use of qualities that emphasized the manliness of working-class masculinity—'fiery independence', 'rock-hard patriotism', a man who 'curses'. There also was no doubt about the manliness of the 'dock worker' as portrayed in *Britain To-Day*, a publication for foreign distribution produced by the British Council. James Hanley described these working men using language that workers in many industries would use to refer to themselves, and to depict their own masculinity. The docker is a 'technical expert . . . He is an out and out individualist and has always been opposed to regimentation.'[136] The dock worker is 'a highly efficient man at his job . . . The case for the dockers is simply this, that under the most appalling conditions they have carried on, and done the job well . . . indomitable courage, superb will, and unshakable belief have kept ports and men still standing'.[137] The writer combined will, courage, and individuality with the attributes of rationalized workmanship.

Not surprisingly the self-representations of the roles of working men by trade unions in their publications reinforced the importance of the work they were doing for the war effort. But some union leaders and farmers, aware perhaps that true wartime masculinity required military service, expressed anxiety that their significance would not be recognized either by the public or by the military. They worried specifically that their skill and expertise at their jobs would not count for much in garnering esteem.

Until new measures were passed in 1941 men had to be between the ages of 20 and 45 to be eligible for call up, and those in particular occupations were exempt from serving. But the shortage of manpower led to a change of policy. The age of conscription was lowered to 18 and raised to 51; men and women 18 to 60 were required to undertake some form of national service. Women too were to be conscripted for the first time. And crucial to this discussion of masculinity and war work, no longer were men in particular occupations reserved. The system was replaced by one in which individual deferments were given to employers for key workers on a case-by-case basis.[138]

Even before the stepped up mobilization, union spokespersons were apprehensive about the 'combing out' of workers from their ranks. The Editor of the *A.E.U. Monthly Journal* commented about how difficult it was to

teach the military . . . that successful prosecution of the war necessitated the maintenance of industry, agriculture, and trade . . . Those of us whose memories carry us back to those days [World War I] still remember the stigma which seemed to attach to men who remained at home to serve the nation in the factories, fields, and mines. There were times when reserved and badged workmen seemed to be expected to apologise for their existence because they were not in the army.

---

[136] James Hanley, 'The Docker', *Britain To-Day*, 65 (31 Oct. 1941), 9.
[137] Ibid. 10.   [138] Calder, *The People's War*, 267.

And again in May 1941, the Editor commented on the lack of appreciation 'of the demands [war] makes upon the product of skilled workmanship in the war industries'. He went on to complain that skilled workers who were conscripted were not used for jobs for which they were qualified. Skilled men should not be asked to 'peel potatoes or scrub floors'.[139]

As men left their regular employment for the services, their jobs were taken up by women or men with less training and experience. In February 1940 when the Chamberlain Government was still in office, unions such as the AEU were highly critical of the Government's industrial policy. The Editor of the *A.E.U. Monthly Journal* wrote in February 1940 that 'skilled workers are not born . . . they have to be trained, and have to acquire experience and craftsmanship by working at their trade . . . Women cannot be summoned into industry as young men are assembled by age groups in camps and barracks'.[140] And after the new registration orders for essential work were announced in the spring of 1941 by the Churchill Government, the Editor's Notes remarked,

There are limits to the capacity of the war trades to absorb these reserves . . . You don't enlarge the field of employment in the engineering trades by combing out young engineers of military age and substituting the labour of women or other entrants to the industry who lacked the experience, the skill and the trained aptitudes of the men who have been combed out . . . There is no substitute for a skilled man except another worker of equal skill.[141]

And again several months later, the Editor complained that the 'Call-ups are automatic, peremptory and in the literal sense indiscriminatory . . . Similarly with the recruitment of women war workers to take the jobs of qualified men of military age. The method is a slap-dash registration of workers in less essential trades'.[142]

The replacement of men by women at work had the potential to stir up apprehension about the possible dissolution of the association between masculinity and highly paid industrial labour. Union agreements such as the one negotiated by the Associated Engineers Union that formalized such substitution as 'for the duration only' may have dampened such anxieties.

But, while public expressions of gender antagonism may have been muted, what the Ministry of Information termed 'sex jealousies' were widespread.[143] One report by Home Intelligence, for example, said that men were exercised about the

---

[139] *A.E.U. Monthly Journal*, May 1941, 116. MS 259/4/14/55, at the MRC.

[140] *A.E.U. Monthly Journal*, Feb. 1940, 49. MS 259/4/14/54, at the MRC.

[141] *A.E.U. Monthly Journal*, Apr. 1941, 90–1. Also see Editor's Notes, for the June 1941 issue. MS 259/4/14/55, at the MRC.

[142] *A.E.U. Monthly Journal*, Oct. 1941, 358. MS 259/4/14/55, at the MRC.

[143] A Home Intelligence report for the last week of Apr. 1942 indicated that 'bad feeling between the sexes' existed in Birmingham, Clydeside, and Durham because of pay rates for women and men. There were complaints that women were not as good workers as men but Home Intelligence attributed this to 'sex jealousies rather than accurate information'. Home Intelligence Weekly Reports, 20–27 Apr. 1942. PRO/INF 1/292 Part 2.

decreasing pay differential between skilled and unskilled work. 'Men do not like to find their daughters bringing home pay packets that are as big and in some cases bigger than their own, for work that they regard as being much lighter and less arduous.'[144] As had been the case in the late nineteenth and earlier part of the twentieth century, particular forms of work and higher pay levels were associated with masculinity. This positioned skilled and higher-waged men as exemplifying respectable manhood in contrast to women and the many men in more menial, casual, and low-waged jobs.[145]

In World War II men's discomfort with women as workmates often was expressed in jokes, cartoons, and satire. The Shop Stewards' newspaper, *New Propeller*, for example, regularly included jokes about women workers.[146] Not infrequently the jokes or cartoons in 'New Propeller' poked fun at women's vanity. An 'elderly lady trainee' according to one of the jokes, when asked to bring in a snapshot to be attached to her works identity badge brought an enlargement of a photograph taken of her twenty years ago.[147] A cartoon in December 1944 showed two women having tea—one a factory worker, the other possibly in uniform. The factory worker says to her friend, 'I'm glad I went into war work. I lost twenty pounds and the men are whistling at me again.'[148] A cartoon in the *A.E.U. Monthly Journal* referred to the difficulty that men had relating to women as workers rather than as sex objects. Two men are shown working side by side, one of them is speaking to the other. Striding towards them with sleeves rolled up, fists clenched, was another man (perhaps the foreman). Behind him was a woman working alone making ammunition. The caption read, 'Don't look now—but here comes the answer to the little note you sent the girl on the end bench.'[149]

The same issue of the *A.E.U. Journal* contained an editorial about the fraternal ties between AEU union members and 'our brothers in the Forces' and their 'wives and sisters and daughters' who are replacing them in the factories. 'We are learning to welcome and assist them in a true spirit of fraternity, and that is an important strengthening of the chain.'[150]

The publication of this editorial comment and the cartoon in the same issue underscores both the men's fraternal responsibilities to their brothers and their duties as men to protect women. The AEU welcomed women workers not as

---

[144] 'Complacency in Factories', Home Intelligence Special Report No. 51, 24 Sept. 1943, 4. INF 1/293.

[145] Sonya O. Rose, 'Respectable Men, Disorderly Others: The Language of Gender and the Lancashire Weavers' Strike of 1878 in Britain', *Gender & History*, 5 (Autumn 1993), 382–97.

[146] See e.g. *New Propellor*, Mar. 1944, 8, MS 233/5/NP at the MRC. This issue had seven jokes, two of them about women—usually about how women workers misunderstood directions; one was about an Irishman, and another was about a deaf and dumb man.

[147] Ibid.

[148] *New Propellor*, Dec. 1944, 2. MS 233/5/NP, at the MRC.

[149] Giles cartoon, *A.E.U. Monthly Journal*, Mar. 1943, 63, MS 259/4/14/57, at the MRC.

[150] Ibid. 62.

comrades, but because of the male workers' ties of brotherhood with the women's fathers, husbands, or sons that the women were replacing. The men were 'assisting' the women to do the jobs that ordinarily belonged to their menfolk. Furthermore the cartoon suggests that the men's relationships with their female workmates were either protective or sexual.

Several months later R. M. Fox, writing in the *A.E.U. Monthly Journal*, reiterated working men's obligations to protect women. In an article on London in war-time, Fox talked about women working alongside men. He wrote, 'it is for the brothers and fathers of these girls to see that they get a fair deal, and that their enthusiasm and lack of industrial experience are not exploited by private interests under the guise of war work.'[151]

Fox had already expressed himself a few months earlier on the topic of 'protecting women workers' in an article devoted to women at work. He linked women gaining industrial opportunities with 'progress' and 'modernity', using the oft-quoted statement (which he attributed to the German socialist, August Bebel), '[T]he test of any social order is the place occupied by its women.' Fox maintained that because of pressure from Labour, Britain had enacted many safeguards to protect women and children from 'bearing burdens unsuited to their strength. It is vital that these safeguards should remain.'[152] State protection of women workers had been central to the agenda of male workers in the nineteenth century.[153] In the context of the World War II deployment of women in all sorts of jobs, the discourse protected traditional assumptions about manhood.

Male workers resented unskilled women and men joining them at their work. Skill was crucial to maintaining their wage levels, and it was also critical to their own understanding of working-class masculinity. By stressing the status of their work and the technical expertise needed to do it, they were accenting the importance of their industry to the war effort. Thus, workers emphasized features of their work such as skill, strength, and danger to underscore its manly nature. For example, R. M. Fox, the writer for the *A.E.U. Monthly Journal* wrote, 'So far as the industrial front is concerned, it is the factory workers—the men of metal—who must be relied upon. In the skill and the strong arms of labour is the final guarantee that the battle for personal freedom, independence and manhood will be maintained.'[154] Fox referred not only to the battle being fought against the Germans, but to the struggles of the industrial worker with capitalist employers.

[151] R. M. Fox, 'London in War Time', *A.E.U. Monthly Journal*, May 1942, 130. MS 259/4/14/56, at the MRC.

[152] R. M. Fox, 'Marching Women', *A.E.U. Monthly Journal*, Jan. 1943, 12. MS 259/4/14/57, at the MRC.

[153] See e.g. Sonya O. Rose, *Limited Livelihoods: Gender and Class in Nineteenth-Century England* (Berkeley and Los Angeles: University of California Press, 1992), chap. 3, and Mariana Valverde, ' "Giving the Female a Domestic Turn": The Social, Legal and Moral Regulation of Women's Work in British Cotton Mills, 1820–1850', *Journal of Social History*, 21 (1988), 619–34.

[154] R. M. Fox, 'Men of Metal', *A.E.U. Monthly Journal*, Aug. 1940, 256. MS 259/4/14/54, at the MRC.

There have been elements who have sought to crush manhood out of the factories and to make the factory workers merely 'hands' without any rights or claims. These elements have always secretly sympathised with the brute force that has ridden roughshod over labour wherever it has been victorious. They have contributed to the strength of Nazism by anti-labour prejudices and hailed Hitler as the man who would keep down the working class—until he threatened their possessions![155]

Fox replayed a much older male working-class discourse about the connection between manhood and skill, and inserted it into contemporary language that confirmed that the industrial front was part of the battle against the Nazis.

When it came time for the Union to demand a pay raise, these arguments were rehearsed again.[156] Jack Tanner, the AEU head, wrote in a national newspaper, '[I]ndustrial worker(s) . . . are not onlookers, but participants in the battle. The machines which come from their hands are the means to victory on land, sea and in the air. The responsibility of the workers is as great, and their skill, physical fitness and sustained effort as essential as those of the airmen, soldiers and sailors who man the machines.'[157]

Skill and expertise were themes also stressed by farmworkers. At the Agricultural Workers' spring Biennial Conference in 1942 Union President Gooch railed against the farmers' plans to employ 12 to 14 year-olds to replace men. 'For a good many years past the land has been the happy hunting ground of theorists and experimentalists in the matter of labour. Those people thought that if there was nothing else for men to do they should bring them on the land, and with no regard for the fact that farm work to-day required a greater degree of skill than ever before in our history.'[158] Gooch also spoke on the BBC Home Service programme about farming. He maintained that the farm worker

has always been a skilled man and to-day his work calls for more skill than ever. The modern farmworker [is] an expert on many different machines, master of all country crafts, strong, versatile, skilled, a blend of trained carpenter and bricklayer, with a dash of engineer and scientist thrown in . . . He is bending to the task doing everything possible to defeat all that the enemy stands for.[159]

In addition to making a case for their status as skilled workers, farmworkers also were sensitive about the stereotyped and negative portrayal of them in popular culture. *Picture Post* addressed this issue in an extensive and amply illustrated article

---

[155] Ibid.

[156] *A.E.U. Monthly Journal*, Dec. 1941, 314. MS 259/4/14/55, at the MRC.

[157] Quoted in John Logan, 'Production Committees', *A.E.U. Monthly Journal*, May 1942, 129. MS 259/4/14/56, at the MRC.

[158] *Land Worker*, July 1942, 3.

[159] Alderman E. G. Gooch, 'Labour and Land', on 'Farming Today', 27 Feb. 1941, Home Service, p. 2 in Radio Talks Scripts Film T 185 at the BBC WAC.

arguing that the farm labourer, 'is one of the most highly skilled workers in the community'. The article went through a typical day for a farm labourer stressing the versatility of the work, the endurance and skill required, and the long hours it demanded.[160]

Rather than speaking of skill as justification for their work, the iron and steel trades workers spoke of endurance and effort. Using the language of wartime sacrifice, the journal of their confederation wrote:

The British artisan is not only the best in the world, he has a tradition of sacrifice when a great cause is at stake . . . No better example could be found than the case of a Midlands steel bender, who in times of peace, was regarded as something of a 'rebel'. Like all the rest of the employees in his factory, he is now working long hours, and has taken on him himself the task of collecting 6d. a week from the workers in his district, towards a fund for the purchase of a bomber or fighter aircraft to be known as the 'Steel Benders' plane.[161]

The news media also praised working men for their effort. *Picture Post* featured a story about munitions workers that focused on a 42-year-old man, Ronald Hubble. Like the story about the farmworker, it outlined Hubble's ordinary day, and described him as doing 'three weeks' work in every fortnight'.[162] 'Every hour— sixty-seven hours a week—Ronald Hubble adds his quota to the weapons— anti-aircraft guns among them—which keep Germany and her bombers at bay. He and his mates are front-line workers.'[163] The caption under a close-up shot of Hubble's face read, 'The Face of a Man at Work, Sweating through double shifts, Ronald Hubble is making up lost time for Britain; giving us the guns long overdue.'[164] The article depicted Hubble as a family man reporting that before the war he used to spend a great deal of time playing with his son. But now, according to the article, he had little time for family life. He also used to read serious literature, but now he had trouble concentrating and so he read 'thrillers'.[165] *Picture Post* suggested that the 'home-loving' anti-hero of the inter-war period had changed. Hubble had always been a stalwart worker, but he was going to even greater effort for the war. While he had been a family man and an avid reader of serious fiction before the war, he has now put family and literature aside for the war effort. He has become more stereotypically masculine.

In addition to the re-articulation of skill and endurance as essential to home front workers' masculinity, workers' spokesmen often depicted working men on the home front using battle imagery. To signify their involvement with the war effort *Man and Metal* not infrequently reproduced verses written either by their members or other steelworkers. To make the connection between their work in the steel mills and the soldiers fighting on the front, *Man and Metal* reprinted a poem:

[160] *Picture Post*, 20 Apr. 1940, 41.   [161] *Man and Metal*, Aug. 1941, 90. MS 36, at the MRC.
[162] *Picture Post*, 12 Oct. 1940, 22.   [163] Ibid. 23.   [164] Ibid.   [165] Ibid. 25.

The Song of Steel
by Stanley Truman Brooks
So must we sing to industry,
For from the fruitful sod
Steel has in growing majesty
Shown man the might of God.
March on, march on, you men of steel,
The heart blood of our nation
Flows from the blast and raging hearth
To fiery re-creation.

The plunging main is furrowed o'er
By mighty ships of steam
And mirrored rivers glow with light
From ruddy furnace gleam.
So up and fight, you men of steel;
Ring out your battle cry,
And be the victors over all
From earth to sea and sky.[166]

The poem clearly created steelworkers in the image of soldiers.

Farmers and farmworkers, too, were depicted as essential participants—often in terms such as, 'the first line of civilian defence against being starved and diseased'.[167] Using a tone similar to that in the steelworker's poem above, the National Savings Committee issued a 'tribute to the farmer' entitled 'Marshal of the Soil'. The advertisement to encourage workers to increase their savings showed a rugged man with greying mustache. On his head was a plaid cap. Shown smoking a pipe, and with his hands on what might have been a hoe, he was dressed in a vest, jacket, and tie. He was clearly a farmer, not a farmworker.

Marshal of the Soil
His sword
a tough ash wand
from the copse yonder,
and his quiet fields are the
fields of his war.
He marshals his panzers—
the tractors;
He trains his commandos—

---

[166] Stanley Truman Brooks, 'The Song of Steel', Carnegie Museum, Pittsburg, with acknowledgements to 'united Effort', house journal of United Engineering and Foundry Company, Pittsburg. *Man and Metal*, Mar. 1942, 3. MS 36, at the MRC.

[167] Ralph Wightman, Postscript, 26, 1943 Dec., Home Service in Radio Talks Scripts Film T 649, p. 2 at the BBC WAC.

the land girls and his cowmen
and carters . . .[168]

One wonders how this advertisement for savings bonds, published as it was in the agricultural union's journal, was received by farmworkers as it glorified the contributions of their employers rather than their own.

The agricultural workers themselves borrowed the language of the soldier-hero to extol their contributions to the war effort. In early 1941 an article in the *Land Worker* described the courage of the farmworkers in Kent, East Anglia, and other areas vulnerable to enemy attack. 'On farm and field the murderous attack of the sky raider has been met with the same defiant fortitude with which they face up to the vagaries of wind and weather. Official recognition may oftimes have passed them by, but they are nevertheless upholding the finest traditions of the sons of the soil.'[169] The concluding paragraph was subtitled 'Heroes All'.

Farm workers have stood up to the test with the same stolid cheerfulness and have shown the same unbreakable spirit as their fellow-workers in the workshops and factories. So when you hear of bombs falling on open country do not think there is no danger or that no damage is done. Spare a thought for the farm worker living where the bombs fell. He, like the townsman, is glad to have them fall in the wide open spaces rather than in a crowded town. But let the farm worker be honoured as also being in the front line with his fellow-workers in our industries throughout the country.[170]

Using the language of heroism they protested their denigrated status as compared with industrial workers and city dwellers who had been constant targets of enemy bombers.

The Fire Brigades Union which, as I have suggested elsewhere in this chapter, maintained a militant class position throughout the war, often connected the national war and their class battle to improve working conditions and salaries. The connection was made clear by John Horner, the head of the union, in his address to a meeting of the Lancashire District Committee, 'the members were engaged "right in the front line" in carrying on the war against Hitler, [and] the union was forced to carry on a war within a war to win justice and the most elementary rights for these men from the Government.'[171] Giving the Brigades a role as one of the Forces, Horner went on to say, 'The new importance we enjoy as the front line in the fight for freedom has not brought in its wake a new realisation on the part of the authorities of their responsibilities towards the men who comprise the British Fire Fighting Service.'[172]

Class unity was also promulgated by stalwart union members using the rhetoric of war. H. S. Richardson wrote to *The Firefighter* about the industrial struggle in

---

[168] *Land Worker*, Sept. 1943, 3.
[169] Harry Pearson, 'The Courage of the Farm Worker', *Land Worker*, Feb. 1941, 2.
[170] Ibid.   [171] *Firefighter*, Nov. 1940, 5. MS 346/88, at the MRC.   [172] Ibid. 7.

which the union was engaged: 'This fight is not secondary to the war, it is part of it. It is a fight which is vital to the interests and for the well-being of all members . . . It is a fight which is part of the great battle which the whole working-class is waging for its very existence. It is a fight which demands unity of action, and determination of purpose.'[173] He went on to suggest, 'If any good is to come from this carnage which is . . . killing our women and children, or driving them into holes and caverns to exist like the beasts of the earth', it must produce working-class unity. Working-class unity, he said, would make firefighters into men.

After Hitler focused his military efforts on the Eastern Front, and Russia rather than Britain was the primary target for German bombardment, the Fire Brigades Union continued to use the language of battle as it demanded that union members assist the industrial production effort by working in factories or elsewhere doing productive labour.[174] The July 1942 issue of *The Firefighter* featured the front-page headline, 'All for the Front, Smash the Bottlenecks'.[175] 'All for the Front' was a Soviet slogan that the article adopted to argue that the Fire Service had to 'sweep aside all remaining obstacles blocking our productive work schemes'. The issue also included pictures showing firemen brought into factories on short-term release, representatives calling on firms engaged in vital war work, and a brief article on the possibility of manufacturing munitions boxes in fire stations.[176] Like the firefighters shown in Plate 14, by becoming engaged in wartime production when they were no longer needed on a regular basis to fight fires, the firemen were claiming a special patriotic dedication to the war effort. In effect they proclaimed themselves to be so patriotic that they refused to rest on the laurels they had earned during the Blitz. Firemen in their two wartime roles as firefighters and as civilians engaged in wartime manufacturing (when they were not on the line) symbolized in one iconic figure the characteristics of Britishness and masculinity that had become hegemonic.

Volunteers in the National Fire Service in Scotland went even further to promulgate their masculine image. Instead of doing 'monotonous chores' such as cleaning brasses, The *Sunday Post* of Glasgow trumpeted they were 'undergoing a commando course that's tougher in parts than that given a famous Guard's regiment . . . Although it was snowing the men, stripped to the waist, were doing complicated physical exercises to toughen up muscles and endurance powers. Boxing, wrestling, and unarmed combat followed in rapid succession.'[177]

Drawing on and reacting to the centrality of the figure of the soldier-hero to wartime hegemonic masculinity as well as to a longer discursive tradition that

---

[173] *Firefighter*, Jan. 1941, 6. MS 346/4/87i, at the MRC.

[174] John Horner, the union president discussed the idea at a London Conference on Productive Work at which the delegates demanded that the Government increase productivity. *Firefighter*, Apr. 1942, 1. MS 346/4/89, 1941–51. 'Miscellaneous Copies of *Firefighter*', at the MRC.

[175] *Firefighter*, July 1942, 1. MS 346/4/89, 1941–51, 'Miscellaneous Copies of *Firefighter*', at the MRC.

[176] Ibid. 4.   [177] 'Scotland's New Commandos', *Sunday Post* (Glasgow), 24 Jan. 1943, 9.

14. London firemen manufacturing paddles.
ACME

depicted workers' struggles with battle imagery, working men attempted to position themselves as patriotic and manly heroic figures. Workers emphasized their manly skill, strength, endurance, their fighting spirit, and their capacity to protect women and children, fashioning themselves as worker-heroes who were as important to the nation as soldier-heroes. In the case of the Fire Brigades, they fought two wars at once—both the war against Germany and the class war. Such self-portraits were drawn in a way that produced wartime masculinity in the mould of a courageous, strong, and skilled working-class hero; one whose loyalty to the nation was above reproach, and who stood ready to protect his working-class sisters temporarily employed at his side.

Hegemonic masculinity combined, I have argued, two potentially contradictory masculinities—one exemplified by the soldier-hero, and the other generated from the anti-heroic mood of the inter-war period and fashioned in opposition to the hyper-masculine German other. But to perform it successfully men had to be in uniform. Lacking a military uniform, working men stressed the heroic features of their masculinity. They drew upon both a language of military battle and a language of working-class manhood in their self-representations.

Given the conceivably contradictory combination of traits associated with heroic military and temperate masculinities, how did they coexist and become so dominant in World War II Britain? As I have already suggested, the connections between masculinity and national identity made it crucial to oppose Britishness and Germanness. Additionally, some of the characteristics of this composite masculinity had long-standing historical connections to middle-class and elite Britishness.

But there is something that is also more fundamental to masculinity in British culture (or indeed western cultures more generally) at work here. Military/heroic masculinity, because it symbolized power, allowed for the assimilation to masculinity of what, in other contexts and articulations, might be considered soft, feminine traits.[178] In the Gulf War in the United States, for example, Norman Schwartzkopf, the US Commander-in-Chief, expressed sentimentality, and made it possible for grown men to cry and remain masculine. Analogously, as Graham Dawson has so elegantly shown, T. E. Lawrence, portrayed by Lowell Thomas as a veritable model of the British Imperial hero, could assume Bedouin dress and emulate Bedouin ways without losing his Britishness.[179] As Dawson put it, 'the meeting of cultures is not reciprocal. Lawrence the European can "go native"; but the natives are not enabled to "go civilized." '[180]

Feminist theorist Rosi Braidotti has proposed that masculinity and femininity

[178] This point is also made by Segal, *Slow Motion*, 103.
[179] Dawson, *Soldier Heroes*, chap. 6, 'The Blond Bedouin: Lawrence of Arabia and Imperial Adventure in the Modern World', 167–90.
[180] Ibid. 186.

are not symmetrically opposed to one another.[181] I am interpreting this to suggest that while women could not assume masculine characteristics without jeopardizing their femininity, 'real men', and in World War II those 'real men' were soldiers, could absorb and claim for masculinity those characteristics and behaviours primarily associated with women.

The nation itself is linguistically gendered, although its gendering is unstable. As a 'homeland', as a space of belonging, the nation can be either masculine or feminine—fatherland or motherland.[182] So too as a subject of history the gendering of the nation is not fixed. When under attack, the nation often is portrayed as a violated but supremely moral feminine body. But as the active subject of history, especially when the nation is waging war, it is cloaked in masculinity. But as this chapter has suggested, the form of masculinity that defines the nation is unstable. It is envisioned in relation to others—to the enemies without and within. In World War II Britain, the nation-at-war was a masculine subject, but this was a temperate masculinity. Combining good humour and kindliness with heroism and bravery was an unstable mix. Pushed too far in one direction, it could uncomfortably resemble the hyper-masculine Nazi enemy. Pushed too far in the other direction, it could slide into effeminacy.

In order for men to be judged as good citizens, they needed to demonstrate their virtue by being visibly in the military. It was only then that the components of hegemonic masculinity could cohere. It is no wonder then that male workers on the home front likened themselves to battle heroes while attempting to make the case that their contributions to the nation and those of men in the armed services were equivalent.

---

[181] Rosi Braidotti, *Nomadic Subjects: Embodiment and Sexual Difference in Contemporary Feminist Theory* (New York: Columbia University Press, 1994), 160.

[182] See Prasenjit Duara, 'Historicizing National Identity, or Who Imagines What and When', in Geoff Eley and Ronald Grigor Suny (eds.), *Becoming National* (Oxford and New York: Oxford University Press, 1996), 167.

6

Geographies of the Nation

In popular imagination nations are presumed to be 'natural' groupings that incline people to experience a sense of belonging, identity, and commonality of sentiment. The metaphoric relationship between the family and the nation links what is supposed to be 'natural', the family, constituted with both gender difference and a hierarchy of age and generation as central components, with the nation, containing at its centre power differentials such as those based on gender, class, and race. But other images—images that combined unity with non-hierarchical diversity were necessary to depict Britain as a nation constituted as both a multiplicity of regions and as a cultural, if not political, 'multi-nation' composed of four distinctive 'national' cultures: Northern Ireland, Wales, Scotland, and England.[1]

As a number of scholars have proposed, verbal and visual depictions of landscape are powerful ways of representing the idea of the nation as a unitary entity and of

---

[1] The term 'multi-nation' is derived from J. G. A. Pocock's term, 'multiple nation'. See J. G. A. Pocock, 'Conclusion: Contingency, Identity, Sovereignty', in Alexander Grant and Keith J. Stringer (eds.), *Uniting the Kingdom? The Making of British History* (London and New York: Routledge, 1995), 301. For discussions of what has come to be known as 'the new British history' and its fluid geographic boundaries, see J. G. A. Pocock, 'British History: A Plea for a New Subject', *Journal of Modern History*, 47 (1975), 601–21 and his 'The Limits and Divisions of British History: In Search of the Unknown Subject', *American Historical Review*, 87 (1982), 311–36. Also see Hugh Kearney, *The British Isles: A History of Four Nations* (Cambridge and New York: Cambridge University Press, 1995); Michael Hechter, *Internal Colonialism: The Celtic Fringe in British National Development, 1536–1966* (Berkeley and Los Angeles: University of California Press, 1975); Keith Robbins, *Great Britain: Identities, Institutions and the Idea of Britishness* (London and New York: Longman, 1998). Also see, David Cannadine, 'British History as a "New Subject": Politics, Perspectives and Prospects', in Grant and Stringer (eds.), *Uniting the Kingdom?*; Eric Evans, 'Englishness and Britishness: National Identities, c.1790–1870', in ibid.; and Keith Robbins, 'An Imperial and Multinational Polity: The Scene from the Centre, 1832–1922', in ibid. Also see Raphael Samuel's 'deconstruction' of the regional and ethnic homogeneity of Great Britain in his *Theatres of Memory, ii. Island Stories: Unravelling Britain* (London and New York: Verso, 1998), esp. 50–73.

stimulating national identity.[2] But landscape, while often symbolizing the whole, and meant to depict something generic, is necessarily a depiction of particular locales, since all the various geographic features and styles of living that exist within the nation state cannot be portrayed simultaneously. As this chapter will suggest, during the war, visions of the English countryside commonly were invoked to conjure the whole.[3] Less frequently, urban landscapes also were deployed, especially those of war-ravaged London, most notably symbolized by the famous December 1940 photograph of St Paul's Cathedral surrounded by billowing black smoke with its dome lit by a sky glowing with fire. This urban representation, however, depicted the nation at war, whereas the countryside symbolized its historical permanence. The British remained profoundly ambivalent during the war about whether countryside or city could lay claim to representing 'the authentic nation', an ambivalence born, in part, from the place of the rural in the nation. The countryside in twentieth-century Britain was both central and peripheral to the nation, its positioning underscored by a war that revealed an ongoing conflict between rural and urban/industrial interests and ways of life in spite of, and often in response to the unifying pressures of wartime.

Furthermore, the tension between Welsh and Scottish identity, on the one hand, and understandings of Englishness and Britishness, on the other, very overtly complicated the idea that the nation was an organic community even as the multi-nation was threatened from without. This tension was one that the British Government, and the agencies and allied organizations that participated in constructing the diverse country as a unitary nation recognized and took into account. They attempted, in doing so, to show Britain as a unitary and culturally diverse nation, a tactic that often ran afoul of local sentiment. This chapter, then, examines the diversity of regional cultures and its consequences for the national imaginary. The chapter begins with the subject of rural life and its contrasts with urban and industrial Britain, and then moves on to an exploration of Welsh and Scottish identities.

Country and City

As Raymond Williams suggested, for some centuries the contrast between country and city has been a major way of envisioning social transformation.[4] For Williams,

---

[2] See e.g. Stephen Daniels, *Fields of Vision: Landscape Imagery and National Identity in England and the United States* (Cambridge: Polity Press, 1993); Simon Schama, *Landscape and Memory* (New York: Alfred A. Knopf, 1995); and the very well argued and highly relevant book by David Matless, *Landscape and Englishness* (London: Reaktion Books, 1998).

[3] On the 'rural myth' in wartime films and its significance to national identity, see Jeffrey Richards, 'National Identity in British Wartime Films', in Philip M. Taylor (ed.), *Britain and the Cinema in the Second World War* (London: Macmillan, 1988).

[4] Raymond Williams, *The Country and the City* (New York: Oxford University Press, 1973, paperback edition 1975), 189.

glorification of the country was a backward-looking nostalgia that evaded directly critiquing capitalist social and economic transformation. Yet the representation of 'authentic England' (that often was conflated with Britain) as a particular form of rural landscape dates from the late nineteenth century. To a large extent, as Alun Howkins has claimed, it is a vision of the 'south country', formed in contrast to 'outcast London' and to Britain's decline as an industrial and imperial power.[5] In contrast to urban places, especially to London, the country and its people were envisioned as 'the essence of England, uncontaminated by racial degeneration and the false values of cosmopolitan urban life'.[6]

The rural ideal emerging in the years prior to World War I stood for continuity in contrast to change, community as opposed to social fragmentation, and class harmony as compared with social discord. This was later to become an increasingly domesticated landscape rather than one envisioned as rugged or wild. It was also the early years of the twentieth century that saw the birth of the English Folk Revival a movement that valorized folk songs and dances, and the preservation of 'traditional' modes of performing them.

The English Folk Revival, particularly under the tutelage of Cecil Sharp, who maintained that the folk song was 'the faithful expression in musical idiom of the qualities and characteristics of the nation', was part and parcel of the construction of 'authentic England' set in a rural landscape.[7] As historian of the English Folk Revival, Georgina Boyes, put it, 'the musical idiom which characterised the nation emerged as the product of a pre-industrial idyll, devoid of politics, urbanism, social disquiet and any contemporaneity'.[8] But it was Sharp's critic, the eccentric Rolf Gardiner, who was actively promulgating the development of a culture of folk dance and song in the 1930s and 1940s.[9] As Boyes has argued, Gardiner's fundamentalist view of folk music and dance counterposed the authenticity of the rural folk with the failure of community in urban settings. In contrast to Sharp's dictates prescribing exacting technique and precise performance of the forms of folk culture, Gardiner's approach stressed the ' "original" motivation for ceremonial dance' to counter a morally bankrupt materialist and mechanized civilization.[10]

---

[5] Alun Howkins, 'The Discovery of Rural England', in Robert Colls and Philip Dodd (eds.), *Englishness: Politics and Culture 1880–1920* (London: Croom Helm, 1986), 62–88, esp. 63–7. For other analyses of rural communities, see Brian Short (ed.), *The English Rural Community: Image and Analysis* (Cambridge: Cambridge University Press, 1992).

[6] Howkins, 'The Discovery of Rural England', 69.

[7] Cecil Sharp as quoted in Georgina Boyes, *The Imagined Village: Culture, Ideology and the English Folk Revival* (Manchester: Manchester University Press, 1993), 97.

[8] Ibid.

[9] For informative discussions of Gardiner, see Patrick Wright, *The Village that Died for England: The Strange Story of Tyneham* (London: Vintage, 1995), 151–62, 176–202, and Matless, *Landscape and Englishness*, 119–30.

[10] See Boyes, *Imagined Village*, 156–7.

The years after World War I saw a 'back to the land' enthusiasm among the middle and elite classes with both a boom in the market for fiction and nonfiction concerning country life, and an increasing search for outdoor recreation by city dwellers.[11] H. V. Morton's *In Search of England*, an illustrated guide and reflection on the necessity of seeing the English countryside 'as a living thing' and as 'guarding the traditions of the race' published in 1927, was in its twenty-sixth edition by November 1939, and in its thirtieth edition in 1943.[12] Accessed by motor cars for those who could afford them, and by railway excursions and charabancs for those who could not, the countryside became the setting for holiday camps and the destination for tourists, ramblers, and cyclists, extending formerly elite preoccupations to those who were less privileged. The appeal of the countryside spread to numerous urban and town dwellers who looked to the rural as a place of tranquility and rest, making access to privately held land an issue that has persisted since. It was also in the inter-war years that England's 'rural tradition' was accorded attention by commentators across the political spectrum.[13] As art historian Alex Potts has observed, it was then 'that a nationalist ideology of pure landscape came into its own'.[14] This rural village life and landscape symbolized historical continuity, simplicity, and spiritual renewal. Thus it is not surprising that during the war the Government, the news media, and public figures not to mention motion pictures rendered their national celebratory images as vistas of a rural landscape.[15] Here is Vera Brittain writing in *England's Hour*, published in 1941:

But more than all, England for me means the fields and lanes of its lovely country; the misty, soft-edged horizon which is the superb gift to the eyes of this fog-laden island; the clear candour of spring flowers; the flame of autumn leaves; the sharp cracking of fallen twigs on frosty paths in winter. These are the things which, no matter where I may travel, I can never forget; this is the England which will dwell with me until my life's end.[16]

---

[11] Martin J. Wiener, *English Culture and the Decline of the Industrial Spirit, 1850–1980* (Cambridge and New York: Cambridge University Press, 1981), 73. See the discussion by Howard Newby, *Country Life: A Social History of Rural England* (Totowa, NJ: Barnes & Noble Books, 1987); Robert Graves and Alan Hodge, *The Long Week-End: A Social History of Great Britain, 1918–1939*, 2nd edn. (New York: W. W. Norton, 1994 [1940]), 254–69. For a richly textured description of the recreational uses of the countryside, see Matless, *Landscape and Englishness*, chap. 2.

[12] H. V. Morton, *In Search of England*, 30th edn. (London: Methuen, 1943), p. x.

[13] Sian Nicholas, *The Echo of War: Home Front Propaganda and the Wartime BBC, 1939–45* (Manchester: Manchester University Press, 1996), 233; for a discussion of this point, see Raphael Samuel, *Theatres of Memory, i. Past and Present in Contemporary Culture* (London: Verso, 1994), esp. 295–9. See also Alison Light, *Forever England: Femininity, Literature, and Conservatism between the Wars* (London and New York: Routledge, 1991).

[14] Alex Potts, 'Constable Country between the Wars', in Raphael Samuel (ed.), *Patriotism: The Making and Unmaking of British National Identity, iii. National Fictions* (London: Routledge, 1989), 166.

[15] Jeffrey Richards, 'National Identity in British Wartime Films', in Philip M. Taylor (ed.), *Britain and the Cinema in the Second World War* (London: Macmillan, 1988), esp. 44–7.

[16] Vera Brittain, *England's Hour* (New York: Macmillan, 1941), 197.

Similarly J. L. Hodson described his reactions to the ringing of church bells to celebrate the Allies' victory in Egypt in the fall of 1942.

That in me which has kinship with the soil and woods begins to stir; I seem to be aware
of older generations dead and gone moving within me. Home and England and wooded
Lancashire come welling up and much of the shell I've grown since boyhood begins to drop
away and I feel young and small. I am aware of a boy in an Eton collar going to church to sing
in the choir.[17]

For Hodson, the rural recalled the innocence of childhood and his belonging to the
England whose 'older generations dead and gone' were within him. And journalist
C. Henry Warren wrote in *England is a Village* that 'England's might is still in her
fields and villages, and though the whole weight of mechanized armies roll over
them to crush them, in the end they will triumph'.[18]

A. G. Street was a farmer as well as a popular writer and in the 1930s and
1940s generally attempted to portray farm life without the gloss of the picturesque.[19]
But Street too drew upon the nationalist imagery of 'authentic England' by
picturing for a BBC radio audience the 'mythical Wessex village of Sedgebury
Wallop'.[20]

The time is Sunday afternoon at three o-clock, the sun is shining brightly, and the old
dairyman is toddling along the lane behind his cows with his little grandson helping him
to drive them into milking. Suddenly the siren begins to scream, giving warning that enemy
aircraft are in the district. 'Hitler's whistle, granfer, Hitler's whistle,' pipes the child, and
whacks Buttercup to make her hurry up. 'Let she bide,' says the ancient, 'an let un blow. Thaass
cows maun be milked whatever.'

The siren gave its last wail, as two local wardens in Sunday suits and steel helmets cycled
by. Apart from this the English scene remained unaltered. The cows plodded on slowly.
Parents and children pursued their Sunday walk towards the primroses in the woods. The
crops continued to grow. The village still nestled serenely under the downs, its houses and
cottages rallying round the church and the inn as from time immemorial. The sparrows still
twittered in the thatch, and the starlings still gurgled on the roof of the barn. That was the
picture of Sedgebury Wallop in war time while danger threatened.[21]

Street portrayed his Wessex village using many of the tropes of England as a
rural landscape. His use of dialect reinforces the distinctiveness of rural people,

---

[17] James Lansdale Hodson, *Home Front* (London: Victor Gollancz, 1944), entry for 15 Nov. 1942, 240.

[18] C. Henry Warren, *England is a Village* (London: Eyre and Spottiswoode, 1941), p. ix, as quoted in
John Taylor, *A Dream of England: Landscape, Photography and the Tourist's Imagination* (Manchester:
Manchester University Press, 1994), 199.

[19] B. A. Holderness, 'The Farmers in the Twentieth Century', in G. E. Mingay (ed.), *The Vanishing
Countryman* (London: Routledge, 1989), 110.

[20] A. G. Street, 'Country Days', Home Service broadcast, 9 May 1942, Radio Talks Scripts Films 519 and
520, at the BBC Written Archives Centre, Cavisham Park, Reading (BBC WAC).

[21] Ibid. 5.

emphasizing their imperviousness to change in their 'country' mode of speaking in spite of nearly seventy years of public education, and the influence of BBC English daily brought into many rural dwellers' homes on the wireless.[22] It also establishes Street as a knowledgeable interpreter of and guide to the countryside. The association between rural life and innate stability is reinforced by 'granfer's' persistence in seeing to the milking despite the threat of enemy bombs. It is underscored as well by images of the countryside as a domesticated landscape and of the village itself, with its inn, church, and thatched cottages that lie outside politics.[23] Street also depicted country people as having the supreme ability, touted again and again as characterizing the British in wartime, to 'carry on' in the face of adversity. Street entitled his published diaries of the early war years *Hitler's Whistle*, and he used the above story, 'The Alert', as the introduction to the volume.[24]

On 27 October 1939 he recorded in his diary his impressions of his journey to London and again used the countryside to symbolize stability while describing London as dramatically altered.

To the uninitiated the countryside looks just the same as it always did in November. As even the wheat is coming up and the flame of the leaves flutters down. The elms have turned from lemon to amber, and the oaks shown ginger-brown according to their habit.[25]

The only visible change, Street wrote, was the

increased activity of the plough . . . For the rest it is the November as of old.
. . . the one to which I journeyed was changed out of all knowledge. The contrast was so great that I suddenly realised just how heavy the hand of war has been laid upon London Town.[26]

He noticed, in particular, the lack of traffic in Bond Street, the black-out, and the sandbags everywhere.

During the 1930s the uses of the countryside were subject to dispute among ramblers, conservationists, and landowners.[27] In 1932, for example, there was a mass trespass of Kinder Scout in the Derbyshire Peaks District. Although it was organized by the British Workers Sports Federations, a communist organization, members of rambling clubs also participated, and the event energized a growing access move-

[22] Street had written before about his imaginary village of Sedgebury Wallop, and also about a dialect-speaking 'granfer' in a story, 'The Wisdom of the Ancient', originally published in 1932 but reprinted in a collection of stories published in 1941. See A. G. Street, *Harvest by Lamplight* (London: Faber and Faber Limited, 1941), 18–25.

[23] As Howkins has pointed out, straw thatching is regionally specific to the south of England (Howkins, 'The Discovery of Rural England', 62).

[24] Interestingly, he changed 'granfer' to 'grandad', although he retained grandad's dialect in the published version.

[25] A. G. Street, *Hitler's Whistle* (London: Eyre & Spottiswoode, 1943), 23.   [26] Ibid. 24.

[27] Tom Stephenson, *Forbidden Land: The Struggle for Access to Mountain and Moorland* (Manchester: Manchester University Press, 1989).

ment.[28] But such open contestation ended with the war, as the depiction of common purpose became primary, and the countryside came increasingly to stand for the England that the people were defending.[29] During 1941, as cities across Britain were coping with continued bombing, Mass Observation asked people, 'What does Britain mean to you?' Like Vera Brittain, they responded by imagining the countryside, and when talking about the cities, they counterposed them with 'authentic England'.[30]

Images of rural England served also to contrast visually England and Germany. In the summer of 1940 as the Battle of Britain was raging, *Picture Post* published an essay describing what the British would lose if the Nazis were to succeed in conquering the country. On the left side of the two-page article was a photograph of sheep being herded down the street of an English village passing in front of its church. The caption read, 'Sunday Afternoon in England: All is Peace.' The caption for the picture on the opposite page read, 'Sunday Afternoon in Germany: All is Peace,' underscoring with irony the contrast with Britain—Germany being represented by a photograph of a mass of marching soldiers stretching as far as the eye could see down the main thoroughfare of a German town.[31] The countryside not only symbolically contrasted England and Germany, but peace and war as well. This theme also was represented in films. *Went the Day Well?*, directed by Alberto Cavalcanti and produced by Michael Balcon for Ealing Studios in 1942, shows a peaceful, rural village of cottages and wooded lanes, seemingly safe and secure. The script, based on a Graham Greene short story, pits the villagers against a small group of armed German soldiers there to survey the countryside preparatory to installing equipment that would disrupt England's radio network prior to a massive German invasion. When the villagers discover that the intruders are German soldiers, the Germans imprison them in the church; the rest of the film deals with the villagers' attempts to get help or to escape. The film contrasts the Nazi menace with the peacefulness and serenity of the English countryside. The countryside was also powerfully celebrated in Michael Powell's *A Canterbury Tale*, and in Humphrey Jennings's *Listen to Britain* which opens with a field of wheat blowing gently in the wind.

The countryside as symbolic of peace constituted a central theme in artist Edward Seago's book of paintings and essays, *Peace in War*.[32] When on leave from the army, Seago went to East Anglia, Somerset, Wiltshire, Norfolk, and Sussex to paint. Seago wrote about his time in Norfolk, 'as I worked I forgot the cry of the birds, I forgot that I was on leave; I forgot that our country was at war'.[33] In the essay

---

[28] Michael Bunce, *The Countryside Ideal: Anglo-American Images of Landscape* (London and New York: Routledge, 1994), 180.

[29] For a good discussion of the English landscape and wartime England, see Taylor, *A Dream of England*, 198–211.

[30] Wiener, *English Culture*, 74.   [31] *Picture Post*, 13 July 1940, 10–11.

[32] Edward Seago, *Peace in War* (London: Collins, 1943).   [33] Ibid. 12.

15. National Savings advertisement: soldier dreaming of home, portrayed as a rural landscape. Public Record Office

The letter home

Each lad as he writes to his Mother
Is conjuring up in his mind
All the scenes and sounds of his homeland
And the folk that he's left far behind.

The tinkle of sheep on the hillside,
The chime of the village church bells,
The tang of the spray off the Solent,
The grandeur of Cumberland dells.

Some yearn to be tramping the moorland,
Some sigh for the Yorkshire dales —
The warm sunny slopes of the Mendips —
The blue hazy hilltops of Wales.

So let's give Salute to our Soldiers,
And remember, wherever they roam,
That when they're not fighting, they're thinking
And dreaming of England and home.

SALUTE THE SOLDIER

Salute the men thousands of miles from home, who seldom think of danger but often think of those they left behind. Save more and yet more — not only during your Special Week, but all the time — to Salute the Soldier.

Issued by the National Savings Committee

'The Flooded River', accompanying a painting of a swollen river he deployed the rhetoric about patriotism and citizenship prominent at the time:

It is simplicity of purpose, rather than selfishness, which makes me still seek . . . Beauty to-day. Am I an escapist? I know the path of my purpose, and it is a path now obstructed by war; to follow that path I must enter the conflict. Maybe there are alternative routes. The way of the Conscientious Objector, for what has war to do with an artist? Or the other route, with the field of battle for its goal; Patriotism, the Rights of Nations, Justice. No, I have taken neither of these alternatives. I am a Patriot because I love the English countryside, and the simple life of its country folk; I am not a politician. And a Conscientious Objector? In my heart I feel that the carnage of war is the vile and wicked of all evil. But I am a Citizen of the land I love, where I have found happiness in Peace, therefore in adversity I shall still share the rights of that citizenship.[34]

In spite of, or more accurately, along with such elegiac depictions of 'authentic' England, conflict over the representation and meanings of rural life continued throughout the war out of the direct gaze of national publicity.

The Land Worker, the journal of the National Union of Agricultural Workers—one of the two unions representing farm workers, frequently commented with wry humour on the portrayal of 'picture-book' rural village life, as contrasted with the 'real country'.[35] For example, in May 1940, a journalist wrote,

[s]tory-books and picture postcards do not let water in through the roof . . . They show the smoke from the chimney rising gracefully and perpendicularly . . . they do not show the smoke coming down and out of the wrong end of the chimney, chased by a howling wind, and ultimately finding egress through the open door, which is ever-open for more reasons than the artist would like to admit even if he knew.[36]

On the same page, in a column about 'Our Visitors', there were printed popular derisive witticisms about children who were evacuees, townsmen who made idiotic statements and asked stupid questions, and jokes about Cockneys.[37]

As a union publication, *The Land Worker* focused on class issues, especially the question of wages, and 'tied cottages'. Articles complained bitterly about farmworkers' low wages relative to workers in industry. While both the farmers and the farmworkers decried the loss of agricultural labourers to other industries, the workers frequently blamed the farmers for the situation. Norman Douglas, a farmworker from Basingstoke, Hants., for example, wrote to the *Farmer's Weekly*, the magazine of the farm employers' association, the National Farmers Union, accusing farmers of paying such low wages that agricultural workers had to work long

---

[34] Ibid. 25–26.
[35] The other union was the Transport and General Workers' Union which the NUAW joined in 1982. The NUAW had tripled in size by 1945, and reached its peak membership of 137,000 in 1948. See W. A. Armstrong, 'Farmworkers in the Twentieth Century', in Mingay (ed.), *The Vanishing Countryman*, 129.
[36] 'The Picture Postcard Country Cottage', *The Land Worker*, 21 (May 1940), 9.   [37] Ibid.

hours 'simply to exist'. He complained as well of farmworkers' housing conditions. He wrote, 'Some of them are nothing more than slums. We don't need to look in the large cities for the depressed areas. We have them here in our own countryside.'[38]

Farmworkers often lived in cottages owned by their employers, and were subject to rent increases as well as eviction. After securing a rise in the minimum wage in May 1940, for example, the National Agricultural Workers' Union journal complained that now that wages were being increased, farmers were demanding an increase in rents.[39] A year later, *The Land Worker* argued that the minimum wage had to be increased, and complained that the forces opposing an increase again gave the picture of

the happy countryman with a cheap charming cottage, a nice little garden, a pig, and a few fowls. The nice little garden is often a dung-heap where he buries the contents of the earth closet once or twice a week, and there are thousands of farm workers who cannot keep pigs and poultry, or even grow vegetables in a backyard. Men living in tied cottages are frequently forbidden to keep livestock.[40]

In July 1942, the paper demanded the elimination of the 'tied cottage system . . . a system which has sapped the independence of the rural worker'.[41]

Agricultural workers sometimes used sarcastic tones, deploying gendered imagery in their expressions of 'class feeling', as in the following example,

The Honorable Phyllis Plushbotham will, now talk on Agriculture from a Worker's Point of View! She will explode many of the existing false ideas and show that a lot of nonsense is talked about long hours, low wages, bad cottages, and petty tyranny. The Hon. Phyllis Plushbotham joined the W.L.A. [Women's Land Army] last week so she speaks as an expert.[42]

Although the Union eventually recruited members of the Women's Land Army, very early in the war the union publication ridiculed them. Here, it portrays the women who join as part of the elite icily commenting on the class divide.

Increasingly, both farmers and farmworkers expressed pride and patriotism in what they saw as the growing importance of agriculture to wartime Britain. The *Farmer's Weekly* trumpeted in the summer of 1940,

Food is news to-day. Every man and woman in Britain is interested in it . . . For the first time in a decade the town housewife looks beyond the shop to the fields . . . at last food has become . . . something more than the stuff [delivered] to the door every day . . . For much longer than most of us care to remember there has been misunderstanding, suspicion and bad faith between town and country . . . What matters now is that, given goodwill in all

[38] *Farmer's Weekly*, 31 May 1940, 14.
[39] *The Land Worker*, July 1940, 2. The new minimum weekly wage was set at 48 shillings a week.
[40] *The Land Worker*, July 1941, 6.   [41] *The Land Worker*, July 1942, 7.
[42] 'She Knows It All', *The Land Worker*, 20 (Aug. 1939) (article printed on the inside of the cover at the back of the journal).

sections of the community throughout Britain and the essence of life in England to-day is that there is present mutual goodwill in all classes—then we may stand at the dawn of a new era . . . The farmers are doing a magnificent job of work for the country. The Government admits that and the public is gradually realising it.[43]

Here we see a refrain that farmers repeated over and over again, one that both contributed to the wartime ideal of class harmony and confirmed the notion that class tensions were muted in village life. Although the farmworkers rarely, if ever, touted class harmony in their publication, they too shared the farmers' pride in their industry assuming a new importance.

We do not need to glorify the war to recognise that it lays bare artificial and false values. This war should have convinced the average townsman that he is very small fry indeed as compared with The Land Worker. When the history of the war effort comes to be written it will do serious injustice . . . to those who have played so magnificent a part . . . if it does not place The Land Worker in a special place of honour.[44]

But even as they applauded farmwork, both farmers and farmworkers emphasized the separation of country and town. The distinction between country people and town residents assumed a particularly important role in commentary about the evacuation.

The *Farmer's Weekly* framed the problems presented by the evacuation of urban children to rural areas as symptomatic of the contrast between city and country. At the end of September 1939 the journal indicated that the evacuees were the major subjects of conversation among people in the country. The writer commented, 'not all of them to understate it a little, are agreeable ones.' Using language redolent with the trope of the city child as urban savage popular in the late nineteenth century, the writer went on to say, '[W]e find that the small human animal, out of its element, shows itself to be a wild and undisciplined creature quick to wriggle away from the conventions of civilisation.'[45] A month later, the *Farmer's Weekly* published the following 'evacuees story': 'A temporary "mother" was cooking eggs and bacon for breakfast. The little Cockney boy lodging with her asked what it was. She told him . . . The reply was 'For your breakfast.' And the little boy, disgusted, answered at once, "Oh, I'm not eating that. At home we have chips and ale". '[46] Making the country-and-town distinction central to the story, the writer discounted the idea that poverty was at the root of what they were observing about their wartime guests, writing, 'It is just that there is evidently such a difference between town poverty and country poverty . . . I think of the country cottage women living near me who are managing splendidly to bring up their large families on labourers' wages . . .

---

[43] *Farmer's Weekly*, 26 July 1940, 14.
[44] Ernest Green, 'Why This Inferiority Complex?' *The Land Worker*, Jan. 1943, 2. Green was the General Secretary of the Workers' Education Association (WEA).
[45] *Farmer's Weekly*, 29 Sept. 1939, 30.   [46] *Farmer's Weekly*, 27 Oct. 1939, 30.

Poverty in the country hasn't the same ugly look as in towns.'[47] The writer of the 'Home Section' of the *Farmer's Weekly* suggested that poor house-hold management by mothers was the cause of many of the evacuee children being 'unfamiliar with what we reckon to be "a good square meal" '. Mary Day concluded her article by surmising that after their experiences in the country 'our town dweller visitors . . . will go back with a changed point of view about housewifery'.[48]

And a letter writer to *Home and Country*, the magazine of the Women's Institutes (the organization for women in rural regions of the country), wrote, 'We have learnt by actual contact now how differently the other half of the world lives; we have seen too the other half appreciates us as little as we appreciate them.'[49] By 'other half', the writer referred not to the poor, but rather to the urban poor. In an attempt, perhaps, to leaven the complaints about the evacuees by injecting humour, the editor of *Home and Country* invited readers to write in, telling of their 'funniest experience in connection with Evacuees'.[50] But, of course, this too underscored the inherent difference between town and country.

Complaints about the evacuation experience were not all one-sided. The teachers who accompanied urban schoolchildren to the countryside expressed disapproval of the reception of city dwellers in country villages. A writer for the *London Schoolmasters' Association Bulletin* was of the opinion that,

[T]eachers have learnt a great deal. Of the snobbery and hypocrisy of the countryside they had read in novels. Of the pettiness and paltriness and limitations of local authorities they had no conception. Shakespeare's Dogberry and Dickens' Bumble live to-day clothed in the dignity of petty offices. The exaggeration of the Press has made teachers physically sick . . . Children think too. One such graded her various hostesses thus: the 'kindly-pass's'; the 'reach yerself'; the 'pass the ruddie—'.[51]

The evacuation scheme, as Chapter 2 has shown, became a central lens through which the British focused on 'the social question' throughout the war. But it also became the focal point of tension between what were imagined to be two opposing ways of life—urban and rural. The cultural construction of the country and the rural village and home as the heart of 'authentic England' were very much a part of public commentary and debate about the evacuation. As Maggie Andrews has perceptively noted, this construction was central to rural women's sense of identity— an identity with boundaries drawn 'through difference and against what was identified . . . as . . . their ideological opposite', urban ways.[52] As the Minister of Health told an audience at the Annual General Meeting of the National Federation of Women's Institutes,

---

[47] *Farmer's Weekly*, 27 Oct. 1939, 30.   [48] *Farmer's Weekly*, 10 Nov. 1939, 30.
[49] *Home and Country*, Nov. 1939, 401.   [50] *Home and Country*, Jan. 1940, 13.
[51] *L. S. A. Bulletin*, Mar. 1940, 3. MS 38A/6/ME/1/14, at the Modern Records Centre, Warwick.
[52] Maggie Andrews, *The Acceptable Face of Feminism: The Women's Institute as a Social Movement* (London: Lawrence & Wishart, 1997), 113.

The land is the mother of us all, but the members of the Women's Institutes are the mothers of the land. Here we have the wives and daughters of the farmers of England and Wales, who are the people who really have made the land of England and Wales in thousands of years of patient toil . . . the land is . . . the home of the nation, the foundation of the folk, the place we summon to our minds when we make the word England with our lips. We do not think of England as London, Manchester or Birmingham, and we . . . do not think of Wales as Cardiff or Swansea: we think of those innumerable valleys, those great smiling countrysides, those areas covered with the oldest industry in the world where really the vital activities of the nation are carried on.[53]

The broader construction of the 'authentic nation' as a rural landscape, and the association of the land as the 'mothers' of the people were also incorporated by rural people themselves in establishing a rural identity.[54] As a consequence, the evacuation produced, as Maggie Andrews has argued, a discourse of 'towneyism'.[55]

This discourse amplified the outrage over the dirty slum children who were supposedly not trained 'in decent habits'. Writing in the Fabian Society's report on the evacuation about the reactions of people in North Norfolk to the children from central London, Lady Sanderson, an organizer for a Women's Voluntary Services Centre, wrote, 'It is . . . unfortunately true that many children from apparently good homes, where the father is in work and conditions are good, have shown a complete ignorance of the purpose of a lavatory.'[56] *Our Towns*, a study of the evacuation by the Women's Group on Public Welfare that was read widely when it was published in 1944, stated:

Rural life has advantages of great price: clean air and sleep-giving quiet, ready access to a diet balanced by fruit and vegetables, few temptations to extravagance . . . juxtaposition of the social classes, the force of public opinion in small communities, the influence of tradition and the extraordinary interest, discipline and emotional enrichment of tending growing things which brings an element of personal responsibility and creativeness into the humblest lives. The life of the countryman is nearer to that of the long ago ages which have fashioned man's subconscious self and is more deeply satisfying to instinct. So many aids and incentives to self-respect are lacking in the mean streets of a great city and in the mass-handling to which their denizens are subjected, that a resultant weakening in personal discipline can cause little surprise.[57]

---

[53] *Home and Country*, July 1939, 261.

[54] James Vernon makes a very similar theoretical argument about the construction of Cornish identity. See James Vernon, *Border Crossings: Cornwall and the English (Imagi)nation* (Manchester: Manchester University Press, 1998), 153–72.

[55] Andrews, *Acceptable Face of Feminism*, 113.

[56] Lady Sanderson, 'North Norfolk', in Richard Padley and Margaret Cole (eds.), *Evacuation Survey: A Report to the Fabian Society* (London: George Routledge, 1940), 226.

[57] Women's Group on Public Welfare, *Our Towns: A Close-up* (London: Oxford University Press, 1943), 6.

The long-lived belief that country life was morally and psychologically healthier than city life was commonly expressed. A. G. Street, for example, wrote in his published diary, 'My firm conviction is that country life produces a saner, more wholesome human being than any town life can produce; that the real heart of Britain is still to be found in her rural districts; and that in time to come . . . this truth will be plain to all the world.'[58]

And writing in the 'Design for Britain' series about post-war reconstruction, C. E. M. Joad, the moral philosopher, wrote about Britons being aware during the war,

of a curious stirring of affection, a wistful and nostalgic affection, as for something that we once had and have lost and forgotten that we ever had—now it is stirred to dim remembrance—when we come into contact with country things and country ways . . . Now we would not so talk and boast (about escapes from civilisation) and lovingly remember, and invent, when remembrance fails us, unless these things had a hold upon us, redressing something that is one-sided in our way of living, appealing to a need, that was submerged and giving us something of which we stand desperately in want but have somehow missed.[59]

Writing in the Fabian evacuation report, Lady Sanderson applauded village foster mothers for their patience in training the children and the children's subsequent acquisition of 'clean and tidy habits'. She also commented on how much country life improved the children's physical and mental health.[60] Drawing on common tropes of rural life that imagined the land as 'mother', she wrote,

There could have been no better proof of the belief that the country is a child's spiritual home than the reactions . . . of the evacuees to the freedom of the countryside and the shore. Some could hardly believe that they could roam at will, that they could pick the flowers, that they could climb in and out of boats on the beach. The bigger boys spent much of their time 'helping' the farmers, and indeed they were a very real help in many cases.[61]

Sanderson concluded her observations on the North Norfolk experience of the evacuation by maintaining that 'a home in which the mother has to go out to work is no home for the children', and that some sort of evacuation scheme should be instituted in peacetime so that the country or the seaside would be an 'integral part of the life of every town child'.[62]

Mary Day, writing in the 'Home Section' of the *Farmer's Weekly*, went even further. She claimed that evacuation children did not wish to go back to their city life and live as they had before. The children were proud of their responsibilities:

feeding the hens, collecting eggs, helping to bring in the cattle—all this is beginning to make them realise that their town amusements were dull in comparison. They are, in fact, coming

---

[58] Diary entry for 29 Dec. 1939, in Street, *Hitler's Whistle*, 38.
[59] C. E. M. Joad, *An Old Countryside for New People* (London: J. M. Dent, undated), 5.
[60] Ibid. 226.   [61] Ibid. 227.   [62] Ibid. 231.

16. News photograph entitled 'Evacuee Treat',
1 January 1940. Hulton Archive

into the heritage every child should have, and of which our sophisticated civilisation has deprived them until now.[63]

The restorative power of the countryside was so significant to Mary Day's vision of a healthy and 'authentic England' that she insensitively commented,

for the town children this war has been a blessing. No single reformer, nor worthy-purposed body, had achieved for them the chance Hitler has given them to inherit a world in which old values have become sharp again, and old bad conditions have been bombed out of existence.[64]

Using an imperial metaphor in another essay, Day likened the city and its way of life to a morally bankrupt society that lacked true civilization. She proposed that the city children who had been evacuated to the country and had learned country ways should become

colonisers of their own country. They are learning, as the colonists learned, to forget the less satisfying trappings of an easy existence; and are discovering for themselves how to come to terms with the real business of living . . . If we can pass it on to these boys and girls who would probably otherwise have grown up to know only the worst and most imitative and dependent aspects of civilisation, then—like colonists everywhere—they will be able to take a full part as citizens in the new world it is our duty to hand over to them; and build up new cities according to a way of life they themselves must be left to shape.[65]

The belief that the health of urban children was degraded, and that life in the countryside was rehabilitative while shoring up popular images of country life, was not supported by the evidence about the children that was collected. Surveys conducted in 1940, in fact, showed no significant difference in the growth rate of evacuated London County Council children as compared with an equivalent group of London children in 1938.[66] But even philosopher C. E. M. Joad believed that the countryside would nourish evacuee children spiritually changing their lives forever.

For the first time a generation of town's children, evacuees, growing up in the country, with a familiarity with country ways, country sights and sounds. Some will never go back to the towns. In those who do, there will remain an abiding memory . . . a memory which will break out in a continual solicitation to return if only for a brief period, to the scenes of childhood; a memory then, which will never wholly let them alone.[67]

---

[63] *Farmer's Weekly*, 7 Mar. 1941, 47.   [64] Ibid. 47.   [65] *Farmer's Weekly*, 23 May 1941, 41.

[66] For a discussion, see John Macnicol, 'The Effect of the Evacuation of Schoolchildren on Official Attitudes to State Intervention', in Harold L. Smith (ed.), *War and Social Change: British Society in the Second World War* (Manchester: Manchester University Press, 1986), 3–31. The Women's Group on Public Welfare, however, reported evidence that the percentages of elementary schoolchildren found dirty and/or verminous by School Nurses in 1938 was generally higher in 'specimen evacuation areas' than it was in 'specimen reception areas'. See Women's Group on Public Welfare, *Our Towns*, 7.

[67] Joad, *An Old Countryside*, 5–6.

The definition of the 'authentic nation' as a rural community that framed discussion about evacuees both reinforced the distinctiveness of rural areas as contrasted with urban ones, and created a language that exposed some of the tensions between country and town that were inherent in conjuring Britain as a unitary national entity. Like Lady Sanderson's depiction of Norfolk, the responses to the Blitz collected by the National Federation of Women's Institutes from its member organizations across the country both expressed how shocking the evacuation-produced exposure to urban life was to the rural women, and reinforced the idea that rural life could transform and heal the ills caused by urban society.

Belief in the restorative value of country life contributed, as well, to depictions of 'healthy' femininity constructed in contrast to 'city girls'. *Sunday Chronicle* columnist Beverley Nichols described a 'typical' member of the Women's Land Army,

Her hair, a few weeks ago, had been a shimmering synthetic gold. Now it was reverting to its natural chestnut, and it seemed to me a much prettier colour.

Her lips, a few weeks ago, had vied with her nails. And the words that came from them were 'yes, moddom,' 'No, moddom.'

To-day those lips were parted in a perpetual, rippling smile. And the words that came from them, as she looked up from her milking stool were, 'Oh, I'm so happy!' . . . They have learned the beauty of the soil . . . its sanity and its sweetness. And the office desk, the factory, the flat, the hotel, the shop-counter—will never see them again.[68] Not only would these city girls become purified by their work on the land, they would not want to return to their former lives,

John Masefield, the Poet Laureate, celebrated the work of the countryside in a poem he published in 1942. The first part of the poem recalled farms of old and farmworkers in times past. Then the poem dealt with the war,

> Soon after dawn the other day
> I saw a tractor rive the clay,
> Sped by a girl of seventeen
> With hair of gold and trousers green,
> With fag against her dainty tongue.
> Her sister led a cart of dung.
> Beside the lane where she was going
> Boy-Scouts in shorts were busy hoeing,
> And as the leader of the band
> The local parson bore a hand,
> And further on, a girl apart
> Was loading up a turnip-cart.
> The same old work was being done
> With pleasure, comradeship and fun;
> And at the days-work-end for these

[68] *Sunday Chronicle*, 5 May 1940, 2.

Even in war-time, there was ease,
And strength remaining for delight
In other joy than gin or fight.[69]

Contrasting country women and city-reared 'Land Girls' also confirmed the opposition between the two forms of femininity represented during the war—maternal femininity and sexualized femininity—discussed in Chapter 4. J. R. Allan, writing for the *Glasgow Herald*, told a story about 'The Merry Widow', a 'womanly woman' and mother of eight children who supported her family by being a farmworker: '[s]he was so completely of the countryside . . . Now what chance has the Land Girl against the memory of such a woman?' He introduced his comparison by claiming that the Land Girls have a 'stiff drill to hoe'. He explained that since she comes from a town, '[s]he probably uses the make-up . . . more effectively than the locals. She probably wears breeches on a figure that shows them off to an advantage not common in country working clothes. The men are inclined to despise her in the fields because she doesn't know her job, and the women to fear her in the fields in case she knows too much.'[70] Here, the country 'mother of eight' both illustrated maternal femininity in contrast to sexualized femininity, and was used to highlight the values of country life in contrast to those of city life. Country life fostered a more fundamental set of commitments than those of the city, represented here as superficial and possibly dangerous.

Discourses that made rural England emblematic of the 'authentic nation' figured rural life styles as more healthy than urban ones, and imagined exposure to the land as curatives of social ills. They contrasted, however, with the sense that agricultural workers and farmers had of their 'second place' status in the nation. Agriculture, they believed, was not recognized as the essential industry that it was, and they were concerned that rural folk, especially farmworkers, were perceived as country bumpkins. The concern of agriculturalists that they were less valued members of the national community than urban dwellers and industrial workers was a primary reason for the BBC's inauguration of 'Country Magazine' in the spring of 1942. The programme turned out to be extremely popular and was on the air on alternating Sundays into the 1950s. It had been so popular during those years that Francis Dillon, one of the hosts of the show, published *Country Magazine: Book of the BBC Programme* in the 1950s.

The theme song of the programme was the folk song 'The Painful Plough', with words dating from the nineteenth century set to a tune that was much older. Its words expressed the sensitivity of agriculturalists about the importance of their livelihoods.

[69] John Masefield, *The Land Workers* (London: William Heinemann, Ltd., 1942), 10.
[70] J. R. Allen, 'Immemorial Land Girl, The Merry Widow', *Glasgow Herald*, 25 May 1940, 3.

The Painful Plough
Come, all you trusty ploughmen
of courage bright and bold,
Who labour all the winter
in the stormy wind and cold.
To clothe our fields with plenty,
Our farmyards to renew;
That bread may not be wanting
Behold the painful plough.

The townsman in his turmoil,
The gentleman at ease
Forgets the honest sailor
in peril on the seas.
But we do give him sustenance
And this he knows be true;
He sails upon the ocean
By virtue of the plough.

We are but humble ploughmen;
No calling we despise.
Each man for his own living
Upon his trade relies.
But were it not for ploughmen
Both rich and poor would rue,
For we are all dependent
Upon the faithful plough.

The words of the song expressed a major theme of the programme, the material centrality of agriculture to the nation.

The idea for such a programme seems to have come from multiple sources. The Secretary of State for Agriculture suggested in the fall of 1941 that the BBC produce a programme about country life, but it was not until the winter that plans were firmly underway to initiate the programme. Internal memos suggest that those at the BBC who were favourable to such a programme believed that the BBC had not up to this point addressed the fact that 'the great number of people who live in the country, are real country folk, and country-minded. There is an entirely different mentality among these people, they are interested in things which are scarcely known to townspeople, think in a different way, have a different outlook.'[71] Although the BBC received some complaints that the resulting show did not fairly

---

[71] Memo from Mr MacLurg to C(F) through A.D.V. 14/2/42. R 19/219/1 'Country Magazine 1: 1941–1946', at the BBC WAC.

present farmers and agricultural workers 'as at least as educated and efficient as they are', the programme was enormously popular.

In focusing on particular regions, however, the programme could stimulate complaints. For example, letters to the BBC charged that the North-East was not being given its fair share of representation on the general programmes of 'Country Magazine'.[72] The BBC also received criticism from people who did not like the way that their regions were portrayed. One comment, for example, suggested that a programme on Cornwall was 'largely spoilt by a "cultivated" Cornish accent apparently to conform with BBC requirements'. The person protesting said he had spent his whole life in the district from which the particular Cornish participants were drawn, and even knew some of them personally. But, 'it was the first time I ever heard them speak with quite the accent and the exaggerated colloquialisms they employed in their broadcast . . . if any of them were to talk in just the same way when mixing with their fellows . . . the general verdict would be "Old Bill's come over queer like, hidn'a?" '[73]

Most of the programmes featured the performance of a folk song and short talks by a variety of different local people. But controversy about how properly to represent the countryside was evident in any number of broadcasts; even the music was the topic of dispute. A. G. Street made it known on the first programme aired that he did not approve of the 'folksey wolksey', having 'no use for hey-nonny-nonny with a band . . . it'll confirm the countryman's worst suspicions about this Magazine.' And another participant from Worcestershire concurred saying, 'It certainly hasn't got much to do with the English Countryside of 1942.'[74] But the participants reluctantly agreed that the show should have a 'signature tune'.

Predictably farmers appeared on the programme. But so too did the district nurse, a birdscarer, a circus horse rider, postmen, architects, beekeepers, bird-watcher, a wherryman, a dairywoman and dairy farmer, and tradesmen of various sorts. The point of presenting the programme was to forge unity through exposing and articulating diversity, and to bring the country into the front parlours of city dwellings, thereby reassuring rural dwellers that they were a part of 'the People' in the People's War. Yet the anxieties experienced by agriculturalists that they were not being taken seriously by the rest of the country were intermittently expressed on 'Country Magazine' throughout the war. On a programme centring on Warwickshire that was aired in February 1943, for example, one of the participants observed that 'the townsman's beginning to appreciate the work of the farmer'. Another participant retorted, 'There's been a lot of nonsense talked about the way town and

---

[72] See memo of John Polwarth, Aug. 8 1944, ibid.

[73] 'Country Magazine, General. June 1942–1943, File 1', 25/11/44 in R 19/220/2, at the BBC WAC.

[74] Radio Play Library and Features Scripts, 'Country Magazine'. Transmission date 3 May 1942, Home Service, p. 1, at the BBC WAC.

country people mix . . . what concerns us are the ordinary people getting together.' And A. G. Street complained in April 1944,

I'm fed up to the teeth with those people who bleat about farming being a charming way of life and of farmers and their employees being such good fellows, don't you know, so unspoilt . . . take it from me that as long as farming here is treated politically as a charming way of life it will remain a hopeless way of misery.[75]

Street suggested that the only way to change things was to legislate to ensure that people could earn a livelihood from farming. He continued,

It's all very well for townsfolk to bleat about the beauty of the old thatched cottage, and the traditional lay-out of farm buildings. If you think those chaps in the Eighth Army are coming back to splash about in the dark up to their knees in muck with an oil lantern and for a low wage I don't.[76]

Attempting to represent unity through regional diversity continued to be problematic.

It is likely that Street's objection to 'folksey wolksey' songs and his arguments about the future of agriculture reflected his concern not just that the rural would once again be relegated to and depicted by the musical equivalent of the visual picturesque, but that the rural would remain old-fashioned and backward in the rest of Britain's eyes. As Chapter 5 has suggested, farmers and farmworkers were keen to emphasize the skill and technology that went into farming. These depictions by rural dwellers underscored that the countryside was a participant in and contributor to Britain as a modern society, and therefore was materially central to the nation both at war and in the future. As geographer David Matless has persuasively argued, many rural enthusiasts, preservationists, and town and country planners emphasized a form of modernity that combined an emphasis on technological progress with a focus on tradition.[77] Ruralists' depictions of the countryside were, to use Tom Nairn's famous phrase about the nation, 'janus-faced,' looking both backward to the past and forward to the future.[78]

Anxieties about the fate of rural areas in the future unsurprisingly surfaced as Britain looked forward to reconstruction.[79] Addressing a London crowd visiting a Food Exhibition in January 1944, the president of the National Farmers' Union, Captain J. Templeton, said that the Exhibition gave Londoners 'a glimpse of the economic haven which the countryside afforded to Britain in peace and war'. He warned, '[s]ocial and industrial security will be a mere shell if we don't put first

---

[75] Radio Play Library and Features Scripts, 'Country Magazine', Transmission date 23 Apr. 1944, Home Service, p. 14, at the BBC WAC.

[76] Ibid. 16.

[77] This is a major theme of Matless's *Landscape and Englishness*.

[78] Tom Nairn, *The Break-up of Britain* (London: New Left Books and Verso, 1980).

[79] See Matless's discussion of reconstruction, *Landscape and Englishness*, 189–205.

things first in post-war reconstruction. Food and clothing are the first material needs of every man, woman and child. Both come from the soil.'[80] But not surprisingly, the Scott Report, the major document dealing with reconstruction in the countryside, aroused controversy. It attempted to marry 'progressive agriculture' and modernization with preservation and aesthetics. As Matless has suggested, the Scott Report disconnected use and beauty. 'The aesthetic is upheld as crucial, yet is potentially disconnected from matters of social and economic functions, opening up the Report to accusations of arbitrary elite aesthetic "taste" and anti-functional aestheticism.'[81]

Although farmers and the Land Workers stressed the importance to the country of modernizing agriculture during the war, the countryside in the national imaginary was an aesthetic space that symbolized an enduring way of life. Rural landscapes symbolically made the countryside central to the nation as did the material dependence of the country and its war effort on agriculture. But rural dwellers and their advocates emphasized the irony of this centrality because they saw that their compatriots in the cities in fact made the material countryside peripheral; that it was given a back seat in an increasingly urban/industrial nation. There was a further irony in the depiction of the authentic nation as a rural landscape. That rural landscape generally was an English one. But England, of course, was just one part of Great Britain.

Scotland and Wales

While the English countryside provided a symbolic landscape for the whole nation that was contested by country people themselves, the Scots, the Welsh, and the Northern Irish were keenly aware of the frequent verbal slippages between England and Britain made by the BBC and Government representatives. If there was anything that could subvert the idea of the nation as unitary, it was when the British nation was referred to as England. That was a sure signal for the Welsh, the Scots, and the Northern Irish to put to the side their internal differences and to protest against the domination of their lands by 'Londoners'.

What follows focuses on Scotland and Wales. The existence of a continuing Irish nationalist movement, given the relative recency of the division between northern and southern Ireland, complicates including Northern Ireland in an analysis of British national identity and citizenship during the war. The Irish Republican Army positioned itself as pro-German and they continued their bombing campaign in 1939 and 1940 which resulted in some of their members being interned in Ulster. Because of concern that it would alienate Roman Catholics and Irish nationalists, as well as causing consternation among Irish-Americans in the United States, the

---

[80] *Farmer's Weekly*, 7 Jan. 1944, 16.   [81] Matless, *Landscape*, 221.

British Government decided against instituting conscription for work or military service in the province. Many men and women from Ulster, however, volunteered to serve in the military and a number worked in British war factories.[82] Adding to this complex situation, the position of Eire vis-à-vis Britain in the war (Eire remained neutral, but British industries recruited large numbers of men and women from the country to work in British war factories with the blessings of the Eamon de Valera Government) was ambivalent at best.[83] This ambivalence undoubtedly had an impact on Northern Ireland, especially because the borders between Ulster and Eire were extremely porous.[84] Because of these complications, especially the potentially explosive issue of Irish nationalism and Roman Catholic–Protestant discord, to have included Ulster in this study of national identity and citizenship in wartime Britain would have meant adding considerable length to an already long and complex chapter.

World War II was not a particularly central moment of political nationalism in either Scotland or Wales. Nationalism was, however, a matter of discussion and contestation—both within the principalities themselves and for the English who were concerned above all with national unity. This produced on the part of those responsible for morale some level of awareness of the sensitivity of the Welsh and Scots about their distinctiveness, but there were continual slips of the tongue and a more general failure to realize the depth and complexity of regional sensitivities. Thus, although political nationalism and the issues of devolution or home rule were matters of some (although limited) public discussion at various points in the war, the more persistently challenging wartime expression of Welsh and Scottish nationhood was in the form of 'cultural nationalism', or what has become known in recent decades, especially in the United States, as 'identity politics'.

Commenting sarcastically on the verbal slippage made by the English between England and Britain, Macnair Reid wrote to the *Glasgow Herald* that the Englishmen's use of the words 'English' and 'England' for 'British' and 'Britain' 'is perfectly consonant with English behaviour in every branch of our common life'.[85] And June Dunlop agreed, saying, 'In times like these every effort should be made to unite all peoples under the British flag—beginning at home. At the present moment the English are doing their level best to cause disruption on the home front by the careless misuse of the aforementioned term.'[86] Arthur McDougal was outraged when

---

[82] For a brief discussion, see Angus Calder, *The People's War: Britain 1939–1945* (London: Pimlico, 1992), 113–14.

[83] For a discussion of Irish migration to Britain during the World War II, see Enda Delaney, *Demography, State and Society: Irish Migration to Britain, 1921–1971* (Liverpool: Liverpool University Press, 2000), esp. 117–44. See also Colin Holmes, *John Bull's Island: Immigration and British Society, 1871–1971* (London: Macmillan, 1988), chap. 2.

[84] Calder, *The People's War*, 414.   [85] *Glasgow Herald*, 27 Nov. 1939, 5.
[86] *Glasgow Herald*, 9 Dec. 1939, 5.

Duff Cooper, the new Minister of Information, gave a speech entitled 'The Soldiers of England' in May 1940. He wrote, 'How long must we in Scotland continue to be irritated, exasperated, and insulted by Englishmen with suburban London minds? It is just this sub-conscious attitude of the English that lost America, lost Ireland, and which . . . may ultimately break up the Empire. When will they think imperially and not in terms of London?'[87] For McDougal, the Government's insensitivity in equating England and Britain, or in making England central to the nation and relegating the principalities to the margins, threatened the end of the British empire as a whole and was not just a problem for the non-English parts of Great Britain.

In June 1941 Scottish complaints about how the nation was often named reached into the House of Commons. A Scottish Labour MP submitted a written question to the Prime Minister suggesting that when Government ministers and other officials used 'England' for 'Britain', they 'cause hurt to Scotland, and Northern Ireland, and the other lands of our common people, who are together in the one purpose and spirit'. The Prime Minister wrote in response that he saw 'no necessity for any further special directions' to ministers and the BBC concerning the precise 'meanings of the terms England, Scotland, and Britain'.[88] The Prime Minister apparently was of the opinion that enough had been said on the subject.

Scottish sensitivity about the use of 'England' for the entire nation was not universal. Occasionally, letters were written to the *Glasgow Herald* by people who were concerned that such sensitivity was detrimental to the war effort. D. Beveridge, who identified himself as 'a Scot living abroad, in England', said that England often was used unthinkingly for Britain, but, in fact, the English had great respect for Scotland. 'So let us all pull together, for I am sure, it is essential, particularly under existing conditions, that we should act as one great loyal and faithful family.'[89] But just how were the Celtic principalities figured as members of the 'loyal and faithful British family'? As distant cousins or as stepchildren, perhaps?

An English journalist who spent two years living in Wales blamed his compatriots on the other side of the Welsh border for their insensitivity and lack of understanding of the Welsh. He wrote, 'it is the fault of that amused intolerance, that ever so slight, graceful, but maddening sense of superiority with which they treat all other races. Have you ever seen the Englishman abroad . . . or in the Empire, in the Colonies, in India? If you have you will know what I mean.'[90] He went on to describe a self-satisfied English nationalism. But he also blamed the Welsh for having 'isolated and insulated yourselves, preserved your national culture almost at

---

[87] *Glasgow Herald*, 22 May 1940, 5.   [88] *Glasgow Herald*, 19 June 1941, 3.
[89] *Glasgow Herald*, 9 Dec. 1939, 5.
[90] Barry Roland, 'Wales Must Wake Up and Scheme!', *Western Mail & South Wales News*, 6 Aug. 1943, 2.

the expense of your national survival'. In effect he accused the Welsh of not being active modernizers, and of doffing 'the cap of national pride to the bowler hat across the border'.[91]

The Ministry of Information was aware that the substitution of England for Britain produced resentment on the part of Northern Ireland, Scotland, and Wales, and warned the BBC in October 1939 to avoid doing so.[92] And to recognize the national sentiments of the Scots and the Welsh, the BBC produced special pro-grammes dealing with their war effort and their distinctive cultures. But this strategy, too, could produce dissonance. As early as November 1940, the Assistant Senior BBC News Editor wrote an internal memo to one of the producers of such programmes, 'I am afraid we are broadcasting so many Scottish postscripts that some English listeners are getting a bit restive, and I think it would be well, therefore, to lay off the subject for a bit unless you have material of quite exceptional quality.'[93]

To highlight the differences amongst the areas of Britain, and also to explore the controversies internal to the regions/nations as to how they configured their own identities, the BBC ran a series of broadcasts on the regularly scheduled programme 'Living Opinion' on such topics as 'What is a Welshman?'. For example, three Welshmen participated in the discussion airing on an evening in mid-January 1943 hosted by a non-Welshman, Frank O'Connor. The hallmark of the programme was to explore disagreements among the participants. The men disagreed about the status of Wales as a 'conquered people', the extent to which the Welsh are a religious people, and the value of preserving the Welsh language.

The programme aired on 22 January and within a few days of the broadcast, let-ters complaining about it began appearing in Cardiff's *Western Mail*. B. Jones wrote to express his 'profound disgust at the feeble way in which Welshmen endeavoured to define themselves, and worst of all their countrymen . . . Our only failing is that we have allowed the Englishman to rule our destinies too long.'[94] D.B. wondered 'Why should Wales be continually represented by those whose platform is the revival of the chapel? Welshmen are keen business men, good organisers, with sound business acumen who can stand alongside any other nationality. I trust that the B.B.C. are not pricking [*sic*] these people with the intention of annoying us.'[95] 'Stick It, The Welch' proposed that 'the B.B.C. officials who arrange these talks should try to enlist the aid of people who know how to put things over in a just manner and not give us any more of this "inferiority complex" type of individual'.[96]

Letters supporting the views of the radio commentators and contesting the

---

[91] Ibid.

[92] Nicholas, *Echo of War*, 231.

[93] ASNE to Miss Orr, 9 Nov. 1940, in 'Postscripts: New File 1b April 1941–1942', R51/422/2 File 1B, at the BBC WAC.

[94] *Western Mail*, 27 Jan. 1943, 5.   [95] Ibid.

[96] *Western Mail & South Wales News*, 30 Jan. 1943, 3.

remarks by the letter-writing critics also were published in the press. A few of them recognized that the BBC was attempting 'to vent quite freely and frankly opinions held by different sections of the community'.[97] The correspondent G.H.T. took issue especially with the critics who were infuriated by the opinion aired by one of the broadcasters about the Welsh language, and maintained that there were 'hundreds of Welshmen to-day who believe . . . that the Welsh language might just as well be dead . . . And . . . on the deeper issues of life language, after all, is of little importance.'[98]

The Welsh language, spoken largely in North Wales and pockets of Welsh-speakers in some of the mining and industrial areas of South Wales, was central to expressions of Welsh nationhood, and was a lively topic of debate among the Welsh themselves during the period. Especially since 1918, the issue of the pre-servation and teaching of the Welsh language had become a significant aspect of Welsh nationalism. Prior to that time, there was relatively little emphasis placed on whether or not people were speaking Welsh.[99] According to historian Kenneth O. Morgan, the increased attention to the Welsh language that came in the inter-war period was a consequence of the growing decline in the proportion of Welsh speakers in Wales. From 43 per cent of the population in 1911, by 1921 the proportion of those 3 years of age or older in the Welsh-speaking areas had declined to 39 per cent.[100] The depression in agriculture in the 1920s contributed to the continued decline in the population of Welsh-speaking rural communities and the widespread economic downturn in Wales during the 1930s further contributed to the migration of Welsh speakers. Thus, in the inter-war period, recognition by Welsh-speaking nationalists that the Welsh language might become eclipsed probably incited their concern for the teaching and use of the Welsh language.[101] In part to foster the Welsh language and Welsh culture more broadly, the *Urdd Gobaith Cymru*, the Welsh League of Youth, was founded in 1922. The movement grew rapidly in the 1930s and actively pressed for the teaching of Welsh in the schools, and for Welsh-language primary education. Originally founded for Welsh-speaking youth, during the war years the *Urdd* expanded to form English-speaking Welsh youth clubs. Among Welsh nationalists there apparently was concern that Welsh culture would be weakened by the wartime efforts at national unification, as well as by increased contact between Welsh people and those from outside Wales. And they continued to foster Welsh-language instruction, the establishment of Welsh-language primary schools, and Welsh-language use throughout the period.

The movement to recognize and foster the Welsh language, because of its

[97] *Western Mail & South Wales News*, 29 Jan. 1943, 3.   [98] Ibid.

[99] See Kenneth O. Morgan, *Modern Wales: Politics, Places and People* (Cardiff: University of Wales Press, 1995), 212.

[100] Kenneth O. Morgan, *Rebirth of a Nation: Wales 1880–1980* (Oxford: Clarendon Press, 1981), 242.

[101] Ibid. 242–6.

symbolic equation with a distinctive Welsh culture and substantively for Welsh speakers who were not bilingual, had some success during the wartime period. Parliament, spurred on by its Welsh members, the majority of whom spoke Welsh as their primary language, passed the Welsh Courts Act granting legal status for the use of Welsh in court proceedings. The fact that Welsh was not officially recognized in the British judicial system had long been a sore point for Welsh nationalists. In Wales, at least, many municipalities paid the fees for Welsh translators when necessary. What the Welsh wanted was to remove the legal restriction against the use of Welsh in the courts by repealing the Act of 1536 that put it there in the first place. Apparently Government officials in London approached the matter with a good deal less seriousness than their Welsh colleagues. For example, Harold Nicholson judged Herbert Morrison's speech supporting the repeal to be unduly flattering to the Welsh Members, and Lady Astor commented, 'I would rather be blown up than suck up'.[102]

Although the Welsh as well as the Scottish radio wavelengths had to be utilized for national purposes during the war, the BBC offered nationwide Welsh-language (and Gaelic) broadcasts on the BBC Home Service. There were daily 5 p.m. 'News in Welsh' broadcasts as well as a daily Welsh children's programme, and after Welsh MPs and Lloyd George intervened, twice monthly religious services from Wales, some in Welsh, were aired. If anything the amount of spoken Welsh broadcast during the war increased over what was offered when the Welsh radio station was fully operational. There were regular features in Welsh on the Forces wavelength as well.

The BBC regularly featured the popular Welsh playwright Emlyn Williams who gave Sunday night Postscripts and other talks to a national BBC audience. In one of these talks, Williams spoke of his Welsh upbringing and by talking about the significance of the Welsh language which he had spoken as a child, he underscored the title of his talk, 'I'm Not English'.

I'm a foreigner. My father and mother speak to each other in this barbaric tongue, my four grandparents spoke no other, and it is doubtful whether any of my eight great-grandparents ever heard one word of the language in which I am speaking to you now. I won't go back further than the eight great-grandparents, partly so as not to bore you with further details of my ancestry, and partly because . . . I don't know any. But I would say that eight non-English-speaking great-grandparents is pretty good proof of foreign blood.[103]

Williams, undoubtedly with some degree of sarcasm, called himself a 'foreigner' at a time when to be foreign might incur suspicion or even hostility to make the point that the Welsh are not English.

[102] Harold Nicolson, diary entry for 14 Oct. 1942 in *Diaries and Letters*, ii. *The War Years: 1939–1945* (New York: Atheneum, 1967), 251.

[103] Emlyn Williams, 'I'm Not English', 22 Sept. 1940, Home Service. Radio Talks Scripts Film T 651/652, at the BBC WAC.

In spite of the efforts of the BBC, agitation for more and better Welsh programming continued. Even the *Western Mail*, a consistent critic of Welsh nationalism, urged the BBC to use the Welsh radio station and wavelength exclusively for programmes about Wales in Welsh and English. The *Western Mail* was concerned that 'the tens of thousands of Wales's sons and daughters now widely dispersed shall feel they are in closer and more frequent touch with home, and tens of thousands of strangers within our gates shall learn more about the people and the land that have adopted them'.[104]

Debates about Welsh BBC programmes, such as the one about 'What is a Welshman?' discussed above, commonly appeared in the 'Reader's Views' columns of the *Western Mail*. For example, a flurry of letters greeted a programme about Monmouthshire entitled 'The Shining Land'. This prompted 'Hostis' to write that protests about Welsh programming were useless. 'It seems as far as Wales is concerned, we are up against the totalitarian outlook that we are supposed to be fighting against. Your readers protest, but no material changes are made in the programmes.'[105] Another writer complained that the programme on Monmouthshire 'might have been produced by "Haw-Haw" to ridicule us'.[106] These letters illustrate how wartime discourse about Nazi Germany could be deployed to express a sense of Welsh subjugation in response to Government efforts to produce national unity.

Thus, while the war could well have diminished expressions of nationalist sentiment on the part of the principalities, increased national attention to Britain's diversity as part of the attempt to foster national unity seems to have encouraged it. Agitation by Welsh and Scottish nationalists continued, and public concern about conserving and strengthening their cultural particularities was coincident with their commitment to the war effort. As Christopher Harvie has said with regard to Scotland, '[T]he war itself ought logically to have killed nationalism *tout court* . . . Nationalism's resilience was remarkable.'[107]

One Government policy in particular aroused nationalist sentiment and was met with animosity, both in Wales and in Scotland—the Ministry of Labour and National Service policy of conscripting young, unmarried women, and moving them to areas of the country where their labour was most needed. This meant that women and girls were required to leave their homes and travel beyond the borders of the principalities into England. The policy was regarded by some of the Welsh as another instance of English insensitivity.[108] And in Scotland, it was one of the most contentious of issues during the war.

[104] John Pennant, 'Wales Wants Its Own Wave-Length', *Western Mail & South Wales News*, 24 Oct. 1942, 3.

[105] *Western Mail & South Wales News*, 23 Dec. 1943, 3.   [106] Ibid.

[107] Christopher Harvie, *Scotland and Nationalism: Scottish Society and Politics, 1707 to the Present*, 3rd edn. (London: Routledge, 1988), 30.

[108] Reginald Coupland, *Welsh and Scottish Nationalism: A Study* (London: Collins, 1954), 339.

The Scottish Trades Union Congress expressed itself against the policy, and the Scottish National Party (SND) held protest rallies against it. In the summer of 1942 numerous letters appeared in the *Glasgow Herald* about the policy.

For example, one letter writer complained bitterly not only about the policy, but about the seeming insensitivity and lack of regard shown by the English in imposing such compulsory service on young Scottish women.

Conscription of Scottish girls for industrial service in England must cause pain to many who feel they have sacrificed a great deal in leaving their native country . . . As the parent of a girl drafted to the South, I know how great a strain this policy of transfer to a strange land whose speech, habits, and outlook are foreign to us can impose . . . If the national feeling of opposition to 'foreign service' . . . is to be overcome it can only be by a frank appeal to patriotism coupled by an admission of mistakes made in the past. Attempts to minimize the sacrifice demanded of Scots girls and their parents can only intensify the discontent already so widely felt.[109]

This letter stimulated a heated exchange of views on Scottish nationalism in the letters column for the next several weeks.

A self-identified English engineer working in Scotland commented that any parent who complained when their daughter was sent to work 'in "foreign" England [displays] an outlook typical of a rabid Scottish nationalist . . . I do not regard Scotsmen as foreigners, but as my fellow countryman . . . Does this whimpering parent reflect on the many young men sent to far outposts of this Empire—many of them never to return?'[110]

His letter, in turn, produced the following retort from J.S.M. to the engineer's remark that he did not consider Scotsmen to be foreigners:

No doubt to him they are just citizens of that England which, judging from the B.B.C. and English newspapers, stretches from the English Channel to the Pentland firth. But his whole letter reveals what a foreigner he is in Scotland.

Mr. Tulip's letter is not much in itself, but alas! it represents a point of view common south of the Border. The sooner Englishmen realise that Scotsmen are utterly opposed to 'gleichschaltung' whether from Berlin or from London, the better it will be for our common effort to save Britain and the world from Nazi domination.[111]

Once again we see anti-Nazi rhetoric being deployed to articulate the claims of regional difference. But not all of the letters expressed opposition to the policy of sending Scottish women to the Midlands.

There also were letters from mothers who said that their daughters were very happy working in the South. One said, 'they have found nothing "alien" in any

---

[109] *Glasgow Herald*, 27 July 1942, 2.   [110] *Glasgow Herald*, 2 Aug. 1942, 2.
[111] 'An Englishman's Comments', *Glasgow Herald*, 6 July 1942, 3.

way.'[112] And a mother from Inverness wrote, 'let us stop giving Hitler the idea that Scotland is not united in her war effort.'[113] But the Scottish National Party used the occasion of a Wallace Day anniversary celebration in Elderslie to pass a resolution condemning the policy. MP Alexander Sloan who spoke at the rally remarked, 'If transportation continued, the government were going to denude Scotland of its womenfolk.' In his comments Sloan accentuated the problems Scotland already faced from a falling birth rate.[114] His remarks constructed Scottish nationalism as the virile defender of national integrity.

Eventually, the debate over the policy of sending Scottish women into England produced an opening for Scottish nationalists to discuss the problems of Scottish economic underdevelopment. This tack was taken by the Scottish National Party and the District Committee of the Communist Party.[115] But this position was not argued solely by political radicals. The very moderate *Glasgow Herald* editorialized,

The need for the transfer of mobile women to English factories . . . is the result of faulty planning in the past. There seems to be no reason whatever why a number of the war factories which make a heavy call on female labour should not have been built in Scotland instead of being concentrated chiefly in the English Midlands. The failure to distribute them properly was a first-class blunder, and it is regrettable that Government spokesmen who have to deal with Scottish complaints do not admit this blunder more frankly, even more apologetically and combine with the admission an appeal to the patriotism of Scots girls and their parents.[116]

The considerable unhappiness in Scotland over the transfer of Scottish 'mobile women' to England also was argued in the House of Commons by Scottish MPs. The Labour MP for South Ayrshire, for example, said that 'nothing in his lifetime had aroused so much resentment in Scotland as this taking away girls to England. Many of them would never come back. That was the way to wipe out a population. Scotland must not be allowed to be denuded of its womenfolk.'[117] Clearly the term 'denuding' was a popular one in the debate. Another Labour MP, the left-leaning David Kirkwood, who complained of the depopulation of Scotland and its 'being denuded of its women', was rewarded with appreciative laughter when he said that the 'Minister of Labour had been left with the baby to hold because the Government had to find labour to fill the English factories'—factories which should have been built in Scotland at the outbreak of the war.[118] Not surprisingly, as these remarks illustrate, gender figured heavily in the rhetoric of protest, a protest that also concerned the underdevelopment of Scottish industry by the Government in London. It figured as well in the reply by the Parliamentary Secretary of the Ministry of

---

[112] *Glasgow Herald*, 8 Aug. 1942, 2. [113] *Glasgow Herald*, 15 Aug. 1942, 2.
[114] *Glasgow Herald*, 24 Aug. 1942, 3. [115] *Glasgow Herald*, 17 Sept. 1942, 3.
[116] *Glasgow Herald*, 7 Aug. 1942, 4. [117] Ibid. [118] Ibid.

Labour who denied that 'there was some sinister design to depopulate Scotland and repopulate England with the best blood. He was a great admirer of Scottish girls but he would be no party to any sinister design of that kind.'[119] This comment also amused a number of the assembled members.

'Class feeling' also informed some of their remarks. The Labour MP for Gorbals who had opened the discussion said that in his district 'there was a widow's daughter being hounded [about leaving Scotland to work in defence], and 10 minutes walk away they saw the servant still working. They felt that they were not being fairly treated.'[120] The fear that 'class feeling' might be provoked by the antagonism generated by moving young Scottish women into the Midlands was also evident in a report by an MOI Staff Speaker who visited Scottish women workers in Midland factories. She wrote, 'Although the discontented are in a minority, they are noisy and influential, and there seems here to be rather fertile ground for Communist propaganda. When I spoke to an audience of about 600 Scots girls their enthusiastic applause for a reference to Russia was noticeable; many of them were wearing the hammer and sickle badge.'[121]

Primarily, however, the objections raised by the Scottish MPs articulated their sense of national cultural difference. Labour MP Mrs Keir Hardie said that young women were sent to England from Scotland on the theory that there would be a married woman in Scotland who could replace her at her former job. But, she said 'most working-class women in Scotland had big families. It was only in London they saw married women hanging on to a dog.'[122] The protesting MPs maintained as had Kirkwood, that to the young Scottish women 'English conditions were entirely foreign . . . The mode of life and the outlook were very different from a Scottish life.'[123]

Although the reception of the Scottish women by fellow workers and management in the Midlands was not always unfriendly, the MOI Staff Speaker reported that she learned that the attitude of their fellow workers and particularly of local girls, was frequently hostile. 'The English say, "We don't want you here; you have come to do us out of our jobs." At Swinnerton there seems to be real ill-feeling between the Pottery girls and the Scots; if the Inspector is English, "she takes it out of the Scots workers". In one hall an advertised "Scottish Night" had the word 'Scottish' deleted and an uncomplimentary term substituted. At another factory I found three newly arrives weeping outside the canteen, having been told by other workers that all the tables were booked.'[124]

In Wales as well there was unhappiness about the transfer of young Welsh women to England, and concern on the part of parents and others about their welfare. A Mrs Hopkin Morris, who chaired the South Wales Welfare Advisory Committee,

[119] *Glasgow Herald*, 7 Aug. 1942, 4.   [120] Ibid.
[121] 'Scotswomen Go South to War Work', M.O.I. Special Report, May 1943. INF 1/292 Part 3.
[122] Ibid.   [123] Ibid.   [124] 'Scotswomen', M.O.I. Report, May 1943, p. 5. INF 1/292 Part 3.

travelled to the Midlands to determine how the young women were adjusting to their new living conditions. She prefaced her report by acknowledging that conscription was viewed with dislike. 'What concerns us now is that the operation of the National Service Act shall be with as little detriment as possible to the values we prize in Welsh life; that the transference of girls from Wales shall not result in a permanent impoverishment of Welsh life.'[125] She alluded to the fine welfare work being done by a joint committee of *Undeb Cymru Fydd* (the Welsh Youth League) and the Welsh churches. But she also complained that the young Welsh women received no information on churches and their social and cultural facilities.

Scottish and Welsh cultural distinctiveness also was expressed positively during the wartime period, not just as a response to English slights, suggesting that regional identities, rather than being flattened by the war, continued to be matters of public attention and awareness. Only a few days after the war had begun, the *Glasgow Herald* expressed Scottish commitment to the war effort by constructing patriotism in the language of Scottish nationalism. It is worth repeating here at length, because of its evocation of history and of national heroes, classic references in nationalist rhetoric.

Scotland to-day, in common with the rest of the British Empire, is facing a crisis in her history. As the oldest of that group of nations, she can perhaps look back on more crises than any of her sisters . . . This, then, is a fitting moment in which to recall the spirit in which Scotsmen have faced previous days of darkness and menace, and to listen to some of the voices of our past for inspiration they can surely provide to us to-day.

The article went on to discuss some of the 'Great men of Scotland'. Readers were reminded that it was a Scot who wrote 'the rousing and audacious verses of "Rule Britannia!" ' . . . Some of the most stirring utterances of Scotsmen in moments of national crisis are anonymous, as though it were the spirit of the nation, rather than an individual citizen that spoke to the threatened people and the world.' The commentary applauded

the defiance by Wallace of the envoys of the English Commander before the Battle of Stirling Bridge . . . Scotland was not often united as a nation; but there were some occasions . . . when a common feeling bound together the greater part of her people, and dissentient minorities were negligible. Then the nation spoke with a singleness of heart and with inflexible resolution. Such was the national spirit when Scotland defended her freedom against Edward I.[126]

Even at the dramatic moment of Britain's declaration of war against Nazi Germany, the usually dispassionate *Glasgow Herald* reminded readers of Scotland's former independence as a way to inspire patriotic fervour.

[125] Mrs G. P. Hopkin Morris, 'Welfare of Welsh Girls in Midlands', *Western Mail & South Wales News*, 11 Apr. 1944, 6.
[126] 'The Week-End Page', *Glasgow Herald*, 9 Sept. 1939, 3.

Newspaper stories of wartime heroism on the part of Welsh and Scottish soldiers commonly appeared in the press. In April 1944, Cardiff gave the Welch Regiment the 'privilege, honour and distinction of marching through the streets of the City of Cardiff on all ceremonial occasions with bayonets fixed, colours flying, and bands playing'.[127] As the *Western Mail* headlined, Cardiff had 'adopted' the regiment. Calling upon a long history of military glory, the newspaper reported, 'Their battle honours tell, in purple, gold and crimson, of their heroism, courage and gallantry from Martinique to Waterloo; from Inkerman to Kimberley, South Africa; on the Somme and at Cambrai in the first World War of 1914–18, and now in the greatest war of all—in Libya, Crete, Sicily and Italy.'[128] Emphasizing the distinctiveness of the Welsh nation within Britain, the newspaper recounted the following 'epic story' of the current war:

After the withdrawal from Crete one of the Welch battalions was re-formed and took a prominent part in the advance to Agheila in December, 1941. When the Germans counter-attacked, units of the Welch, who held advanced positions, were cut off from the main body of troops at Benghazi.

They were forced to fight their way through the enemy lines in small parties and after a 300-mile march reached Tobruk. It was, as a survivor has since recorded, 'a story of 15 days tramping over hills behind the German lines. 15 days of lying low from the Germans, eating any food and living with the Arabs and Bedouins, and somehow getting back to fight again.

Not all reached our lines. Those who did were placed in hospital, and after hearing the story of their ordeal a Welsh medical officer told his orderly, "Don't put just British on their hospital cards; put Welsh." '[129]

Headlines such as 'Scots Battalion Repulse Nazi Brigade', and 'Welshman's Medal for Biggest Rail Smash', were common fare in Scottish and Welsh newspapers after D-Day.[130]

As the end of the war seemed to be in sight, newspapers began to publish commemorative stories such as 'Women of Wales on the War Front', praising the various roles that Welsh women played in the war effort; and 'Record of Scotland's Most Bombed City: Aberdeen's "Front-Line" Ordeal'.[131]

Such commemorative articles also could be the occasion for expressing regional resentment. Commentator John Pennant, for example, wrote of Welsh wartime achievements in the New Year's Day issue of the *Western Mail* in 1944. In addition to touting Wales's industrial achievements and military exploits, he wrote,

[127] J. H. Morgan, 'Cardiff to "Adopt" the Welch Regiment', *Western Mail & South Wales News*, 14 Apr. 1944, 3.
[128] Ibid.   [129] Ibid.
[130] See e.g. *Glasgow Herald*, 1 July 1944, 2; *Western Mail & South Wales News*, 30 Oct. 1944, 6.
[131] Dorothy Dungworth, 'Women of Wales on the War Front', *Western Mail & South Wales News*, 15 Jan. 1944, 3; *Glasgow Herald*, 8 May 1945, 3.

in this war official obtuseness has refused to recognise the value of keeping Welshmen together under Welsh officers in the traditional Welsh regiments. And so Welsh military achievement has been obscured or gains given tardy recognition.

True, the Welsh Guards have retained something of their national character, but even their sterling deeds all through the war have been damped down or get mere incidental mention.[132]

After detailing some of these feats, Pennant reminded his readers that there was a 'strong Welsh element' in the Hampshire Regiment, and 'even in the much-publicised "Scottish Highland Division" there are Welshmen'.[133] Pennant's comment about the Scottish Highland Division reflects Welsh perception of the undue prominence of the Scottish Highland Division, and a general sensitivity of the Welsh about the 'Scot-controlled War Office that gives their own fighting men preferential treatment'.[134] Letters in the Cardiff paper complained about 'Scotsmania' on the BBC and that the Scots forces were being credited on the BBC for all of the victories in North Africa. John Britain quoted the BBC as reporting 'Scottish and British troops [note the distinction] fought side by side. Sturdy Highlanders went right in. Nought could stop them.'[135] These letters prompted a response from 'Jock Britain', a former Highlander living in Wales. He insisted that, 'even if your correspondents are so anti-Scottish, they need not rush to put their biased bickerings into print, for in this war we are all—English, Welsh, and Scottish.'[136]

Welsh sensitivity about Scottish prominence continued to be articulated in the 'Reader's Views' column of the Cardiff newspaper throughout the war. 'Veteran' wrote a letter expressing his Welshman's sense of Scottish privilege:

Every day recently the radio and Press have been recording that 'Scottish troops did this or that' and that 'British troops did something else,' the latter, of course, means English or Welsh. If the Scots are to be specially mentioned as such then in common fairness the name 'British' should be dropped and the correct nationality given. But while we have to suffer a Scottish staffed B.B.C. and Ministry of Information this kind of thing will persist.[137]

To underscore his perception that the extent of recognition given to Scotland was undeserved, 'Veteran' complained that there 'must be quite five or six times as many Scots in reserved occupations, in munitions, shipbuilding, Government offices and Ministries as there are in the Forces, so it is evident that the English are doing the bulk of the fighting'.[138]

For their part, the Scots were unhappy that so many non-Scots were in the 51st Highland Regiment that Glasgow policemen called up for duty found that there were no openings for them.[139] And there was anger that while the kilt could be worn

[132] *Western Mail & South Wales News*, 1 Jan. 1944, 5. [133] Ibid.

[134] Letter from Keidrych Rhys, *Western Mail & South Wales News*, 8 Dec. 1942, 3.

[135] Letters from 'Fairplay' and 'Jock Britain', *Western Mail & South Wales News*, 25 Nov. 1942, 3.

[136] *Western Mail & South Wales News*, 1 Dec. 1942, 3.

[137] 'Are the Scots British?', *Western Mail & South Wales News*, 26 Feb. 1945, 3. [138] Ibid.

[139] 'Glaswegian' letter to *Glasgow Herald*, 6 Aug. 1942, 5.

for dress wear, it could not be worn into battle.[140] Early in the war the War Office sought to abolish the kilt from Scottish regiments on active service. Colonel Norman MacLeod spoke to a meeting called to discuss the ban. He advocated the formation of a select committee composed of Scotsmen to advise the War Office about the kilt.

We have no confidence in a War Office Committee, probably composed of English officers unsympathetic toward the Kilt . . . The ordinary Englishman cannot understand the sentimentalism and clannishness of the Scot, and is apt to sneer at it. But it is that sentimental love of the tartan and clannish spirit which have largely made the Highland regiments the dour fighters they are and for which they are renowned.[141]

In many ways, then, expressions of cultural distinctiveness were activated by wartime circumstances and the various attempts to imagine 'the nation' as unitary. Although there were voices both in Wales and Scotland who argued against those who insisted on emphasizing Welsh or Scottish particularity, even they contributed to a fraught conversation about regional/national difference that continued throughout the war. Even political nationalists, although certainly not a dominant force, did not absent themselves and their agenda for the duration.

Scotland's first nationalist political party, the Scottish National Party was formed by university students and small groups of other radical nationalists in 1928, although there had been calls for a nationalist party beginning in the 1890s. Home Rule had been advocated by Liberals, and with the party's decline the Labour Party took up the issue, although by the late 1920s it was not high on the agenda of either of the two major parliamentary parties. Once the Scottish National Party was established and began its slow growth, Labour's connections to Scottish nationalism withered. A decisive issue in those years was whether nationalism or socialism would be primary on the political agenda. At first the SNP's agenda was 'self-government for Scotland with independent national status within the British group of nations', but it moderated its position in 1934 when it joined forces with the more conservative pro-Home Rule Scottish Party advocating a Scottish Parliament which would govern Scottish affairs.[142]

As war loomed in the late 1930s, a new rent in SNP unity appeared as an anti-imperialist wing of the party declared itself in opposition to a London-led war. But the majority of the SNP subsequently abandoned their opposition to conscription and military service and the party supported the war effort. A group of members however, disgruntled with the SNP leadership, waged a successful challenge at the 1942 Glasgow party conference producing a decisive split. A powerful group left the

---

[140] See e.g. letters to the editor of *The Glasgow Herald*, 30 Nov. 1939, 5; 30 Apr. 1942, 4.

[141] *Glasgow Herald*, 8 Nov. 1939, 9.

[142] For a lively discussion of the people and politics of Scottish Nationalism, see Andrew Marr, *The Battle for Scotland* (London: Penguin, 1992).

SNP and set up the Scottish Convention. The SNP, although greatly weakened still fought by-elections, and its leadership continued their resistance to England by taking up such causes as opposing the transfer of young Scottish women to England. It also formed an alliance with the Welsh National party—the two parties agreeing to cooperate on matters affecting the two countries. At a conference in Glasgow at the end of November 1942 the leadership of the two organizations expressed concern about the 'increased encroachment of the centralised Government on the liberties and privileges of Scottish and Welsh citizens'.[143] But the SNP's membership dwindled, and what small political success it had was short-lived. In contrast the Scottish Convention, advocating Home Rule for Scotland, successfully recruited members and maintained itself as a nonpartisan pressure group establishing branches across the country. After the war it was to propose a 'Blue Print for Scotland', advocating a Scottish Parliament with jurisdiction over most domestic matters. It galvanized support for a 'Covenant' that pledged both loyalty to the Crown and commitment to securing a Scottish Parliament.

Political nationalism took organized form in Wales in the 1880s with the establishment in 1887 of Cymru Fydd League. The League grew out of and promoted the Welsh cultural revival and by 1890, it dedicated itself to a national Welsh legislative body and an Imperial Parliament in which Wales would be represented. This was a movement for devolution not for independence. The cause of Home Rule for Wales was given a parliamentary voice when Lloyd George was elected for Caernarfon Boroughs in April 1890 and the League's influence spread. In 1895 it formally merged with the North Wales Liberal Federation. Their political cause was supported in North Wales, but not in the south, and after 1898, Cymru Fydd foundered.[144] The cause of devolution was raised again when Welsh Liberals introduced a Home Rule Bill for Wales in Parliament in 1914. Shortly after, the war began, and the Bill had only the one reading. Consciousness of Welsh nationhood withstood the war and it emerged somewhat strengthened, in part by the fact that a Welshman, Lloyd George, had led Britain through it, and had fostered the formation of a new Welsh Division in the British Army. The Welch Guards was formed in 1915, and achieved military reknown during the war.[145]

Political nationalism, however, made little headway after the war as the division between North and South Wales became solidified, and the cause of Home Rule stumbled. As interest in Welsh national issues dwindled in both the Liberal and Labour Parties, Plaid Cymru the first nationalist political party in Wales, was formed in 1925.

It was, however, politically unsuccessful at the polls throughout the 1930s,

---

[143] *Glasgow Herald*, 30 Nov. 1942, 5.

[144] For a discussion, see Kenneth O. Morgan, *Rebirth of a Nation: Wales 1880–1980* (Oxford: Clarendon Press, 1981), 115–18.

[145] Ibid. 160–1.

although the activities of its main spokesman, Saunders Lewis, a writer and Lecturer in Welsh at University College, Swansea, gained press attention. He was jailed for nine months for having set fire to buildings at a newly formed RAF bombing school, the installation of which had been opposed by local Welsh residents. His trial was conducted in English at Old Bailey further inflaming his supporters and other Welsh nationalists. When war was declared, Plaid Cymru came out against Welsh involvement in what they termed a 'foreign', 'English imperialistic war'. This stance did not win large numbers of supporters, although it did encourage a small number of men and women to declare themselves conscientious objectors on political grounds.[146] The activities of Plaid Cymru during the war encouraged its vocal critics to keep both the party and its Welsh nationalist sentiments in public awareness.[147] Interestingly, Lewis himself emerged from seclusion to contest a by-election for the Welsh Universities, doing somewhat better than he had in previous elections.[148] And by 1945, according to Plaid Cymru's organizing secretary, J. E. Jones, membership nearly doubled over the wartime period from 3,750 in 1939 to 6,050 in 1945.[149]

Thus, while nationalist political objection to the war was far from popular, the nationalists kept their cause in the public eye. In January 1942, for example, D. Rowland Morgan wrote to the *Western Mail* his concern that their activities were aiding the enemy. He wrote,

The contrivances of the sect . . . implicate the rest of Wales and force a vital question upon all other citizens within the border. It is: What discouragement have this band had at the hands of the Welsh people? Up to now the answer is—none. No Welsh society, council or conference has ever made an explicit utterance which stands out as a condemnation of a group which is actively designing, in the name of Wales, against the safety of Wales.[150]

Ten days later the *Western Mail* published an article analysing the concepts of national culture and nationalism by a barrister, Arthur Lewis. He argued that 'national culture' is a 'synthesis compounded of the ethics, education, music, conventions and traditions of any people bound by a common tie of unity'.

Welsh culture may be homegrown, but the seeds came from small communities—Palestine, Athens, and Rome. To the Jews we owe the Christian ethic; to the Greeks the ideal of human life; and to the Romans law and order. Without these influences Welshmen might still be barbarians . . .

But just as consciousness of self may degenerate to egoism, so national consciousness can develop the cancerous growth of nationalism.[151]

[146] For a discussion of Welsh peace movements and conscientious objection in Wales, see Kenneth O. Morgan, *Modern Wales: Politics, Places and People* (Cardiff: University of Wales Press, 1995), 84–116, esp. 106–16.

[147] Ibid. 113.   [148] Coupland, *Welsh and Scottish Nationalism*, 378.

[149] Cited in Morgan, *Modern Wales*, 113.

[150] D. Roland Morgan, 'Nation and the Nationalists', *Western Mail & South Wales News*, 14 Jan. 1942, 2.

[151] Arthur Lewis, 'Culture and Welsh Nationalism', *Western Mail & South Wales News*, 24 Jan. 1942, 3.

He then went on to talk about German and Japanese nationalism, and the analogous dangers of Welsh nationalism.

Not long after, Tom Jones, former secretary to the Cabinet under Lloyd George, made a scathing attack on the nationalist party in an address to the Cardiff Cymrodorion. The party, in his view, 'would not unite Wales; it would divide Wales more deeply than ever, the more clearly its objectives were understood'. He then accused the party of using 'Hitlerian technique' and claimed that if they pressed their claim for Dominion status,

it would mean civil war . . . for dear as Wales was to many of them there were some things that were dearer, dearer than the preservation of its language, dearer than Dominion status, dearer than a return to the Middle Ages. If they were forced to make a choice, they would fight for Reason, for Freedom, and for the British Commonwealth as a stepping stone to world unity and citizenship . . . the Welsh Nationalist Party had entered with a new, narrow and intolerant dogma, and the vision of a new Promised Land of Fascism.[152]

Anti-nationalists regularly wrote letters published in the 'Readers' Views' column of the Cardiff newspaper. For example, someone calling himself Anglo-Celt from Cardiff wrote in August 1942:

Can the Welsh claim to be a nation? Wales has been incorporated in England for some 400 years and racially, her people are formed substantially of the same elements as are the English. Apart from her moribund language, long ago swept out of England, there is no difference. Why then, should Wales be treated as a separate nation, especially in view of the immense number of hybrids, possibly a majority of the people, formed during the past few decades by immigrants from other countries. All these are taxpayers and have some strong views on Welsh Home Rule.[153]

Notice that 'Anglo-Celt' denied that Wales could be a separate nation because the Welsh are 'hybrids', a point that was not lost on some readers. Several days later two letters protesting 'Anglo-Celt's' remarks appeared in the paper. W. Morgan Davies (a not infrequent letter writer) argued that, 'by any reasonable standards the Welsh are a nation, and if treated with justice the loyal and law-abiding people of Wales should be entrusted with at least the same measure of self-government as that so magnanimously and generously granted to Northern Ireland'.[154] Walter Dowding claimed that 'Anglo-Celt's' letter 'betrays a complete sympathy with the Nazi attitude towards small nationalities . . . all men are hybrids, but I am what "Anglo-Celt" with his quaint terminology would describe as a "recent hybrid," and I am emphatically in favour of Welsh self-government.'[155]

As the campaign for the University by-election progressed, voices arguing for and

[152] 'Home Truths on Welsh Government', *Western Mail & South Wales News*, 28 Feb. 1942, 3.
[153] *Western Mail & South Wales News*, 12 Aug. 1942, 3.
[154] *Western Mail & South Wales News*, 18 Aug. 1942, 3.   [155] Ibid.

against the nationalists became more persistent. Just before the election in January 1943, John Pennant, a regular political columnist for the *Western Mail*, devoted his column to the contest. He described the supporters of Saunders Lewis and the nationalists in the following words:

Many of the young ministers and ministerial students, arrogant in their immunity from bullets and bombs will follow Leader Lewis. In the North there is a small select body of theological students—a self-elected 'Gestapo' . . . whose purpose seems to be to make life uncomfortable for others who will not do homage to 'The Party' and the Leader.

One third of the electors are women graduates, most of them teachers. Among them there is a strong and fanatical following for Leader Lewis. In some cases their devotion amounts to idolatry . . . It is a blind and blinding adulation that has no parallel since Adolf Hitler set up business as the 'saviour of my people'.[156]

Although the nationalists polled more than they had in previous elections, Pennant declared it a 'rout'. This defeat, he said scathingly, was 'Wales's devastating answer to this self-important minority that would have their countrymen flounder in the hopeless bog of outworn political and religious creeds'. Pennant called for 'the complete extinction of Welsh neo-Fascism'.[157]

Prior to the election, in early January 1943, County Alderman Edgar Chappell published a series of three articles discussing the demand for Welsh self-government.[158] He commented on the history of Welsh nationalism and proposals for devolution since the 1880s. Chappell argued that demands for either Dominion Home Rule or a limited federal scheme were not practicable, and that the best first step in gaining autonomy for Wales should be modelled on the Scottish system. He proposed that the 'Welsh Parliamentary Party', that is, all of the Welsh representatives regardless of party, join together to propose such a plan.[159]

In early July 1943, they did just that, approaching the Churchill Government, through questions and debate in Parliament, to support the establishment of a Welsh Office under a Welsh Secretary of State. The request, however, was denied. Shortly after, Home Intelligence reported that there was widespread indignation in Wales at the Government's refusal. The Welsh were saying, 'The time is ripe for Wales to be treated on equal terms with Scotland.'[160]

The Churchill Government made a single concession to Welsh sentiment. One day in each session of Parliament would be 'Welsh Day', parallel to a day in each session of Commons devoted to Scottish affairs. The first 'Welsh Day' was on 17 October 1944, and it was poorly attended. Aneurin Bevin denounced the day as a farce and made it plain that he, for one, saw economic issues for the whole of

---

[156] *Western Mail & South Wales News*, 16 Jan. 1943, 2.
[157] *Western Mail & South Wales News*, 12 Apr. 1943, 2.
[158] *Western Mail & South Wales News*, 5 Jan. 1943, 2; 6 Jan. 1943, 4; and 7 Jan. 1943, 4.
[159] Ibid.   [160] Home Intelligence, 29 June to 6 July 1943. INF 1/292 Part 3C.

Britain as more significant than the issue of national difference.[161] Other Labour representatives, however, were more supportive of devolution.[162]

Clearly there were numerous voices in Wales and in Scotland, and these regional/national identities were no more singular or even coherent than was British or English national identity. Linguistic and religious differences divided North and South Wales; highlanders differentiated themselves from lowlanders in Scotland. But the wartime conjuncture saw a continuing struggle to mark the distinction between these regional nations and England, as well as to determine just what it was that made Britain a national community.

Just as Parliament permitted one day a session for Scotland and one for Wales devoted to consideration of issues concerning the principalities, the BBC allotted national recognition to Wales and Scotland on St David's Day and St Andrew's Day, respectively. Although the celebrations were apparently not as extensive as were those for St George's Day, especially in 1944 when an entire day's programming was devoted to it, commemorative talks were given on the radio to mark the holidays. These were times when commentators could speak to the entire country while specifying the roots of their principality's nationhood and calling attention to the diversity of the British nation state.

Emlyn Williams opened his St David's Day Sunday Postscript in February 1944 speaking in Welsh. He went on to define the Welsh as a people, biologically distinct from the English.

The country that I hail from . . . is a very small one, full of mountains . . . ; a country that we call Cymru, the English call Wales, and the French by a name which I remember well hearing for the first time at school—for it was then I realised with quite a shock that I had more of France in my blood than of England whose language I was daily learning with such difficulty—the French call Wales the Pays de Galles, the country of the Gauls. And so it dawned upon me, a Welsh schoolboy that we Welsh are not, as I had thought, flesh and bone relations of our English neighbours: I began to understand that we are rather betrothed to the English in friendly bondage in the same way as a dutiful but philosophical wife is tied to a successful but slightly overpowering husband.[163]

In this highly gendered and racialized language, Williams proclaimed that Wales was, like a dutiful woman, bound and subordinated to her prosperous and important husband, and that the Welsh were related to their English masters only because of this marriage. He then went on to remind the listening audience that it was his people who were the first to populate the islands.

In ages past, we Cymry started off somewhere on the vast plains of Asia, and were thence blown, slowly, but surely, westward across Europe, to end up, weary and breathless, some-

---

[161] Quoted in Coupland, *Welsh and Scottish Nationalism*, 369–70.

[162] Morgan, *Rebirth of a Nation*, 298.

[163] Emlyn Williams, 'Post Script', 27 Feb. 1944, Home Service, Radio Talks Scripts Film T 651/642, p. 1, at the BBC WAC.

where near Calais. From Calais, we embarked in pitiful coracles and made for this island then unknown and unpeopled . . . across a stormy strip of water which was yet unchristened; my ancestors, with the audacity of the very young and ignorant, may perhaps have called it 'The Welsh Chanel' . . . who knows? We landed, presumably in Kent, and according to our habit, retreated westward, ending up in the hills of Cymru.[164]

St Andrew's Day is the last day of November and in 1944 Ian Finlay broadcast his St Andrew's Day talk on the Home Service from Edinburgh in 'prime time'. He too stressed ancient history and called attention to the fact that Scotland was a 'small country'. His message was one about the future as well as the past.

Scotland has climbed to the summit of the pass. From the summit she can look back or she can look forward. She can look back for just eleven centuries to the year 844, when Kenneth MacAlpin united the thrones of two great Gaelic peoples, the Picts and the Scots, and began the story of Scotland. Or she can look forward to the future and settle the road she must take . . .

. . . there are so many nations like us . . . So many *little* nations [emphasis in the original]. Little nations with tumultuous pasts like ours, facing a future they're a bit uncertain about.[165]

Finlay wondered if the 'grand new world' ahead is to be 'a thing of colossal combines and concentrations all demanding standardisation, in which all individuality is to be sunk? Or is it going to be conducted like a great orchestra: an orchestra in which all the rediscovered loyalties of this war—national, parochial, personal,—will be attuned in harmony?'

Using images sounding much like those of the countryside ideal, he then praised 'the little things, the little old things,—old times, old customs, old associations . . . And little things depend for their existence on little communities—on the family, the village, the parish, ultimately on the nation. Especially on the *little* nation.'[166] He praised Scottish history, its heroes, its fighting past, and made certain that his listeners understood that it was the 'true' (i.e. Scottish) version of Scotland's history that they were hearing. He argued that it was only by remembering Scottish history with pride that they would build the future.

Both Williams and Finlay chose to stress past glories and to point out that theirs were *little* countries, putting them in the league of other little countries on the Continent, or perhaps, in the Commonwealth. What made these little countries British? How was Britishness to be understood—was Britain to be understood as a 'nation' or was it really an empire ruled by England to which Wales and Scotland, like the colonies and dependencies were bound?

---

[164] Emlyn Williams, 'Post Script', 27 Feb. 1944, Home Service, Radio Talks Scripts Film T 651/642, p. 1, at the BBC WAC.

[165] Ian Finlay, 'Talk on St Andrew's Day, 1944', 30 Nov. 1944, Home Service, Radio Talks Scripts Film T 157, p. 1, at the BBC WAC.

[166] Ibid. 2–3.

Early in the war Home Intelligence warned the Ministry of Information not to distribute the booklet 'Growth of the Empire Commonwealth', throughout Wales. The regional intelligence officer was concerned that 'it would only increase the opinion, in Welsh-speaking Wales, that justice was not being done to this part of the Empire. It appears that any stressing of the consideration received by other distinct national cultures within the Commonwealth would lead to unfortunate contrasts.'[167] While it was pointed out that this was the view of only a minority, Home Intelligence feared that Commonwealth propaganda would serve as a foil for the expression of significant Welsh national resentments produced by the war including those inspired by the fact that 'conscripted Welshmen are scattered among other national regiments while Welsh regiments are filled with English and Scots soldiers; Welsh children being evacuated outside of Wales and "away from their country's traditions," etc.'[168]

Thus, as we have seen in the case of class feeling, wartime measures and wartime rhetoric opened spaces for the expression of particular resentments. The persistent articulation of the rural idyll, used to symbolize both the 'authentic nation' and the nation at peace, provoked agriculturalists to vent their profound sense of marginalization when compared with industrial and urban Britain. By stressing the fact that theirs were 'small countries' and, at least in the case of Wales, countries subordinated to another with which they were joined in a larger kind of unit, the Saints' Days talks raised quite different questions about the 'nationhood' of Britain. The very existence of these 'regional' nations, and the continuing issue of national/cultural difference, suggested that 'Britain' both historically and contemporaneously was less a nation and more an empire.[169] And as an empire, the challenges to a unitary British identity were profound. The issues concerning British wartime identity raised by Britain's empire beyond the British Isles are the subject of the next chapter.

[167] Weekly Home Intelligence Report, 21 to 28 May 1941. INF 1/292.
[168] Ibid.
[169] A similar point stemming from a different analytical standpoint was made by sociologist Michael Hechter, *Internal Colonialism*.

7

'The End is Bound to Come'

RACE, EMPIRE, AND NATION

As we have seen in the last chapter, urban–rural contestation and the straining against singularity of Britain's constituent national cultures troubled the idea that the British were one people. As a nation state Great Britain, geographically and politically speaking, was as much an empire as it was a nation for it had been formed by England's incorporation of Wales, Scotland, and Ireland. Moreover, Britain was, of course, an imperial nation, both materially and symbolically dependent upon its ties to lands that were geographically much further removed than Wales, Scotland, and Ireland—the dominions and the colonial dependencies.

While the empire may seem to have been at some remove from Great Britain's wartime national identity as it fought the 'People's War', it was thoroughly imbricated in it. Not only was Britain dependent upon the military, industrial, and diplomatic support of the dominions, colonies, and dependencies; Britain was reliant as well on the empire for its self-image as a virtuous imperial power.

In popular discourse as well as officially, the British understood their colonial relationships as fostering democracy and their nation as a benevolent, paternalistic imperial power. In this chapter I will suggest that these conceptions were persistently undermined by the often contradictory repercussions of racial divisiveness. The consequences of racism in both the metropole and in the colonies threatened the metropole–colonial relations so fundamental to British sensibilities. As a result Government officials in the United Kingdom were involved throughout the war in the ideological labour of repairing Britain's reputation with its imperial subjects as well as with its non-white citizens in the metropole.

The idea that the United Kingdom's identity was crucially dependent upon the empire has been argued persuasively by a number of scholars. Linda Colley, for example, made the argument that the British would not have known themselves as Britons without particular others.[1] Speaking of the period before 1783 the

[1] Linda Colley, *Britons: Forging the Nation, 1707–1837* (New Haven and London: Yale University Press, 1992), 6.

17. Poster depicting imperial unity.
Public Record Office

particular others that she had in mind were primarily French and Catholic. Since that time, however, as Colley has argued, Britain's so-called Second Empire gave a sense of commonality to the constituent entities that made up Great Britain.[2] Catherine Hall's work has shown the importance of England's engagement with the colonies for the constitution of middle-class identity, masculinity, and domestic politics, and Antoinette Burton has demonstrated the centrality of Britain's imperial mission for late nineteenth- and early twentieth-century British feminists.[3]

As Simon Gikandi has so aptly stated, the 'modern British nation cannot be imagined outside the realm of empire.' Indeed, he argued, 'imperialism becomes the raison d'être of Britishness itself.'[4] In what follows I suggest that the impact of racism and colonialism in concert threatened Great Britain's image of itself as a particular kind of imperial power during the war. To do this I trace the imperial presence in the metropole and track the repercussions of metropolitan and colonial racism on Great Britain's colonial relations both 'at home' and 'out there' in the colonies.

Like identifying the nation as England or Britain, the terms used to distinguish this larger political unit also were contested. And the contest over words suggests some of the difficulties posed by the significance of the empire to the nation during the war.

The Secretary of State for India and Burma, L. S. Amery, addressed a gathering of schoolteachers who were beginning in 1943 a summer course of study on the empire mounted by the Board of Education. He began his talk with the question of whether empire or Commonwealth was the correct terminology. 'Commonwealth', he said, was appropriate when speaking of a distinctive political system either characterized by 'free co-operation between its members or to convey our purpose that, with the development of self-governing institutions in every part, the terms 'Empire' and

[2] Linda Colley, 'Britishness and Otherness: An Argument', *Journal of British Studies*, 31 (Oct. 1992), 324.

[3] Catherine Hall, *White, Male and Middle Class: Explorations in Feminism and History* (New York: Routledge, 1992); '"From Greenland's Icy Mountains . . . to Afric's Golden Sand": Ethnicity, Race and Nation in Mid-Nineteenth-Century England', *Gender & History*, 5 (Summer 1993), 212–30; 'Rethinking Imperial Histories: The Reform Act of 1867', *New Left Review*, 208 (Winter 1994), 3–29; and Catherine Hall, 'The Nation Within and Without', chap. 4 in Catherine Hall, Keith McClelland, and Jane Rendall (eds.), *Defining the Victorian Nation: Class, Race, Gender and the Reform Act of 1867* (Cambridge: Cambridge University Press, 2000), 179–221; Catherine Hall, *Civilising Subjects: Metropole and Colony in the English Imagination 1830–1867* (Cambridge: Polity, 2002); Antoinette Burton, *Burdens of History: British Feminists, Indian Women, and Imperial Culture* (Chapel Hill: University of North Carolina Press, 1994); Antoinette Burton, *At the Heart of the Empire: Indians and the Colonial Encounter in Late-Victorian Britain* (Berkeley and Los Angeles: University of California Press, 1998); also see John M. Mackenzie's multivolume series, Studies in Imperialism, e.g. *Imperialism and Popular Culture* (London and Dover, NH: Manchester University Press, 1986) and *Propaganda and Empire* (London and Dover, NH: Manchester University Press, 1984); Ian Baucom, *Out of Place: Englishness, Empire, and the Locations of Identity* (Princeton: Princeton University Press, 1999); Hall, McClelland, and Rendall (eds.), *Defining the Victorian Nation*.

[4] Simon Gikandi, *Maps of Englishness: Writing Identity in the Culture of Colonialism* (New York: Columbia University Press, 1996), 31.

'Commonwealth' shall become completely synonymous.' In contrast, 'Empire' 'brings out the idea of unity comprising infinite variety, but also that of responsibility for peace and good government, of trusteeship towards the weak and backward.'[5] This parsing of terms reveals a great deal of what was at stake at the time. While the avalanche of independence movements that was to obliterate the empire was largely a post-war phenomenon, independence was certainly 'in the air', no more so, of course, than in India. Amery's discussion of terms was a way for him to reiterate Britain's promise of eventual political independence ('Commonwealth'), at some time in an unspecified future, without the dissolution of the whole. At the same time, it was a way for him to restate the paternalist stance of Britain towards its colonies and dependencies ('Empire'), which in an earlier time had been defined as Britain's self-proclaimed 'civilizing mission'. This was the concept of 'trusteeship'.[6] As historian Frederick Cooper has remarked, during the war 'British policy makers were anxious to deflect the discussion from progress toward independence to a broader consideration of the responsibilities of imperial trusteeship.'[7]

Amery's careful discussion of terminology was, on the one hand, a response to the fact that the United States, not to mention colonial peoples themselves, were sharply critical of British imperialism. On the other hand, it emphasized the significance of empire for British nationhood. That significance to men such as Amery was expressed as Britain's special mission to the world—what made Britain unlike Germany a virtual model for world order. As Amery put it, 'the British Empire . . . is the translation into outward shape, under ever varying circumstances, of the British character and of certain social and political principles, constituting a definite British culture or way of life, which, first evolved on British soil, and has since been carried by our people across all the seas.'[8] The idea that the nation and the empire were reflections of one another was voiced in less flowery language by one of the working-class participants in the BBC programme, 'What is a Good Man?'. 'I mentioned the Empire. Well, the Empire's our chance. There's things that has got to be made different out there, same as there is at home, I admit that, but by Jove, it's a better place than most other countries . . . Both this country and the Empire.'[9]

---

[5] L. S. Amery, 'Empire and Commonwealth', in L. S. Amery, *The Framework of the Future* (London: Oxford University Press, 1944), 4–5.

[6] Suke Wolton has argued that during the war, some in the Government, such as Lord Hailey and Harold Macmillan, and Labour Party spokesman on the colonies, Arthur Creech Jones, advocated replacing the term 'trusteeship' with 'partnership'. Hailey preferred partnership because although there could be junior and senior partners, it implied a less fixed hierarchy, and one that would imply economic and social development. Suke Wolton, *Lord Hailey, the Colonial Office and the Politics of Race and Empire in the Second World War* (Houndsmill: Macmillan Press, 2000), 122–3.

[7] Frederick Cooper, *Decolonization and African Society: The Labour Question in French and British Africa* (Cambridge: Cambridge University Press, 1996), 112.

[8] Ibid. 6.

[9] 'What is a Good Man?', 'Living Opinion', 24 Apr. 1942, Home Service, Radio Talks Scripts Film T 405, pp. 9–10, at the BBC Written Archives Centre, Caversham Park, Reading (BBC WAC).

He united the empire and the metropole in a dream of reconstruction that the 'good British man' would actualize.

In praising the nation, those who spoke for the empire used similar themes and were keen to contrast the British empire with others. The President of the Empire Day Movement commented in his Empire Day message of 1943, '[O]ur Empire, so magnificently united in this period of grave emergency, was not founded on conquest and oppression, like some Empires of the past, which the Germans are seeking to copy, but upon bold adventure, love of liberty and justice, and spiritual ideals.'[10] The Empire Day Movement was an organization established in the United Kingdom at the turn of the twentieth century that promoted the active participation by young people in yearly celebrations of the empire. And in his Empire Day radio broadcast in 1942, Duff Cooper, former head of the Ministry of Information, also emphasized the difference between the British empire and its predecessors. Those, he said, were founded by ambitious statesmen with the use of force and were maintained by military power. To illustrate the contrast, he quoted nineteenth-century historian Seeley's famous phrase, 'British people conquered a quarter of the earth in a fit of absence of mind.'[11] Cooper maintained that 'it was not our statesmen who made our empire—it was the common people—or I would rather say the very uncommon people of our land.'[12] Cooper both claimed the empire and denied that the British were imperious.

And defending Britain's imperial policy to the United States, the Editor of *Britain To-Day*, the publication of the British Council, wrote emphasizing Britain's imperial paternalism:

There has been an acute awakening of the public conscience in Great Britain to the need of harmonizing its Colonial policy with British conceptions of individual rights and democratic government. Clearly the populations of some of the dependencies are not ready for full democratic institutions and self-government; none but the Imperial Power can take the measures which are necessary to rescue them from barbarism, to ease the transition from ancient savagery to intercourse with the modern world, to protect them from exploitation, to educate them, to enable them to hold their own and win their way to prosperity.[13]

As Duff Cooper, in an address to the Royal Empire Society put it in January 1943, 'The British Empire is not breaking up; it is growing up.'[14]

Surely, those who spoke in praise of the empire sounded a defensive note. It was not just that British imperialism had been under sustained attack by the colonial

[10] 'Empire Day Message', from Viscount Bledisloe, Empire Day, 1943. PRO/CO 875/19/17.

[11] Duff Cooper, Empire Day Broadcast, 24 May 1942, Home Service, Radio Talks Scripts film T 381, at the BBC WAC.

[12] Ibid. 6.

[13] Editorial, 'Trusteeship of Empire', Introduction to article by Lord Lugard, *Britain To-Day*, 28 Nov. 1941, 2–3.

[14] *Western Mail & South Wales News*, 13 Jan. 1943, 2.

peoples who, since the end of World War I, were actively involved in protest movements of various kinds, most dramatically in the West Indies in the mid- and late 1930s.[15] The Colonial Office had long been keenly aware that the British citizenry were not particularly interested in the empire, and that those who were interested tended to be in favour of granting independence to the colonies. Thus, very early in the war, officials in the Colonial Office discussed how to make the populace at large more 'empire conscious'. Such courses for teachers on the empire as the one at which L. S. Amery presented the keynote quoted above had been actively advocated by the Colonial Office for some time. Members of the Colonial Office staff believed that colonial affairs were rarely mentioned in the schools except, perhaps, for perfunctory references in history or geography classes. Putting the matter in the language of wartime citizenship, Colonial Office staff members maintained that the schoolteachers and the general public need to be educated about 'our colonial responsibilities'.[16] In a letter to Lord Hailey, Margaret Read worried that nine-tenths of the British population developed their views on the empire from cinema and 'ultra-left wing propaganda of an anti-imperialist type'.[17] Reiterating her stress on the responsibilities of British citizens for the empire, Read argued that a significant aspect of popular education about the empire should concern itself with

the nature of our responsibilities as British citizens for the welfare and progress of the colonial peoples. There should be the same unifying principle running through it which is beginning to dawn on us at home; that as a British commonwealth of free peoples, the whole body politic is weakened if any one part of it suffers from maladjustment or poverty, and that conversely there can be no stable prosperity in one section based on exploitation of another.[18]

Frederick Cooper has written about the important connections between 'development' as a goal of the British Colonial Office and 'welfare'—so significant to British politics beginning in about 1940. As he has suggested, health, education, water supplies, and procedures to settle industrial disputes were issues that 'crossed the line between metropole and colony'.[19] This newer definition of the imperial mission was produced, as Cooper informs us, in response to African and West Indian protest, but raised different questions about the stability of the colonial enterprise.[20]

---

[15] For an account, see Ken Post, *Arise Ye Starvelings: The Jamaican Labour Rebellion of 1938 and its Aftermath*. (The Hague: Nijhoff, 1978). For responses in the metropole, esp. by the Left, see Stephen Howe, *Anticolonialism in British Politics: The Left and the End of Empire, 1918–1964* (Oxford: Clarendon Press, 1993), 96–106.

[16] Margaret Read's letter to Lord Hailey, 11 Oct. 1941. PRO/CO 875/11/12.

[17] Ibid. 3. This was a common perception—that esp. among the educated, there was hostility to the British empire. Elspeth Huxley complained that progressive teachers are 'distinctly left-wing in politics, and to them colonies equal Imperialism—the Devil, quite simply' (17.21 letter from Elspeth Huxley to Christopher Cox, n.d. but probably late Jan. or early Feb. 1942, CO 859/80/11).

[18] Ibid. 3. [19] Cooper, *Decolonization and African Society*, 67.

[20] For an account of Left political pressure to move the Government in this direction in the late 1930s, see Howe, *Anticolonialism in British Politics*, 90–105.

The Empire at Home

The colonial question in the war did not only concern Britain's relationship with people living in lands far from Great Britain. Colonial peoples also were resident in the metropole, and their presence represented both an opportunity for the British Government to secure its imperial ties, and a potential threat to those ties abroad and to the British nation at home.

The Colonial Office both supported and encouraged the importation of workers from the colonies to the metropole to aid in the war effort. They hoped that by bringing colonial people to the United Kingdom, when they returned they would speak positively of their experience thereby strengthening the bond between Great Britain and its imperial subjects. But threatening Great Britain's reputation as a beneficent colonial power was the issue of race, and the persistent indications of a 'colour bar' in the metropole in spite of the self-described 'tolerance' that was supposed to characterize the British people as a nation. As a pamphlet issued by the RAF put it, 'It has been said that part of the genius of the British in dealing with other races is their sense of impartial justice, understanding and an ability to see the other man's point of view, without descending either to weak sentiment or to jackboot methods. Now we have our individual parts to play in proving this genius.'[21]

As the reference to 'jackboot methods' suggests, Nazi policy on the issue of race made British racial tolerance a particularly salient aspect of national identity during the war. Thus, while the British were concerned to show colonials who had come to Britain during the war that they were welcome in the 'mother country', the colour bar, strongly protested by non-white Britons during the 1930s, became an even more significant problem.[22] As Hakim Adi has suggested, racial prejudice was clearly 'at odds with government declarations that the war was being fought against the evils of racism'.[23]

There were approximately 7,000 permanent non-white residents in the port cities.[24] Unlike World War I, there were no non-white colonial regiments or battalions stationed in Great Britain except for very short periods of time, although there were non-white colonials in the country who had enlisted in the military. More than 10,000 men and a small number of women from the West Indies were volunteers in the armed services. Almost all of the men were in the RAF; most were from Jamaica, with lesser numbers from Trinidad, British Guiana, and other Caribbean islands; the women enlisted in the Auxiliary Territorial Services (ATS).[25] Additionally,

---

[21] R.A.F., 'The Stranger Within Our Gates', Sept. 1941. RG 160/383.8, at the National Archives, Modern Military History, College Park, Maryland.

[22] For a discussion of instances of racial discrimination, and the responses by West African students, see Hakim Adi, *West Africans in Britain: 1900–1960* (London: Lawrence & Wishart, 1998), 90–2.

[23] Ibid. 91.

[24] Figure from Ian Spencer, 'World War Two and the Making of Multiracial Britain', in Pat Kirkham and David Thoms (eds.), *War Culture: Social Change and Changing Experience in World War Two Britain* (London: Routledge, 1995), 209.   [25] Ibid. 212.

during the war, roughly 800 Indians were brought for training and then sent back to India to boost production of munitions.[26] Approximately 1,000 skilled technicians and trainees from the West Indies were hired in ordnance factories, and about the same number of men from British Honduras were brought to work in the forests of Scotland.[27]

The Colonial Office throughout the war put pressure on other ministries to bring non-white people from the colonies to Great Britain, and to provide them with a welcoming environment and positive experience when they arrived. The first groups of West Indians, mostly from Jamaica, came to the country in February 1941 and were followed by another group in August of that year.

The Colonial Office and the Ministry of Labour reported to the West Indies of the welcome given to the men when they arrived in Scotland, their first UK stop, and described the tours they were given and the entertainment provided for them. Colonial Office staff member Ivor Cummings, whose parents had come from Sierra Leone, broadcast to the West Indies news of their safe arrival, placement in employment, and their welcome by officials in late February 1941.[28] And Learie Constantine, the Trinidadian cricket star, was appointed Local Welfare Officer to look after the Jamaicans in Liverpool. In June 1942 he broadcast the success of bringing 200 technicians to the country from the West Indies:

It would be playing with words to say that all has been well and rosy in the Empire in the past. In fact there are many difficulties and many problems that have surfaced . . . since the commencement of the war. These troubles and difficulties are endeavoured to be solved by this pioneering movement of bringing Colonial workers into the mother country, mixing and merging with their white fellow workers. On both sides there has been a tendency in the direction of understanding and tolerance, not to speak of the educative value of the contact which should be seen to be believed.[29]

He spoke of the fact that the men were gradually being housed in private homes, included in their trade unions, in Whitley Councils and elected as representatives on committees in the factories where they worked.

Not all was so 'rosy' in the metropole, however. The first problem concerned where the West Indians should be housed, and it took the Ministry of Labour

[26] See Laura Tabili, *'We Ask for British Justice': Workers and Racial Difference in Late Imperial Britain* (Ithaca, NY: Cornell University Press, 1994), chap. 8.

[27] Spencer, 'World War Two and the Making', 212. For a description of the experiences of the West Indian technicians and British Honduran foresters, see Marika Sherwood, *Many Struggles: West Indian Workers and Service Personnel in Britain (1939–45)* (London: Karia Press, 1985). For an early sociological study of West Indian residents of Liverpool during the war and early post-war years, see Anthony H. Richmond, *Colour Prejudice in Britain: A Study of West Indian Workers in Liverpool, 1941–1951* (London: Routledge & Kegan Paul, 1954).

[28] Ivor Cummings Broadcast talk for the West Indies. LAB 26/52.

[29] Learie Constantine's Broadcast, 'The Jamaican Technician Scheme', 18 June 1942. LAB 26/52.

months to arrange for private billeting. Until then, they were housed in hostels.[30] The Ministry of Labour also expected that the men from the West Indies would be highly skilled technicians, but the quality of the craftsmanship of the initial groups of men was below the Ministry's expectation. Therefore, they were placed in lower paying positions than the men had anticipated.[31] Furthermore, the West Indian men were very alive to racial prejudice and discrimination against them. As early as November 1941 Arnold Watson, the North-west Regional Controller for the Ministry of Labour wrote about the men who had been sent to Bootle that they are 'quick to put to any sympathetic listener the evidence in their possession of inequalities and disrimations [*sic*] and they are naturally anxious to make full use of every opportunity'.[32] Watson was of the opinion that the men ignored the 'real help' that they had been given by the Welfare Department and the West Indies House (a residential and social club in Liverpool run by the YMCA for the Ministry of Labour) and did not see themselves as the metropole's publicists.[33] Furthermore, *New Statesman* hinted in an article that the men on Merseyside were suffering from blatant racism on the streets, and that they resented the 'patronage' of the Regional Officers of the Ministry of Labour.[34]

Other problems arose. The warden of West Indies House reported that some of the men were troublemakers. He recommended that the house be closed and then be reopened only for those who were members of the club.[35] And because the General Secretary of the YMCA and the warden had complained that the house staff felt endangered, a Ministry of Labour staff member suggested sending the troublemakers back to the West Indies.[36] The charges, however, were not one-sided. The West Indians claimed that the warden was not suited to his position; he had, without adequate cause, called in the police to oust a man from the house.[37]

The residents organized a deputation to protest conditions at the house and their protest was supported by all the Jamaican technicians in the area. Watson then called a meeting with representatives of the Dormitory Committee and a number of Ministry of Labour officials, including Learie Constantine to discuss the problems. At the meeting one of the West Indians said, 'What we want at West Indies House is self-government. The days of school are over. We want democracy.' The West Indian representatives complained that the staff of the house kept them

[30] See memorandum from JJT of the Ministry of Labour to C. G. Carstairs of the Colonial Office, 21 Feb. 1941. LAB 26/52.

[31] Draft Telegram for West Indies, 11 Mar. 1941. LAB 26/52.

[32] Arnold Watson minute, 29 Nov. 1941. LAB 26/52.   [33] Ibid.

[34] *New Statesman*, 6 June 1942, reported by Graham Smith, *When Jim Crow Met John Bull: Black American Soldiers in World War II Britain* (New York: St. Martin's Press, 1988 and London: I. B. Tauris & Co., 1987), 58

[35] Watkinson to Arnold Watson, 11 Mar. 1942. LAB 26/52.

[36] J. J. Taylor to Arnold Watson, 15 Mar. 1942 and Arnold Watson to J. J. Taylor, 17 Mar. 1942. LAB 26/52.

[37] Arnold Watson to Keith, 29 Apr. 1942; A. B. Wellesley Cole to Arnold Watson, 11 Apr. 1942; Watson to Taylor, 29 Apr. 1942. LAB 26/52.

waiting for a long time before they were served, and acted as though they were doing them a great favour to wait on them at all. They reported that one member of the staff was particularly discourteous, and that whenever they complained to the warden, they were told they could leave.[38] After a period of negotiation and discussion following the meeting, the warden was fired and replaced by a Jamaican.[39] But problems at West Indies House persisted.[40]

These initial difficulties involving the West Indians were nothing as compared with those that arose once US troops were in the country.[41] As early as June 1942 (the first troops arrived in the late winter of 1942) the Colonial Office began hearing complaints about how white Americans treated black Britons. The presence of the Americans in any service hostel made it impossible for colonial servicemen to enter.[42] John L. Keith of the Welfare Division of the Colonial Office and others in the Colonial Office discussed the problem throughout that summer. As Keith reminded Sir John Jeffries, discriminatory treatment 'of coloured persons here is bound to react on the work we are trying to do to break down the colour bar and to help coloured people . . . fit into the work and life of this country'.[43] Keith attempted to persuade the War Office, through the person of Colonel Brian Rowe, the Anglo-American liaison officer, to intervene and inform the Americans of the 'attitude of tolerance and non-discrimination' that he and others in the Colonial Office were trying to foster.[44] Although Keith's colleagues in the Colonial Office all were concerned to 'protect our Colonial people' from American racism, they warned Keith that it would cause enormous resentment on the part of the Americans if the British attempted to 'educate' them.[45] As Jeffries wrote, their major objective should be to safeguard the interests of 'our Colonial coloured people who are resident in this country and to maintain for them the policy that there should be no discrimination on grounds of colour. We should be most unwise to force our views on the Americans.'[46] Jeffries advised the Colonial Secretary that it would be helpful if the US Army could explain to their troops the Colonial Office attitude and urge them to avoid ill 'treatment of British coloured persons'. He thought they might create a badge to be worn 'by our coloured workmen in this country so that they can be easily differentiated'.[47] Although it was never adopted, the then Secretary of State for the colonies, Viscount Cranborne, thought the idea of a badge was worth pursuing.

[38] 'Minutes of Meeting to Inquire into Conditions at West Indies House', 5 May 1942. LAB 26/52.

[39] Report of Local Welfare Officer, 15 Sept.–14 Oct. 1942. LAB 26/52.

[40] Sherwood, *Many Struggles*, 64–5.

[41] For a discussion of the impact of US troops on Colonial Office policy, see Wolton, *Lord Hailey*, 88–93.

[42] J. L. Keith minute, 30/6/42. CO 876/14.   [43] J. L. Keith to J. Jeffries, 31 July 1942. CO 876/14.

[44] Colonel Rolleston to Keith, 10 July 1942. CO 876/14.   [45] Gent minute, 8 July 1942. CO 876/14.

[46] J. J. Jeffries to Gent and Keith, 11 July 1942.

[47] Jeffries to Viscount Cranbourne, 14 Sept. 1942. CO 876/14.

Incidents of racial discrimination against black Britons either by or in connection with the presence of American troops persisted throughout the war. Beginning in the autumn of 1942 the welfare officers of the Ministry of Labour found themselves preoccupied with the issue. A fracas between West Indians and white American soldiers took place at the Grafton Ballroom in Liverpool. A West Indian suffered injuries and another British patron was slashed with a razor. The police blamed the Americans for starting it, but the management decided to bar Jamaicans from the Ballroom.[48] By January of 1943 Learie Constantine was reporting a steady deterioration in the relationship of white Americans to 'our own Colonial People'. He told of an instance in which a West Indian technician was attacked by an American while waiting to purchase a ticket to go to the cinema; and reports circulated that men from West Indies House retaliated as a group bearing razors and knives. Learie Constantine was himself subject to abuse by an American when he was eating in a restaurant with a white female colleague from the Ministry of Labour.[49] And several establishments in Merseyside instituted a ban on black British patrons.

Later that year a black Briton first dressed as a civilian and then in his Home Guard uniform was refused entrance to the Grafton Ballroom. He informed the Home Guard that 'as the uniform was "insulted" he was not in future prepared to attend Home Guard duties and that the Home Guard could take whatever action they pleased'.[50] Arnold Watson reported to his superiors that such incidents have aroused considerable 'feeling' among the technicians, and there was talk of the men leaving their work.[51]

By the summer of 1944 Arnold Watson had become increasingly frustrated that nothing positive was being done to stop the discrimination that West Indians were facing in the Liverpool area. A number of restaurants and dance halls in the city had been closed to people of colour, and Watson had evidence that at least in one case, the management of a dance hall had been threatened by white Americans with a 'boycott and perhaps even . . . something worse' if blacks were allowed in.[52]

Watson maintained that the technicians in areas where the Americans were not present were relatively satisfied with their experiences. In Bolton, for example, where there were a number of Jamaicans and Bahamians, the 'men have taken an active part in the social life of the churches, they have given lectures in the Town, they take part in such public functions as Red Army Day, and they have more invitations to private houses than they can accept'.[53] He continued to hope that the

---

[48] Local Welfare Officer's Report, 15 Oct.–14 Nov. 1942. LAB 26/52.

[49] 'Welfare of Colonial People in the UK. Relations with American Forces', ND, probably Jan. 1943. CO 876/15.

[50] 'West Indian Technicians and Trainees', Report by Arnold Watson, 18 Dec. 1943. LAB 26/55.

[51] Ibid.

[52] Arnold Watson, 'West Indian Technicians and Trainees: Discrimination', 24 July 1944. LAB 26/55.

[53] Ibid. 2.

Americans would inform their troops that 'American nationals should accept as normal in the U.K. the presence of coloured British subjects in hotels, dance-halls and pubs'.

Eventually action was taken when the then Secretary of State for the Colonies, Oliver Stanley, interested himself personally in ending the colour bar in Merseyside places of entertainment. Stanley wrote to the President of the Merseyside Committee on Hospitality, Lord Leverhulme, requesting his help, and asked Leverhulme to convey his views to the managements of the offending establishments. These interventions resulted in a lifting of the ban. Finally, although the man who had been denied entry to the dance hall when wearing his Home Guard Uniform was fined by the police for refusing to do Home Guard duty, on appeal the judge reduced the fine to a token one farthing.[54]

Wherever white Americans encountered black British subjects, they tried to use Jim Crow tactics. Ernest Marke wrote extensively about his treatment at the hands of Americans in his memoir. Marke, originally from Sierra Leone, had resided in the United Kingdom since his World War I service in the British army. He had just been called up for possible service in World War II when he was attacked and bloodied by some white GIs in London. He reports having thought, 'No, I decided they would have to come and get me . . . It's a white man's war and I'm not having none of it . . . from that evening until the end of the war, after most of the G.I.s had been sent back home, I kept away from all pubs.'[55] Marke, who ran a colonial social club in Soho during the war, had another run-in with white GIs after Germany had surrendered. His establishment was attacked by uniformed Americans and when he attempted to fight them off, the police intervened.[56]

Incidents such as these often were reported in the press, and their effects rippled far beyond those who were directly involved. The most notorious of them involved Learie Constantine who had been working with Watson to solve the colour bar problems for colonials in Liverpool. Constantine was denied a room at the Imperial Hotel in London on the grounds of race by a manager who claimed that the presence of blacks bothered American officers staying at the hotel. Constantine successfully sued the hotel for damages.[57]

The episode was widely covered in the press and discussed in Parliament, and

<hr>

[54] Arnold Watson minute, 4 Jan. 1945. LAB 26/55.

[55] Ernest Marke, *In Troubled Waters: Memoirs of My Seventy Years in England* (London: Karia Press, 1986; originally published 1975), 117.

[56] Ibid. 142–4. For a discussion of other incidents of racism, see Ben Bousenquet and Colin Douglas, *West Indian Women at War: British Racism in World War II* (London: Lawrence & Wishart, 1991), chaps. 7, 9.

[57] Peter Fryer, *Staying Power: The History of Black People in Britain* (London: Pluto, 1984), 365–75; John Flint, 'Scandal at the Bristol Hotel: Some Thoughts on Racial Discrimination in Britain and West Africa and Its Relationship to the Planning of Decolonisation, 1939–47', *Journal of Imperial and Commonwealth History*, 12 (May 1983), 75–6.

caused an uproar among colonials in the city. Additionally public discussion was widespread throughout the country.[58] Apparently the residents of Colonial Centre in London 'had to be restrained from making a demonstration against the hotel, which might have led to very unpleasant complications'.[59] A Mass Observation 'snap' survey of public opinion about the colour bar, and specifically about what had happened to Learie Constantine, showed extensive popular sympathy for him. According to the Mass Observation report, there was 'general feeling of hostility against "the authorities" and the never very popular management of a "luxury hotel"'. Many of those interviewed commented on the contribution that 'coloured men' were playing in the war, and expressed the view that this entitled them to equality.[60] It also was the subject of protests by various church groups, philanthropic organizations, and trade unions.[61]

Constantine had occasion to protest again to the Ministry of Labour about his treatment by white Americans. This time he was accosted by two white Americans in a London pub in the spring of 1944. He bitterly suggested in his letter that neither the Colonial Office nor any other branch of Government seemed willing to confront the Americans about their treatment of black Britons.[62]

Britain's dependence on colonial support for the war effort, coupled with the perceptible restiveness on the part of people in the West Indies and West Africa concerning their political and/or economic status made such incidents especially troublesome. In addition to these instances of discrimination against black Britons, several ministries of Government were attempting to deal with problems arising from the presence of both black and white GIs in the country.

Black soldiers comprised about 10 per cent of the US military in the country, and their segregation in separate units made them a visible presence. Individual Americans and the US Army attempted to secure both official and unofficial British cooperation in their efforts to keep the races separate, and to avoid racially motivated confrontations.[63] The Colonial Office was extremely apprehensive about the British Government's adopting a stance that would further intensify colonial disaffection with British rule. If the British seemed to sanction or participate in overtly racist practices against the American blacks, such behaviour would exacerbate

---

[58] Report, 23–8 Sept. 1943. INF 1/292 Part 4.   [59] J. L. Keith minute, 6 Aug. 1943. CO 859/80/8.

[60] File Report # 1944, 11 Oct. 1943, 2. Mass Observation Archive, University of Sussex.

[61] See resolutions by the Methodist Church, Hulme & Whalley Range Circuit, Manchester, 13 Sept. 1943; International Order of Good Templars, Grand Lodge of Scotland, 8 Sept. 1943; National Union of Railwaymen, 18 Sept. 1943; Christian Endeavour Union of Great Britain and Ireland, 23 Sept. 1943. CO 859/80/8.

[62] Extract from Constantine to Ministry of Labour and National Service, Liverpool Welfare Office, 8 May 1944. PRO/LAB 26/55.

[63] For an analysis of some of the issues raised by the presence of black GIs in Britain, see Christopher Thorne, 'Britain and the Black GIs: Racial Issues and Anglo-American Relations in 1942', *New Community*, 3 (Summer 1974), 262–71.

anti-British sentiment on the part of colonial elites. As sociologist Kenneth Little wrote in a memorandum to the Colonial Office,

As you yourself know, these representatives of the British colonials over here have been made very uneasy, and justifiably so in my opinion, at the prospects of American methods of Segregation, etc. being copied here as well as re-enforcing existing colour bar mechanisms. What the ordinary statesman or politician apparently does not realize is that news of such events and 'incidents' flies very quickly these days, and particularly at a time like the present when coloured people everywhere are almost morbidly alive to anything over here which savours of discrimination.[64]

Little reported that he had been told of racial incidents by 'various coloured seamen' who manned ships and carried news to 'Freetown, Lagos, Jamaica, etc., and in fact to most important centres in the Colonial Empire'.[65] His report confirmed what the Colonial Office feared, that such news could not be contained within the metropole.

The Foreign Office, however, was concerned that long-term diplomatic ties between the United States and Britain would be damaged if situations resulted that rankled the Americans. The Foreign Office, in fact, hoped to use the American presence as a way to strengthen these ties, and to instil in the Americans a positive opinion and appreciation for the British, just as the Colonial Office hoped to do with the colonials in the United Kingdom.[66] The reluctance by members of the Government to directly confront the Americans about their treatment of black Britons was even greater when it came to how white Americans treated their black countrymen. The War Office was not just reluctant to call the Americans to task, it hoped that the government might issue instructions to encourage the British to accommodate American segregationist attitudes and practices.[67]

For many sections of the civilian British population, however, as well as ordinary British soldiers, the presence of black Americans was a source of fascination. And many viewed the open hostility of white American soldiers towards their black countrymen with disgust. Black Americans were often favourably contrasted by British civilians to white Americans, and were seen as more polite and better mannered than their white compatriots. African-American soldiers, however, became racial 'others' when it came to sexual relations with white British women.

As Chapter 3 has indicated across the country and for the duration of the war there was widespread anxiety about the sexual exploits of British women and girls with African-American soldiers. Even after the war had ended but before the Americans were sent back to the States for demobilization, the anxieties over

[64] Kenneth Little, 'Treatment of Colour Prejudice in Britain', to J. L. Keith, Colonial Office, n.d., probably late Sept. or early Oct. 1942. PRO/CO 875/19/14.

[65] Ibid. 8–9.

[66] For a discussion of the Foreign Office concerns, see David Reynolds, *Rich Relations: The American Occupation of Britain, 1942–1945* (New York: Randorm House, 1995), 164–82.

[67] War Office draft paper, 8 Sept. 1942. PRO/CO 876/14.

interracial sex continued. In Cardiff, for example, the press headlined in September 1945, 'Girl tramps have become a menace to Wales. Aged between 15 and 20 they are sleeping rough and camp-following in the tradition of the Napoleonic days, spreading disease and immorality.'[68] The article focused on Maindy Barracks, Cardiff, where African-American soldiers were billeted. Although the general tenor of the reports blamed the girls, the issue of racial difference was crucial to many of those who wrote letters in response. One of the residents, for example, said, 'My daughter is afraid to go out at night because a coloured man recently followed her. The trouble is that they now think that all girls are alike.'[69]

'Observers', identified by the newspaper as 'two coloured girls' who lived in the Cardiff docks area, wrote to defend the soldiers reporting that they were barred from some dance halls, and that where they were allowed, the (white) British girls refused to dance with them, or they 'make it pretty plain that they are dancing only because politeness demands that they should.'

The Docks, the only area where they would be made welcome and where they would be able to mix in decent surroundings without fear of being snubbed on account of their colour, is out of bounds. As far as we can ascertain not one man in 10 knows the reason why. Little wonder then that the soldiers are ready to talk to anyone who will show them a little friendliness . . . What we really wish to point out is that the blame for what is described in your paper lies not with the soldiers but is due more to the lack of social amenities.[70]

'Observers' were responding to the articles and letters that overtly blamed the girls, but covertly suggested that the soldiers were at fault. A vicar, for example, had described what was going on as 'jungle behaviour', but added, 'all the blame must not be attributed to the coloured men'.[71]

Such messages were not lost on the African-American soldiers. One of them wrote to the newspaper to express his resentment at the charges threatening 'the integrity of the coloured soldier'. As he put it:

I have never felt more down sick on any subject connected with the British and Americans at the moment. [sic] I have heretofore cherished a faint hope that we would establish social and moral understanding while in your locality, and not receive severe and stern rebuke from public opinion.

I am prepared henceforth to do my part to maintain relations between the Forces and Cardiff Civilians, because the consequences of the accusations will probably be fatal and the minute elements of friendship of the past blown asunder.[72]

And the following week a letter signed by Mabel Jackson of the American Red Cross and twenty-five Americans expressed deep outrage at the press coverage because they saw it as blaming the black men.

[68] *Western Mail & South Wales News*, 12 Sept. 1945, 3.   [69] Ibid.
[70] *Western Mail & South Wales News*, 14 Sept. 1945, 3.
[71] *Western Mail & South Wales News*, 17 Sept. 1943, 3.
[72] *Western Mail & South Wales News*, 15 Sept. 1945, 3.

At first reading we thought it a good thing to have such vice cleaned out, but later, to our surprise and disgust, we discovered that you were pinning the blame on the negro troops there . . . The decent women will have nothing to do with them—who can they turn to?

Your paper is saying that all coloured troops are alike . . . When the negro troops first came to England people ran away because they had heard stories that we all had tails which came out at midnight, that we howled; in other words, that we weren't considered human beings. That sounds fantastic, doesn't it? How would you overcome such a handicap?[73]

Fears of both interracial marriage and sex between men of colour and white women had a long cultural history in Britain. As Ann Laura Stoler's work on nine-teenth-century European colonialism has suggested, the policing of interracial sex-uality to maintain 'racial purity' is intimately bound up with constructing and maintaining white supremacy.[74] While her work explicitly deals with maintaining the boundaries of the empire abroad, the empire 'came home' during World War I when non-white colonial troops were stationed in Britain. They were closely guarded while on leave and not allowed to participate in the victory celebrations held in London. Their being attended by white female nursing staff in hospitals that treated wounded soldiers in Britain aroused considerable controversy as well.[75] During the inter-war period, the Cardiff chief constable argued for the desirability of such anti-miscegenation legislation as had recently been passed in South Africa to secure the 'welfare' of the British.[76] Paul Rich has suggested in his discussion of inter-war racial ideology that 'welfare . . . was assumed to accrue from implicit racial separation and the prohibition on inter-racial marriage and sexual contact'.[77]

The extant records do not reveal that such anxieties plagued the Colonial Office or the Ministry of Labour and National Security as they dealt with matters con-cerning West Indian technicians in the north-west.[78] The two Ministries arranged for local hospitality to be offered in Bolton including 'informal dances' and having

---

[73] *Western Mail & South Wales News*, 17 Sept. 1945, 3.

[74] See Ann L. Stoler, 'Making Empire Respectable: The Politics of Race and Sexual Morality in 20th-Century Colonial Cultures', *American Ethnologist*, 16 (Nov. 1989), 634–60; Stoler, 'Rethinking Colonial Categories: European Communities and the Boundaries of Rules', *Comparative Studies in Society and History*, 13 (May 1992), 134–61.

[75] Philippa Levine, 'Battle Colours: Race, Sex and Colonial Soldiery in World War I', *Journal of Women's History*, 9 (1998), 104–30. On the treatment of Indian troops in Britain during World War I, see Rozina Visram, *Ayahs, Lascars and Princes: Indians in Britain, 1700–1947* (London and Dover, NH: Pluto Press, 1986), 122–39. On West Indians, see Fryer, *Staying Power*, 294–7.

[76] As reported in Paul Rich, *Race and Empire in British Politics* (Cambridge and New York: Cambridge University Press, 1986), 127–8.

[77] Ibid. 128.

[78] An article in the 1944–5 League of Coloured People's Annual Report, however, expressed concern about the treatment of West Indians in the services due to reports that they were addressed by officers and their white compatriots as 'darkies'. Also the League noted that orders had been given to WAAF (Women's Auxiliary Air Force) personnel not to be seen 'walking out with West Indian airmen in their company although in other respects they must be treated like any other airmen' (*League of Coloured Peoples 14th Annual Report, 1944–45*, 4).

'ladies interested in the Colonial problem to accompany the coloured men to the-atres and dances'.[79] And a report indicated that the West Indians' association with white British women did not 'appear to give rise to really serious problems in Bolton'. Indicating his surprise the official suggested that this felicitous state of affairs was probably due to the small number of black men in Bolton and the fact that the community already included a few black professional men.[80]

Such a relatively benign attitude towards interracial heterosexual associations applied as well to the British Hondurans in Scotland when they first arrived. A report on their welfare in January 1941 indicated that the 'men seem to have found many friends amongst the local inhabitants; they visit the neighbouring villages and towns and are well received . . . dances are given and attended'.[81] But this propitious atmosphere did not last. In August 1942, Harold Macmillan, Parliamentary Under-secretary of State for the Colonies, received a complaint from the Duke of Buccleuch about the British Honduran unit:

The people in the neighbourhood were encouraged to be friendly to them and the girls have interpreted this rather widely . . . I . . . learned that there have been a number of marriages and births, and much intercourse is allowed, even in the Camp itself . . . Personally, I dislike this mixture of colour and regret that it should be allowed with no discouragement. There are already sufficient births of foreign extraction in the country without the additional compli-cation of colour . . . I feel that unsophisticated country girls should be discouraged from marrying these black men from Equatorial America.[82]

Macmillan ordered an inquiry and responded to the duke, reassuring him that there was no evidence that the British Hondurans had abused the social hospitality given by local residents, although several women of 'an undesirable type' from Edinburgh had gained access to one of the camps and prompted immediate police action.[83]

Not to be quieted, the duke characterized Macmillan's response as having a 'not unexpectedly official tone which puts the matter in a more favourable light than is factual . . . I think it can be admitted that loose relations between black men of totally different standards, both moral and material and our simple country girls has unpleasant features, and that improper intercourse with decent young women should be strongly discouraged.'[84]

---

[79] Colonel Matthews, Memo to J. L. Keith, Welfare Section of the Colonial Office, 'Visit to West Indian Technicians in Bolton', 15 Nov. 1943. PRO/CO 876/48.

[80] Matthews to Keith, CO 876/48.

[81] Report on Health, Welfare, etc. of British Honduras Unit, 5 Jan. 1941. PRO/CO 876/41. For a study of the British Honduran Forestry Unit, see Marika Sherwood, *The British Honduran Forestry Unit in Scotland, 1941–43* (London: Karia Press, 1982).

[82] Duke of Buccleuch, Drumlanrig Castle, Thornhill Dumfriesshire, to Colonial Office, 10 Aug. 1942. PRO/CO 876/41.

[83] See Harold Macmillan to J. L. Keith, 13 Aug. 1942; Macmillan to Buccleuch, 13 Aug. 1942; and draft of Macmillan to Buccleuch, 31 Aug. 1942. PRO/CO 876/41.

[84] Buccleuch to Macmillan, 30 Sept. 1942. CO 876/41.

The duke also contacted the Ministry of Supply alerting its officials to the trouble caused by the British Hondurans' presence. The Ministry of Supply, already hostile to the idea of having Caribbean workers in the country, became involved in monitoring the situation.[85] Its officials took a dire view of what they saw as the 'increasingly difficult' problem of sexual relations between British Honduran men and white British women.[86] In addition to relations with women of an 'undesirable type', the idea that the British Hondurans were associating with farmers' daughters and with white wives of British soldiers was of particular concern.[87] Eventually, the Ministry of Supply insisted that the British Honduran units be repatriated, claiming that there was no longer any need for their labour.[88] As J. L. Keith of the Colonial Office put it,

The problem of association between members of the Unit and women is serious, but it can be exaggerated. There is no real evidence that the Unit behaves in a worse way than the Newfoundlanders and the other 'foreigners' in Scotland, but they are coloured men, and therefore their immoralities get more publicity and are more shocking to the susceptibilities of persons like the Duke of Buccleuch and his friends than would be the goings on of non-coloured persons.[89]

Although the Colonial Office opposed their repatriation, most of the men were sent back to British Honduras and the rest were transferred to industrial work.

The contrast between the Newfoundlanders and the British Hondurans made by Keith is instructive. The Newfoundlanders were recruited shortly after the war began, and were hired on six-month contracts. By February 1940, around 2,000 men were in the country. Complaints about the Newfoundlanders concerned their work rather than their sexual habits, and the main difficulty that the British officials confronted was how to provide various amenities and provisions for welfare and recreation to the men in remote areas. The Dominions Office was particularly worried because the Newfoundland Government had been disturbed by the fact that many of the loggers had returned and refused to renew their contracts because they had received 'inadequate treatment at the hands of this country'.[90] The Dominions Office requested and finally was granted special approval to have two lorries a week

[85] Memo from official (illegible signature) to J. L. Keith, Colonial Office, 21 Aug. 1942. PRO/AVIA 22/1239.

[86] T. Fitzgerald, Home Timber Production, to W. H. Ekins, Ministry of Supply, 2 Dec. 1942. AVIA 22/1239.

[87] Report of meeting of representatives of Ministry of Supply and the Department of Home Timber Production, 30 Jan. 1943. PRO/AVIA 22/1349.

[88] See report of Ivor G. Cummings to J. L. Keith, 3 Sept. 1943; and telegraphed memo, Colonial Secretary to Governor of British Honduras, 9 Sept. 1943. PRO/CO 876/42.

[89] J. L. Keith to J. J. Jeffries, accompanying memo from Ministry of Supply, 14 Apr. 1943. CO 876/42.

[90] Clement Atlee, Dominions Office to Andrew Duncan, Ministry of Supply, 11 Mar. 1942. PRO/AVIA 22/1352.

running from each camp to an agreed town so that the men could visit friends or go to a 'place of amusement'.[91]

Similarly in contrast both to the British Hondurans and to the African-Americans, there were laudatory stories in both the national and local press about the relationships between Polish soldiers and Scottish women. In early February 1941 *Sunday Chronicle*, a national newspaper, featured an article by Beverley Nichols on the Poles in Scotland. The headline proclaimed, 'Scotland has taken the Poles to its heart . . . they have brought new colour and romance to the North.' Below the headline was a picture of Polish soldiers dancing with young Scottish women and the caption, 'One of the best ways to get a girl in Scotland is to be a Polish soldier!'[92] Nichols suggested that there was 'a sort of *chic* about them with their charming manner and their flashing smiles', and reported there had been already over 70 Anglo-Polish marriages. The remainder of the article told stories detailing the heroic feats of some of the soldiers who had fought and then escaped from the Nazis and the Russians.

A number of the Poles were living in and around Kelso, a town in the Scottish Borders. In December 1942 the local newspaper featured a fulsome tribute to the goodwill shared between the Kelso locals and their Polish guests. The Poles had invited a number of Kelsonians to a Christmas Eve dinner. The spokesman for the Kelsonians, Bailie Boles talked of the admiration of the local residents 'for your fine qualities of courtesy, consideration and kindness and your high standard of culture . . . With the young ladies of the town your conquest was immediate and lasting.'[93] On the same day that the Poles were entertaining their Scottish hosts, the newspaper reported that there had been a raid on a nearby lumber camp and twelve white women and two British Honduran men had been taken into custody.[94] This was not the first of such articles—they had been appearing since at least June of that year.[95]

Although the duke in his letter to Macmillan had complained about 'foreign marriages', undoubtedly referring to the marriages between Scottish women and Polish soldiers, interracial unions were far less welcome. The prospect of interracial sex and marriage was extremely disconcerting to the British authorities. What is crucial, however, is that this discomfort jeopardized their attempts to establish both good will with colonial peoples, and a clear policy with regard to the non-white men present in such large numbers on British soil.

While there was no official support for the colour bar, the potential of any

---

[91] Draft Report on Visit to Newfoundland Forestry Camps, Free Transport to Nearest Town, Feb. 1942. AVIA 22/1352.

[92] *Sunday Chronicle*, 2 Feb. 1941, 2. Angus Calder reports, however, that while the Poles may have been popular with Scottish women, their popularity was in 'inverse ratio to the liking felt for them by British servicemen' (Angus Calder, *The People's War, Britain 1939–1945* (London: Pimlico, 1992), 308).

[93] *Border Mail and Gazette*, 31 Dec. 1942, 3.   [94] *Border Mail and Gazette*, 24 Dec. 1942, 3.

[95] See e.g. *Border Mail & Gazette*, 23 June 1942, 4.; 3 Nov. 1942, 4.; 10 Nov. 1942, 4; 8 Dec. 1942, 3.

'darkening of the residents of the metropole' and sexual intimacy between men of colour and white women was frightening. Thus, efforts to stop the Americans from imposing segregation on British communities were at best half-hearted, and there were reports of Britons without being prompted imposing a colour bar of their own. At the same time, with the exception of the War Office, most officials desired not to be seen to be supporting US segregationist practices. The British understood themselves to be tolerant of racial difference, identifying racialist practices with the United States, Germany, and South Africa. They wished to deny the existence of a colour bar operating in Britain because of colonial relations, and a long-standing national self-image of being a paternalist colonial power that would welcome colonial peoples as independent and equal citizens of the empire/Commonwealth once they had 'grown up'. But at the same time, officials were extremely concerned that ordinary British citizens were insufficiently 'race conscious'. What follows are some examples of the confusing assortment of British responses to the black Americans.

The West Country Regional Commissioner for Home Security reported in the summer of 1942 on conditions in his area where there was a considerable number of African-American troops, after consulting, as he put it, 'responsible persons' in his area. On the basis of what they had told him, he was concerned that 95 per cent of the people in the Region had no idea that the presence of 'coloured troops is a problem'. They had already encountered minor difficulties such as British troops resenting the making of YMCA canteens out of bounds for the black soldiers and Baptist churches welcoming men from the South who had never attended a chapel with whites.[96] In one locality, according to the report, residents did not understand why there should be any differentiation in the treatment given to 'coloured Americans and Czechs'. 'Charitably disposed persons' were shocked that 'there should be any form of differentiation in the treatment of coloured troops. Sentimental persons are inclined to look upon this as being entirely unethical, and that view is conscientiously held by persons of many shades of religious conviction.' For this Regional Commissioner 'the problem' was an insufficiency of appropriate race consciousness on the part of ordinary Britons. What made this an urgent problem, the report suggested, was the necessity of 'protecting from deplorable consequences certain of our womenkind, and of averting, should those consequences develop into fact, possible trouble between ourselves and the Americans'.[97]

Apparently, in the western counties, the US Army had segregated the towns that white and black soldiers could visit. The writer of the report on the Westcountry feared that in Tewkesbury, which was out of bounds to white American troops, black men would have 'relations with the wives of absent soldiers'. On the basis of these concerns, the report writer concluded that a word-of-mouth propaganda

[96] Minute Sheet (signature illegible), Bristol, 12 Aug. 1942. HO 45/25604 (probably from Regional Commissioner for Home Security).

[97] HO 45/25604.

campaign should be set in motion to educate the citizenry about the problem based on an 'authorised description of the background of the colour problem in the United States'.[98]

I should like to emphasise the need for speed. Broad and large the darky is a simple minded child. But like other children, if you give him an inch he will take an ell, and once has taken an ell, the trouble will have started. What is very necessary is that the ell should be reduced to something less than a foot. The problem is an urgent one, in my view. Only yesterday I was given an authentic account by a responsible person of two young girls coming out of a public house, escorted by one buck nigger, all of them in drink. Speculations on this sort of incident are rather frightening.[99]

While this official wrote rather hysterically about the potential for problems and suggested a 'whispering campaign' to prevent it, the Chief Constable of Oxford was opposed to such a campaign. He suggested that what was required instead was 'an intensive propaganda campaign among the American white soldiers, particularly the Officers, that: "When in Rome they must do as the Romans do." ' Yet although this Chief Constable had suggested that in Oxfordshire people did not object to see-ing white women with 'members of the coloured races', he added, 'of course, every step must be taken to stop British women misconducting themselves with coloured troops, if for no other reason than that we do not desire to have a certain proportion of the population semi-coloured, in rural districts in this Country in the future.' He advised sending Ministry of Information speakers to the Women's Institutes to warn women about this.[100] Finally, he concluded that the American military authorities 'should arrange for coloured American females to be stationed in each district where coloured American troops are quartered'.[101] The authorities were unquestionably haunted by the spectre of interracial sexual relations.[102]

Judging from reports throughout the war of white British women associating with black Americans, the efforts to channel female desire in racially appropriate ways through education were not very successful. The threat to reputation and respectability of the women who would do so, however, is suggested by a letter inter-cepted by British censors: 'Perhaps the most dreadful experience I have yet gone through in life happened not so long ago. We were given instructions on how to act on the Negro problem in England. All the girls were told that they were not to com-ment on other white ladies dating negroes. However, we were not to date them, for

---

[98] Ibid.   [99] Ibid.

[100] Letter from T. E. Johnston, Chief Constable Oxford to Under Secretary of State, Home Office, 22 July 1942. HO 45/25604.

[101] Ibid.

[102] For fuller analyses and accounts of the American presence and how it was handled by the British than can be offered here, see Smith, *When Jim Crow Met John Bull*; Reynolds, *Rich Relations*; Sonya O. Rose, 'Girls and GIs: Race, Sex, and Diplomacy in Second World War Britain', *International History Review*, 19 (Feb. 1997), 146–60; Sonya O. Rose, 'The "Sex Question" in Anglo-American Relations in the Second World War', *International History Review*, 20 (Dec. 1998), 884–903.

nice girls don't.'[103] Adding to the potentially negative consequences of such an official response for British colonial policy, such instructions and their implementation were vilified in the press.[104]

First-person accounts from the period that are available suggest that while some Britons were highly critical of American-style segregation and of being told not to associate with African-American soldiers, others were concerned about interracial contact. Shirley Joseph wrote in her 1946 memoir of her years in the Women's Land Army about having hitch-hiked rides with Americans. She noted, 'I drew the line, however, at traveling with coloured men. I knew I shouldn't be prejudiced, but I couldn't face it.'[105] A diarist, Miss P. Arnold from Hampstead, who wrote about her extensive social life during the war noted in one entry that one of her boyfriends made her promise that she would never go out with a black man.[106] A Mass Observation report, based on a survey of the organization's National Panel of Observers (primarily middle-class, of 'more than average intelligence and broadmindedness') about their personal attitudes towards people of colour suggested that the observers held complicated views.[107]

One in five respondents were 'rationally in favour of equality for all races' and one in fifteen 'spontaneously criticized the white American attitude on race', while others in the sample had some 'deep-seated prejudice' . . . One male Mass Observeration correspondent, for example, wrote that 'North American Negroes' were 'good natured fellows, and several have distinguished themselves well above the average white', but 'I am horrified at the idea of a British girl marrying a black man including Indians. The wars have not changed my opinion on this.' Another wrote that he did not differentiate 'between any coloured people. I have . . . no desire to associate myself with them, but on the other hand I do not think I would go out of my way to avoid social or business relations with coloured people. I do on the other hand feel very strongly about intimate relations with coloured folk, and consider the laws of the land should prohibit inter-marriage of white people with coloured.' And another observer responded that he felt 'ashamed' that he 'understood' why some people would discriminate and would want segregation.[108]

---

[103] Field censors, 1944, p. 191. FO 371/34126. Some British male soldiers also did not receive their instructions about race with approval. See response by Mass Observer Denis Argent to Directive Reply, 'Directive on Attitudes towards People of Colour', Directive Reply, June 1943, Mass Observation Archive, Sussex.

[104] See e.g. *New Statesman*, 22 Aug. 1942, reported by Smith, *When Jim Crow Met John Bull*, 58, and *Sunday Pictorial*, 6 Sept. 1942, Smith, *When Jim Crow Met John Bull*, 45.

[105] Shirley Joseph, *If their Mothers Only Knew: An Unofficial Account of Life in the Women's Land Army* (London: Faber & Faber, 1946), 93.

[106] Miss P. Arnold diary. 88/3/1, at the Imperial War Museum.

[107] 'Attitudes to Coloured Races', File Report 1885, Aug. 1943 (microfilm). For a discussion of Mass Observation, see Penny Summerfield, 'Mass Observation: Social History or Social Movement?', *Journal of Contemporary History*, 20 (1985), 439–52.

[108] Directive Replies, June 1943. Mass Observation Archive, Sussex.

Fundamentally, the British Government wished to avoid conflict with the Americans over the race issue and wanted them to take 'the colour problem' back to the United States with them after the war. This was implied in the Army Bureau of Current Affairs publication 'The Colour Problem as the American Sees It', one of the educational pamphlets that served as a vehicle for group discussions by the British troops. Like the other government statements, it also stressed the issue of interracial sex, and advised British soldiers on how they should conduct themselves with regard to the presence of both black and white American soldiers in Britain.

We need not go into a long discussion as to whether mixed marriages between white and coloured are good or bad. What is fairly obvious is that in our present society such unions are not considered desirable, since the children resulting from them are neither one thing nor the other and are thus badly handicapped in the struggle for life.

To the Americans, the report continued,

it is a first-hand problem, while to us it is a second-hand one. There is no reason why we should adopt the average American attitude to the problem, but we should certainly respect that attitude and appreciate the reasons for it.[109]

This statement both underscores British concern about interracial sex, and suggests that it stemmed, in part, from the hope that once the Americans had gone home Britain would return to the pre-war state of affairs in which most areas did not confront the issue of racial difference in their daily lives. As Simon Gikandi has noted, Britain was both proud of being an imperial power and threatened by the physical presence of the empire 'at home'.[110]

There was never any expectation on the part of the British Government that the non-white colonial people who came to Great Britain for the war effort would stay. In fact, the whole idea was that they would return as 'good-will ambassadors' to their places of origin. The attitude towards these workers and their repatriation is evident in a conference convened by the Colonial Office and called 'Conference on Disposal of Colonial War-Workers'.[111] A memorandum from Arthur Dawes to Sir George Gater about the conference suggested that it was essential to formulate a policy without delay, in order

to aim at an orderly and systematic liquidation of the Colonial labour force. The political reasons for doing this are very obvious and need not be emphasised here. We have I think among these workers a considerable volume of goodwill towards this country and the British

---

[109] Army Bureau of Current Affairs, 'The Colour Problem as the American Sees It', 21 Nov. 1942, London.

[110] Gikandi, *Maps of Englishness*, 6.

[111] 'Welfare: Labour from the Colonies for War Purposes: Conference on Disposal of Colonial War-Workers'. CO 876/77.

connection: and the aim should clearly be to capitalise on it and not allow it to be dissipated through some turn of the economic kaleidoscope.[112]

As the war was drawing to a close in the spring of 1945, Learie Constantine had the impression that not more than half of the West Indians in the Liverpool area wanted to return to their colonial countries at all. A Ministry of Labour staff member commented about Constantine's observation: 'As they are British subjects we cannot force them to return, but it would be undesirable to encourage them to remain in this country. We should, therefore, take immediate advantage of every expression in favour of repatriation as the longer the men stay here, the less ready they will be to go.'[113]

After the war with Germany had ended, Constantine worried:

A wave of feeling is beginning to rise (restiveness) and I make the strong recommendation that men who wish to return home should have their wishes considered immediately . . . English workers on the floor of factories constantly ask the men when they are returning home, as it is obvious that their services could be dispensed with. That, of course, is creating the impression (erroneously of course) that West Indians are not now wanted because the war is over.[114]

After the Colonial Office received a petition signed by 50 or 60 West Indians describing their fear of being unemployed when they returned to their homes, the ministry pressured the Government to fund a training scheme for the West Indian Technicians and other colonials, as was being offered to demobilized servicemen. By late autumn 1945 the employment situation of West Indians in Lancashire had deteriorated, and it was increasingly difficult for the Ministry of Labour to find employment for them. There was a 'growing tendency for employers to seek English labour rather than accept the Colonials sent to them'.[115] Eventually the Treasury funded the training scheme, but the Ministry of Labour became increasingly anxious that those on the scheme accept repatriation.

This section of the chapter has considered fears about interracial sex and its potential consequence—a 'darkening' of the British population. Being British meant being white. It also meant being tolerant, at least more tolerant than white Americans; it meant a paternalist stance that helped people of colour to 'develop' and eventually 'earn' their independence. But that independence was always seen as involving a Commonwealth of Nations—that is retaining a political tie to Britain. I have tried to indicate that particularly in a war when Britain was in fact dependent on the colonies for loyalty and support, these aspects of Britishness worked against

---

[112] AJD to Sir George Gater, 6 Oct. 1944. CO 876/77.

[113] Barbara Green, Note, 27 Apr. 1945. LAB 26/134.

[114] Learie Constantine, Minute on Repatriation, 27 June 1945. PRO/LAB 26/134.

[115] Note on Present Position of West Indian Technicians and Trainees in NW Area. 17 Nov. 1945. PRO/LAB 26/134.

one another. Additionally, long-standing racial ideologies and attitudes continued to subvert Great Britain's image of itself as a benign imperial power. As Kenneth Little said in a memorandum to J. L. Keith,

I have . . . become somewhat depressed at the poor state of what I may call Anglo-Colonial relations . . . I have never had any doubt that a very great improvement could be brought about if the Government and others concerned would adopt a more imaginative and even a more constructive attitude towards the implications which arise simply out of the question of 'colour'.[116]

Indigenous Colour Bars in the Metropole

Even if most Britons, prior to the war, had little or no personal contact with non-whites, especially people from Africa and the West Indies, numerous scholars have pointed out that they certainly had exposure to stereotyped ideas through various forms of cultural representation.[117] Minstrelsy was apparently a popular style of entertainment prior to the war, as it had been since the nineteenth century.[118] Several groups, some white and some black, were broadcast on the BBC and featured in *Radio Times*, the BBC magazine. In August 1939, *Radio Times* featured programmes by 'Uncle Mack and His Minstrels', the Kentucky Minstrels, and on 1 September 1939, 'Nosmo King' was pictured in the magazine.[119] During the same time period, *Radio Times* was publishing a serialized story that in one episode focused on a scene at the 'Three Nations Cafe-bar' when the group was interrupted by 'a gigantic Negro of such repulsive appearance that the man who sat just inside the door stared at him in frank amazement'.[120]

Even though there was sympathy for Learie Constantine and overt antagonism towards white Americans for their treatment of blacks, racial discrimination in employment, housing, and hotel accommodation that had nothing to do with American influence existed in the United Kingdom. At least since 1932 Harold Moody, President of the League of Coloured Peoples had complained to the Home Office about the regulation of the British Boxing Board of Control that prohibited 'a coloured person from fighting for the British boxing championship'.[121] Again in

---

[116] PRO/CO 875/19/14.

[117] See e.g. Kim F. Hall, *Economies of Race and Gender in Early Modern England* (Ithaca, NY: Cornell University Press, 1995); Patrick Brantlinger, *Rule of Darkness: British Literature and Imperialism, 1830–1914* (Ithaca, NY: Cornell University Press, 1988).

[118] See Paul Gilroy's discussion of the difficulty black artists like the Fisk Jubilee Singers had in establishing an audience for their music because of 'black face' minstrelsy towards the end of the 19th century. *The Black Atlantic: Modernity and Double Consciousness* (Cambridge, Mass.: Harvard University Press, 1993), 88–9.

[119] *Radio Times*, 22 Aug. 1939, 35; 26 Aug. 1939, 64; 1 Sept. 1939, 64.

[120] Sidney Horler, 'Here is an SOS', *Radio Times*, 4 Aug. 1939, 15.

[121] 'Previous Consideration of the Colour Bar Question', n.d., probably early July 1941. HO 45/25604.

April 1941 Moody wrote to the Secretary of the British Board of Boxing Control ask-ing that the Board reconsider the ban, 'in the light of recent happenings such as the effect of the Nazi racial theory and also the rallying of the Colonial members of the Empire' in the war effort. The Board decided not to discuss the question 'particu-larly during the present War'.[122]

In the late 1930s and continuing during the war, women from the colonies who wanted to obtain nurses' training in hospitals in England and especially in London were denied admission.[123] In 1937, for example, a member of the League of Coloured Peoples received a letter from the Matron at the Manchester Royal Infirmary responding to one sent supporting the application of a colonial woman that read, 'We have never taken coloured nurses for training here . . . there was a definite rule that nobody of negroid extraction can be considered. If the lady about whom you write has no Negro blood perhaps you would kindly let me know, and I will bring your letter to the notice of the Nursing Committee at their next meeting.'[124] As a consequence of the League's pressure, the colonial Office established a committee to investigate questions concerning the training of Colonial nurses in UK hospitals. But years later, in the spring of 1944, the committee was still meeting and working out how to have 'coloured' women from the colonies accepted at a number of dif-ferent English hospitals.[125]

Discrimination against non-white colonial visitors to the United Kingdom by hotel keepers also was common. Some of the colonial people attending the Coronation festivities had been denied rooms at hotel and boarding-houses.[126] A Maori choir under the direction of a Maori minister from New Zealand, giving con-certs for charity in 1937 or 1938, was denied hotel rooms in Cornwall.[127] In an article reporting on Learie Constantine's experience at a London hotel, a Bath newspaper recalled a similar incident that took place in Somerset some time previously in which a 'famous coloured entertainer was asked to leave a leading hotel'.[128]

In the summer of 1941, two years before the Learie Constantine episode, the Secretary of State for the Colonies, Lord Moyne, at the urging of J. L. Keith of the Welfare Office, wrote to Home Office Secretary Herbert Morrison recommending that there be a statute to enforce what was implicit in the common law, that innkeepers had an obligation to provide accommodation and refreshment for trav-

---

[122] *League of Coloured Peoples' News Letter*, June 1941, 65–6. Beginning in around 1910 the Home Office and other ministries were concerned about permitting championship fights between black and white boxers. For an interesting discussion, see Patrick McDevitt, 'May the Best Man Win: Sport, Masculinity and Nationalism in Great Britain and the Empire, 1884–1933 (Ireland, West Indies, Australia)', Ph.D. thesis (Rutgers University, 1999).

[123] League of Coloured People's Annual Report, 1937–8, 3–5.   [124] Ibid. 2.

[125] 'Training of Colonial Nurses in the UK', May–July 1944. CO 876/79.

[126] Letter to *The Times*, reprinted in LCP Annual Report, 1937–8, 6.   [127] Ibid. 9.

[128] *Bath and Wiltshire Chronicle*, 2 Sept. 1943, 4.

ellers to prevent their discriminating against persons of colour.[129] A conference about the matter was scheduled, but the participants recommended not pursuing the proposal. Both the representatives of the India Office and the Home Office opposed raising the issue of race in the law, and any other positive action was dismissed as unworkable.[130]

The rebuff of Learie Constantine at the Imperial Hotel in the autumn of 1943 provided an urgency to the Colonial Office desire to sponsor legislation that would make it an offence for an innkeeper or hotel manager to deny accommodation on the grounds of race. The purpose of the legislation, according to Colonial Office records, however, was to 'prevent insults' rather than to stop hotel keepers from discriminating against non-whites which they could 'easily do . . . in some other way than referring to their colour'.[131] As J. L. Keith of the Colonial Office suggested, this would be purely 'declaratory legislation' which would 'satisfy Colonial opinion . . . it is either now or never. We shall never have a better case.'[132] In other words, hotel managers could discriminate on the basis of race as long as they had another more palatable excuse. The law was meant to be 'window dressing'. The proposal was again discussed at a conference at the Home Office, but because of Constantine's legal action against the hotel, it was felt unwise to pursue the possibility of legislation further at that point. The Permanent Under-Secretary of State for the Home Office, Alexander Maxwell, was of the opinion that in any case, such legislation was impracticable.[133]

People of colour in the United Kingdom generally faced various forms of overt discrimination. In the summer of 1940 the *Evening Standard* reported the case of a man who was arrested for breaking a telephone at a labour exchange. When asked why he was so troublesome, the man replied that he had been refused work because of his colour. He said, 'I have nowhere to go, nowhere to eat, because I am a coloured man. I seek the humblest employment. I would chop wood; I would wash plates! But not even jobs like that can I get!'[134] A Nigerian who had applied at the Camden Town Employment Exchange for a job with the Post Office was denied employment in the autumn of 1940 because the Divisional Post Office had insisted that they would not 'employ coloured persons, unless they were a very light colour'.[135] In the summer of 1942 an Indian, Dhandru Ram Dehil, complained in a letter to the *Coventry Evening*

---

[129] Letter from Lord Moyne, Secretary of State for the Colonies to Herbert Morrison, Home Secretary, 27 June 1941. CO 859/80/7.

[130] Report of Meeting, 15 July 1941. CO 859/80/7.

[131] J. L. Keith minute, 13 Sept. 1943, CO 859/80/8.   [132] Ibid.

[133] C. J. Jeffries Minute. 17 Sept. 1943. CO 859/80/8.

[134] From *Evening Standard*, 19 July 1940, as reported in the *League of Coloured Peoples' News Letter*, Aug. 1940, 87–8; also see G. H. Hall, Colonial Office letter to Ralph Assheton, M. P. Minister of Labour, Aug. 1940, encouraging the Ministry to look into the general treatment of non-white people at Labour exchanges.

[135] Letter from H. Gosney, Ministry of Labour and National Security to J. L. Keith, Colonial Office, 15 Nov. 1940.

Telegraph that there was a 'malicious attitude towards Indians' on the part of officers at Labour Employment Exchanges. And at the end of 1944 the Church Missionary Society complained to the Colonial Office about a shortage of accommodations, high prices, and poor facilities for African students in the country because of colour prejudice.[136] These are just some examples of racial discrimination confronted by organizations such as the League of Coloured Peoples, and welfare officers in the Colonial Office.

Racial discrimination, however, was practised not just by private citizens and employers, but also by members of the Government, and in particular by the military. Until October 1939, the three services had prohibited the possibility of non-white men enlisting in the regular peacetime services and being given commissions. Under pressure both for manpower and by the Colonial Office, they agreed to relax the 'colour bar' subject to three limitations: it was to be relaxed only in the present emergency; the relaxation applied only to 'coloured persons who are in this country', and it applied only to 'emergency commissions'.[137] The War Office refused to mount a West Indian regiment (there were such regiments in India, Kenya, and West Africa), claiming that West Indians had not made good soldiers in World War I. This was a profound source of difficulty for the Colonial Office who were under pressure from West Indians to allow them to participate as combat troops in defence of the empire. The Colonial Secretaries beginning with Lord Moyne in the middle of 1940 were at odds with the War Office over the policy. The RAF, however, did allow individual West Indians to enlist during the war on a case-by-case basis, and eventually the War Office allowed individual West Indian women to enlist in the ATS.

The Colonial Office attempted, until early in 1942 when it gave up, to have the 'for the duration only' policy of the services made permanent, but the services were intransigent on the issue. The best that Lord Moyne, who spearheaded the Colonial Office contestation with the War Office, could hope for was that 'no action should be taken which might prejudice the examination of the general question afresh at the end of the war'.[138] In addition to these policies of discrimination in the military, the Women's Land Army rejected the application by a woman of colour. This incident occurred about the same time as Learie Constantine's rejection from the London hotel, also was covered by the press, and was widely and critically discussed.

---

[136] Church Missionary Society Memorandum, 'Accommodation for African Students at Educational Centres in This Country'. In file, 'Welfare of Colonial People in the UK Advisory Committee, 1944–46'. CO 876/69, 968/38/10.

[137] 'Colour Bar in the Armed Forces', 10 Nov. 1941. CO 968/38/10.

[138] Letter from C. H. Thornley of the Colonial Office to E. B. B. Speed, Under-secretary in the War Office, approved by Secretary of State, 6 Jan. 1942. CO 968/38/10.

Race in the Colonies

Colour bars existed not only in the metropole but in the colonies as well, and incidents of discrimination there were well-publicized for local, metropolitan, and imperial consumption. For example, a West Indian journalist, Garnet H. Gordon, wrote a letter that went to newspapers in Bermuda, to the Governor of Bermuda and to Lord Moyne, Secretary of State for the Colonies in the autumn of 1941. Gordon was on a flight to London that was grounded in Bermuda because of weather with six other non-white journalists. The six black West Indians were assigned to one hotel while the other grounded passengers were assigned elsewhere. When they arrived they found the hotel to be 'dirty and drab; third rate in appearance', and were told by an attendant that they were not wanted as guests there. He wrote:

Suffice it to say that despite our widely proclaimed war aims, despite Bermuda's vaunted patriotism, despite (or because of) the influence of many whose honesty of purpose it may be 'sacreligious' to call into question, we who left our homes and security on War and Empire service were scurvily treated and not provided with, or offered any accommodation in keeping with what we were accustomed to or with our official status.

This rude insult hurled at strangers . . . may have consequences beyond the expectation of myopic prejudice. Under a liberal system of government the theories of race superiority can only be enforced in the proportion with the supine complacency of those who through numbers and otherwise should have the courage to resist and strike at this evil wherever and whenever it protrudes its ugly, venomous head.

I desire to do no more than to place before the Bermuda Public as I shall place before other publics the 'broadminded' restrictions which obtain in the most 'advanced' and peculiarly 'distinguished' part of the British Empire.

It might be quite desirable to perpetuate this state of affairs if a Hitler victory is really wished for.[139]

Under-Secretary of State Parkinson conferred with Gordon in London and attempted to convince him that the Colonial Office would do anything 'practicable' to break down the colour bar in the Colonies. Correspondence about the Gordon incident between Secretary of State Lord Moyne and the Governor of Bermuda, Viscount Knollys, mentioned Bermuda's dependence on American tourists as the cause of the colour bar in hotels there. Knollys and Moyne seemed to agree that 'in the present state of feeling' rather than intervene against hotel proprietors, the solution was to 'arrange that, with the co-operation of one of the leaders of the coloured population accommodation in private houses of suitable members of the coloured community should be available in the future'.[140] Knollys attempted to reassure Lord Moyne that he would do everything he could

---

[139] Letter from Garnet H. Gordon, 30 Oct. 1941. CO 859/80/16.

[140] See Lord Moyne to Viscount Knollys, 13 Nov. 1941, and Viscount Knollys to Lord Moyne, 4 Dec. 1941. CO 859/80/16.

by example or persuasion, to mitigate the very firmly and deep-seated policy of effective discrimination which in practice, though not in law, exists here. I am sure you will agree that on a question so full of dynamite as is the colour problem here, it would be harmful for me to do anything which might during the war and at this particular time affect adversely any influence I may have in guiding opinion on matters connected with the prosecution of the war in the widest sense . . . opinion here is such that I am quite prepared to find that even my gesture in arranging for my A.D.C.—not too conspicuously—to express my regret at the incident, might be criticised as pandering to coloured feeling. But I will do what I can.[141]

Clearly, neither Moyne nor the Governor were about to do anything to prohibit racial discrimination or even to denounce it in the colonies.

During the period the Colonial Office also was dealing with criticism about racism in the colonies that had absolutely nothing to do with American tourists. For example, the League of Coloured Peoples complained that Barclays Bank in the West Indies refused to hire non-white staff, and that West Indian Governments refused to employ non-white inspectors of police.[142]

The League approached the Colonial Office about Barclays Bank in 1941. Apparently, not much was done about the problem then, because in 1944 there was another round of correspondence in the Colonial Office files about it—this time between the Colonial Office and Barclays Bank. T. K. Lloyd, a Colonial Office official, described his unsuccessful interview on the subject with William Goodenough, Chair of Barclays Bank's overseas branches. He described Goodenough as 'charming', but he had 'a distinct element of stubbornness in his attitude on the question of employing coloured staff at West Indian branches of Barclays Bank'.[143] Goodenough said that it would not be feasible to do anything in wartime, but that he hoped to initiate a scheme for the employment of coloured staff sometime in the future. Lloyd said in his note to the files that he was not asking the bank for dramatic action; just a token measure 'that the Bank was moving in the right direction'. 'I pointed out the importance of the matter to us at a time when the West Indian islands, particularly Jamaica, were becoming very politically conscious.'[144]

Barclays gave as its excuse for not actively pursuing the matter the competitive pressure from Canadian banks operating in the West Indies which also maintained a colour bar.[145] When the Canadian banks were contacted, the head office of the Commercial Bank of Canada said that because they hoped to further trade in the

---

[141] Knollys to Moyne, 12 Dec. 1941. CO 859/80/16.

[142] George Gater, Colonial Office to William Goodenough, Chair Barclays, 8 June 1943; Minutes, 3 Dec. 1941; 6 Dec. 1941; 20 Dec. 1941; 23 Dec. 1941. CO 859/80/16.

[143] T. K. Lloyd, Note of Interview with Sir William Goodenough, 24 Feb. 1944. CO 859/126/6.

[144] Ibid.

[145] See letter from A. E. F. Benson of the Colonial Office to the Under-Secretary of State, Dominions Office, 23 Mar. 1944. CO 859/126/6.

area, they had top posts in these communities 'occupied by officers of mature Canadian experience'.[146] Cables from the Royal Bank of Canada and the Bank of Nova Scotia claimed not to discriminate against Jamaicans, but their policies mandated filling key positions with senior officers who had experience in other countries, and/or who had training in Canada. The Canadian banks continued to resist changing their policies, or even announcing a policy in which posts would be open to all West Indians regardless of colour.[147]

The League of Coloured Peoples also was active in pressuring the Colonial Office to employ non-whites in the higher echelons of the Colonial Service. The Colonial Office maintained that if black men were not employed, it was not due to a colour bar, but rather to the fact that officers must be able to serve in any part of the empire and 'must be acceptable wherever they may have to go'. What the Colonial Office feared was that they could not transfer a black West Indian official to Kenya, for example. The League took the view 'that if the only reason why we cannot have a black governor of (e.g.) the Gold Coast, is that when the time comes to transfer him to (e.g.) Nyasaland either he will not want to go, or the people of Nyasaland will not want to have him, then the principle of having a unified colonial service must be brought under review'.[148] In one of its annual reports the League of Coloured Peoples quoted Dr J. B. Danquah, a barrister and newspaper editor from the Gold Coast,

Is it really true that it is a policy of the Colonial Office to-day that no matter how well an African may be qualified for taking a share in the Government of his own country he will not be given that opportunity to participate . . . for the simple reason that he is a native? If so, where are Africans to get experience for the promised self-government? If so, why make declarations of trusteeship?[149]

Danquah's statement continued with a thinly veiled threat: 'If, that is, the Government of the West African Colonies is, by *policy*, going to be kept always in the hands of British-born subjects until such time as the Africans in the mass become as politically conscious as Indians, are we not creating conditions for another "Indian problem"— . . . another Gandhi, in West Africa?[150] This sort of thing cannot last for a thousand years. The end is bound to come. Life is short, but art is long.'[151] Danquah saw that racism and colonial domination went hand-in-hand. After

---

[146] Cable from Canada, 6 July 1944. CO 859/126/6.

[147] See letters from Royal Bank of Canada, 8 Nov. 1944, 28 Nov. 1944; Bank of Nova Scotia, 18 Nov. 1944; 30 Nov. 1944; and Canadian Bank of Commerce, 7 Dec. 1944. CO 859/126/6.

[148] 'The Colour Bar', Report on Deputation by League of Coloured Peoples to Secretary of State for the Colonies MacDonald, 23 Jan. 1940. CO 859/40/1.

[149] League of Coloured Peoples 11th Annual Report, 1941–1942, 8.

[150] For an analysis of racial discrimination and colonial policy in the West African colonies, see Flint, 'Scandal at the Bristol Hotel', 74–93.

[151] League of Coloured Peoples 11th Annual Report, 1941–1942, p. 8 (emphasis in the original).

the war Danquah was to become a key player in the Gold Coast's independence movement.[152]

Incidents of discrimination against Africans in British African colonies were subjects of sharp criticism by some anti-imperialist Members of Parliament. John Dugdale, a Labour MP for West Bromwich, for example, unfavourably compared the treatment of colonial peoples in the British empire with those in the French empire, and 'in what I might refer to as the Russian Empire. There are large numbers of people of different races in Russia and among none of those peoples is there any sense of a colour bar. All are treated as equal. If we followed their example we might do much to improve our relations with Colonial peoples.'[153] He was concerned especially about the treatment of African soldiers in the colonies, and suggested that it would be a 'slur on our Colonial Empire' if there were public places in the cities of the various colonies to which natives were not admitted. Dugdale undoubtedly had in mind the example of the treatment of West African troops stationed in Kenya.

A year prior to Dugdale's remarks the Colonial Office was questioned in the House of Commons about colour bar restrictions that prevented West Africans from going to the cinema in Nairobi. In preparing their reply the Colonial Office queried the Governor of Kenya and learned that it was the Government of Kenya's practice to censor films 'as suitable for exhibition to non-Africans only'.[154] The discussion about the matter of access of West Africans to cinema houses in Nairobi between Secretary of State Lord Moyne and Governor Moore of Kenya continued for over six months with no seeming resolution. Moyne learned that individual West Africans could apply for permission to go to a particular film. But he was concerned that there was different treatment meted out to different Africans, and informed Moore that he placed 'great importance to questions of discrimination on racial grounds, and I am particularly anxious to be in a position to meet Parliamentary or other criticism to the effect that such discrimination is being shown where members of the forces are concerned'.[155] The Governor in his response some months later insisted that there had been no complaints about the differential treatment among different African groups, and that Africans rarely attended the cinema because of the high admission prices. In any case, he argued, the problem was moot in the case of West Africans because they had all left.[156] The internal minutes in Colonial Office files about discrimination in Nairobi cinemas indicated a range of views on the part of Colonial Office officials. J. L. Keith, responsible for

[152] Danquah was instrumental in forming the United Gold Coast Convention (UGCC) and he invited Kwame Nkrumah back to the region after years of exile to act as Secretary-General of the UGCC. After Ghana's declaration as a republic in 1960, the newly elected President Nkrumah placed Danquah, his main opponent for the presidency, in prison where he was to remain until his death.

[153] As reported in *The Town Crier* (Birmingham), 25 July 1941, 8.

[154] Governor of Kenya to Secretary of State, 24 June 1941. CO 859/80/15.

[155] Lord Moyne to Governor Moore, 30 Sept. 1941. CO 859/80/15.

[156] Governor of Kenya to Lord Moyne, 16 Dec. 1941. CO 859/80/15.

the welfare of colonials residing in the United Kingdom, maintained that the real reason Africans were excluded in both Nairobi and Northern Rhodesia 'is that the Europeans object to their presence in places of amusement which the European community regard as their own'.[157] Another official, W. Beckett, advocated a cautious response in order not to 'precipitate a walk-out of Europeans'. He also objected to Keith's having blamed the cinema owners for using discrimination as a way of 'profit-mongering' to keep Europeans paying high prices for their seats.[158]

The extent to which formal colour bars ruled the lives of Africans in Kenya and the Rhodesias was detailed in the anthropologist Norman Ley's, *The Colour Bar in East Africa*, published in 1941. Ley made it clear that the kinds of statutory colour bars he was describing did not exist in French, Portuguese, or Belgian Africa, and ended his book by advocating that the British Government by decree mandate their abolition.[159] Such publicity and the operation of the colour bar in the colonies was every bit as potentially troublesome for the Colonial Office as was its operation within the metropole. Racism clearly threatened Great Britain's hold over its colonies.[160]

Anti-racist propaganda also was not welcome by white officials in a number of the colonies. The Bermuda Information Office, for example, requested that the Ministry of Information not send propaganda to Bermuda concerning 'the abolition of the colour bar in Britain and various parts of the Empire', because the 'white population strongly resents this'.[161] The letter, which the writer meant to be 'private and confidential', said:

The white people of Bermuda are a minority (about 1/3 to 2/3) but for the most part we are of pure British stock—a matter in which we take pride—and the truth is we regard the coloured people as lacking in many of the characteristic which we regard as important and there is a deep, traditional objection to any policy which will lead to social and cultural association with them and which may lead to a mixed race.[162]

The press in Bermuda was strictly censored by the Bermuda Information Office to reinforce what was described as the 'cast-iron social colour-bar'.[163]

In 1943 BBC personnel in London began to consider broadcasting a programme with a script on colour prejudice. The script was in the form of a discussion among a West African student at Cambridge, Harold Moody head of the League of Coloured Peoples, Robert Adams, a West Indian from British Guiana who was an actor, Kenneth Little the anthropologist, and a white real estate broker.

---

[157] J. L. Keith minute, 30 June 1941. CO 859/80/15.

[158] W. Beckett minute, 2 July 1941. CO 859/80/15.

[159] Norman Ley, *The Colour Bar in East Africa*, repr. (New York: Negro Universities Press, 1970).

[160] For an interesting study examining ideas about race both in London and in African colonies, see Wolton, *Lord Hailey*.

[161] Letter from Bermuda Information Office to Noel Sabine, early May 1943. CO 875/5/22.

[162] Ibid.   [163] Overseas Planning Committee, 3 Feb. 1944, #8. INF 1/561.

Although fearful that it would offend 'Chinese, Maoris, Indians', the Director of Talks, G. R. Barnes, originally seemed to favour broadcasting it on the Home Service. He thought the programme should be introduced with brief biographies of the speakers so that the listeners understood that the discussion concerned feelings of West Africans and West Indians. The Colonial Office was strongly in favour of doing the broadcast. With regard to the concern that the discussion of colour prejudice would be offensive to some, Elspeth Huxley, the BBC Liaison Officer for the Colonial Office, opposing such a tepid approach suggested,

It would seem rather unfortunate if we were to reach the stage when we cannot discuss an urgent Colonial and domestic problem in a way which might do a lot of good, for fear of offending some of the more reactionary among our Allies who are temporarily over here. As regards the Indians they are, no doubt, very touchy, though they can hardly be more so than the Colonials. As I understand it, what Colonials object to is not a frank and open discussion of difficulties, but the hypocrisy which they see in our attitude of official non-discrimination and unofficial prejudice.[164]

Huxley's reference to 'reactionary Allies' was to the Americans; earlier in her note she had said, 'the Americans cannot have it both ways. They are always criticising us for our imperialistic and oppressive policy of rule and exploitation in the Colonies and they cannot, with justice, then turn round and criticise us for trying to treat our Colonials more as equals'.[165]

In spite of Colonial Office support for the project, Barnes was apparently persuaded that such a broadcast would be too sensitive at that time for the Home Service.[166] Then, he considered possibly broadcasting the discussion on the Overseas Service. While the Assistant Controller thought the script somewhat superficial, he ventured that it might be a good thing to produce as some discussion of 'the superficial effects of the colour bar in this country and its hurtfulness to British colonial subjects would serve a useful purpose'. He was concerned, however, that the script should be clear that the programme was talking 'about negroes [*sic*] and not about coloured people generally'. He worried that the programme would offend 'Chinese and others'.[167]

In the meantime, a letter about publicity on the colour bar written by Frank Stockdale, the Comptroller for the West Indies, circulated at the BBC. Stockdale advocated extreme caution in referring to the 'colour question' in propaganda, and

---

[164] Elspeth Huxley to Director of Talks, 25 June 1943, 'Coloured People'. R 51/92, at the BBC WAC.
[165] Ibid.
[166] See G. R. Barnes (Director of Talks) to Miss Bucknall, 21 June 1943; DT to C(H), 'Colour Prejudice Discussion', 26 June 1943, in 'Colonies: Personal', R 51/90; Barnes (DT) to Miss Bucknall, 30 June 1943, RCONT 1 Learie Constantine File 1 (1943–1962) both at the BBC WAC.
[167] R. A. Rendall (Assistant Controller, Overseas Service) to D.T., 22 July 1943. Learie Constantine File 1, at the BBC WAC.

said the less done by direct reference to it the better.[168] Stockdale argued that '[c]olour in the West Indies is basically a class distinction and there are as keen feeling [*sic*] between shades of coloured people as there are between white and black'.[169] He suggested that one indirect method of attacking the 'colour question' would be to stress 'the breaking down of class barriers and distinctions which have been such a feature of the social revolution in England during the war and also by stressing the steps which have been taken by industrial concerns in the United Kingdom in the development of welfare services and community centres for their workers'.[170] Stockdale proposed that there should be more extensive employer-sponsored welfare measures for workers, and enhanced economic opportunity for the 'intelligent and educated coloured people' in the West Indies. His suggestions were very influential at the Ministry of Information in shaping their propaganda campaigns.[171]

There were efforts early in 1944 to reactivate interest in the script on colour prejudice, but there was still insufficient support at the BBC for doing so. The subject of the colour bar and its abolition was simply 'too hot to handle'. The Acting Governor of British Honduras felt that the question of colour prejudice should not be made the subject of propaganda at all; any propaganda from London on the topic might be harmful unless 'handled most delicately indeed'.[172] He added, 'it would presumably be necessary to consider the very sensitive American reaction. Embarrassment is already caused to a large body of opinion in the United States by the activities of such a lady as Mrs. Roosevelt; it might not be desirable that additional embarrassment should be attributed to official British sources'.[173]

In sharp contrast, the Jamaican Information Officer urged propaganda 'showing that colour discrimination is disapproved by the British Government'. His concern was that racial antagonism was being 'stirred up by local agitators . . . The Americans have lately blotted their copy-book by advertising for "White" employees.' In Jamaica, he argued, it would be helpful to stress the idea that the empire was a 'Commonwealth of many and diverse races'.[174] The various sensitivities about racism compounded problems for the Colonial Office and the Ministry of Information in constructing propaganda extolling Britain's virtues as an imperial power.[175]

[168] Extract from Letter to Mr Beckett from Sir Frank Stockdale, 15 July 1943, #15, p. 3 in 'Coloured People', R 51/92, at the BBC. The full letter from Frank Stockdale to H. Beckett of the Colonial Office is also in PRO/INF 1/560.

[169] Stockdale Letter, 20 June 1943, #12, p. 1. in 'Coloured People', R 51/92, at the BBC WAC.

[170] Stockdale Letter, 29 June 1943, #13, p. 2. in 'Coloured People', R 51/92, at the BBC WAC.

[171] See 'Plan of Propaganda to the West Indies, First Revision of Aims', Overseas Planning Committee, 20 Mar. 1944, #4. PRO/INF 1/561.

[172] R. E. Turnbull, Acting Governor to Oliver Stanley, 27 May 1943. PRO/INF 1/560.   [173] Ibid.

[174] Jamaican Information Officer, Secret letter to Usill (Empire Division, M.O.I.), 12 Jan. 1944. PRO/INF 1/560.

[175] In Frank Furedi's estimation, the only propaganda campaign during the war that was designed to present a positive view of race relations was considered for the Caribbean but never implemented. In the

The various attempts to deal with racism either at home or in the colonies suggest that officials in the Colonial Office and in the colonies were exquisitely aware that racism was a highly explosive issue. As Frank Furedi has so aptly argued, this fostered a pragmatic approach that would avoid conflict—an approach preoccupied with 'the reaction to racism rather than with racism as such'.[176]

Imperial Heterogeneity

The twin issues of colonialism and race continued throughout the war to upset any unifying conception of 'the Empire'. Even Colonial Office officials referred to the colonial empire as a 'convenient myth'.[177] They were acutely conscious not only of the potential weakening of the attachment of particular colonial dependencies to the 'mother country', but also of the extraordinary heterogeneity within the empire itself. The question of heterogeneity arose when the Colonial Office concerned itself with entertaining people from different colonies who were in the United Kingdom. As one of the officials said,

If you just throw an assortment of miscellaneous people from the Colonies together in a room it won't work. I am all for mixing them—judiciously: but the mixer has to bear in mind that they don't think of themselves as members of that convenient myth, the Colonial Empire. They think of themselves as say, Jamaicans or Mauritians, and they recognise a relationship to this country, but they find it a lot harder to recognize any relationship to Mauritians or Jamaicans.[178]

Commenting on the difficulties in arranging social occasions for people from the diverse colonies, another official made the issue of race central to the problem of imperial unity:

it is one thing for some kindly people to entertain a batch of soldiers or airforce men whose homes are overseas . . . But it is quite another for the Colonial—i.e. largely if not entirely, coloured, people to be picked out from the airforce, as curious specimens and brought together in an artificial atmosphere. West Indians are said to despise West Africans and Asiatics are said to despise both. If they were included with a batch of *white* overseas airmen it would be excellent provided [that the latter] did not feel and show that they were insulted—which is likely enough.[179]

Imperial unity, and the British Government's efforts to deal with it by means of propaganda were continually being undermined by the issue of race.

end, 'official consensus concurred that "colour feeling" had to be handled "delicately" and never confronted directly.' Frank Furedi, *The Silent War: Imperialism and the Changing Perception of Race* (London: Pluto Press, 1998), 187.

[176] Frank Furedi, *The Silent War*, 107.

[177] Minute (signature illegible), 19 Jan. 1942. CO 875/12/18.   [178] Ibid.

[179] Minute (initials illegible), 20 Jan. 1942. CO 875/12/18.

BBC plans for an Empire Day broadcast that would bring together men from different regions of the empire together for a broadcast foundered on the issue of race. As an internal memo put it,

one would have to be careful with an Indian in the kind of set-up proposed. He would be very likely, I think, to resent being asked to broadcast with 'black men'—if the other two were black. (Racial feeling is not, of course, confined to whites!) and an Indian might conceivably object to broadcasting *as an Empire type* with other speakers from the *Colonies*. I imagine a man from the dominions might also object to broadcasting in these circumstances.[180]

There also were problems in attempting to consider a particular region of the empire or a specific colony as unitary for propaganda purposes. For example, concerns about how to deal with the colonial, racial, and national identities of West Indians were discussed at a meeting of the Overseas Planning Committee of the Ministry of Information.

The white elements of the population of these islands, are, on the whole proud of their traditions and longstanding family connections with the West Indies, and consider themselves West Indians as well as Englishmen: they are therefore inclined to express some resentment 'at the prevailing tendency in broadcasts of speeches in England and elsewhere' to think of West Indians as coloured people exclusively.

Equally, coloured West Indians react unfavourably if they are subjected to propaganda designed to extol negro [*sic*] exploits and activities and drawing attention to their racial affinities with African negroes and the negro population [*sic*] in the U.S.A.[181]

Additionally the Committee was concerned that when West Indians were depicted in Britain or elsewhere as 'coloured men exclusively, and therefore as having paramount interests in the West Indies as the sole native inhabitant', these representations were used by blacks agitating for political reform. Because of these complications of race, national/colonial identity, and nationalist politics, the Committee recommended that 'the achievements of both white and coloured West Indians should be stressed as a matter of pride to all West Indians'.[182]

When the revised plan for propaganda to the West Indies was sent to the colonies in the winter of 1943, the Information Officer from Antigua, Hilda McDonald, strongly supported not 'drawing attention to a Colour Problem (e.g. we should refer to West Indians rather than to Coloured men)'. She protested that this policy was not in practice being carried out,

There is a tendency in B.B.C. Broadcasts, as well as among Politicians, to identify the West Indian not only as a Coloured Man, but as having the same status in the West Indies as the

---

[180] Controller (Home Service) to Director of Talks, 5 April 1943, in 'Postscripts: Sunday', R51/423/4, at the BBC WAC.

[181] Overseas Planning Committee. Plan of Propaganda to the West Indies. First Supplement to the Basic Appreciation. Paper No. 471B, 30 Mar. 1944, 5. PRO/INF 1/161.

[182] Ibid. 5.

African has in Africa . . . this misconception is deliberately fostered for political and racial purposes, in order that the Coloured West Indian may enjoy that preference indicated in the much quoted principle of British Colonial Policy that 'If in any Colony the interests of the natives and the immigrants, including white immigrants, conflict, the former must be paramount.'[183]

She complained, as well, that the American Broadcasting Service to the West Indies, under the control of the Anglo-American Caribbean Commission, had programmes directed to the 'Negro Race, and so designed to encourage Race Consciousness and Race Antagonism . . . there is constant reference to and stress on the achievements of Africans, having no connection with the West Indies.'[184] She also blamed communists for instituting 'the drive to embitter the negro [sic]', and complained that editors of newspapers in the Leeward and Windward Islands exclusively criticized white government officials.

It was not just race that was a destabilizing issue when it came to pro-empire/pro-British propaganda. Although full-blown independence movements in many of the Caribbean and African colonies were still a few years away, white officials were alive to the potential threat that they might pose. Wartime rhetoric emphasizing freedom and democracy, therefore, could be very threatening indeed to colonial whites.

For example, distributing an anthology of writings on the 'virtues of liberty and democracy' compiled by Alan Nevins, Professor of American History at Oxford and Josiah Wedgwood MP, and sponsored by the Ministry of Information proved exceedingly problematic for the Colonial Office. The proposal for distributing the book, *Forever Freedom*, to schools in the colonies came first from Christopher Cox, a Colonial Office official concerned with education at the behest of Wedgwood and the Ministry of Information.[185] Colonial Office officials decided to send copies of the book to Information Officers in all the Colonies, the nature of its use to be left to each of the Colonial Governments. The Governor of Bermuda responded,

I hope I may say without fear of being misconstrued that it is the general opinion among my advisers that the youthful population of Bermuda are in no present need of being educated in the virtues of freedom, of which they already have a pretty wide conception; their needs are rather centred upon the obligations which these virtues impose on good citizens, particularly on that of discipline . . . This would not tend to encourage constructive thinking with regard to reforms; it might also foster undesirable discontent.[186]

The book also was not well-received in Colombo, Northern Rhodesia, or Antigua.[187]

---

[183] Hilda McDonald, 'Comments on Propaganda to the West Indies', 10 Mar. 1943. INF 1/560.

[184] Ibid.   [185] Cox Minute, 10 Feb. 1941; Thornley Minute, 7 Mar. 1941. CO 859/44/7.

[186] Governor of Bermuda to Secretary of State Moyne, 12 Sept. 1941. CO 859/44/7.

[187] Letter from Colombo (signature illegible) to Gent, 8 Sept. 1941; from Acting Governor of Northern Rhodesia, 26 Sept. 1941; Hilda McDonald, Publicity Officer, Antigua to Acting Governor of Antigua, 17 Sept. 1941. PRO/CO 859/44/7.

The Publicity Officer of Antigua, Hilda McDonald, was particularly antagonistic towards the book. She wrote,

in backward communities such as this, where the sense of responsibility is practically non-existent, and the sense of rights growing apace, it is all the more necessary that when the citizen is being taught to demand his rights, he should at the same time, be taught the necessity for developing those rights into duties; and when he is being encouraged to demand the right of self-Government, he should at the same time be taught to realise that the right to Govern carries with it the obligation to Serve.

. . . In this connection I wish to stress the need for care in issuing material from the MoI which while easy of digestion in a fully educated community, is liable to cause moral and mental indigestion when administered to a half-educated community; and I submit for consideration a paragraph which I 'edited' out of a Ministry of Information article recently sent to me for distribution, because I felt that it 'preached the virtue of resistance' and was unsuitable for publicity in this territory.[188]

Eventually, Lord Moyne, Secretary of State, decided that the Colonial Office could not recommend the book for general use in the schools in the colonies.[189]

In Jamaica, the Information Officer was concerned that there was an anti-British separatist movement advocated by an 'extremist group' of the People's National Party. His desire for anti-racist British propaganda was motivated by fear of race being used to advocate Jamaican independence. He believed it important that the propaganda stress empire solidarity, and the advantage of 'being a part of a great Commonwealth, [given] the fate of isolated unprotected countries in the world of to-day'.[190]

India

Events in India must have been closely watched by colonial critics as well as defenders of Britain's imperial policies. Throughout the war, the Indian independence movement was a symbol of resistance to British rule for colonial subjects in other parts of the empire, and there was continuing support for India's independence by various critics of colonialism within the metropole itself.[191] When the Viceroy of India declared that India would fully participate in the war effort, the Indian National Congress ministers in the provinces of the sub-continent resigned because neither Congress nor any other political parties or elected representatives had been been consulted by the Viceroy prior to his announcement. Efforts to negotiate with

---

[188]   Hilda McDonald to Acting Governor, 17 Sept. 1941. CO 859/44/7.

[189]   Confidential Circular from Lord Moyne to Colonies, 5 June 1951. PRO/CO 859/44/7.

[190]   Jamaican Information Officer, Secret letter to Usill, 12 Jan. 1944. PRO/CO 859/44/7.

[191]   For a discussion of the response by African-Americans in the United States to the Indian independence movement, as well as to British colonialism in Africa, see Penny M. Von Eschen, *Race Against Empire: Black Americans and Anticolonialism, 1937–1957* (Ithaca, NY: Cornell University Press, 1997), chaps. 1 and 2.

Congress failed when Churchill refused to discuss the issue of self-government in spite of criticism of British Government policy by other influential British politicians, such as Sir Stafford Cripps and others on the left in and out of the House of Commons as well as the Secretary of State for India, L. S. Amery. Congress's price for supporting the war was immediate independence or at least setting a definite date when independence would be granted.

Both Gandhi and Nehru, as well as the India League in Great Britain argued that for India to support Britain in a war against Fascism, it needed to have true democracy.[192] In India Congress continued to demand immediate independence, and began to advocate *satyagraha* or non-cooperation. The Government of India retaliated by arresting 2,000 members of Congress including Nehru in the autumn of 1940.

Although Nehru had been sentenced to four years' imprisonment, he was released in December 1941 along with the others. But while he was in prison, the British press published letters from Krishna Menon and others protesting the prison conditions under which Nehru and the others were kept, charges that were denied by other letter writers and also by the Government of India.[194] The India Office was concerned that the press was giving too much credence to Krishna Menon's claims, and the office arranged for propaganda to be released to the UK press about how well cared for were the prisoners, and that the number of prisoners was declining. The propaganda arm of the India Office also attempted to play up the fact that a former Home Minister of the Congress Government in Bombay had resigned from Congress because he disagreed with Congress's policy of non-cooperation in the war effort.[195]

During this period, India Office files show a marked Ministry concern about those in Great Britain who were supporting Indian independence as well as about Krishna Menon. They worried, for example, about meetings of the National Council for Civil Liberties and the Left Book Club in which Krishna Menon and others from the India League actively participated. They seemed convinced that Krishna Menon was a communist and that he used 'Communist devices'. As the Adviser on Publicity Questions for the India Office put it, 'It is scandalous that Krishna Menon and his associates should abuse the liberty and freedom of speech accorded to them in this country and devote all their energies towards attempting to blacken the face of the British Government by the dissemination of lies and half truths about the situation in India.'[196]

[192] For discussion and quotes, see Keshava Chandon Arora, *Indian Nationalist Movement in Britain* (New Delhi: Inter-India Publications, 1992), 87–9.

[193] Ibid. 88.

[194] India Office Archives. L/I/1/886 File 46/39A. Letters were in the *New Statesman and Nation*, 24 May 1941, and letters contesting the charge were solicited by the India Office, 30 May 1941.

[195] Ibid.   [196] 'Anti-British Propaganda', 1/I/1/890 file 462/41 at the India Office Archives.

As the war in the Far East worsened with the loss of both Burma and Singapore to the Japanese in 1942, the British Government sent Sir Stafford Cripps to India in the late winter hoping that he could convince Congress to cooperate. In exchange for promising India freedom and self-government 'the moment the war was over and the Indians had framed a new Constitution for their country', Cripps wanted Congress to participate in the government and in the defence of the country.[197] But the leaders of Congress were not satisfied with the proposals and refused to trust the British Government's promises.

The Government's relationship with Congress went from bad to worse. In early August 1942, the All-India Congress ratified Gandhi's proposal for mass non-violent resistance unless Britain withdrew from India immediately. The day following the ratification, the Government of India imprisoned all the leaders of Congress, including Gandhi. Protests across India followed and Congress workers went into hiding. They continued to operate clandestinely as an underground movement.

In the metropole Home Security reported that the British public generally reacted with hostility to Gandhi, and were concerned that the disorder in India would adversely affect the war against Japan, but warned of the existence of a vocal minority sharply critical of the Government's position.[198] To respond to its critics, the Government of India published a pamphlet that set out the case against Congress describing Congress's alleged participation in the disturbances of the summer and fall of 1942. The pamphlet was issued in London as a Government White Paper. Congress was portrayed as 'an underground revolutionary movement with all the trappings of terrorism . . . sabotage, unscrupulous opportunism and complete disregard of the safety and welfare of the general public'.[199]

In London V. K. Krishna Menon's India League publication, *About India*, attempted to counter anti-Congress propaganda in the British metropole. Menon claimed that the Government controlled what could be printed about the situation in India. He described mass arrests, beatings, floggings, shootings and 'other acts of repression familiar to those who know India under Police Raj'.[200] Menon was supported by a number of trade unions and labour leaders, students and local branches of the Labour Party.[201]

The India League organized 'India Week' celebrations in late January 1943 to coincide with Indian Independence Day, a day commemorating the date that Congress launched its initial campaign for freedom from British rule; large meetings and demonstrations were held in London as well as in other cities throughout

---

[197] Sir Stafford Cripps, MP, 'My Mission to India', *Current Affairs*, 6 June 1942, Army Bureau of Current Affairs.

[198] PRO/INF 1/292 Part 3, p. 3.   [199] L/I/i/887 file 462/39B, at the India Office Library, London.

[200] India League, 'Realities in India', *About India*, Dec. 1942.

[201] Arora, *Indian Nationalist Movement*, 106.

Great Britain where the India League had branches. In London British and Indian speakers demanded that the Government release the prisoners, grant civil liberties in India, and reopen negotiations. In Birmingham the Labour Party's newspaper, *The Town Crier*, announced the week of demonstrations, and urged trade unionists to send resolutions to the Government and to the Viceroy. 'What a challenge to Democracy! Every sincere socialist, every active co-operator, every ardent trade unionist will strive to link Birmingham with India next week,' wrote Victor Yates for the newspaper.[202]

Pressure grew on the British Government to release Gandhi, especially because of his deteriorating health. Churchill approved his release on 6 May 1944. But the sense of urgency about finding a solution to the Indian situation continued. In early June 1944 a group of well-known British writers and intellectuals wrote to the Secretary of State for India supporting the more than 100 Indian newspaper editors who had urged the Government of India to free Congress leaders still in prison. The signatories included Vera Brittain, Fenner Brockway, Victor Gollancz, Julian Huxley, C. E. M. Joad, Harold Laski, J. B. Priestley, E. M. Forster, Herbert Reed, G. D. H. Cole, and Tom Wintringham, a virtual all-star cast of left intellectuals. Labour MPs also demanded their release and the establishment in India of a representative government. And on 9 August the anniversary of the arrest of Congress leaders, a large group of Americans appealed to the British Ambassador in Washington[203] on behalf of the imprisoned members of Congress. Labour Party candidates made India an issue in their speeches in the run-up to the June 1945 election. Finally in July 1945, the leaders of Congress remaining in prison were released. Clearly, the British Government's India policy had been politically divisive.

Subjects or Citizens?

The difficulties in constructing propaganda for consumption in the various regions of the empire that either dealt explicitly with the issue of race or in any way imagined the empire as some sort of unity through its connection with the metropole (the 'mother-country') clearly show that racism and colonialism separately and in concert posed problems for British policy throughout the war. British propaganda efforts attempted to deny, mask, or circumvent the power relations that were at the heart of both race and empire. As I have already suggested, the British, especially those in the Colonial Office and in the Ministry of Information, commonly attempted to portray Britain's relationship to India and the colonies using a paternalist metaphor. This translated into familial imagery in which the white British were the parents who would benevolently guide their charges to their full adulthood. The

---

[202] *The Town Crier*, 23 Jan. 1943, 8.
[203] 'Indian National Congress', L/I/1/884/ File 462/39. India Office Library, London.

colonial powers were even called 'parent states' in British Government discussion.[204] Economic development and welfare were to be nurturing potions to be dispensed from and by Great Britain. The paternalist relationship between empire and colony was contained within and occluded by 'trusteeship', a concept used repeatedly to describe the obligations of Britain to its imperial dependencies. Increasingly, and in response to the political and ideological currents set in motion by a war against Fascism, the term 'partnership' came into the Colonial Office lexicon during the war years. The term was meant to suggest a more equal relationship than trusteeship, but one which at first would be structured as involving senior and junior partners. It downplayed a fixed hierarchical sensibility and, as Suke Wolton has argued, made the notion of development crucial to the imperial relationship.[205]

In Secretary of State for India L. S. Amery's speech to the attendees at the Teachers' Course on Empire Problems that I quoted at the beginning of this chapter, Amery stressed the role of England in 'creating the British Empire and making it what it is'. And in saying this, he clearly meant England as contrasted with Britain. For men like Amery, England was the parent and Britain was the imperial offspring.

The Empire is the embodiment of a tradition of political life in which all are free to co-operate and which knows no formula of exclusion. The main bearers of that tradition, as they were its creators, have been the English people. Theirs has been the quickening and guiding spirit. Their language has enshrined that tradition in a great and glorious literature. But they have claimed no monopoly for themselves or for their speech . . . Scots and Irish, French-Canadian and Afrikander, Moslem and Hindu, have carried forward, and, each in his own way, enriched the British tradition as they have contributed to the strength of the Empire.[206]

Using a maternal metaphor Amery simultaneously portrayed England as a nurturer of the empire as well as its paternal progenitor. England was the 'guiding spirit', leading the others to form a whole. But this was not a homogeneous unity; it was a unity of difference. How was it to be consolidated?

Amery suggested that its consolidation stemmed from two features. First, England set a lofty example of a country exemplifying the characteristics of tolerance, charity, and comprehension; the recognition of the rights and point of view of others . . . who have come under our control. Britain, he maintained has, 'on the whole, regarded her government over other peoples as a trust, and has striven to live up to the spirit of trusteeship'.[207] Second, the empire was 'one single, indissoluble body corporate composed of the King and his subjects . . . As subjects of the King all inhabitants of the Empire owe loyalty not only to the King, but in virtue of their loyalty to him, to each other.'[208] These characteristics, he maintained, had brought

---

[204] Cited in Cooper, *Decolonization*, 112.
[205] Wolton, *Lord Hailey*, 122–5, esp. 124.
[206] Amery, 'Empire and Commonwealth', 10.
[207] Ibid. 11.
[208] Ibid. 13.

the parts together, sharing 'a common tradition interwoven with each local tradition, a common patriotism of Empire not excluding but embracing and enlarging the narrower patriotism of nation or community'.[209] Amery proposed that Great Britain's ethical and beneficent policies and actions led to ties of loyalty between the colonies and dominions and the mother-country. Additionally, their common allegiance to the King produced a shared patriotism, a loyalty 'transcending more immediate loyalties'. His vision of common subjecthood, 'loyalty to the Throne', as he put it, provided the glue that made the empire's parts adhere into a whole.

Other representatives of the British Government used a more contemporary trope than that of the ties between subjects of the same monarch to describe the bonds of loyalty among and between imperial subjects and Great Britain. They spoke of those subjects as 'citizens of the empire'. Describing Harold Moody to Secretary of State for the Colonies, Malcolm McDonald, the Secretary General of the International Institute of African Languages and Cultures wrote, 'Dr. Moody is at heart, I am perfectly sure, a most loyal subject of the King and extremely proud to be a citizen of the Empire.'[210] Urging the Colonial Office to encourage the public towards a 'more enlightened public opinion', J. L. Keith, then newly appointed to the Welfare Division of the Colonial Office, wrote that white people in the metropole and the colonies should 'regard men and women of colour as fellow human beings and fellow citizens of the Empire with the same fundamental needs as themselves, rather than as anthropological specimens of curious appearance'.[211] And in a speech to the Board of Education in Jamaica, B. H. Easter, Director of Education and Information Officer, referred to the 'wider citizenship enjoyed by the people of the British Empire'.[212]

As a Jamaican newspaper editorial wryly commented this 'wider citizenship' was a 'mere figure of speech'. Yet it was a telling one. It was 'subject-hood' under a more 'enlightened' rubric—one that signified belonging. It also suggested 'rights' of a sort—the 'rights' that a child had from its parents, or that subjects had from a benevolent monarch, and the 'obligations' of fealty that those subjects owed in return. In its editorial, the *Evening Post* retorted: 'But the people of Jamaica are not British citizens . . . To be sure, the legal nationality of a Jamaican is British. But unless he possesses the full rights of a citizen, he is no more on a footing of equality with a real British citizen than is a bunch of bananas, which is also legally British.'[213] At the heart of the notion of imperial citizenship lay that most fragile of national self-understandings: Great Britain as an imperial and paternal benefactor.[214]

---

[209] L. S. Amery, 'Empire and Commonwealth,' 11–12.

[210] Letter from H. Vischer to the Colonial Office, 29 Mar. 1940. CO 859/40/1.

[211] J. L. Keith, 'Colour Prejudice in the U.K.', 7 Nov. 1940. CO 859/40/4.

[212] Extract from Colonial press Summary No. 42, n.d., probably summer 1941. CO 875/6/11.

[213] Extract from Colonial Press Summary No. 42. CO 875/6/11.

[214] Interestingly, Suke Wolton has noted that the common ground between the United States, which had been sharply critical of British imperialism, and the United Kingdom was a 'shared paternalism towards the non-white peoples' (*Lord Hailey*, 147).

Britain's imperial relations across the globe subverted the framing of the war as one being fought to secure freedom and democracy for both the country and the empire, and this was quite obvious to Britain's critics both at home and abroad. The League of Coloured Peoples, for example, reprinted a letter that had been published in a regional newspaper in the fall of 1942. I quote it here at length because it expresses so explicitly the perception by at least some non-white residents of the metropole of the contradictions in Britain's self-proclaimed moral stance in the war.

With the crescendo of battle, with the visions of victory, with the hunt for allies comes the unfolding of promises; re-assuring messages echo and re-echo through the ether, each in sharp contrast to the letter foretold in the 'Atlantic Charter'. Each vibration fills the hearts of white men with drunken satisfaction; each utterance lays the foundation-stone for the next great terrible war that of Coloured v. White.

Mr. Churchill and Mr. Roosevelt solemnly promised in mid-ocean that they were fighting this war for the freedom of mankind—or should I be distorting if I said for the freedom of Europeans to exercise pressure for the preservation of vested interest, coming to this conclusion through the statement by Mr. Churchill in retort to Mr. Willkie that he, Mr. Churchill was not fighting this war for the dismemberment of the British Empire, and the promise by Mr. Roosevelt that the French colonies would be returned to France directly after the war. This contradiction might pass with honour so far as Europe is concerned.

But what is the position of the Asiatic and the African? Are they to be used as hard cash in an effort to make a rich European peace; or used as machines to enrich the white man's larder? Is it not time for us to demand a full statement before assisting our white administrations in bringing revenge and hatred upon themselves?

Take care, England and America! It does not require a prophet to foretell the result of such utterances. A federal white union that is to possess the power to subdue the world by force of arms can only lead to one result—a federal union of coloured men to blast their way to liberty and equality.

Was the ringing of church bells an echo of victory or the death-rattle of humanity? Always remember that 'a governing Power is not only answerable for the evils it commits, but also for those evils it might have prevented.'

And is not Hitler a product of our evils?[215]

Churchill had made it plain that the promises of the Atlantic Charter, to which the letter writer was referring, would only apply to Europeans, giving Britain's general wartime anti-Fascist ideological stance an undeniably hollow ring. The sensitivity of at least some non-white Britons to the contradictions in Britain's wartime rhetoric was palpable. Across the empire many colonial subjects were convinced that the message of the Atlantic Charter must apply to them in the not too distant future.[216]

---

[215] Letter written by Basil A. L. Rodgers of Salcombe to *Western Morning News*, 28 Nov. 1942; *League of Coloured Peoples' News Letter*, Jan. 1943, 114–15.

[216] As Furedi comments, many colonial nationalists 'believed that their time had arrived' (*Silent War*, 175).

The fragility of Britain's image as a paternalist imperial nation clearly went beyond the contradictions imposed by fighting a war against Fascism and for 'liberty, equality, and fraternity', although wartime rhetoric certainly underscored the contradictions of racism and colonialism. It was fragile because at the core of paternalism was a clearly unequal power relation, but one in which the more powerful figure in the relationship was dependent upon the weaker one. This dependence surely was economic, but the relationship also was necessary to Great Britain for its national image as a great and benign imperial power; one that existed to 'do good in the world'. Furthermore, Great Britain was also dependent upon the empire for the loyalty of its colonial dependencies and dominions, both for its existence as an empire, and for the war effort, a loyalty that was continually challenged by issues of race and difference. Fear of racial mixing and the supreme importance of securing the United Kingdom as a 'white nation' subverted its imperial project. Whiteness was central to rule, but it was also central to the imposition of colour bars that continually threatened to weaken the loyalties of black British subjects.

Indeed, the war had been over just a matter of months when the Fifth Pan-African Congress met in Manchester in October 1945. The Congress was attended by 90 delegates, 26 of whom were from various regions of Africa. The attendees included W. E. B. Dubois, the inspiration behind the Pan-African movement, and those who were later to become independence advocates and political leaders including Hastings Banda, Kwame Nkrumah, Jomo Kenyatta, George Padmore, Arthur Lewis, and Peter Abrahams (for the African National Congress). The Congress demanded an end to both colonial rule and racial discrimination. It marked a significant step along the political road to decolonization.

8

Conclusions and Afterthoughts

Nothing is sudden. Not an explosion—planned, timed,
wired carefully—not the burst door. Just as the earth invisibly prepares its
cataclysms, so history is the gradual instant.

(Anne Michaels, *Fugitive Pieces*)

I began to think about patriotism and national identity when the United States
went to war with Iraq in 1990. Almost overnight, or so it seemed, yellow ribbons
were everywhere. Initially, when the bombing of Baghdad first started, there were
protests in college and university towns—I distinctly remember the sounds of
'Give Peace a Chance', that wonderful Beatles song from another age booming over
loudspeakers. But in a matter of days, the yellow ribbons adorned clothing and
decorated campus buildings. I wondered at how easily patriotic sentiment and the
sense of belonging to a nation under threat—even if that threat was so far away—
could be aroused. My previous work had convinced me that collective identities like
gender and class were difficult to forge, and so I looked with amazement as so many
of my compatriots rallied to the flag. As I was finishing the book, patriotism and
national unity once again had become central to US political culture following the
terrorist attack on New York City in September 2001. And, as this book goes into
production the US, abetted by Britain, threatens a new war with Iraq and again the
drums of patriotism are beating loudly and persistently. Once again flags wave, proclaiming that we, the people, are united.

My research for this book quickly revealed that like gender and class identities,
indeed like all collective identities—all definitions of who 'we' are—national identity and concepts of nationhood are fragile. Even as they are articulated, once they
move beyond the generality that 'we are all in this together', once who the 'we' is, and
what 'together' means are specified, the singularity of that identity is exposed as
being false.

'We' are one people in both the most profound and the most qualified of senses.
We are profoundly one in that we are all human; but once that humanity is delin-
eated—like the political subject of liberal theory—the definition excludes some and

includes others. We are also significantly 'one people' when we say we are British, or Canadian or Australian or whatever it is that has been stamped on our passports— that fundamental marker of identity in a world of nation-states. Without a pass- port, as Philosopher Seyla Benhabib insists, 'the refugee, the illegal immigrant, the asylum seeker . . . has no protection from the collective and organized power of her or his fellow human beings.'[1] Being a member of a particular national 'community', however, may say nothing else about who 'we' may be. But it is precisely those national identifications that become so extremely powerful at some historical junc- tures. There is something about national belonging, and about feeling oneself as a member of an organic community that is incredibly emotionally compelling. And, in part, it is that very emotional power of the idea of being one with others that makes the definition of the national community so fraught.

This book has explored the instabilities at the centre both of British nationhood and the meanings of citizenship in a historical period in which the people of Britain were, in fact, unified. That is, they agreed that they were not German; they agreed, if they lived in the United Kingdom that they were British citizens—that their nation- ality was British. And they recognized that because Britain was at war, they were all 'in it together'. But they did not agree as to what it meant to be British, or what it meant to be a citizen. There was no one-size-fits-all Britishness even when the peo- ple of Britain were at war. The pull to unity was haunted by the spectre of division and difference. And to add further to this complexity, there were different ways of being citizens.

Great Britain was an imperial nation, and while many in Britain were critical of imperialism of any sort, mostly the British thought that their country was a be- nevolent imperial power. Especially when Britain was fighting against an aggressive and racist country that was bent on conquest, it was important to underscore the image of British tolerance and Britain's humanitarian and philanthropic stance towards the colonies and dependencies. But racism both at home and in the empire, and the presumption of being a white nation tested the perception that the British were both tolerant and benevolent, and threatened to weaken the very ties that made Britain an imperial nation in the first place. World War II produced strains within the empire confirming that its dissolution was just a matter of time.

The question of empire also was at issue geographically closer to 'home', as those who lived in national cultures that were a part of Great Britain but were outside of England contested just what was Britain as a nation. It seemed almost as though the very efforts on the part of the Government to recognize Britain's cultural hetero- geneity in order not to antagonize those who felt themselves to be equally Welsh or Scottish and British fostered identity politics.

And the long established vehicle for representing England to the English, the

---

[1] Seyla Benhabib, 'Sexual Difference and Collective Identities: The New Global Constellation', *Signs*, 24 (Winter 1999), 357.

rural landscape and the ways in which the rural became critical to the war effort—as both a destination for evacuees and as the only source of food—also stimulated the expression of long held resentments. For those living on farms and in villages, the symbolic and material centrality of the rural was at odds with what they saw as their peripheral political status.

The British prided themselves on being a virile nation, but its virility was temperate. They were fighting a war with their sense of humour intact; they were 'good tempered' and modest. The qualities of being British, what then might have been called British 'national character' also were those that characterized hegemonic masculinity. Hegemonic masculinity was comprised of an unstable mix of the traits of the soldier-hero, and those that drew upon the homely, more feminine ideals of masculinity inherited from the inter-war years. This was a 'kinder, gentler' manliness that was equated with Britishness. But it was a balancing act—one that required a military uniform for its successful performance. Any male of apparently military age who was not in uniform was at risk of being seen as a 'bad citizen', even though there were men on the home front 'doing their bit' for the country. Also those who behaved in too aggressive or too strident a manner, or advocated 'toughness' over 'goodness' risked being thought of as fascistic. The masculine version of Britishness and citizenship, like masculinity itself, was fragile.

The meanings of women's citizenship have always been a source of contestation. And so they were in wartime Britain. 'Good citizenship' for women was demonstrated by being sexually virtuous and by being a good mother. Participating in the war effort as a soldier or as a worker could jeopardize women's civic virtue if they were suspected of sexual promiscuity or if they were thought to be irresponsible mothers. Additionally, the emphasis on unity and participating in the war effort by accepting increased civic responsibilities produced contestation over women's rights. This contestation, like the protests of striking workers, openly challenged the idea that the British were one people.

Furthermore the symbolic roles of women as guardians of the home and representatives of stability were continually tested over the course of the war. Women were both necessary as workers to the war effort and urged to continue being feminine. Their accomplishments in their jobs or their participation in the services, however, provoked continuing challenges to the idea that after the war women and family life would go on as though the war had not happened. As Steven Fielding has put it, women's wartime roles were 'equivocal'—while they 'were expected to perform previously male tasks, and for less pay, they were also required to uphold traditional expressions of femininity.'[2] Furthermore, traditional expressions of femininity were themselves conflicted—sexualized femininity and maternal femininity both, in their own ways, were potentially destabilizing.

---

[2] Steven Fielding, 'The Good War: 1939–1945', in Nick Tiratsoo (ed.), *From Blitz to Blair: A New History of Britain since 1939* (London: Phoenix, 1998), 39.

The meanings of 'good citizenship' and Britishness focused on self-sacrifice and placing the common good over individual interest. The singularity of the nation of good citizens was imagined by identifying and excluding those who did not fit; sexually promiscuous young women, 'good-time girls', were constructed as 'lacking good citizenship' while Jews were viewed as inherently unBritish—as perpetual aliens—regardless of their citizenship status.

There were strong populist overtones to the war's popular description as the 'People's War', and the promise of 'equality of sacrifice' became crucial to wartime unity. This was so especially following a decade of high unemployment and economic insecurily when, as Tony Mason has put it, 'old ideas that the poor were divided between the deserving and the undeserving resurfaced in the form of a belief that the working class were responsible for their own misfortune.'[3] What I have called, following the language used by the Ministry of Information, 'class feeling', was omnipresent during the war years. Produced in part by the experience of the 'hungry thirties', and by a rearticulation of the 'social question' during the war, class feeling for many in Britain fueled the desire for social change along with the pervasive fear that the 'old gang' would successfully thwart it.

Three images served as tropes for the nation as an organic community. The idea of the 'People'—the 'Common People'—an idea with a long, radical past that became renewed during the hungry thirties and with the rhetoric of the popular front was mobilized to signify that the British were inherently one people. The 'People' made their appearance in documentary and feature film, in speeches, in newspapers and magazines. In 1942, for example, *Meet '. . . The Common People . . .'*, compiled by the filmmaker Edward Carrick and based on photographs from documentary films made between 1939 and 1942, appeared in book shops on both sides of the Atlantic. The book ended with the following message:

We have told our story of the common people at war. This is a little island. A people packed and concentrated in a small space, a few hundred miles from verge to verge. Within its bounds great changes have forced new shapes into being, for good or evil. A tremendous surgery is going on all round us. We shall lose a lot that is moribund and decaying, but we shall gain a new strength and vitality. Yes, whether we like it or not, great changes are in the air . . . A new world is in being, even though the pangs of travail have still to be endured.[4]

This enunciates perfectly the tone of populism and utopian longing that was omnipresent at the time. The people may still have to endure, but there will be a new world. But as we have seen, class feeling continued to be expressed, articulated in and by a variety of antagonisms, along with the desire for social transformation coupled with deep abiding cynicism.

[3] Tony Mason, ' "Hunger . . . is a Very Good Thing": Britain in the 1930s', in Tiratsoo (ed.), *From Blitz to Blair*, 21.

[4] Gerry Bradley, 'Commentary', in Edward Carrick (ed.), *Meet . . . 'the Common People . . .'* (London and New York: Studio Publications, 1942), 94.

The English countryside that stood for peace, tranquility, stability, harmony, and timelessness was emblematic of what I have referred to as the 'authentic nation'. But, as Michael Bunce has written, this landscape is an aesthetic built upon ironies:

The British, and especially the English countryside is valued as a landscape aesthetic. This is evident in virtually every aspect of its idealisation from its literary and artistic treatment to its use as an amenity and the campaign for its protection from development . . . However, the aesthetic appreciation of the countryside is inseparable from the social order which created it . . . the bulk of the English countryside . . . was created by the process of enclosure and gentrification which accompanied the spread of landed estates. Although it evolved within the framework of agricultural progress, it was a form of progress constrained by the entrenched hierarchical structure of rural society, in which agrarian objectives were often subordinate to the requirements of gentrification.[5]

As Bunce explains, the harmonious and timeless countryside, a highly domesticated one, was created by a social order that was anything but harmonious. This mode of creation continued to affect the lives of people who inhabited the countryside during the war. As a symbol, the English landscape glossed over or even misread the history of the countryside, picturing it as a place absent of politics and conflict. By producing the sense that the countryside was locked in past time, it denied the fact that technologies had transformed agriculture, thus making it seem marginal to Britain viewed as a modern, technologically advanced society.

Finally, if any image was central to depictions of the nation, it was the trope of family. As Anne McClintock has so ably written, the family image figured 'social hierarchy within a putative organic unity of interests'.[6] Or, as Anne Phillips has suggested, the family metaphor identifies 'a common heritage, some shared experience that sets us apart from the rest of the world. It draws the boundaries between my family and yours, pulling us inexorably into its ghettoized confines.'[7] One might scrutinize the familial metaphor further to underscore the centrality to the projected image of 'the family' of the persistence of 'natural' emotional bonds regardless of inequalities of power, differences in interests, and conflict. As an imagined organic community, like the members of a family who belong 'naturally', the nation is characterized by affective rather than instrumental bonds. Given such a powerful trope, more homology than analogy, it is understandable that there was so much anxiety expressed in public culture about how women, potential 'mothers of the race', might be changed by the war.

The presumed homologous relationship between family and nation had other correlates. The fear of miscegenation was one—the fear that stymied British

---

[5] Michael Bunce, *The Countryside Ideal: Anglo-American Images of Landscape* (London and New York: Routledge, 1994), 34.

[6] Anne McClintock, *Imperial Leather: Race, Gender and Sexuality in the Colonial Context* (London and New York: Routledge, 1995), 45.

[7] Anne Phillips, *Democracy and Difference* (Cambridge: Polity Press, 1993), 33.

attempts to both manage the presence of African-Americans within the United Kingdom and remain in good standing with colonial peoples.[8] Furthermore, when it came to the colonies, the familial metaphor again provided a useful image. Britain was the 'mother-country' that would benevolently care for her youthful charges while simultaneously giving paternal guidance until they became adults and could manage for themselves.

How then does this examination of the national imaginary during World War II accord with other histories of Britain in the war? Paul Addison has noted that the history of Britain in World War II has been undergoing substantial revision. He writes that

historians have been trying to disentangle the truth as they see it from the myths of wartime propaganda and the self-interested accounts of politicians and others. The patriotic interpretation of the British at war as a united people, ennobled by the struggle against an evil dictatorship, has been replaced by a more streetwise account in which the divisive and discreditable aspects of wartime society are well to the fore. Once full of neighbourly Cockneys defying the Blitz, the home front has been repopulated with factious politicians, incompetent managers, malingering workers, unfaithful husbands and wives, racists, looters, black marketeers and other prototypes of Essex Man.[9]

This book is not meant to debunk the historical memory of World War II as the 'good war'. The British were united in fighting the enemy; there was a coalition Government that agreed to agree on basic wartime policy; it was a time of high idealism when visions of a better society were dreamt, and when being an engaged citizen counted for more in the public culture of the time than did the pursuit of individual happiness. The war did lead numbers of people to turn from solely focusing on their private lives to becoming civic actors.

Because the British could not articulate a unitary national identity, a singular version of Britishness, did not mean that they were not unified; it did not mean that they failed to 'pull together' in defeating the enemy. They were unified and they did pull together. They understood themselves as being members of the nation, even if they could not agree on how the nation was constituted; on who belonged and who did not, on what made Britain distinctive, or on what membership entailed. The sheer fact of the matter was that being unified did not depend on a single core of national identity. Being British and living in the United Kingdom, regardless of what Britishness meant, was enough. The nation was at war, and the personal as well as collective threat of that armed conflict was enough to forge solidarity. National

---

[8] See Ann Stoler's critique of Foucault's analysis of the 'symbolics of blood' and the rise of racism in *Race and the Education of Desire: Foucault's History of Sexuality and the Colonial Order of Things* (Durham, NC and London: Duke University Press, 1995), chap. 2.

[9] Paul Addison, 'Churchill and the Price of Victory: 1939–1945', in Tiratsoo (ed.), *From Blitz to Blair*, 54.

unity of the magnitude that occurred during the war needed only to last the duration. It did.

What does this tell us about the nature of identity and its implications for collective action? I think it points to what a number of social theorists have suggested—that collective action is possible when identities are taken up strategically; an essential core to those identities is not a necessary component. As sociologist Craig Calhoun has suggested, 'the choice between deconstructing and claiming identities (or identity as such) may be one that needs to be shaped by strategic considerations, not dictated by theoretical and normative first principles'.[10] Political theorist Kathleen Jones has put it this way: 'The strategic assertion of identity remains necessary to the development of any political movement. Yet identity should not be the goal itself.'[11] Collective solidarity need not be premissed either on denying the differences among those who are involved or on imposing some form of homogeneity on them. Rather, it could entail 'building unity without denying social difference' in the words of Anne Phillips.[12]

But if the cultural construction of a common core identity of 'the people' failed (as it inevitably would), but the British were (relatively) unified anyway, did the multiple attempts to forge a common national identity have no impact on Britain in World War II? Should scholars abandon the analysis of processes involved in the creation of identities and their meanings if, as in this case, they made no apparent difference to the success or failure of the war effort; if that is, they are simply an effect of discourse period? One might answer this question by pointing to other cases in which the construction of national or ethnic identity has had dramatic and devastating consequences, as in the former Yugoslavia. This suggests that it would be worth investigating under what conditions national identities can make such a profound difference. But what about Britain in World War II? Did the discursive politics of identities have no bearing at all on the wartime conjuncture and its aftermath?

Clearly, Britishness and its definition—how the nation was imagined—was something people at the time cared about. A great deal of wartime rhetoric espoused high-minded principles and grand aspirations, and promoted altruistic behaviour—ideals that many people readily embraced and that they probably experienced as uplifting. Furthermore national identities were real to the people who debated, contested, and protested them. It is precisely because people seem to care so much about them that they demand study. But more than that, as Stuart Hall has

---

[10] Craig Calhoun, 'Social Theory and the Politics of Identity', in Craig Calhoun (ed.), *Social Theory and the Politics of Identity* (Cambridge, Mass. and Oxford: Blackwell, 1994), 22. See also his analysis of the Chinese student movement of 1989, in which he suggests that a common emotionally powerful identity was created in the course of the movement, itself. Craig Calhoun, *Neither Gods Nor Emperor: Students and the Struggle for Democracy in China* (Berkeley and Los Angeles: University of California Press, 1994).

[11] Kathleen Jones, 'Identity, Action and Locale', *Social Politics*, 1/3 (1994), 262.

[12] Phillips, *Democracy and Difference*, 69.

argued, 'identity is a matter of considerable political significance', and analysis of the question of identity 'is only likely to be advanced when both the necessity and the "impossibility" of identities, and the suturing of the psychic and the discursive in their constitution, are fully and unambiguously acknowledged.'[13] I understand this to mean that collective identities are a consequence of peoples' emotional needs to belong or to be 'one' with others, and are generated as diverse people forge bonds of group membership. But these discursively constructed identities are fragile because they inevitably fail fully to meet those needs. This dynamic produces cultural contestation generating both obstacles and opportunities for action.[14]

The contestation over identities during the war years produced 'identity politics' or rather several different kinds of politics of difference. And even if the processes of cultural identification that I discussed in this book did not articulate an explicit or programmatic politics of difference, these processes forged openings—created the potential, even if not the likelihood, for people to think differently and to raise questions that previously they might not have considered. In other words, they intimated that there were possibilities for various social and cultural transformations.

Surely the rhetorics of equality of sacrifice, and the expressions of class feeling that were articulated in the context of the memory of the 'hungry thirties' moved the British public to insist that the Government not bury, but act on the Beveridge Report. The Government's initial recalcitrance about taking up the report was publicly chastised, but when the Government began to propose reforms, they were remarkably modest. The dynamics of race during the war thwarted the Government's hope that the loyalties of colonial people would be strengthened. The ambivalent representations of femininity during the war produced meanings that were available to women, some of whom insisted that the status of the housewife and mother be elevated, and some of whom could begin to imagine that contributing to civic affairs and in economic matters outside their private households would not make them less feminine. Although Scottish and Welsh nationalism may not have intensified during the war years, it did not die out either; rather it continued to be an issue that would simply not go away. Temperate masculinity was a model that persisted into the immediate post-war period, as self-discipline and emotional restraint were valued characteristics that fit well with 'Labour's faith in reason and dispassionate expertise,' as historian Martin Frances has proposed.[15] But he suggests

[13] Stuart Hall, 'Introduction: Who Needs Identity', in Stuart Hall and Paul du Gay (eds.), *Questions of Cultural Identity* (London: Sage, 1996), 16.

[14] Prasenjit Duara, 'Historicizing National Identity, or Who Imagines What and When', in Geoff Eley and Ronald Grigor Suny (eds.), *Becoming National* (Oxford and New York: Oxford University Press, 1996), 152. Also see his provocative meditation on history and the nation, *Rescuing History from the Nation: Questioning Narratives of Modern China* (Chicago: University of Chicago Press, 1995).

[15] Martin Frances, 'The Labour Party: Modernisation and the Politics of Restraint', in Becky Conekin, Frank Mort, and Chris Waters (eds.), *Moments of Modernity: Reconstructing Britain, 1945–1964* (London and New York: Rivers Oram Press, 1999), 157.

that this masculine/political language of restraint was to be challenged by the ethics of the restored consumer society that developed in Britain in the late 1950s.

If the many possibilities for social transformation created during the war through the contestation over identities did not eventuate in specific discernable changes, it is still important to recognize, at least at a theoretical level, the significance involved in the cultural work of the process of identity construction and contestation. On this point, anthropologist James Clifford, building on the theoretical groundwork laid by Stuart Hall has commented recently on identity politics in the following way:

One suspects that 'identity politics' needs to be contained, even scapegoated at times, because it is a figure for chaotic cultural and political articulations that exceed systemic, progressive determination. Collective agency, for better and worse, has long been exercised at discrepant scales: particular colonial and neo-colonial contact zones; regional, religious, ethnic mobilizations and resistance, specific transnational and diasporic circuits. It is on this uneven terrain, grasped with ethnographic complexity, that we can begin to track less heroic, more contradictory and multivalent processes of historical transformation. History without guarantees.[16]

Collective agency in World War II Britain clearly operated at different registers. Utopian dreams, the politics of recognition and inclusion, and the high ideals stressing self-sacrifice and civic-mindedness were produced in and by the public culture of national identity; but so too were anti-Semitic expressions and other manifestations of racial thinking.

I understand this book on World War II Britain to be a historical ethnography of sorts—an exploration of the conditions of possibility—of future possibilities— produced by the various contestations over identities and citizenship during the People's War.

---

[16] James Clifford, 'Taking Identity Politics Seriously', in Paul Gilroy, Lawrence Grossberg, and Angela McRobbie (eds.), *Without Guarantees: In Honour of Stuart Hall* (London and New York: Verso, 2000), 96.

Bibliography

Unpublished Primary Sources

Archival Collections

BBC Written Archives Centre, Caversham Park, Reading
    BBC Radio Talks Scripts
    BBC Administrative and Programme Files
City Records Office, Liverpool
Imperial War Museum, London
    Papers of Miss P. Arnold
    Papers of Miss E. M. Bolster
    Papers of F. P. Foster
    Papers of the Ministry of Information
    Papers of C. Ruffoni
    Papers of John L. Sweetland
    Papers of Mrs L. White
India Office, London
Mass Observation Archive, University of Sussex
    File Reports (Microfilm)
    Directive Replies
Modern Records Centre, Warwick University
    Papers of the Amalgamated Engineering Union, MS 259
    Papers of the Fire Brigades Union, MS 346
    Papers of the Iron and Steel Trades Confederation, MS 36
    Papers of Harry Meigh, MS 38/A/6/ME
    Papers of David Michaelson, MS 233
    Papers of the National Association of Schoolmasters, MS 38
National Archives, Modern Military History, College Park, Maryland
Policy Federation, Surbiton
    National Council of Women Papers
Public Records Office, Kew
    Cabinet Office Files (CAB)

BIBLIOGRAPHY

Colonial Office Files (CO)
Foreign Office Files (FO)
Home Office Files (HO)
Ministry of Agriculture and Food Files (MAF)
Ministry of Education Files (ED)
Ministry of Health Files (MH)
Ministry of Information Files (INF)
Ministry of Labour and National Security Files (LAB)
Ministry of Pensions Files (PIN)
Ministry of Supply Files (AVIA)
War Office Files (WO)

Religious Society of Friends Library, London
The Woman's Library, London Guildhall University

Published Sources

Newspapers and Magazines
Bath and Wiltshire Chronicle and Herald
Border Mail and Gazette
Chard and Ilminster News
Coventry Evening Telegraph
Daily Express
Daily Herald
Daily Sketch
Glasgow Herald
Huddersfield Daily Examiner
Jewish Chronicle
Journal and Guardian (Bolton)
Kelso Chronicle and Border Pioneer
Labour Woman
Leicester Evening Mail
Liverpool Daily Post
Norfolk News and Weekly Press
Picture Post
Preston Herald
Radio Times
Sunday Chronicle
Sunday Pictorial
Sunday Post (Glasgow)
Time and Tide
Town Crier (Birmingham)

Weekly Mail and Cardiff Times
Western Mail & South Wales News
Western Morning News (Plymouth)
Woman's Own

Pamphlets and Publications of Non-Governmental Organizations
Association of Education Committees, *Education*
British Council of Churches, *Home and Family Life*
British Federation of Business and Professional Women, *Women at Work*
Church of England Moral Welfare Council, *Quarterly Leaflet*
Engineering and Allied Trades Shop Stewards National Council, *New Propellor*
Fire Brigades Union, *Firefighter*
India League, *About India*
League of Coloured Peoples, Annual Reports 1939–45; News Letters 1939–45
Liverpool Council of Social Services, Conference Report 1946; *National Emergency Bulletin*;
    Wartime Information Bulletin
London Association of Schoolmasters, *The L. S. A.*
National Council for the Unmarried Woman and Her Child, Reports
National Farmer's Union, *The Farmer's Weekly*
National Federation of Women's Institutes, *Home and Country*; *Town Children through
    Country Eyes*
Official Organization of the National Agricultural Labourers' and Rural Workers' Union, *The
    Land Worker*
Organization of the Amalgamated Engineering Union, *A. E. U. Monthly Journal*
Organization of the British Constabulary, *Police Review*
Organization of St Joan's Social and Political Alliance, *The Catholic Citizen*
Organization of the Transport and General Workers' Union, *T. and G. W. Record*
Woman's Gas Council, *Fanfare*
Women's Freedom League, *The Bulletin*
Women's Publicity Planning Association, *International Women's News*
Young Woman's Christian Association, *The Blue Triangle*; *News for Citizens*

Government Sources
Army Bureau of Current Affairs, *Current Affairs* (1939–45); 'War Pamphlets'
British Council, *Britain To-Day*
Medical Advisory Committee (Scotland), *Report on Venereal Diseases* (Cmd. 6518, 1944)
Ministry of Information, *Eve in Overalls* by Arthur Water (pamphlet 1942); *Warwork News*
Parliamentary Debates, 5th ser., vol. 371 (1941), cols. 639–40; 5th ser., vol. 391 (1943), col. 606
United Kingdom, *Youth Registration in 1942* (Cmd. 6446, May 1943)
Youth Advisory Council to the Office of the Minister of Education, 'The Purpose and
    Content of Youth Service' (report, 1945); 'The Youth Services after the War' (report, 1943)

BIBLIOGRAPHY

Films

A Canterbury Tale. Directed by Michael Powell and Emeric Pressburger, 1944.

Diary for Timothy. Directed by Humphrey Jennings, Crown Film Unit, 1945.

Fires Were Started. Directed by Humphrey Jennings, produced by Ian Dalrymple, 1943.

The Foreman Went to France. Directed by Charles Frend, Ealing Studios, 1942.

Listen to Britain. Directed by Humphrey Jennings, Crown Film Unit, 1942.

London Can Take It. Directed by Humphrey Jennings, GPO Film Unit, 1940.

Went the Day well. Directed by Alberto Cavalcanti and Michael Balcon, Ealing Studios, 1942.

Books and Articles

Addison, Paul, 'Churchill and the Price of Victory: 1939–1945', in Nick Tiratsoo (ed.), *From Blitz to Blair: A New History of Britain since 1939* (London: Phoenix, 1998).

—— *The Road to 1945: British Politics and the Second World War*, rev. edn. (London: Pimlico, 1994).

Adi, Hakim, *West Africans in Britain: 1900–1960* (London: Lawrence & Wishart, 1998).

Aldgate, Anthony, and Richards, Jeffrey, *Britain Can Take It: The British Cinema in the Second World War* (Oxford: Basil Blackwell, 1986).

Alexander, Sally, 'Becoming a Woman in London in the 1920s and 1930s', in Sally Alexander (ed.), *Becoming a Woman and Other Essays in 19th and 20th Century Feminist History* (New York: New York University Press, 1995).

Allen, Margaret, 'The Domestic Ideal and the Mobilization of Woman Power', *Women's Studies International Forum*, 6 (1983), 401–12.

Amery, L. S., 'Empire and Commonwealth', in L. S. Amery, *The Framework of the Future* (London: Oxford University Press, 1944).

Anderson, Benedict, *Imagined Communities: Reflections on the Origin and Spread of Nationalism*, rev. edn. (London: Verso, 1991).

Andrews, Maggie, *The Acceptable Face of Feminism: The Women's Institute as a Social Movement* (London: Lawrence & Wishart, 1997).

Armstrong, W. A., 'Farmworkers in the Twentieth Century', in G. E. Mingay (ed.), *The Vanishing Countryman* (London: Routledge, 1989).

Arora, Keshava Chandon, *Indian Nationalist Movement in Britain* (New Delhi: Inter-India Publications, 1992).

Babha, Homi, 'Of Mimicry and Man: The Ambivalence of Colonial Discourse', in Homi Babha (ed.), *The Location of Culture* (London and New York: Routledge, 1994).

Balibar, Etienne, 'The Nation Form: History and Ideology', in Etienne Balibar and Immanuel Wallerstein (eds.), *Race, Nation, Class, Ambiguous Identities* (London and New York: Verso, 1991).

Barker, Rachel, *Conscience, Government and War: Conscientious Objection in Great Britain, 1939–45* (London: Routledge, 1982).

Baucom, Ian, *Out of Place: Englishness, Empire, and the Location of Identity* (Princeton: Princeton University Press, 1999).

Bauman, Zygmunt, 'Allosemitism: Premodern, Modern, Postmodern', in Bryan Cheyette and Laura Marcus (eds.), *Modernity, Culture and 'the Jew'* (Cambridge: Polity Press, 1998).

Beach, Abigail, 'Forging a "Nation of Participants": Political and Economic Planning in Labour's Britain', in Richard Weight and Abigail Beach (eds.), *The Right to Belong: Citizenship and National Identity in Britain, 1930–1960* (London: I. B. Tauris, 1998).

Bederman, Gail, *Manliness & Civilization: A Cultural History of Gender and Race in the United States, 1880–1917* (Chicago and London: University of Chicago Press, 1995).

Beisel, Nicola, 'Morals versus Art: Censorship, the Politics of Interpretation, and the Victorian Nude', *American Sociological Review*, 58 (Apr. 1993), 145–62.

Bell, P. M. H., *John Bull and the Bear: British Public Opinion, Foreign Policy and the Soviet Union 1941–1945* (London: Edward Arnold, 1990).

Bella, Anna, 'Take a Chance on Being Beautiful', *Fanfare*, 3 (Winter 1940), 8.

Bellah, Robert N., *et al.*, *Habits of the Heart: Individualism and Commitment in American Life* (New York: Harper & Row, 1986).

Benhabib, Seyla, 'Sexual Differences and Collective Identities: The New Global Constellation', *Signs*, 24 (Winter 1999), 335–62.

Benson, Theodora, *Sweethearts and Wives: Their Part in the War* (London: Faber and Faber, 1942).

Benton, Sarah, 'The 1945 "Republic"', *History Workshop Journal*, 43 (Spring 1997), 249–57.

—— 'Women Disarmed: The Militarization of Politics in Ireland 1913–23', *Feminist Review*, 50 (Summer 1995), 148–72.

Berezin, Mabel, *Making the Fascist Self: The Political Culture of Interwar Italy* (Princeton: Princeton University Press, 1997).

Berlant, Lauren, *The Queen of America Goes to Washington City* (Durham, NC and London: Duke University Press, 1997).

Beveridge, William, *Voluntary Action: A Report on the Methods of Social Advance* (London: G. Allen & Unwin, 1948).

Biagini, Eugenio F., *Citizenship and Community: Liberals, Radicals and Collective Identities in the British Isles, 1865–1931* (Cambridge and New York: Cambridge University Press, 1995).

—— and Reid, Alastair J., *Currents of Radicalism: Popular Radicalism, Organized Labour and Party Politics in Britain, 1850–1914* (Cambridge and New York: Cambridge University Press, 1991).

Bland, Lucy, 'In the Name of Protection: The Policing of Women in the First World War', in Julia Brophy and Carol Smart (eds.), *Women-in-Law: Explorations in Law, Family and Sexuality* (London: Routledge, 1985).

—— and Mort, Frank, 'Look Out for the "Good Time" Girl: Dangerous Sexualities as a Threat to National Health', in Bill Schwarz (ed.), *Formations of Nation and People* (London and Boston: Routledge and Kegan Paul, 1984).

Bonnell, Victoria E., *Iconography of Power: Soviet Political Posters under Lenin and Stalin* (Berkeley and Los Angeles: University of California Press, 1997).

BIBLIOGRAPHY

Bonnell, Victoria E., 'The Peasant Woman in Stalinist Political Art of the 1930s', *American Historical Review*, 98 (Feb. 1993), 55–82.

—— 'The Representation of Women in Early Soviet Political Art', *Russian Review*, 50 (1991), 267–88.

Bourke, Joanna, *Dismembering the Male: Men's Bodies, Britain and the Great War* (London: Reaktion Books, 1996).

—— *Working-Class Cultures in Britain, 1890–1960: Gender, Class and Ethnicity* (London and New York: Routledge, 1994).

Bousenquet, Ben, and Douglas, Colin, *West Indian Women at War: British Racism in World War II* (London: Lawrence & Wishart, 1991).

Boyes, Georgina, *The Imagined Village: Culture, Ideology and the English Folk Revival* (Manchester: Manchester University Press, 1993).

Bradley, Gerry, 'Commentary', in Edward Carrick (ed.), *Meet . . . 'the Common People . . .'* (London and New York: Studio Publications, 1942).

Braidotti, Rosi, *Nomadic Subjects: Embodiment and Sexual Difference in Contemporary Feminist Theory* (New York: Columbia University Press, 1994).

Brantlinger, Patrick, *Rule of Darkness: British Literature and Imperialism, 1830–1914* (Ithaca, NY: Cornell University Press, 1988).

Braybon, Gail, *Women Workers in the First World War: The British Experience*, repr. (London: Routledge, 1990).

—— and Summerfield, Penny, *Out of the Cage: Women's Experiences in Two World Wars* (London: Pandora, 1987).

Brittain, Vera, *England's Hour* (New York: Macmillan, 1941).

Brivati, Brian, and Jones, Harriet (eds.), *What Difference Did the War Make?* (London and New York: Leicester University Press, 1993).

Brooke, Stephen, *Labour's War: The Labour Party during the Second World War* (Oxford: Clarendon Press, 1992).

Brubaker, Rogers, *Citizenship and Nationhood in France and Germany* (Cambridge, Mass.: Harvard University Press, 1992).

—— *Nationalism Reframed: Nationhood and the National Question in the New Europe* (Cambridge: Cambridge University Press, 1996).

—— and Cooper, Frederick, 'Beyond "Identity"', *Theory and Society*, 29 (Spring 2000), 1–47.

Bruley, Sue, ' "A Very Happy Crowd": Women in Industry in South London in World War Two', *History Workshop Journal*, 44 (Autumn 1997), 58–76.

Budd, Michael Anton, *The Sculpture Machine* (New York: New York University Press, 1997).

Bunce, Michael, *The Countryside Ideal: Anglo-American Images of Landscape* (London and New York: Routledge, 1994).

Burchell, Graham, 'Peculiar Interests: Civil Society and Governing "The System of Natural Liberty" ', in Graham Burchell, Colin Gordon, and Peter Miller (eds.), *The Foucault Effect: Studies in Governmentality* (Chicago: University of Chicago Press, 1991).

—— Gordon, Colin, and Miller, Peter (eds.), *The Foucault Effect: Studies in Governmentality* (Chicago: University of Chicago Press, 1991).

Burton, Antoinette, *At the Heart of the Empire: Indians and the Colonial Encounter in Late-Victorian Britain* (Berkeley and Los Angeles: University of California Press, 1998).

—— *Burdens of History: British Feminists, Indian Women, and Imperial Culture* (Chapel Hill: University of North Carolina Press, 1994).

—— 'A "Pilgrim Reformer" at the Heart of the Empire: Behramji Malabari in Late-Victorian London', *Gender & History*, 8 (Aug. 1996), 175–96.

Caine, Barbara, *English Feminism, 1780–1980* (Oxford: Oxford University Press, 1997).

Calder, Angus, *The Myth of the Blitz* (London: Jonathan Cape, 1991).

—— *The People's War: Britain 1939–1945* (London: Pimlico, 1992).

Calhoun, Craig, *Nationalism* (Minneapolis: University of Minnesota Press, 1997).

—— *Neither Gods nor Emperor: Students and the Struggle for Democracy in China* (Berkeley and Los Angeles: University of California Press, 1994).

—— 'Social Theory and the Politics of Identity', in Craig Calhoun (ed.), *Social Theory and the Politics of Identity* (Cambridge, Mass. and Oxford: Basil Blackwell, 1994).

Cannadine, David, 'British History as a "New Subject": Politics, Perspectives and Prospects', in Alexander Grant and Keith J. Stringer (eds.), *Uniting the Kingdom? The Making of British History* (London and New York: Routledge, 1995).

Canning, Kathleen, *Languages of Labour and Gender: Female Factory Work in Germany, 1850–1914* (Ithaca: Cornell University Press, 1996).

Ceadel, Martin, *Pacifism in Britain 1914–1945: The Defining of a Faith* (Oxford: Clarendon Press, 1980).

Cesarani, David, 'An Alien Concept? The Continuity of Anti-Alienism in British Society before 1940', in David Cesarani and Tony Kushner (eds.), *The Internment of Aliens in Twentieth Century Britain* (London: Frank Cass, 1993).

Chatterjee, Partha, 'Whose Imagined Community?', in Partha Chatterjee, *The Nation and Its Fragments: Colonial and Postcolonial Histories* (Princeton: Princeton University Press, 1993).

Clifford, James, 'Taking Identity Politics Seriously', in Paul Gilroy, Lawrence Grossberg, and Angela McRobbie (eds.), *Without Guarantees: In Honour of Stuart Hall* (London and New York: Verso, 2000).

Colley, Linda, 'Britishness and Otherness: An Argument', *Journal of British Studies*, 31 (Oct. 1992), 309–29.

—— *Britons: Forging the Nation, 1707–1837* (New Haven and London: Yale University Press, 1992).

Collini, Stefan, *Liberalism and Sociology: L. T. Hobhouse and Political Argument in England, 1880–1915* (Cambridge: Cambridge University Press, 1979).

Connell, R. W., *Masculinities* (Berkeley and Los Angeles: University of California Press, 1995).

Cooper, Frederick, *Decolonization and African Society: The Labour Question in French and British Africa* (Cambridge: Cambridge University Press, 1996).

BIBLIOGRAPHY

Cooper, Frederick, Holt, Thomas C., and Scott, Rebecca J., *Beyond Slavery: Explorations of Race, Labor, and Citizenship in Post-Emancipation Societies* (Chapel Hill and London: University of North Carolina Press, 2000).

Coupland, Reginald, *Welsh and Scottish Nationalism: A Study* (London: Collins, 1954).

Dagger, Richard, *Civic Virtues, Rights, Citizenship, and Republican Liberalism* (New York and Oxford: Oxford University Press, 1997).

Daniels, Stephen, *Fields of Vision: Landscape Imagery and National Identity in England and the United States* (Cambridge: Polity Press, 1993).

Davidoff, Leonore, and Hall, Catherine, *Family Fortunes: Men and Women of the English Middle Class, 1780–1850*, 2nd edn. (forthcoming).

Davin, Anna, 'Imperialism and Motherhood', *History Workshop Journal*, 5 (Spring 1978), 9–65.

Davis, John, *A History of Britain, 1885–1939* (New York: St Martin's Press, 1999).

Dawson, Graham, *Soldier Heroes: British Adventure, Empire and the Imagining of Masculinities* (London and New York: Routledge, 1994).

Delaney, Enda, *Demography, State and Society: Irish Migration to Britain, 1921–1971* (Liverpool: Liverpool University Press, 2000).

Delano, Page Dougherty, 'Making Up for War: Sexuality and Citizenship in Wartime Culture', *Feminist Studies*, 26 (2000), 33–69.

Den Otter, Sandra M., *British Idealism and Social Explanation: A Study in Late Victorian Thought* (Oxford: Clarendon Press, 1996).

Douglas, Mary, *Purity and Danger: An Analysis of Concepts of Pollution and Taboo* (New York: Praeger, 1966).

Downs, Laura Lee, *Manufacturing Inequality: Gender Division in the French and British Metalworking Industries, 1914–1939* (Ithaca, NY, and London: Cornell University Press, 1995).

Duara, Prasenjit, 'Historicizing National Identity, or Who Imagines What and When', in Geoff Eley and Ronald Grigor Suny (eds.), *Becoming National* (Oxford and New York: Oxford University Press, 1996).

——— *Rescuing History from the Nation: Questioning Narratives of Modern China* (Chicago: University of Chicago Press, 1995).

Dudink, Stefan, 'The Trouble with Men: Problems in the History of "Masculinity"', *European Journal of Cultural Studies*, 1–3 (Sept. 1998), 419–31.

Easthope, Antony, *Englishness and National Culture* (London and New York: Routledge, 1999).

Edwards, A. Trystan, *A Hundred New Towns?* (London: J. M. Dent & Sons, 1944).

Eley, Geoff, 'Finding the People's War: Film, British Collective Memory, and World War II', *American Historical Review*, 106 (June 2001), 818–38.

——— and Suny, Ronald Grigor (eds.), *Becoming National* (New York and Oxford: Oxford University Press, 1996).

——— ——— (eds.), 'Introduction: From the Moment of Social History to the Work of Cultural Representation', *Becoming National: A Reader* (New York and Oxford: Oxford University Press, 1996).

Elshtain, Jean Bethke, *Women and War* (Chicago and London: University of Chicago Press, 1995).

Endelman, Todd M., 'Anti-Semitism in War-time Britain: Evidence from the Victor Gollancz Collection', *Michael*, 10 (1986), 75–95.

Epstein, James A., *Radical Expression: Political Language, Ritual, and Symbol in England, 1790–1850* (Oxford and New York: Oxford University Press, 1994).

Eschen, Penny M. Von, *Race Against Empire: Black Americans and Anticolonialism, 1937–1957* (Ithaca, NY: Cornell University Press, 1997).

Evans, Eric, 'Englishness and Britishness: National Identities, c.1790–1870', in Alexander Grant and Keith J. Stringer (eds.), *Uniting the Kingdom? The Making of British History* (London and New York: Routledge, 1995).

Fantasia, Rick, *Cultures of Solidarity: Consciousness, Action, and Contemporary American Workers* (Los Angeles and Berkeley: University of California Press, 1988).

Featherstone, Simon, 'The Nation as Pastoral in British Literature of the Second World War', *Journal of European Studies*, 16 (Summer 1986), 155–68.

Field, Geoffrey, 'Perspectives on the Working-Class Family in Wartime Britain, 1939–1945', *International Labor and Working-Class History*, 38 (Fall 1990), 3–28.

—— 'Social Patriotism and the British Working Class: Appearance and Disappearance of a Tradition', *International Labor and Working-Class History*, 42 (Fall 1992), 20–39.

Fielding, Steven, 'The Good War: 1939–1945', in Nick Tiratsoo (ed.), *From Blitz to Blair: A New History of Britain since 1939* (London: Phoenix, 1998).

—— 'The Second World War and Popular Radicalism: The Significance of the "Movement Away from Party"', *History*, 80 (1995), 38–58.

—— 'What Did "The People" Want?: The Meaning of the 1945 General Election', *Historical Journal*, 35 (1992), 623–39.

—— Thompson, Peter, and Tiratsoo, Nick, *'England Arise!': The Labour Party and Popular Politics in 1940s Britain* (Manchester: Manchester University Press, 1995).

Finlayson, Geoffrey, 'A Moving Frontier: Voluntarism and the State in British Social Welfare 1911–1949', *Twentieth Century British History*, 1/2 (1990), 183–206.

Flint, John, 'Scandal at the Bristol Hotel: Some Thoughts on Racial Discrimination in Britain and West Africa and Its Relationship to the Planning of Decolonisation, 1939–47', *Journal of Imperial and Commonwealth History*, 12 (May 1983), 74–93.

Frances, Martin, 'The Labour Party: Modernisation and the Politics of Restraint', in Becky Conekin, Frank Mort, and Chris Waters (eds.), *Moments of Modernity: Reconstructing Britain, 1945–1964* (London and New York: Rivers Oram Press, 1999).

Freedan, Michael, *The New Liberalism: An Ideology of Social Reform* (Oxford: Clarendon Press, 1978).

Fryer, Peter, *Staying Power: The History of Black People in Britain* (London: Pluto, 1984).

Furedi, Frank, *The Silent War: Imperialism and the Changing Perception of Race* (London: Pluto Press, 1998).

Gardiner, Juliet, *'Over Here': The GIs in Wartime Britain* (London: Collins & Brown, 1992).

BIBLIOGRAPHY

Geyer, Michael, 'War and the Context of General History in an Age of Total War: Comment on Peter Paret, "Justifying the Obligation of Military Service", and Michael Howard, "World War One: The Crisis of European History"', *Journal of Military History*, Special Issue 57 (Oct. 1993), 145–63.

Gikandi, Simon, *Maps of Englishness: Writing Identity in the Culture of Colonialism* (New York: Columbia University Press, 1996).

Gilbert, Sandra, 'Soldier's Heart: Literary Men, Literary Women, and the Great War', in Margaret Randolph Higonnet et al. (eds.), *Behind the Lines: Gender and the Two World Wars* (New Haven and London: Yale University Press, 1987).

Giles, Judy, ' "Playing Hard to Get": Working-Class Women, Sexuality and Respectability in Britain, 1918–40', *Women's History Review*, 1/2 (1992), 239–55.

Gilman, Sander L., ' "I'm Down on Whores": Race and Gender in Victorian London', in David Theo Goldberg (ed.), *Anatomy of Racism* (Minneapolis and London: University of Minnesota Press, 1990).

—— *The Jew's Body* (New York: Routledge, 1991).

—— *Making the Body Beautiful: A Cultural History of Aesthetic Surgery* (Princeton: Princeton University Press, 1999).

—— 'The Visibility of the Jew in the Diaspora: Body Imagery and Its Cultural Context', The B. G. Rudolph Lecture in Judaic Studies, Syracuse University, 1992.

Gilroy, Paul, *The Black Atlantic: Modernity and Double Consciousness* (Cambridge, Mass.: Harvard University Press, 1993).

Gledhill, Christine, and Swanson, Gillian (eds.), *Nationalising Femininity: Culture, Sexuality and British Cinema in the Second World War* (Manchester: Manchester University Press, 1996).

Goldsmith, Margaret, *Women and the Future* (London: Lindsay Drummond, 1946).

Goodman, Philomena, *Women, Sexuality and War* (Basingstoke, Hants.: Palgrave, 2002).

Graves, Robert, and Hodge, Alan, *The Long Week-End: A Social History of Great Britain, 1918–1939*, 2nd edn. (New York: W. W. Norton, 1994 [1940]).

Grayzel, Susan R., *Women's Identities at War: Gender, Motherhood and Politics in Britain and France* (Chapel Hill: University of North Carolina Press, 1999).

Griffiths, Richard, *Patriotism Perverted: Captain Ramsay, the Right Club and British Anti-Semitism, 1939–40* (London: Constable, 1998).

Gullace, Nicoletta F., 'White Feathers and Wounded Men: Female Patriotism and the Memory of the Great War', *Journal of British Studies*, 36 (Apr. 1997), 178–206.

—— *'The Blood of Our Sons': Men, Women, and the Renegotiation of British Citizenship During the Great War* (New York and Basingstoke: Palgrave MacMillan, 2002).

Hall, Catherine, ' "From Greenland's Icy Mountains . . . to Afric's Golden Sand": Ethnicity, Race and Nation in Mid-Nineteenth-Century England', *Gender & History*, 5 (Summer 1993), 212–30.

—— 'The Nation Within and Without', in Catherine Hall, Keith McClelland, and Jane

Rendall (eds.), *Defining the Victorian Nation: Class, Race, Gender and the Reform Act of 1867* (Cambridge: Cambridge University Press, 2000).

—— 'Rethinking Imperial Histories: The Reform Act of 1867', *New Left Review*, 208 (Winter 1994), 3–29.

—— *White, Male and Middle Class: Explorations in Feminism and History* (New York: Routledge, 1992).

—— McClelland, Keith, and Rendall, Jane (eds.), *Defining the Victorian Nation: Class, Race, Gender and the Reform Act of 1867* (Cambridge: Cambridge University Press, 2000).

Hall, Kim F., *Economies of Race and Gender in Early Modern England* (Ithaca, NY: Cornell University Press, 1995).

Hall, Stuart, 'Encoding, Decoding', in Simon During (ed.), *The Cultural Studies Reader* (London: Routledge, 1993).

—— 'Gramsci's Relevance to the Analysis of Racism and Ethnicity', *Journal of Communication Inquiry*, 10 (1986), 5–27.

—— 'Introduction: Who Needs Identity?', in Stuart Hall and Paul du Gay (eds.), *Questions of Cultural Identity* (London: Sage Publications, 1996).

Harris, Elbert L., 'Social Activities of the Negro Soldier in England', *Negro History Bulletin*, 11/7 (Apr. 1948), 152–6, 164–6.

Harris, Jose, 'Political Thought and the Welfare State, 1870–1940', *Past and Present*, 135 (1992), 116–41.

—— 'Political Values and the Debate on State Welfare', in Harold L. Smith (ed.), *War and Social Change: British Society in the Second World War* (Manchester: Manchester University Press, 1986).

—— *William Beveridge: A Biography* (Oxford: Clarendon Press, 1977).

Harrison, Brian, *Separate Spheres: The Opposition to Women's Suffrage in Britain* (London: Croom Helm, 1978).

Hartley, Jenny, *Millions Like Us: British Women's Fiction of the Second World War* (London: Virago Press, 1997).

Harvie, Christopher, *Scotland and Nationalism: Scottish Society and Politics, 1707 to the Present*, 3rd edn. (London: Routledge, 1988).

Hayes, Denis, *Challenge of Conscience: The Story of the Conscientious Objectors of 1939–49* (London: Allen and Unwin, 1949).

Hechter, Michael, *Internal Colonialism: The Celtic Fringe in British National Development, 1536–1966* (Berkeley and Los Angeles: University of California Press, 1975).

Hennessy, Peter, 'Never Again', in Brian Brivati and Harriet Jones (eds.), *What Difference Did the War Make?* (London and New York: Leicester University Press, 1993).

Hinton, James, '1945 and the Apathy School', *History Workshop Journal*, 43 (Spring 1997), 266–72.

—— *Shop Floor Citizens: Engineering Democracy in 1940s Britain* (Aldershot, Hants.: Edward Elgar, 1994).

BIBLIOGRAPHY

Hobsbawm, Eric, 'Man and Woman: Images on the Left', in *Worlds of Labour: Further Studies in the History of Labour* (London: Weidenfeld and Nicolson, 1984).

Hodson, James Lansdale, *Home Front* (London: Victor Gollancz, 1944).

Holderness, B. A., 'The Farmers in the Twentieth Century', in G. E. Mingay (ed.), *The Vanishing Countryman* (London: Routledge, 1989).

Holmes, Colin, *John Bull's Island: Immigration and British Society, 1871–1971* (London: Macmillan, 1988).

Honey, Maureen, *Creating Rosie the Riveter: Class, Gender, and Propaganda during World War II* (Amherst: University of Massachusetts Press, 1984).

Hopkinson, Tom (ed.), *Picture Post 1938–1950* (London: Chatto and Windus, 1984).

Howe, Stephen, *Anticolonialism in British Politics: The Left and the End of Empire, 1918–1964* (Oxford: Clarendon Press, 1993).

Howkins, Alun, 'The Discovery of Rural England', in Robert Colls and Philip Dodd (eds.), *Englishness: Politics and Culture 1880–1920* (London: Croom Helm, 1986).

Humphries, Stephen, *Hooligans or Rebels?* (Oxford: Basil Blackwell, 1981).

Hunt, Lynn, *Politics, Culture, and Class in the French Revolution* (Berkeley and Los Angeles: University of California Press, 1984).

Ignatieff, Michael, 'Citizenship and Moral Narcissism', in Geoff Andrews (ed.), *Citizenship* (London: Lawrence and Wishart, 1991).

Inman, Patricia, *Labour in the Munitions Industries* (London: HMSO, 1957).

Jeffries, Kevin, 'British Politics and Social Policy during the Second World War', *Historical Journal*, 30 (Mar. 1987), 123–44.

Joad, C. E. M., *An Old Countryside for New People* (London: J. M. Dent, undated).

Jones, Gareth Stedman, *Outcast London: A Study in the Relationship between Classes in Victorian Society*, repr. (Harmondsworth, Middlesex: Penguin, 1984).

Jones, Kathleen, 'Identity, Action and Locale', *Social Politics*, 1–3 (1994), 256–70.

Joseph, Shirley, *If their Mothers Only Knew: An Unofficial Account of Life in the Women's Land Army* (London: Faber & Faber, 1946).

Joyce, Patrick, *Visions of the People: Industrial England and the Question of Class, 1848–1914* (Cambridge: Cambridge University Press, 1991).

Kandiyoti, Deniz, 'From Empire to Nation State: Transformations of the Woman Question in Turkey', in Susan Jay Kleinberg (ed.), *Retrieving Women's History: Changing Perceptions of the Role of Women in Politics and Society* (Oxford and New York: Berg, 1988).

—— 'Women and the Turkish State: Political Actors or Symbolic Pawns?', in Nira Yuval-Davis and Floya Anthias (eds.), *Woman-Nation-State* (Basingstoke: Macmillan, 1989).

Katin, Zelma, *Clippie* (London: Gifford, 1944).

Kearney, Hugh, *The British Isles: A History of Four Nations* (Cambridge and New York: Cambridge University Press, 1995).

Kent, Susan Kingsley, *Making Peace: The Reconstruction of Gender in Interwar Britain* (Princeton: Princeton University Press, 1993).

Kerber, Linda, 'The Meanings of Citizenship', *Journal of American History*, 84 (Dec. 1997), 833–52.

—— *No Constitutional Right to be Ladies: Women and the Obligations of Citizenship* (New York: Hill and Wang, 1998).

—— 'The Republican Mother: Women and the Enlightenment', *American Quarterly*, 27 (1976), 187–205.

Kirkham, Pat, 'Fashioning the Feminine: Dress, Appearance and Femininity in Wartime Britain', in Christine Gledhill and Gillian Swanson (eds.), *Nationalising Femininity: Culture, Sexuality and British Cinema in the Second World War* (Manchester: Manchester University Press, 1996).

Kohn, Marek, *Dope Girls: The Birth of the British Drug Underground* (London: Lawrence and Wishart, 1992).

Kushner, Tony, *The Persistence of Prejudice: Antisemitism in British Society during the Second World War* (Manchester: Manchester University Press, 1989).

—— 'Remembering to Forget: Racism and Anti-Racism in Postwar Britain', in Bryan Cheyette and Laura Marcus (eds.), *Modernity, Culture and 'the Jew'* (Cambridge: Polity Press, 1998).

Lake, Marilyn, 'The Desire for a Yank: Sexual Relations between Australian Women and American Servicemen during World War II', *Journal of the History of Sexuality*, 2 (Nov. 1992), 621–33.

—— 'Female Desires: The Meaning of World War II', in Joy Damousi and Marilyn Lake (eds.), *Gender and War: Australians at War in the Twentieth Century* (Cambridge: Cambridge University Press, 1995).

Landes, Joan, 'Representing the Body Politic: The Paradox of Gender and the Graphic Politics of the French Revolution', in Sara E. Melzer and Leslie W. Rabine (eds.), *Rebel Daughters: Women and the French Revolution* (New York and Oxford: Oxford University Press, 1992).

—— *Women and the Public Sphere in the Age of the French Revolution* (Ithaca, NY and London: Cornell University Press, 1988).

Lant, Antonia, 'Prologue: Mobile Femininity', in Christine Gledhill and Gillian Swanson (eds.), *Nationalising Femininity: Culture, Sexuality and British Cinema in the Second World War* (Manchester: Manchester University Press, 1996).

Levine, Philippa, 'Battle Colours: Race, Sex and Colonial Soldiery in World War I', *Journal of Women's History*, 9 (1998), 104–130.

—— ' "Walking the Streets in a Way No Decent Woman Should": Women Police in World War I', *Journal of Modern History*, 66 (Mar. 1994), 34–78.

Lewis, Jane, *The Politics of Motherhood: Child and Maternal Welfare in England, 1900–1939* (London: Croom Helm, 1980).

Ley, Norman, *The Colour Bar in East Africa*, repr. (New York: Negro Universities Press, 1970).

Light, Alison, *Forever England: Femininity, Literature, and Conservatism between the Wars* (London and New York: Routledge, 1991).

Lister, Ruth, *Citizenship: Feminist Perspectives* (New York: New York University Press, 1997).

London, Louise, *Whitehall and the Jews, 1933–1948: British Immigration Policy, Jewish Refugees and the Holocaust* (Cambridge: Cambridge University Press, 2000).

Lowe, Rodney, 'The Second World War, Consensus, and the Foundation of the Welfare State', *Twentieth Century British History*, 1 (1990), 152–82.

McClintock, Anne, *Imperial Leather: Race, Gender and Sexuality in the Colonial Context* (London and New York: Routledge, 1995).

McDevitt, Patrick, 'May the Best Man Win: Sport, Masculinity and Nationalism in Great Britain and the Empire, 1884–1933 (Ireland, West Indies, Australia)', Ph.D. thesis (Rutgers University, 1999).

Mackenzie, John M., *Imperialism and Popular Culture* (London and Dover, NH: Manchester University Press, 1986).

—— *Propaganda and Empire: The Manipulation of British Public Opinion, 1880–1960* (London and Dover, NH: Manchester University Press, 1984).

McKibbin, Ross, 'Class and Conventional Wisdom: The Conservative Party and the 'Public' in Inter-war Britain', in *The Ideologies of Class: Social Relations of Britain 1880–1950* (Oxford: Clarendon Press, 1994).

—— *Classes and Cultures: England 1918–1951* (Oxford: Oxford University Press, 1998).

McLaine, Ian, *Ministry of Morale: Home Front Morale and the Ministry of Information in World War II* (London: George Allen & Unwin, 1979).

Macnicol, John, 'The Effect of the Evacuation of Schoolchildren on Official Attitudes to State Intervention', in Harold L. Smith (ed.), *War and Social Change: British Society in the Second World War* (Manchester: Manchester University Press, 1986).

Mangan, J. A., 'Social Darwinism and Upper-Class Education in Late Victorian and Edwardian England', in J. A. Mangan and James Walvin (eds.), *Manliness and Morality: Middle-Class Masculinity in Britain and America, 1800–1940* (Manchester: Manchester University Press, 1987).

Marke, Ernest, *In Troubled Waters: Memoirs of My Seventy Years in England* (London: Karia Press, 1986 [1975]).

Marr, Andrew, *The Battle for Scotland* (London: Penguin, 1992).

Marriott, John, 'Labour and the Popular', *History Workshop Journal*, 43 (Spring 1997), 258–65.

Marwick, Arthur, *Britain in the Century of Total War: War, Peace and Social Change, 1900–1967* (Boston: Little and Brown, 1968).

Masefield, John, *Land Workers* (London: William Heinemann, Ltd., 1942).

Mason, Tony, ' "Hunger . . . is a Very Good Thing": Britain in the 1930s', in Nick Tiratsoo (ed.), *From Blitz to Blair: A New History of Britain since 1939* (London: Phoenix, 1998).

—— and Thompson, Peter, ' "Reflections on a Revolution?" The Political Mood in Wartime Britain', in Nick Tiratsoo (ed.), *The Attlee Years* (London and New York: Pinter, 1991).

Mass Observation, *People in Production* (Harmondsworth: Penguin, 1942).

Matless, David, *Landscape and Englishness* (London: Reaktion Books, 1998).

Mayhall, Laura, *Rethinking Suffrage: Citizenship and Resistance in Britain, 1860–1930* (New York and Oxford: Oxford University Press, forthcoming).

Mehta, Uday Singh, *Liberalism and Empire: A Study in Nineteenth-Century British Liberal Thought* (Chicago: University of Chicago Press, 1999).

Melman, Billie, *Women and the Popular Imagination in the Twenties: Flappers and Nymphs* (London: Macmillan Press, 1988).

Mitchell, W. J. T., *On Narrative* (Chicago and London: University of Chicago Press, 1981).

Moore, John Hammond, *Over-Sexed, Over-Paid and Over Here: Americans in Australia, 1941–1945* (St Lucia: University of Queensland Press, 1981).

Morgan, David, and Evans, Mary, *The Battle for Britain: Citizenship and Ideology in the Second World War* (London and New York: Routledge, 1993).

Morgan, David H. J., *Discovering Men* (London and New York: Routledge, 1992).

——'Theater of War: Combat, the Military, and Masculinities', in Harry Brod and Michael Kaufman (eds.), *Theorizing Masculinities* (London: Sage Publications, 1994).

Morgan, Kenneth O., *Labour in Power 1945–1951* (Oxford: Clarendon Press, 1984).

——*Modern Wales: Politics, Places and People* (Cardiff: University of Wales Press, 1995).

——*The People's Peace* (Oxford: Oxford University Press, 1990).

——*Rebirth of a Nation: Wales 1880–1980* (Oxford: Clarendon Press, 1981).

Mort, Frank, *Dangerous Sexualities: Medico-Moral Politics in England since 1830* (London and New York: Routledge and Kegan Paul, 1987).

Morton, H. V., *In Search of England*, 30th edn. (London: Methuen, 1943).

Mosse, George L., *The Image of Man: The Creation of Modern Masculinity* (New York: Oxford University Press, 1996).

——*Nationalism and Sexuality: Middle-Class Morality and Sexual Norms in Modern Europe* (Madison: University of Wisconsin Press, 1985).

Mouffe, Chantal, 'Democratic Citizenship and the Political Community', in Chantal Mouffe (ed.) *Dimensions of Radical Democracy* (London: Verso, 1992).

——'Feminism, Citizenship and Radical Democratic Politics', in Judith Butler and Joan W. Scott (eds.), *Feminists Theorize the Political* (New York and London: Routledge, 1992).

Nairn, Tom, *The Break-up of Britain* (London: New Left Books and Verso, 1980).

Nathanson, Constance, *Dangerous Passage: The Social Control of Sexuality in Women's Adolescence* (Philadelphia: Temple University Press, 1991).

Nava, Mica, 'Wider Horizons and Modern Desire: The Contradictions of America and Racial Difference in London, 1935–45', *New Formations*, 37 (1996), 71–91.

Newby, Howard, *Country Life: A Social History of Rural England* (Totowa, NJ: Barnes & Noble Books, 1987).

Nicholas, Sian, *The Echo of War: Home Front Propaganda and the Wartime BBC, 1939–45* (Manchester: Manchester University Press, 1996).

Nicolson, Harold, *Diaries and Letters*, ii. *The War Years: 1939–1945* (New York: Atheneum, 1967).

Noakes, Lucy, *War and the British: Gender, Memory and National Identity* (London: I. B. Tauris, 1998).

Nugent, David, *Modernity at the Edge of Empire: State, Individual and Nation in the Northern Peruvian Andes, 1885–1935* (Stanford, CA.: Stanford University Press, 1997).

Nye, Robert, *Masculinity and Male Codes of Honor in Modern France* (Berkeley and Los Angeles: University of California Press, 1998).

Okin, Susan Miller, *Is Multiculturalism Bad for Women?* (Princeton: Princeton University Press, 1999).

Oldfield, Adrian, *Citizenship and Community: Civic Republicanism and the Modern World* (London and New York: Routledge, 1990).

Oram, Alison, ' "Bombs Don't Discriminate!" Women's Political Activism in the Second World War', in Christine Gledhill and Gillian Swanson (eds.), *Nationalising Femininity: Culture, Sexuality and British Cinema in the Second World War* (Manchester: Manchester University Press, 1996).

—— *Women Teachers and Feminist Politics 1900–1939* (Manchester: Manchester University Press, 1996).

Orwell, George, *The Lion and the Unicorn: Socialism and the English Genius* (London: Secker and Warburg, 1941).

Parker, Andrew, 'Introduction', in Andrew Parker et al. (eds.), *Nationalisms & Sexualities* (London: Routledge, 1992).

Pateman, Carole, 'The Fraternal Social Contract', in Carole Pateman, *The Disorder of Women: Democracy, Feminism, and Political Theory* (Stanford, CA.: Stanford University Press, 1989).

Paul, Kathleen, *Whitewashing Britain: Race and Citizenship in the Postwar Era* (Ithaca, NY: Cornell University Press, 1997).

Pelling, Henry, *Britain and the Second World War* (London: Penguin, 1970).

Phillips, Anne, *Democracy and Difference* (Cambridge: Polity Press, 1993).

Pitkin, Hanna, *Fortune is a Woman: Gender and Politics in the Thought of Nicolo Machiavelli* (Berkeley and Los Angeles: University of California Press, 1984).

Pocock, J. G. A., 'British History: A Plea for a New Subject', *Journal of Modern History*, 47 (1975), 601–21.

—— 'Conclusion: Contingency, Identity, Sovereignty', in Alexander Grant and Keith J. Stringer (eds.), *Uniting the Kingdom? The Making of British History* (London and New York: Routledge, 1995).

—— 'The Limits and Divisions of British History: In Search of the Unknown Subject', *American Historical Review*, 87 (1982), 311–36.

—— *Machiavellian Moment: Florentine Political Thought and the Atlantic Republican Tradition* (Princeton: Princeton University Press, 1975).

—— 'Virtue and Commerce in the Eighteenth Century', *Journal of Interdisciplinary History*, 3 (1972), 119–34.

Poovey, Mary, 'Curing the "Social Body" in 1832: James Phillips Kay and the Irish in Manchester', *Gender & History*, 5 (Summer 1993), 196–211.

Post, Ken, *Arise Ye Starvelings: The Jamaican Labour Rebellion of 1938 and its Aftermath* (The Hague: Nijhoff, 1978).

Potts, Alex, 'Constable Country between the Wars', in Raphael Samuel (ed.), *Patriotism: The Making and Unmaking of British National Identity*, iii. *National Fictions* (London: Routledge, 1989).

Priestley, J. B., 'Broadcast from June 5, 1940', *Postscripts* (London, 1940).

—— ' "Postscript", Sunday, 9th June, 1940', *All England Listened: The Wartime Broadcasts of J. B. Priestley* (New York: Chilmark Press, 1967).

Procacci, Giovanna, 'Omnes or Singulatum? Citizenship as Government Strategies', paper presented at the CSST Faculty Seminar, University of Michigan, 28 Jan. 1999.

—— 'Social Economy and the Government of Poverty', in Graham Burchell, Colin Gordon, and Peter Miller (eds.), *The Foucault Effect: Studies in Governmentality* (Chicago: University of Chicago Press, 1991).

Pugh, Martin, *Women and the Women's Movement in Britain, 1914–1959* (London: Macmillan, 1992).

Purdom, C. B., *Britain's Cities Tomorrow: Notes for Everyman on a Great Theme* (London: King, Littlewood & King, 1942).

Reynolds, David, *Rich Relations: The American Occupation of Britain, 1942–1945* (New York: Random House, 1995).

Rich, Paul, *Race and Empire in British Politics* (Cambridge and New York: Cambridge University Press, 1986).

Richards, Jeffrey, 'National Identity in British Wartime Films', in Philip M. Taylor (ed.), *Britain and the Cinema in the Second World War* (London: Macmillan, 1988).

Richmond, Anthony H., *Colour Prejudice in Britain: A Study of West Indian Workers in Liverpool, 1941–1951* (London: Routledge & Kegan Paul, 1954).

Riley, Denise, ' "The Free Mothers": Pronatalism and Working Women in Industry at the End of the Last War in Britain', *History Workshop Journal*, 11 (1981), 59–118.

—— *War in the Nursery: Theories of the Child and Mother* (London: Virago, 1983).

Robbins, Keith, *Great Britain: Identities, Institutions and the Idea of Britishness* (London and New York: Longman, 1998).

—— 'An Imperial and Multinational Polity: The Scene from the Centre, 1832–1922', in Alexander Grant and Keith J. Stringer (eds.), *Uniting the Kingdom? The Making of British History* (London and New York: Routledge, 1995).

Roper, Michael, *Masculinity and the British Organization Man since 1945* (Oxford and New York: Oxford University Press, 1994).

—— and Tosh, John (eds.), *Manful Assertions: Masculinities in Britain since 1800* (London and New York: Routledge, 1991).

Rorty, Richard, *Contingency, Irony, and Solidarity* (Cambridge and New York: Cambridge University Press, 1989).

Rose, Sonya O., 'Cultural Analysis and Moral Discourses: Episodes, Continuities, and Transformations', in Victoria E. Bonnell and Lynn Hunt (eds.), *Beyond the Cultural Turn* (Berkeley and Los Angeles: University of California Press, 1999).

—— 'Girls and GIs: Race, Sex, and Diplomacy in Second World War Britain', *International History Review*, 19 (Feb. 1997), 146–60.

—— *Limited Livelihoods: Gender and Class in Nineteenth-Century England* (Berkeley and Los Angeles: University of California Press, 1992).

—— 'Respectable Men, Disorderly Others: The Language of Gender and the Lancashire Weavers' Strike of 1878 in Britain', *Gender & History*, 5 (Autumn 1993), 382–97.

—— 'Sex, Citizenship and the Nation in World War II Britain', *American Historical Review*, 103 (Oct. 1998), 1147–76.

—— 'The "Sex Question" in Anglo-American Relations in the Second World War', *International History Review*, 20 (Dec. 1998), 884–903.

Ross, Ellen, *Love and Toil: Motherhood in Outcast London, 1870–1918* (New York: Oxford University Press, 1993).

Rubinstein, W. D., *A History of the Jews in the English-Speaking World: Great Britain* (London: Macmillan, 1996).

Rupp, Leila, *Mobilizing Women for War* (Princeton: Princeton University Press, 1978).

Salecl, Renata, 'The Fantasy Structure of Nationalist Discourse', *Praxis International*, 13 (Oct. 1993), 213–23.

Samuel, Raphael, 'Introduction: Exciting to Be English', in Raphael Samuel (ed.), *Patriotism: The Making and Unmaking of British National Identity*, i (London and New York: Routledge, 1989).

—— *Theatre of Memory*, i. *Past and Present in Contemporary Culture* (London: Verso, 1994).

—— *Theatres of Memory*, ii. *Island Stories: Unravelling Britain* (London and New York: Verso, 1998).

Sanderson, Lady, 'North Norfolk', in Richard Padley and Margaret Cole (eds.), *Evacuation Survey: A Report to the Fabian Society* (London: George Routledge, 1940).

Saunders, Kay, 'In a Cloud of Lust: Black GIs and Sex in World War II', in Joy Damousi and Marilyn Lake (eds.), *Gender and War: Australians at War in the Twentieth Century* (Cambridge: Cambridge University Press, 1995).

Saville, John, 'May Day 1937', in Asa Briggs and John Saville (eds.), *Essays in Labour History, 1918–1939* (London: Croom Helm, 1977).

Scarry, Elaine, *The Body in Pain: The Making and Unmaking of the World* (New York and Oxford: Oxford University Press, 1985).

Schama, Simon, *Landscape and Memory* (New York: Alfred A. Knopf, 1995).

Scottish Women's Group on Public Welfare, *Our Scottish Towns: Evacuation and the Social Future* (Edinburgh: William Hodge, 1944).

Seago, Edward, *Peace in War* (London: Collins, 1943).

Segal, Lynn, *Slow Motion* (London: Virago, 1991).

Sennett, Richard, *The Fall of Public Man* (New York: Vintage Books, 1974).

Seton-Watson, Hugh, *Nations and States* (London: Methuen, 1977).

Sherwood, Marika, *The British Honduran Forestry Unit in Scotland, 1941–43* (London: Karia Press, 1982).

——*Many Struggles: West Indian Workers and Service Personnel in Britain (1939–45)* (London: Karia Press, 1985).

Short, Brian (ed.), *The English Rural Community: Image and Analysis* (Cambridge: Cambridge University Press, 1992).

Skinner, Quentin, 'On Justice, the Common Good and the Priority of Liberty', in Chantal Mouffe (ed.), *Dimensions of Radical Democracy* (London: Verso, 1992).

Smith, Graham, *When Jim Crow Met John Bull: Black American Soldiers in World War II Britain* (New York: St Martin's Press, 1988).

Smith, Harold L. (ed.), *Britain in the Second World War: A Social History* (Manchester and New York: Manchester University Press, 1996).

——(ed.), *British Feminism in the Twentieth Century* (Aldershot, Hants: Edward Elgar, 1990).

——'The Effect of the War on the Status of Women', in Harold L. Smith (ed.), *War and Social Change: British Society in the Second World War* (Manchester: Manchester University Press, 1986).

——'The Problem of "Equal Pay for Equal Work" in Great Britain during World War II', *Journal of Modern History*, 53 (Dec. 1981), 661–5.

——(ed.), *War and Social Change: British Society in the Second World War* (Manchester: Manchester University Press, 1986).

——'The Womanpower Problem in Britain during the Second World War', *Historical Journal*, 27 (1984), 928–31.

Smith, Malcolm, 'The Changing Nature of the British State, 1929–59: The Historiography of Consensus', in Brian Brivati and Harriet Jones (eds.), *What Difference Did the War Make?* (London and New York: Leicester University Press, 1993).

Smith, Rogers M., *Civic Ideals: Conflicting Visions of Citizenship in U.S. History* (New Haven and London: Yale University Press, 1997).

Smith-Rosenberg, Carroll, 'Beyond Roles, Beyond Spheres: Thinking about Gender in the Early Republic', *William and Mary Quarterly*, 3rd ser., 46 (1989), 565–81.

Somers, Margaret, 'Citizenship and the Place of the Public Sphere', *American Sociological Review*, 58 (1993), 587–620.

Spencer, Ian, 'World War Two and the Making of Multiracial Britain', in Pat Kirkham and David Thoms (eds.), *War Culture: Social Change and Changing Experience in World War Two Britain* (London: Routledge, 1995).

Springhall, John, 'Building Character in the British Boy: The Attempt to Extend Christian Manliness to Working-Class Adolescents, 1880–1914', in J. A. Mangan and James Walvin (eds.), *Manliness and Morality: Middle-Class Masculinity in Britain and America, 1800–1940* (Manchester: Manchester University Press, 1987).

Stains, Penny, *Nurses at War: Women on the Frontline, 1939–45* (Stroud, Glos.: Sutton, 2000).

313

Steinmetz, George, *Regulating the Social: The Welfare State and Local Politics in Imperial Germany* (Princeton: Princeton University Press, 1993).

Stephenson, Tom, *Forbidden Land: The Struggle for Access to Mountain and Moorland* (Manchester: Manchester University Press, 1989).

Stevenson, John, 'Planners' Moon? The Second World War and the Planning Movement', in Harold L. Smith (ed.), *War and Social Change: British Society in the Second World War* (Manchester: Manchester University Press, 1986).

Stinchcombe, Arthur, 'The Deep Structure of Moral Categories', in Jeffrey C. Alexander (ed.), *Durkheimian Sociology: Cultural Studies* (Cambridge and New York: Cambridge University Press, 1988).

Stoler, Ann Laura, 'Making Empire Respectable: The Politics of Race and Sexual Morality in 20th-Century Colonial Cultures', *American Ethnologist*, 16 (Nov. 1989), 634–60.

—— *Race and the Education of Desire: Foucault's History of Sexuality and the Colonial Order of Things* (Durham, NC and London: Duke University Press, 1995).

—— 'Rethinking Colonial Categories: European Communities and the Boundaries of Rules', *Comparative Studies in Society and History*, 13 (May 1992), 134–61.

Strachey, Mrs Amy St Loe, *Borrowed Children: A Popular Account of Home Evacuation Problems and Their Remedies* (London: John Murray, 1940).

Street, A. G., *Harvest by Lamplight* (London: Faber and Faber, Limited, 1941).

—— *Hitler's Whistle* (London: Eyre & Spottiswoode, 1943).

Sturma, Michael, 'Public Health and Sexual Morality: Venereal Disease in World War II Australia', *Signs*, 13 (1988), 725–40.

Summerfield, Penny, 'Approaches to Women and Social Change in the Second World War', in Brian Brivati and Harriet Jones (eds.), *What Difference Did the War Make?* (London and New York: Leicester University Press, 1993).

—— ' "The Girl that Makes the Thing that Drills the Hole that Holds the Spring . . ." ': Discourses of Women and Work in the Second World War', in Christine Gledhill and Gillian Swanson (eds.), *Nationalising Femininity: Culture, Sexuality and British Cinema in the Second World War* (Manchester: Manchester University Press, 1996).

—— 'Mass Observation: Social History or Social Movement?', *Journal of Contemporary History*, 20 (1985), 439–52.

—— *Reconstructing Women's Wartime Lives: Discourse and Subjectivity in Oral Histories of the Second World War* (Manchester: Manchester University Press, 1998).

—— ' "She Wants a Gun Not a Dishcloth!": Gender, Service and Citizenship in Britain in the Second World War', in Gerald J. DeGroot and Corinna Peniston-Bird (eds.), *A Soldier and a Woman: Sexual Integration in the Military* (Harlow, England: Pearson Education Ltd., 2000).

—— *Women Workers in the Second World War: Production and Patriarchy in Conflict* (London and Dover, NH: Croom Helm, 1984).

—— and Penniston-Bird, Corinna, *Contesting Home Defence: Women, Men and the Home Guard in the Second World War* (Manchester: Manchester University Press, forthcoming).

—— 'Women in the Firing Line: The Home Guard and the Defense of Gender Boundaries in Britain in the Second World War', *Women's History Review*, 9 (2000), 231–55.

Suny, Ronald Grigor, *The Revenge of the Past: Nationalism, Revolution and the Collapse of the Soviet Union* (Stanford, Calif.: Stanford University Press, 1993).

Tabili, Laura, *'We Ask for British Justice': Workers and Racial Difference in Late Imperial Britain* (Ithaca, NY: Cornell University Press, 1994).

Taylor, Charles, 'Cross-Purposes: The Liberal–Communitarian Debate', in Nancy Rosenblum (ed.), *Liberalism and the Moral Life* (Cambridge, Mass. and London: Harvard University Press, 1989).

—— 'The Politics of Recognition', in Amy Gutmann (ed.), *Multiculturalism: Examining the Politics of Recognition* (Princeton: Princeton University Press, 1994).

Taylor, John, *A Dream of England: Landscape, Photography and the Tourist's Imagination* (Manchester: Manchester University Press, 1994).

Taylor, Miles, 'Patriotism, History and the Left in Twentieth-Century Britain', *Historical Journal*, 33 (Sept. 1990), 971–87.

Thelweleit, Klaus, *Male Fantasies*, i and ii (Minneapolis: University of Minnesota Press, 1989).

Thom, Deborah, *Nice Girls and Rude Girls: Women Workers in World War I* (London: I. B. Tauris, 1998).

Thompson, Derek, 'Courtship and Marriage between the Wars', *Oral History*, 3/2 (1975), 42–3.

Thorne, Christopher, 'Britain and the Black GIs: Racial Issues and Anglo-American Relations in 1942', *New Community*, 3 (Summer 1974), 262–71.

Tilly, Charles, *Coercion, Capital, and European States, AD 990–1992*, rev. edn. (Cambridge, Mass. and Oxford: Basil Blackwell, 1992).

Tiratsoo, Nick (ed.), *From Blitz to Blair: A New History of Britain Since 1939* (London: Phoenix, 1998).

—— ' "New Vistas": The Labour Party, Citizenship and the Built Environment in the 1940s', in Richard Weight and Abigail Beach (eds.), *The Right to Belong: Citizenship and National Identity in Britain, 1930–1960* (London: I. B. Tauris, 1998).

—— *Reconstruction, Affluence and Labour Politics: Coventry 1945–60* (London: Routledge, 1990).

Titmuss, Richard M., *Problems of Social Policy* (London: HMSO, 1950).

Tosh, John, 'Domesticity and Manliness', in Michael Roper and John Tosh (eds.), *Manful Assertions: Masculinities in Britain since 1800* (London and New York: Routledge, 1991).

Tubbs, Ralph, *The Englishman Builds* (Harmondsworth: Penguin Books, 1945).

Turner, Bryan, *Citizenship and Social Theory* (Newbury Park, CA.: Sage Publications, 1993).

Valverde, Mariana, *'The Age of Light, Soap, and Water': Moral Reform in Turn of the Century English Canada* (Toronto: McClelland and Stewart, 1991).

—— ' "Giving the Female a Domestic Turn": The Social, Legal and Moral Regulation of Women's Work in British Cotton Mills, 1820–1850', *Journal of Social History*, 21 (1988), 619–34.

Valverde, Mariana, 'The Rhetoric of Reform: Tropes and the Moral Subject', *International Journal of the Sociology of Law*, 18 (1990), 61–73.

Vance, Norman, *Sinews of the Spirit: The Ideal of Christian Manliness in Victorian Literature and Religious Thought* (Cambridge: Cambridge University Press, 1985).

Verdery, Katherine, 'Whither "Nation" and "Nationalism"?', *Daedalus*, 122 (Summer, 1993), 37–46.

Vernon, James, *Border Crossings: Cornwall and the English (Imagi) nation* (Manchester: Manchester University Press, 1998).

Vincent, Andrew, and Plant, Raymond, *Philosophy, Politics and Citizenship: The Life and Thought of the British Idealists* (Oxford: Basil Blackwell, 1984).

Visram, Rozina, *Ayahs, Lascars and Princes: Indians in Britain, 1700–1947* (London and Dover, NH: Pluto Press, 1986).

Voeltz, Richard A., 'The Antidote to "Khaki Fever"? The Expansion of the British Girl Guides during the First World War', *Journal of Contemporary History*, 27 (1992), 627–38.

Walker, Pamela J., ' "I Live but Not yet I for Christ Liveth in Me": Men and Masculinity in the Salvation Army, 1865–90', in Michael Roper and John Tosh (eds.), *Manful Assertions: Masculinities in Britain since 1800* (London and New York: Routledge, 1991).

Walkowitz, Judith, *City of Dreadful Delight: Narratives of Sexual Danger in Late-Victorian London* (Chicago: University of Chicago Press, 1992).

Walvin, James, 'Symbols of Moral Superiority: Slavery, Sport and the Changing World Order, 1800–1950', in J. A. Mangan and James Walvin (eds.), *Manliness and Morality: Middle-Class Masculinity in Britain and America, 1800–1940* (Manchester: Manchester University Press, 1987).

Wasserstein, Bernard, *Britain and the Jews of Europe, 1939–1945*, 2nd edn. (London and New York: Leicester University Press, 1999).

Waters, Chris, 'J. B. Priestley 1894–1984, Englishness and the Politics of Nostalgia', in Susan Pedersen and Peter Mandler (eds.), *After the Victorians: Private Conscience and Public Duty in Modern Britain, Essays in Memory of John Clive* (London and New York: Routledge, 1994).

Waters, Elizabeth, 'The Modernisation of Russian Motherhood, 1917–1937', *Feminist Review*, 33 (Autumn 1989), 3–18.

Watney, Simon, *Policing Desire: Pornography, AIDS, and the Media*, 2nd edn. (Minneapolis: University of Minnesota Press, 1989).

Weight, Richard, and Beach, Abigail, 'Introduction', in Richard Weight and Abigail Beach (eds.), *The Right to Belong: Citizenship and National Identity in Britain, 1930–1960* (London: I. B. Tauris, 1998).

Weiler, Peter, *The New Liberalism: Liberal Social Theory in Great Britain 1889–1914* (New York and London: Garland Publishing, 1982).

White, Hayden, *The Content of Form: Narrative, Discourse and Historical Representation* (Baltimore and London: Johns Hopkins University Press, 1987).

Wiener, Martin J., *English Culture and the Decline of the Industrial Spirit, 1850–1980* (Cambridge and New York: Cambridge University Press, 1981).

Williams, Raymond, *The Country and the City* (New York: Oxford University Press, 1973).

Wilson, Kathleen, 'Citizenship, Empire, and Modernity in the English Provinces, c.1720–90', in Catherine Hall (ed.), *Cultures of Empire* (New York: Routledge, 2000).

Winship, Janice, 'Women's Magazines: Times of War and Management of the Self in *Woman's Own*', in Christine Gledhill and Gillian Swanson (eds.), *Nationalising Femininity: Culture, Sexuality and British Cinema in the Second World War* (Manchester: Manchester University Press, 1996).

Wolfe, Lawrence, *The Reilly Plan—A New Way of Life* (London: Nicholson & Watson, 1945).

Wolton, Suke, *Lord Hailey, the Colonial Office and the Politics of Race and Empire in the Second World War* (Houndsmill: Macmillan Press, 2000).

Women's Group on Public Welfare, *Our Towns: A Close-up* (London: Oxford University Press, 1943).

Woollacott, Angela, ' "Khaki Fever" and Its Control: Gender, Class, Age and Sexual Morality on the British Homefront in the First World War', *Journal of Contemporary History*, 29 (Apr. 1994), 325–47.

—— *'On Her Their Lives Depend': Munitions Workers in the Great War* (Berkeley and London: University of California Press, 1994).

—— 'Women Munitions Makers, War and Citizenship', *Peace Review*, 8 (Sept. 1996), 373–8.

Wright, Patrick, *The Village that Died for England: The Strange Story of Tyneham* (London: Vintage, 1995).

Yeo, Eileen, *The Contest for Social Science: Relations and Representations of Gender and Class* (London: River Orams Press, 1996).

Index